STO

ANNEX

ACPL IT
DISCARDED

YO-BWS-094

1-19-59

MODERN AMERICAN ANTITRUST LAW

A Guide To Its Domestic And Foreign Application

INSTITUTE FOR INTERNATIONAL AND FOREIGN TRADE LAW
OF THE GEORGETOWN UNIVERSITY LAW CENTER
WASHINGTON, D. C.

MODERN AMERICAN

ANTITRUST LAW

A Guide To Its Domestic And Foreign Application

by

HEINRICH KRONSTEIN
J.D., S.J.D.

JOHN T. MILLER, Jr., *J.D.*

in cooperation with
IVO E. SCHWARTZ, *LL.M.*

OCEANA PUBLICATIONS • NEW YORK 1958

COPYRIGHT © 1958, BY GEORGETOWN UNIVERSITY,
WASHINGTON, D. C.

LIBRARY OF CONGRESS CATALOG CARD NUMBER 58-9196

Printed in the United States of America
by Oceana Publications, Inc., New York, N. Y.

CONTENTS

1067344

INTRODUCTION

Congress has laid down America's policy against restraints of trade and monopoly in three basic statutes, the Sherman Antitrust Act of 1890,[1] the Clayton Act of 1914[2] and the Federal Trade Commission Act of 1914.[3] While these statutes and their underlying philosophy have remained essentially unchanged, there are few fields where the law has developed more dynamically than in antitrust. At the same time, there are few areas where it has had more difficulties in dealing effectively with the expanding business and technology of our economy. The recent *du Pont-General Motors* decision[4] is an impressive illustration for these propositions. One specific question which it raises, how to deal with oligopolistic enterprises, is becoming increasingly important in itself. Other recent cases raising new issues of law and economics or throwing new light on old antitrust problems could easily be added. In the distribution sector of our economy, the Robinson-Patman Anti-Price Discrimination Act[5] and the "Fair Trade" statutes of numerous states are under renewed attack for both their legal and economic implications. Recent cases involving restraints of our trade with foreign nations have emphasized the delicate problem of applying the American antitrust laws to foreign commerce. Concurrently with the judicial developments, Congress has investigated numerous antitrust problems and, in a few instances, amended the antitrust laws.

---

[1] 26 STAT. 209 (1890), as amended, 15 U.S.C. §§ 1 *et seq.* (Supp. IV, 1957). For an excellent study on the history of the Sherman Act, see THORELLI, THE FEDERAL ANTITRUST POLICY, ORIGINATION OF AN AMERICAN TRADITION (1955). *Cf.* also Dewey, *The Common-Law Background of Antitrust Policy*, 41 VA. L.REV. 759 (1955).

[2] 38 STAT. 730 (1914), as amended, 15 U.S.C. §§ 15 *et seq.* (1952).

[3] 38 STAT. 717 (1914), as amended, 15 U.S.C. §§ 41 *et seq.* (1952). For the convenience of the reader we have set out these statutes, as amended, in the appendix.

[4] United States v. E. I. du Pont de Nemours & Co., 353 U.S. 586 (1957), discussed in chapter 3.

[5] 49 STAT. 1526 (1936), 15 U.S.C. § 13 (1952) .

At such a time, it may be helpful to review the present state of the law in those matters which most concern Congress, the courts, the Federal Trade Commission and the Department of Justice today. In doing so, we do not attempt to evaluate our antitrust law and policy.[6] Nor is this book a study of the present state of competition and concentration in the United States.[7] Its purpose is simply to help provide a clear understanding of the legal developments. It is divided into ten chapters, each dealing with a major current antitrust problem and subdivided as seemed appropriate to clarify the subject. For those who desire to go beyond such a brief orientation, as well as to compare materials on the more settled areas of the law, the book is designed to be a ready and reliable, though selective, reference tool.

Today, American antitrust problems are of interest not only

---

[6] For recent studies, see, *e.g.*, REPORT OF THE ATTORNEY GENERAL'S NATIONAL COMMITTEE TO STUDY THE ANTITRUST LAWS (1955) and Schwartz, *The Schwartz Dissent*, 1 ANTITRUST BULL. 37 (1955); ADAMS and GRAY, MONOPOLY IN AMERICA (1955); CARLSTON, LAW AND STRUCTURES OF SOCIAL ACTION c. 7 (1956); DIRLAM and KAHN, FAIR COMPETITION, THE LAW AND ECONOMICS OF ANTITRUST POLICY (1954); EDWARDS, BIG BUSINESS AND THE POLICY OF COMPETITION (1956); GRIFFIN, AN ECONOMIC APPROACH TO ANTITRUST PROBLEMS (1951); HAMILTON, THE POLITICS OF INDUSTRY (1957); MACHLUP, THE POLITICAL ECONOMICS OF MONOPOLY 226 *et seq.* (1952); MASON, ECONOMIC CONCENTRATION AND THE MONOPOLY PROBLEM 327-401 (1957); MUND, GOVERNMENT AND BUSINESS (2d rev. ed. 1955); Oppenheim, *Federal Antitrust Legislation: Guideposts to a Revised National Anti-Trust Policy*, 50 MICH. L.REV. 1139 (1952); PAPANDREOU and WHEELER, COMPETITION AND ITS REGULATION (1954); STOCKING and WATKINS, MONOPOLY AND FREE ENTERPRISE (1951); WILCOX, PUBLIC POLICIES TOWARD BUSINESS (1955).

[7] See, *e.g.*, *Concentration in American Industry*, Report of the Subcommittee on Antitrust and Monopoly to the Senate Committee on the Judiciary, S. REP. No. ...., 85th Cong., 1st Sess. (1957); FEDERAL TRADE COMMISSION, REPORT ON INDUSTRIAL CONCENTRATION AND PRODUCT DIVERSIFICATION IN THE 1,000 LARGEST MANUFACTURING COMPANIES: 1950 (1957); THE STRUCTURE OF AMERICAN INDUSTRY, SOME CASE STUDIES (Adams ed., 2d. rev. ed. 1954); GALBRAITH, AMERICAN CAPITALISM, THE CONCEPT OF COUNTERVAILING POWER (2d rev. ed. 1956); KAPLAN, BIG ENTERPRISES IN A COMPETITIVE SYSTEM (1954); MASON, *op. cit. supra* n.6 at 13-54 (1957); QUINN, GIANT CORPORATIONS: CHALLENGE TO FREEDOM (1956); BUSINESS CONCENTRATION AND PRICE POLICY, A CONFERENCE (National Bureau of Economic Research ed., 1955).

at home, but also abroad[8] where trade with the United States calls for careful study of our law. For example, several European countries have, in part influenced by our law and philosophy, enacted new antitrust statutes requiring mutual attention and study. The Treaty on the new European Economic Community includes strong-worded and far-reaching general provisions against restraints of trade and monopoly. There is thus a growing need being felt abroad for more and reliable information on current American antitrust law and experiences. We hope that by its systematic approach this book will also be of assistance in this respect.

There are areas of antitrust in which no important recent developments can be reported at this time. This is, *inter alia,* the situation with respect to horizontal and vertical price fixing agreements (except on branded articles) as well as to agreements among competitors to limit production, divide markets, or boycott third parties, which the courts continue to prohibit under the principle of *"per se"* unreasonableness as they have for decades.[9] Nevertheless, a recent Supreme Court decision, *Northern Pacific Railway Co.* v. *United States,*[10] involving the same principle in another area, covers these fields in the course of an excellent summary of the policy laid down by the Sherman Act and of the rationale and applicability of the *"per se"* principle. It is reprinted in chapter 4.

The chapter on the restraints in international trade owes much to the diligent research and writing skills of Jan M. Z. Kaczmarek, LL.B., fellow, Institute for International and For-

---

[8] See *Foreign Legislation Concerning Monopoly and Cartel Practices,* Report of the Department of State to the Subcommittee on Monopoly of the Select Senate Committee on Small Business, 82d Cong., 2d Sess. (1952); U.N. ECONOMIC AND SOCIAL COUNCIL OFF. REC., 16th Sess., Supp. No. 11a (Doc. No. E/2379 and E/AC. 37/2 and Add. 1) (1953); Supp. No. 11b (Doc. No. 2379/Add. 2, E/AC. 37/2/Add. 2) (1953); 19th Sess., Supp. No. 3 (Doc. No. E/2671) (1954); Supp. No. 3a (Doc. No. E/2675) (1955); MONOPOLY AND COMPETITION AND THEIR REGULATION, Papers and Proceedings of a Conference held by the International Economic Association (Chamberlin ed., 1954); ANTITRUST LAWS, A COMPARATIVE SYMPOSIUM (Friedmann ed., 1956); NEWMAN, PUBLIC CONTROL OF BUSINESS, AN INTERNATIONAL APPROACH (1956).

[9] A number of cases involving application of most of these practices in foreign commerce are discussed in chapter 10. See also United States v. McKesson & Robbins, 351 U.S. 305, at 309-310 (1957), discussed in chapter 6. *Cf.* HANDLER, ANTITRUST IN PERSPECTIVE 3-28 (1957).

[10] 78 S.Ct. 514 (1958).

eign Trade Law of the Georgetown University Law Center in Washington, D. C. We were greatly assisted in the collection of material by Kate Kronstein. We wish to thank Charlott Weyersberg for her untiring help in preparing the manuscript.

Chapter 1

TRADE AND INTERSTATE COMMERCE

Sections 1, 2 and 3 of the Sherman Act[1] apply only to restraints of "trade or commerce among the several States, or with foreign nations."[2] Hence, the Act frequently raises two questions: (1) What is the functional scope of the terms "trade or commerce"? and (2) what is the scope of the term "interstate" as contrasted with "intrastate" commerce?

The Supreme Court has held that the term "trade" as used in the Sherman Act applies to any occupation, employment, or business carried on for the purpose of profit, or gain, or a livelihood, not in the liberal arts or in the learned professions.[3] There is some authority for the proposition that the term "trade" so used covers *all* occupations in which men are engaged for a livelihood.[4] The terms "trade or commerce" as used in the Sherman Act may be regarded as synonymous.[5]

The interstate-intrastate jurisdictional problem arises from the fact that Congress enacted the Sherman Act by exercising its power to regulate interstate commerce under the commerce clause of the Constitution of the United States.[6]

Recently, the definition of the terms "trade or commerce among the several States," as used in the Sherman Act, came

---

[1] 26 STAT. 209 (1890), as amended, 15 U.S.C. §§ 1-3 (1952).

[2] Section 1 reads in part:

"Every contract, combination in the form of trust or otherwise, or conspiracy, in restraint of trade or commerce among the several States, or with foreign nations, is hereby declared to be illegal."

[3] United States v. National Association of Real Estate Boards, 339 U.S. 485, 490-491 (1950), quoting Justice Story in The Schooner Nymph case, 18 Fed. Cas. 506.

[4] United States v. American Medical Association, 110 F.2d 703, 710 (D.C. Cir. 1940). *Contra,* Riggall v. Washington County Medical Society, 249 F.2d 266 (8th Cir. 1957); United States v. Oregon State Medical Society, 95 F.Supp. 103 (D. Ore. 1950), *affirmed,* 343 U.S. 326 (1952).

[5] See Atlantic Cleaners & Dyers, Inc. v. United States, 286 U.S. 427, 434 (1932) (*dictum*).

[6] Article I, section 8, clause 3 of the Constitution of the United States reads: "The Congress shall have power . . . to regulate commerce with foreign nations and among the several states, and with the Indian Tribes."

once more before the courts. The cases involved several industries which had already been the subjects of antitrust litigation in earlier decades: professional sports, the theatre and the insurance businesses. In the new cases the courts were required to resolve the following issues:

(1) Do professional sports and the theatre business constitute trade?

(2) If so, when are such activities and the insurance business interstate trade?

(1) Professional Baseball[7]

Preliminary to a discussion of *Toolson* v. *New York Yankees, Inc.*[8] a brief look into the structure of professional baseball may be helpful. In this connection the Subcommittee on Study of Monopoly Power of the House Committee on the Judiciary in its Report on Organized Baseball stated:[9]

"A study of professional baseball in America today is largely a study of 'organized baseball.' The term is used to refer to the many professional clubs and leagues which have subjected themselves to the jurisdiction of the commissioner of baseball and have contracted with one another to abide by certain rules and regulations. . . . Organized baseball . . . is composed of 51 leagues rating in performance from the 2 major leagues at the top, down through 6 classifications to the D leagues at the bottom of the structure. These 51 leagues comprise 382 clubs, operating in 42 of our 48 States, and in 4 foreign countries. [Footnote omitted.]

* * *

"The 16 major-league clubs are 16 separate corporate entities. The two leagues are unincorporated associations each operating under its own constitution. But—in interleague relations they are governed by the Major League Agreement, which establishes and recognizes the office of commissioner and gives to the commissioner broad authority for disciplinary action against any club, any player, or any official where there is involved a question of conduct detrimental to baseball. [Footnote omitted.]

"The present Major League Agreement was executed by the two leagues and 16 clubs on November 1, 1946, and provides that it shall remain in force until January 1, 1970. In form it is an amendment to the agreement executed on January 12, 1921,

---

[7] *Cf.* Johnson, *The Law of Sports: The Unique Performer's Contract and the Antitrust Laws,* 2 ANTITRUST BULL. 251 (1957); Johnson, *Baseball, Professional Sports and the Antitrust Acts, id.,* at 678; Note, *Monopsony in Manpower: Organized Baseball Meets the Antitrust Laws,* 62 YALE L.J. 576 (1953).

[8] 346 U.S. 356 (1953).

[9] H.R. REP. No. 2002, 82d Cong., 2d Sess. 12-14 (1952).

when the office of commissioner was formally established. The agreement defines the functions of the commissioner and creates an executive council comprised of five men — the commissioner, the two league presidents, and one other representative from each league.

"Broadly speaking, the powers of the commissioner may be described as investigative and judicial. He is given broad discretion to investigate any acts or practices —

alleged or suspected to be detrimental to the best interests of the national game of baseball —

and to determine what —

preventive, remedial, or punitive action is appropriate in the premises.

His only powers, which might be considered legislative in nature, are limited to proposing changes in the rules, compelling a reconsideration of a rule after its adoption, and resolving disagreements between the two leagues over a proposed amendment to the rules or to the standard contracts.

"The executive council is authorized to exercise all of the powers of the commissioner in the event of a vacancy in the office. In addition, it acts as a sort of board of directors with jurisdiction, among other matters, to survey, investigate, and submit recommendations for changes in any rules, regulations, agreements, proposals, or other matters in which the major leagues have an interest. The executive council has power to act for the major leagues in the interim between the annual joint meetings of all clubs in the two major leagues. When the council is considering matters which concern the standard form of player's contract, the players are represented on the council by one active player from each league. These player representatives, however, do not have any vote on the council.

"The major-league rules were prepared by the executive council and 'duly accepted by the clubs of both major leagues.' These rules comprise a comprehensive schedule regulating the relationships among clubs and between clubs, players, and other officials. Among the provisions covered in the rules, for example, are the composition of the circuits of each league, the form of the standard major-league contracts, the reserve rules, and such matters as the player draft and the waiver rules.

"The minor-league organization, though much more extensive, is comparable in structure to the majors'."

Specifically, the agreements between the leagues and the clubs comprising them require players to be bound to their respective clubs by what is known as the standard player contract. Such a contract includes the so-called *reserve clause* "which requires a player who is under contract to play with any club to refrain, at the expiration of the period of his employment, from contracting to play for, or playing for, any other club other than the one to which he has been under contract or its assignee."[10] This reserve clause has been called "The keystone of the entire structure of organized professional baseball . . . together with its attendant rules and regulations. . . . [P]rofessional baseball could not operate without some form of a reserve clause."[11]

The present Commissioner of Baseball has recently attempted to justify the use of the reserve clause as follows:[12]

> "If the result of the proposed statute [H.R. 5319, H.R. 5307] should be the elimination of the reserve clause, a chaotic scramble for player talent will ensue. The result will be a concentration of the best player talent in the clubs which are able and willing to spend the money necessary to outbid other clubs. Weaker clubs will be unable to compete.
>
> * * *
>
> "However, my greatest concern is with the effect on the integrity of the game. . . . I am thoroughly convinced that abolishing or seriously modifying the reserve clause will tend to destroy public confidence in the game and impair the morale of clubs and players.
>
> * * *
>
> "How could public confidence in player loyalty and will to win be maintained if the player, while playing for one club, may shop around for a job with another club against which he is directly competing on the field, or may be approached with offers from several other clubs? It is not merely a matter of player honesty. In sports competition, players must be above suspicion. Public suspicion is bound to arise in a situation like this — Player A is a star on Club X. In a crucial series between Clubs X and Y, Player A commits a run-yielding error and strikes out with the bases full. Club X loses the game. It then develops that Club Y has been negotiating with Player A for his services for the next season and signs him. Even though Player A was playing his very best, public criticism and loss of respect for A and for the game are inevitable. Moreover, as the early history of the game

---

[10] Gardella v. Chandler, 172 F.2d 402, 403-404 (2d Cir. 1949). See Note, 53 COLUM. L.REV. 242, 243-244 (1953); Comment, 62 YALE L.REV. 576, 585-594 (1953). For an example of a major league baseball contract containing a reserve clause see *Hearings Before the Subcommittee on Study of Monopoly Power of the House Committee on the Judiciary*, 82d Cong., 1st Sess., ser. 1, Part 6, at 1248-1252 (1951).

[11] *Organized Baseball*, Report of the Subcommittee on Study of Monopoly Power of the House Committee on the Judiciary, H.R. REP. No. 2002, 82d Cong., 2d Sess. 228 (1952); *cf.* also *id.*, at 208-228.

[12] Statement of Ford C. Frick, Commissioner of Baseball, in *Hearings Before the Antitrust Subcommittee of the House Committee on the Judiciary*, 85th Cong., 1st Sess. (June 19, 1957), Official Verbatim Transcript (mimeographed) 218-219, 238, 240, 243-244.

demonstrates, cases may arise in which the suspicion might be justified.

* * *

"Player loyalty, team integrity, and will to win—these are indispensable ingredients of public respect for the game. I have yet to hear of a proposal for elimination or modification of the reserve clause which will give any assurance on these points.

"It has been suggested that a player be released from reservation after three, five, seven or ten years. Mr. Hillings' second bill [H.R. 8023], for example, would exempt from the antitrust laws a reserve clause which operated for three years, subject to a two-year extension if the player's salary were increased 15% in each of the fourth and fifth years. At whatever the point of his release from reservation, the player becomes then subject to these questions of loyalty. The suggestion that some but not all players be reserved raises the same problem as to the unreserved players. Also, the players not reserved might object to discriminatory treatment as they did when the practice of a limited number of reservations was given a trial.

"The reserve clause has advantages for the player in that it increases the incentive of the club to exercise patience and make expenditures of time and money in his development. Many of our Major League players, including some of the stars, were slow in developing into Major League caliber. The active Major League players in 1956, other than 25 bonus players, had an average of 4.13 years in the Minor Leagues. The production of Major League players is an expensive process."

In *Toolson* v. *New York Yankees, Inc.*[13] the Supreme Court dealt with a private antitrust action of a professional baseball player who had been barred from playing in organized baseball.

Toolson was under a standard player contract with the Newark International Baseball Club, Inc., one of the signatories of the Major League Agreement. Pursuant to this agreement one club has the power to assign a player to play with another club. When the Newark Club assigned Toolson's contract to Binghamton Exhibition Co., Toolson refused to report to the latter club. For his breach of the player contract and pursuant to the regulations governing organized baseball, Toolson was placed on the ineligible list of the Binghamton team and defendants refused to allow Toolson to play professional baseball. Toolson brought suit under sections 1 and 2 of the Sherman Act and the Clayton Act, alleging that, as a result of the alleged monopoly to which all of the defendants were allegedly parties, he had been deprived of his livelihood. The district court dismissed the

---

[13] 346 U.S. 356 (1953).

action for want of jurisdiction over the subject matter[14] on the basis of *Federal Baseball Club of Baltimore, Inc.* v. *National League of Professional Baseball Clubs.*[15] The Supreme Court affirmed the decision and disposed of the *Toolson* case with the following short majority *per curiam* opinion:[16]

> "In *Federal Baseball Club of Baltimore* v. *National League of Professional Baseball Clubs,* 1922, 259 U.S. 200, this Court held that the business of providing public baseball games for profit between clubs of professional baseball players was not within the scope of the federal antitrust laws. Congress has had the ruling under consideration but has not seen fit to bring such business under these laws by legislation having prospective effect. The business has thus been left for thirty years to develop, on the understanding that it was not subject to existing antitrust legislation. The present case asks us to overrule the prior decision and, with retrospective effect, hold the legislation applicable. We think that if there are evils in this field which now warrant application to it of the antitrust laws, it should be by legislation. *Without re-examination of the underlying issues,* the judgments below are affirmed on the authority of *Federal Baseball Club of Baltimore* v. *National League of Professional Baseball Clubs, supra,* so far as that decision determines that Congress had no intention of including the business of baseball within the scope of the federal antitrust laws." [Emphasis added.]

Indeed the majority ruled without any determination on the basis of the present facts. This is vividly illustrated by Justice Burton in his dissenting opinion, concurred in by Justice Reed:[17]

> "Whatever may have been the situation when the *Federal Baseball Club* case [Footnote omitted] was decided in 1922, I am not able to join today's decision which, in effect, announces that organized baseball, in 1953, still is not engaged in interstate trade or commerce. In the light of organized baseball's well-known and widely distributed capital investment used in conducting competitions between teams constantly traveling between states, its receipts and expenditures of large sums transmitted between states, its numerous purchases of materials in interstate commerce, the attendance at its local exhibitions of large audiences often traveling across state lines, its radio and television activities which expand its audience beyond state lines, its sponsorship of interstate advertising, and its highly organized 'farm system' of minor league baseball clubs, coupled with restrictive contracts and understandings between individuals and among clubs or leagues playing for profit throughout the United

---

[14] 101 F.Supp. 93 (S.D. Cal. 1951).
[15] 259 U.S. 200 (1922).
[16] 346 U.S. 356 (1953).
[17] 346 U.S. 356, at 357 and 360.

States, and even in Canada, Mexico and Cuba, it is a contradiction in terms to say that the defendants in the cases before us are not now engaged in interstate trade or commerce as those terms are used in the Constitution of the United States and in the Sherman Act . . .

* * *

"In the *Federal Baseball Club* case the Court did not state that even if the activities of organized baseball amounted to interstate trade or commerce those activities were exempt from the Sherman Act. The Court acted on its determination that the activities before it did not amount to interstate commerce."

In addition, Justice Burton set forth some of the facts and figures contained in the 1952 *Report on Organized Baseball* of the Subcommittee on Study of Monopoly Power of the House Committee on the Judiciary.[18] That Report stated:[19]

"After full review of all of the foregoing facts and with due consideration of modern judicial interpretation of the scope of the commerce clause, it is the studied judgment of the Subcommittee on the Study of Monopoly Power that the Congress has jurisdiction to investigate and legislate on the subject of professional baseball."

(2) The Theatrical Business

The refusal of the Supreme Court to re-examine the application of the antitrust laws to organized baseball suggested to other segments of the entertainment industry that they might similarly obtain exemptions from the antitrust laws. Their efforts were based either on the fact that the industry concerned was akin to baseball and, therefore, not engaged in interstate trade or commerce, or on the ground that the Supreme Court had ruled on the facts in the industry concerned at some time in the past and, at that time, found the business practices now being attacked by the federal government or private parties to be lawful under the antitrust laws.[20]

---

[18] H.R. REP. No. 2002, 82d Cong., 2d Sess. (1952). Thus the combined revenue of the 16 major-league clubs rose from $10,519,500 in 1929 to $32,035,500 in 1950. During the same period, receipts from radio and television rose from nothing in 1929 to $3,365,500 in 1950. *Id.*, at 5-6, quoted by Justice Burton in 356 U.S. at 359.

[19] *Id.*, 4, 7, and see 111-139.

[20] It is interesting to note that in their dissenting opinion in United States v. Employing Plasterers Association, 347 U.S. 189, 190 *et seq.* (1954), Justices Minton and Douglas on the basis of the Federal Baseball case took the position that contracting to plaster a building in Chicago by a contractor located outside the state is not interstate commerce even though the contractor intends to bring his men from outside to do the job.

In *United States* v. *Shubert*[21] Chief Judge Knox dismissed a civil antitrust action alleging restraint of trade in the theatre field with the following brief opinion:

> "In principle, I can see no valid distinction between the facts of this case and those which were before the Supreme Court in the cases of *Federal Baseball Club of Baltimore* v. *National League of Professional Baseball Clubs,* . . . and *Toolson* v. *New York Yankees,* . . ."

The defendants were engaged in the business of producing theatrical attractions, booking attractions in theatres throughout the United States, and operating about forty theatres in eight states, including all the theatres in almost all key "try-out" cities and about 50 per cent of the theatres in New York City. The economic importance of the business was emphasized by the fact that in 1953 it generally cost from $60,000 to $100,000 to produce a play, while musicals required from $200,000 to $300,000.

The Supreme Court reversed the district court and held that the business of producing, booking, and presenting legitimate attractions on a multistate basis constitutes "trade or commerce" that is "among the several States" within the meaning of those terms in the Sherman Act.[22] Chief Justice Warren stated that in *Hart* v. *B. F. Keith Vaudeville Exchange*[23] the Court established that *Federal Baseball*[24] "did not automatically immunize the theatrical business from antitrust laws."[25] In the *Hart* case the "Court took note of the plaintiff's argument 'that in the transportation of vaudeville acts the apparatus sometimes is more important than the performers' and concluded that the complaint, at least to that extent, sufficiently alleged a violation of the [Sherman] Act to go to trial."[26] *Toolson* could not be relied upon by the defendants in *Shubert* because in *Toolson* " '[w]ithout re-examination of the underlying issues', the Court adhered to *Federal Baseball* 'so far as that decision determines that Congress had no intention of including the business of baseball within the scope of the federal antitrust laws.' 346 U.S. at 357. In short, *Toolson* was a narrow application of the rule of *stare decisis*."[27]

---

[21] 120 F.Supp. 15, 16 (S.D. N.Y. 1953), *reversed,* 348 U. S. 222 (1955).

[22] United States v. Shubert, 348 U.S. 222 (1955).

[23] 262 U.S. 271 (1923), decided in the term following that in which Federal Baseball was decided.

[24] Federal Baseball Club of Baltimore, Inc. v. National League of Professional Baseball Clubs, 259 U.S. 200 (1922).

[25] United States v. Shubert, 348 U.S. 222, at 229 (1955).

[26] *Id.,* at 228-229.

[27] *Id.,* at 230.

Thus by narrowly construing the immunity granted in *Federal Baseball,* the Supreme Court staved off this attempt to bring the theatrical business under the *Federal Baseball* exemption. It is noteworthy that Justice Burton, retaining the views expressed in his dissent in the *Toolson* case,[28] joined the opinion and judgment of the Court and Justice Reed joined in this concurrence.[29]

(3) Professional Boxing

In 1954, a district court dismissed a civil antitrust suit involving the business of promoting professional championship boxing contests on a multistate basis on the ground that there was no valid distinction between the case and *Federal Baseball* and *Toolson.*[30]

On the same day the Supreme Court decided the *Shubert* case, it reversed the district court and held that the promotion of professional championship boxing contests on a multistate basis, coupled with the sale of rights to televise, broadcast and film the contests for interstate transmission, constitutes "trade or commerce among the several States" within the meaning of the Sherman Act.[31] The Court noted that it had never before considered the antitrust status of the boxing business but that, absent *Federal Baseball* and *Toolson,* the Government's allegations brought the defendants within the scope of the Sherman Act. The Court held that the exemption sought by the defendants in the boxing case could not be granted without substantially repealing the antitrust laws. Said the Court:[32]

> "We have held today in the Shubert case that *Toolson* is not authority for exempting other businesses merely because of the circumstance that they are also based on the performance of local exhibitions. That ruling is fully applicable here.
> "Moreover, none of the factors underlying the *Toolson* decision are present in the instant case. At the time the government's complaint was filed, no court had ever held that the boxing business is not subject to the antitrust laws. [References

----

[28] 346 U.S. 356, 357.

[29] United States v. Shubert, 348 U.S. 222, at 231 (1955).

[30] United States v. International Boxing Club, Inc. (S.D. N.Y. 1954). The judge gave an oral opinion. The grounds for dismissal are to be found in the assignment of errors and prayers for reversal filed with the Supreme Court on March 12, 1954.

[31] United States v. International Boxing Club, Inc., 348 U.S. 236 (1955). See subsequent decision in United States v. International Boxing Club, Inc., 150 F.Supp. 397 (S.D. N.Y. 1957); judgment partially stayed pending appeal, 78 S.Ct. 4 (1957).

[32] *Id.,* at 242-243.

omitted.] Indeed this Court's decision in the *Hart* case less than a year after the *Federal Baseball* decision, clearly established that *Federal Baseball* could not be relied upon as a basis of exemption for other segments of the entertainment business, athletic or otherwise. Surely there is nothing in the Holmes opinion in the *Hart* case to suggest, even remotely, that the Court was drawing a line between athletic and nonathletic entertainment. Nor do we see the relevance of such a distinction for the purpose of determining what constitutes 'trade or commerce among the several States.' The controlling consideration in *Federal Baseball* and *Hart* was, instead, a very practical one—the degree of interstate activity involved in the particular business under review. It follows that *stare decisis* cannot help the defendant here; for, contrary to their argument, *Federal Baseball* did not hold that all businesses based on professional sports are outside the scope of the antitrust laws. The issue confronting us is, therefore, not whether a previously granted exemption should continue, but whether an exemption should be granted in the first instance. And that issue is for Congress to resolve, not this Court."

Thus, in the *Toolson* opinion the failure of Congress in 1951 to pass laws exempting all professional sports from application of the antitrust laws was used as an argument to uphold the ruling in *Federal Baseball*. By contrast, in the boxing case that failure was used by the Court to support its holding that Congress did not wish to exempt other professional sports from the application of those laws.

Justice Minton, unable to agree with the rationale of the majority, stated:[33] "What this court held in the *Federal Baseball* case to be incident to the exhibition now becomes more important than the exhibition."

Justice Frankfurter also dissented against what he considered a capricious application of *stare decisis*.[34] Indeed the interstate aspects of baseball and the extent of the exploitation of baseball through mass media are far more extensive than is true of boxing. Again Justice Burton, retaining the views expressed in his dissent in the Toolson case, joined the majority opinion and judgment of the Court, and Justice Reed joined in the concurrence.[35]

---

[33] *Id.*, at 251.

[34] *Id.*, at 248.

[35] *Id.*, at 245. Based on International Boxing, a district court recently held: "The business of *professional basketball*, as conducted by the National Basketball League and its constituent teams on a multistate basis, *coupled with* the sale of rights to televise and broadcast the games for interstate transmission, is trade or commerce among the several States within

(4) Professional Football

In *United States* v. *National Football League*[36] the plaintiff sought an injunction against certain bylaws of the League restricting radio broadcasting and televising of professional football games played by member clubs on the ground that it violated section 1 of the Sherman Act. The court easily distinguished the *Toolson* case, on the ground that *National Football* primarily concerned restrictions on the sale of radio and television rights, and rendered judgment for the plaintiff.

In *Radovich* v. *National Football League*[37] a professional football player sued for treble damages under section 4 of the Clayton Act. Radovich alleged that he was denied employment in organized professional football by illegal conspiracy between a football league and its ten member clubs to monopolize interstate commerce in professional football; and that pursuant to agreement, defendants boycotted Radovich and prevented him from becoming a player coach in the Pacific Coast League. The trial court dismissed the case for lack of jurisdiction and failure to state a claim on which relief could be granted. The court of appeals affirmed.[38]

The Supreme Court held that the business of professional football, as conducted by a football league and its member clubs on a multistate basis, is within the coverage of the antitrust laws and that the complaint stated a cause of action thereunder. Justice Clark stated for the majority:[39]

> "[B]ut since *Toolson* and *Federal Baseball* are still cited as controlling authority in antitrust actions involving other fields of business, we now specifically limit the rule there established to the facts there involved, *i.e.*, the business of organized professional baseball. As long as the Congress continues to acquiesce we should adhere to—but not extend—the interpretation of the [Sherman] Act made in those cases. We did not extend them to boxing or the theatre because we believed that the volume of interstate business in each—the rationale of *Federal Baseball*— was such that both activities were within the Act. Likewise, the volume of interstate business involved in organized football places it within the provisions of the Act."

---

the meaning of the Sherman Act." Washington Professional Basketball Corp. v. National Basketball Ass'n, 157 F.Supp. 154 (S.D. N.Y. 1956).

[36] 116 F.Supp. 319 (E.D. Pa. 1953).

[37] 352 U.S. 445 (1957).

[38] 231 F.2d 620 (9th Cir. 1956).

[39] Radovich v. National Football League, 352 U.S. 445 at 451-452 (1957). Justices Frankfurter, Harlan and Brennan dissented. See Note, 57 COLUM. L.REV. 725 (1957).

The Supreme Court also noted that if the amount of revenues from radio and television interstate transmission which are a "significant, integral" part of the League's business is substantial "as alleged, it alone is sufficient to meet the commerce requirements of the Act."[40]

(5) Legislative Reaction to Court Decisions Regarding Professional Sports

Congressman Celler, Chairman of the Antitrust Subcommittee of the House Committee on the Judiciary recently summarized pending legislation:[41]

". . . [T]he obligation rests upon the Congress to determine whether the Supreme Court decisions are discriminatory and, if so, how this discrimination should be resolved.

"Each of the bills pending before the Antitrust Subcommittee is designed to rectify what is regarded as a disparate situation; each is designed to reemphasize the fundamental premise of American jurisprudence of equality of legal treatment.

"Three types of solution to the present problem are suggested by the pending proposals. My bill, H.R. 5319 and H.R. 5307, introduced by Representative Hillings, a member of this Committee, of California, provides that baseball, like other professional sports activities, shall be subject to the antitrust laws. Under these bills, the courts would be permitted to determine upon the facts in each individual case whether or not any particular agreement or trade practice constituted an unreasonable restraint of trade.

"Several other bills, namely, H.R. 6876 introduced by Representative Keating, one of our colleagues on this Committee, of New York, H.R. 6877 by Representative Byrnes of Wisconsin and H.R. 8023 by Representative Hillings, include all professional sports under the antitrust laws with the exception of certain enumerated practices that are specifically exempted. Representative Hillings' bill, H.R. 8023, contains an additional proviso that a reserve clause in a player's contract of employment would enjoy an antitrust exemption only if it did not exceed 5 years in duration and if the amount of compensation for the last 2 years were increased by 15 percent each year.

"H.R. 5383, introduced by the distinguished Chairman of the Committee on Foreign and International Commerce, Representative Harris of Arkansas, provides for a complete antitrust exemption for all professional sports enterprises, as well as for acts in the conduct of such enterprises."

---

[40] *Id.*, at 453.
[41] Professional Sports, *Hearings Before the Antitrust Subcommittee of the House Committee on the Judiciary*, 85th Cong., 1st Sess. (June 17, 1957), Official Verbatim Transcript (mimeographed) 2-4.

(6) Insurance Business

In *United States* v. *South Eastern Underwriters' Association*[42] the Supreme Court held that the antitrust laws apply to the insurance business to the same extent as they do to other businesses conducted across state lines. As a result of the vigorous reaction of the insurance companies to this decision, Congress enacted the McCarran-Ferguson Insurance Regulation Act.[43] Section 2 (b) of the Act provides, *inter alia,* that after June 30, 1948, the Sherman Act, the Clayton Act, and the Federal Trade Commission Act, as amended, "shall be applicable to the business of insurance *to the extent that such business is not regulated by state law.*"[44] [Emphasis supplied.]

In 1954, the Federal Trade Commission, acting under section 5 of the Federal Trade Commission Act, began a nationwide investigation of alleged false and misleading advertising of health and accident insurance companies. This investigation has resulted in Federal Trade Commission complaints against forty-one companies. Thirty-six of the firms contended that the Commission lacked jurisdiction.[45] See, *e.g., American Hospital and Life Insurance Co.;*[46] *Travellers Health Assn.;*[47] and *National Casualty Co.*[48]

The arguments of both sides have been summarized in the following case wherein the court reversed and set aside the cease and desist order issued by the Federal Trade Commission.

NATIONAL CASUALTY CO. v. FEDERAL TRADE COMMISSION
United States Court of Appeals for the Sixth Circuit
245 F.2d 883 (1957)[49]

"MILLER, Circuit Judge.

"The petitioner seeks a review of an order of the Federal Trade Commission requiring the petitioner to cease and desist from engaging in acts and practices in the conduct of its insurance business found by the Commission to be unfair and deceptive, in violation of the Federal Trade Commission Act, as amended. Sect. 45(a) (1) (6) and (c), Title 15, U.S. Code.

"The complaint filed by the Commission alleged that the petitioner in the course of its interstate business of selling accident

---

[42] 322 U.S. 533 (1944).

[43] 59 STAT. 33 (1945), 15 U.S.C. §§ 1011 *et seq.* (1952).

[44] 59 STAT. 34 (1945), 15 U.S.C. § 1012 (f) (1952).

[45] 3 CCH TRADE REG. REP. p. 35, 837 (10th ed. 1956).

[46] F.T.C. Dkt. No. 6237 (April 24, 1956).

[47] F.T.C. Dkt. No. 6252 (December 20, 1956, initial decision March 29, 1956).

[48] F.T.C. Dkt. No. 6311 (May 2, 1956).

[49] *Cert. granted,* 355 U.S. 867 (1957).

and health insurance and for the purpose of inducing purchases of such insurance policies, was making statements and representations concerning the benefits of said policies of insurance which were false and deceptive, were to the prejudice and injury of the public, and constituted unfair and deceptive acts and practices in commerce within the meaning of the Federal Trade Commission Act. Petitioner by its answer admitted that it had advertised its accident and health insurance policies as charged in the complaint, but denied that its advertising was false or misleading, or was to the prejudice and injury of the public, or that it had violated the Federal Trade Commission Act. The petitioner affirmatively alleged that the Commission was without jurisdiction over its interstate insurance business because of state statutes regulating unfair and deceptive acts or practices within the respective boundaries of the states, within the scope and meaning of the McCarran Act, Sections 1011-1015, Title 15 U.S. Code.

"At the hearings which followed, the facts were shown to be as follows. Petitioner is a stock company incorporated under the laws of Michigan for the purpose of selling accident, health and all types of casualty insurance, with its principal office in Detroit, Michigan. It is licensed to sell such policies in all states of the United States, the District of Columbia and Hawaii, through resident agents located therein. It sells its insurance policies by solicitation from 350 to 400 direct, but independent, insurance agents throughout the nation, who operate under contract on commission only. Petitioner prepares and sends to these agents direct-mailing cards, advertising material and applications. The agents mail locally or distribute personally this material to likely prospects, secure leads thereby and then call and personally solicit the prospect. A small percent of direct mail advertising is sent by petitioner from its offices in Detroit to the public. 80% or more of petitioners' accident and health policies are issued by it from its home office after receipt, checking and consideration by it of the prospect's signed application which has been secured by the agent. Any policy issued by petitioner is forwarded to the agent for delivery to the insured. Premium notice forms are printed by the petitioner and furnished to the agents who mail them out locally. Premium collection is the agent's responsibility, only 5% or less being remitted directly to the petitioner in cases of unusual or temporary situations.

❋ ❋ ❋

". . . Since, in our opinion, this case will be disposed of on the jurisdictional issue, it is unnecessary to discuss petitioner's contentions that its advertising was not false or misleading and that the proceeding and the issuance of a Cease and Desist order did not serve any public interest. The jurisdictional question involves the construction and application of the McCarran Act referred to above.

"The background giving rise to the McCarran Act is important.

"In 1869, the Supreme Court upheld the validity of a Virginia statute which regulated foreign insurance companies, on the ground that the statute did not offend the Commerce Clause of the U. S. Constitution because 'issuing a policy of insurance is not a transaction of commerce.' *Paul* v. *Virginia,* 8 Wall 168, 183. Thereafter, in similar cases, the Supreme Court consistently ruled that the business of insurance was not commerce. In *New York Life Insurance Company* v. *Deer Lodge County,* 231 U.S. 495, 503-504, 510, the Supreme Court, as late as 1913, held to this view, stating in its opinion in that case that 'contracts of insurance are not commerce at all, neither state nor interstate.' However, in 1955, the Supreme Court in *United States* v. *South-Eastern Underwriters' Association,* 322 U.S. 533, a case involving alleged violations of the Sherman Antitrust Act, again considered the question and in a four-to-three decision, held that the business of insurance conducted across state lines was interstate commerce subject to regulation by Congress under the Commerce Clause.

"The Supreme Court's decision was vigorously protested in the insurance field. The insurance companies, relying upon the Court's previous rulings, had engaged in practices which were prohibited under the federal antitrust laws but which were permitted under the laws and regulations of the various states. The states feared the loss of large revenues under their laws taxing insurance sold within the states, which, under the new ruling, might be held discriminatory of interstate commerce and, therefore, unconstitutional. As a result of this vigorous reaction to the decision, Congress passed the so-called McCarran Act in 1945.

* * *

"The petitioner contends that the purpose of the Act was generally to restore the insurance business to the situation existing prior to the decision in the *South-Eastern Underwriters* case, and that in states in which the insurance business was regulated by state law, such business was not subject to regulation by the Federal Trade Commission.

"The Commission does not challenge the validity of any state statute regulating the business of insurance, nor the validity of the McCarran Act. It points out that state laws have no extraterritorial effect and cannot regulate the business of insurance beyond the borders of the particular state; that prior to the *South-Eastern Underwriters Association* case, the states were authorized to regulate the intrastate aspects of the insurance business, even though state regulation might affect interstate commerce in insurance; that following the decision in the *South-Eastern Underwriters Association* case there was a field of interstate business of insurance which the states could not regulate and which Congress did not intend to leave unregulated; that in enacting the McCarran Act, Congress intended only to authorize the states to exercise their police power in the same manner they had exercised it when the business of insurance was not considered to be commerce, and gave the states until January 1, 1948, later extended by statute to June 30, 1948, in which to define a reasonable area of state police power, beyond which they could not go; that after that date the Commission was authorized to regulate insurance on different grounds, namely, regulating the use of the interstate channels of commerce; and that the Federal and state laws in the field of insurance supplement and reinforce one another in order to provide full protection to the public.

"The wording of the Act clearly indicates that, regardless of the ruling in the *South-Eastern Underwriters Association* case, Congress did not intend to take from the states the regulation of insurance within the state. Section 1 declares that the *continued* regulation . . . by the several states of the business of insurance is in the public interest, . . .' (emphasis added). Section 2 states, 'The business of insurance . . . shall be subject to the laws of the several states which relate to the regulation or taxation of such business.' The real question is, to what extent, if any, did Congress provide for federal regulation in addition to state regulation.

"The Act is equally clear, by the express wording of Section 3, that until January 1, 1948, subsequently extended by amendment to June 30, 1948, the business of insurance was not subject to the Federal Trade Commission Act or certain other federal regulatory acts. After January 1, 1948, according to Section 2 of the Act, the Federal Trade Commission Act and the Sherman and Clayton Acts were made 'applicable to the business of insurance to the extent that such business is not regulated by state law.' That is the only express grant of power to the Federal Trade Commission over the business of insurance contained in the Act. It is a grant expressly limited by its terms to insurance business which 'is not regulated by state law.' We do not find in those words the 'clear and specific grant of jurisdiction' to the Federal Trade Commission which the Commission claims is given to it by the Act. On the contrary, we find the logical and reasonable conclusion from the two sections to be that jurisdiction over the business of insurance was granted to the Federal Trade Commission after January 1, 1948, *only* where the business was not regulated by state law.

"There is some merit in the Commission's contention that since the decision in the *South-Eastern Underwriters Association* case there is a field of interstate insurance, outside the jurisdiction of the states, which should be subject to federal regulation. But it does not follow that it was the purpose of the McCarran Act to accomplish such result, desirable though it might be. Congress realized that by reason of the Supreme Court decision federal jurisdiction existed over the interstate business of insurance. The enactment of the McCarran Act was to correct that situation . . .

* * *

"It is probable that in the regulation of the business of insurance by both the federal and state governments there will develop a conflict of policies. The parties agree that in such event the federal regulation would control. If so, 'the continued regulation and taxation by the several states,' referred to in Section 1 of the Act as being in the public interest, would no longer exist.

"The general purpose of restoring to the states the right to regulate the business of insurance as it existed prior to the 1944 decision was carried out by the moratorium provided by the Act until January 1, 1948. During the moratorium there was no jurisdiction over the business of insurance in the Commission. During that period the states which did not have such laws had the necessary time in which to pass regulatory legislation. The tie-in between the moratorium and the obvious invitation to enact regulatory legislation while it existed, both recognized the need of regulating the business of insurance and indicated an intention to permit the states to do it to the exclusion of the federal government if they elected to do so. It seems more logical to conclude that it was the purpose of the moratorium to deprive the federal agencies of their newly acquired jurisdiction over the business of insurance in order to restore such jurisdiction to the states if they elected to assume it, than to conclude that it was the purpose of the moratorium to deprive the agencies of their newly acquired jurisdiction for only a short period of time after which it would be given back to them regardless of what the states did in the meantime.

* * *

"We are of the opinion that the Federal Trade Commission was without jurisdiction to regulate the insurance business of the petitioner in those states where such business is regulated by state law. The order of the Commission is set aside and the case remanded to the Commission for further proceedings consistent with this opinion."

The Court of Appeals for the Fifth Circuit reached the same result in *American Hospital and Life Insurance Co.* v. *Federal Trade Commission.*[50] Other cases are at present pending before the courts of appeals.

---

[50] 243 F.2d 719 (5th Cir. 1957), *cert. granted,* 355 U.S. 867 (1957). *Cf.* also Miley v. John Hancock Mutual Life Insurance Co., 148 F.Supp. 299, at 301-302 (D. Mass. 1957); *affirmed per curiam,* 242 F.2d 758 (1st Cir. 1957); *cert. denied,* 355 U.S. 828 (1957). In this case, a suit for treble damages, brought by an insurance broker against several Massachusetts insurance companies, was dismissed because, *inter alia,* it was held that the Massachusetts law fully regulated the acts of the defendants.

Chapter 2

MONOPOLY AND OLIGOPOLY

(1) The Meaning of the Legal Concept "to monopolize"

The Sherman Act prohibits monopolies in the field of inter-state trade and commerce and provides for their restraint and dissolution. Section 2 of the Act reads:

> "Every person who shall monopolize or attempt to monopolize or combine or conspire with any other person or persons to monopolize any part of the trade or commerce among the several states, or with foreign nations, shall be guilty of a misdemeanor, and on conviction thereof, shall be punished by fine not exceeding fifty thousand dollars, or by imprisonment not exceeding one year, or by both said punishments, in the discretion of the court."[1]

The Act does not define monopoly. The burden is thrown upon the courts to determine, case by case, whether the particular facts before them warrant a finding of unlawful monopoly. Facts play the predominant role in such cases, which may account for the lengthy court opinions.

Some general guides or standards may be drawn from the decided cases which are of some help to the courts, the government and industry.

An unlawful monopoly, within the meaning of the statute, exists whenever one person, or a group of persons acting jointly or by conspiracy, has (1) the power to exclude actual or potential competition from a field and (2) the purpose to exercise that power.[2] "[T]he material consideration in determining whether a monopoly exists is not that prices are raised and that competition actually is excluded, but that power exists to raise prices or to exclude competition when it is desired to do so."[3]

---

[1] 26 STAT. 209 (1890), as amended, 15 U.S.C. § 2 (Supp. IV, 1957).

[2] United States v. Griffith, 334 U.S. 100, 107 (1948); American Tobacco Co. v. United States, 328 U.S. 781, 809 (1946). See Handler, *Monopolies, Mergers and Markets—A New Focus,* in SYMPOSIUM of same title, 17-28 (Trade Regulation Series No. 1, Timberg and Hoffmann ed. 1955).

[3] 328 U.S. at 811.

It is no defense that an existing monopoly was lawfully acquired, just as it is no defense to a charge of conspiracy to monopolize that the monopoly power was never acquired.[4]

Purpose to monopolize "is present if the acquisition or retention of the power comes about as a consequence of defendant's conduct or business arrangements."[5]

(a) Determination of the relevant market

Two basic considerations in a monopoly case are factual; the relevant market[6] and the extent of monopoly in that market.

> ". . . The Sherman Act is not limited to eliminating restraints whose effects cover the entire United States; [the Supreme Court has] consistently held that where the relevant competitive market covers only a small area the Sherman Act may be invoked to prevent unreasonable restraints within that area. In *United States* v. *Yellow Cab Co.*, 332 U.S. 218, we sustained the validity of a complaint which alleged that the defendants had monopolized the cab operating business in four large cities. It is the volume in the area which the alleged restraints affect that is important."[7]

The "relevant market" in one case may involve a geographical determination;[8] in another it may turn on product differentiation and the availability of competitive substitutes or alternative products. An excellent illustration of the difficulties underlying the determination of the relevant market is to be found in the *Cellophane* case[9], the most important recent opinion under section 2 of the Sherman Act. There the Supreme Court found substitute competition between cellophane and other flexible wrapping materials by looking to the so-called cross-elasticity of demand between the products. This modern economic test at-

---

[4] Relevant market is also a consideration in other cases under the antitrust laws, *e.g.*, section 7 of the Clayton Act. United States v. E. I. du Pont de Nemours & Co., 353 U.S. 586 (1957).

[5] United States v. Columbia Steel Co., 334 U.S. 495, at 519 (1948).

[6] United States v. Griffith, 334 U.S. 100, 107 (1948). For a critical review of this concept as a criterion limiting the application of the Sherman Act, see Marcus, *Antitrust Bugbears: Substitute Products—Oligopoly,* 105 U.PA.L.REV. 185, 186-204 (1957).

[7] United States v. Aluminum Co. of America, 91 F.Supp. 333, 342 (S.D.N.Y. 1950); see American Tobacco Co. v. United States, 328 U.S. 781, 809-814 (1946). For a presentation of pertinent case material, see our book REGULATION OF TRADE, Chapter 6 (1953).

[8] In United States v. Lehigh Valley Railroad Co., 254 U.S. 255 (1920), the Court was concerned with the anthracite producing territory of eastern Pennsylvania underlying approximately 310,000 acres of land.

[9] United States v. E. I. du Pont de Nemours & Co., 351 U.S. 377 (1956).

tempts to measure the responsiveness of the sales of one product to price changes of the other.

UNITED STATES v. E. I. DU PONT DE NEMOURS & CO.

Supreme Court of the United States 351 U.S. 377 (1956)

"Mr. JUSTICE REED delivered the opinion of the Court.

＊ ＊ ＊

"During the period that is relevant to this action du Pont produced almost 75% of the cellophane sold in the United States, and cellophane constituted less than 20% of all 'flexible packaging material' sales. This was the designation accepted at the trial for the materials listed in Finding 280, App.A, this opinion.

"The Government contends that by so dominating cellophane production du Pont monopolized a 'part of the trade or commerce' in violation of § 2. Respondent agrees that cellophane is a product which constitutes 'a "part" of commerce within the meaning of Section 2.' Du Pont brief, 16, 79. But it contends that the prohibition of § 2 against monopolization is not violated because it does not have the power to control the price of cellophane or to exclude competitors from the market in which cellophane is sold. The court below found that the 'relevant market for determining the extent of du Pont's market control is the market for flexible packaging materials,' and that competition from those other materials prevented du Pont from possessing monopoly powers in its sales of cellophane. Finding 37.

"The Government asserts that cellophane and other wrapping materials are neither substantially fungible nor like priced. For these reasons, it argues that the market for other wrappings is distinct from the market for cellophane and that the competition afforded cellophane by other wrappings is not strong enough to be considered in determining whether du Pont has monopoly powers. Market delimitation is necessary under du Pont's theory to determine whether an alleged monopolist violates § 2. The ultimate consideration in such a determination is whether the defendants control the price and competition in the market for such part of trade or commerce as they are charged with monopolizing. Every manufacturer is the sole producer of the particular commodity it makes but its control in the above sense of the relevant market depends upon the availability of alternative commodities for buyers; *i.e.*, whether there is a cross-elasticity of demand between cellophane and the other wrappings. This interchangeability is largely gauged by the purchase of competing products for similar uses considering the price, characteristics and adaptability of the competing commodities. The court below found that the flexible wrappings afforded such alternatives. This Court must determine whether the trial court erred in its estimate of the competition afforded cellophane by other materials.

* * *

IV. *The Relevant Market.*

"When a product is controlled by one interest, without substitutes available in the market, there is monopoly power. Because most products have possible substitutes, we cannot, as we said in *Times Picayune* v. *United States*, 345 U.S. 594, 612, give 'that infinite range' to the definition of substitutes. Nor is it a proper interpretation of the Sherman Act to require that products be fungible to be considered in the relevant market.

"The Government argues:

'We do not here urge that in no circumstances may competition of substitutes negative possession of monopolistic power over trade in a product. The decisions make it clear at the least that the courts will not consider substitutes other than those which are substantially fungible with the monopolized product and sell at substantially the same price.'

"But where there are market alternatives that buyers may readily use for their purposes, illegal monopoly does not exist merely because the product said to be monopolized differs from others. If it were not so, only physically identical products would be a part of the market. To accept the Government's argument, we would have to conclude that the manufacturers of plain as well as moistureproof cellophane were monopolists and so with films such as pliofilm, foil, glassine, polyethylene, saran, for each of these wrapping materials are distinguishable. These were all exhibits in the case. New wrappings appear, generally similar to cellophane; is each a monopoly? What is called for is an appraisal of the 'cross-elasticity' of demand in the trade. See Note, 54 Col. L. Rev. 580. The varying circumstances of each case determine the result. [Footnote omitted.] In considering what is the relevant market for determining the control of price and competition, no more definite rule can be declared than that commodities reasonably interchangeable by consumers for the same purposes make up that 'part of the trade or commerce,' monopolization of which may be illegal. As respects flexible packaging materials, the market geographically is nationwide.

"Industrial activities cannot be confined to trim categories. Illegal monopolies under § 2 may well exist over limited products in narrow fields where competition is eliminated. [Footnote omitted.] That does not settle the issue here. In determining the market under the Sherman Act it is the use or uses to which the commodity is put that control. The selling price between commodities with similar uses and different characteristics may vary, so that the cheaper product can drive out the more expensive. Or, the superior quality of higher priced articles may make dominant the more desirable. Cellophane costs more than many competing products and less than a few. But whatever the price, there are various flexible wrapping materials that are bought by manufacturers for packaging their goods in their own plants or are sold to converters who shape and print them for use in the packaging of the commodities to be wrapped.

       ❋ ❋ ❋

"It may be admitted that cellophane combines the desirable elements of transparency, strength and cheapness more definitely than any of the others.

       ❋ ❋ ❋

"But despite cellophane's advantages it has to meet competition from other materials in every one of its uses. . . . The overall result is that cellophane accounts for 17.9% of flexible wrapping materials, measured by the wrapping surface. . . .

"Moreover, a very considerable degree of functional interchangeability exists between these products, . . .

       ❋ ❋ ❋

"An element for consideration as to cross-elasticity of demand between products is the responsiveness of the sales of one product to price changes of the other.[10] If a slight decrease in the price of cellophane causes a considerable number of customers of other flexible wrappings to switch to cellophane, it would be an indication that a high cross-elasticity of demand exists between them; that the products compete in the same market. The court below held that the '[g]reat sensitivity of customers in the flexible packaging markets to price or quality changes' prevented du Pont from possessing monopoly control over price. 118 F.Supp., at 207. The record sustains these findings. . . .

"We conclude that cellophane's interchangeability with the other materials mentioned suffices to make it a part of this flexible packaging material market.

"The Government stresses the fact that the variation in price between cellophane and other materials demonstrates they are non-competitive. As these products are all flexible wrapping materials, it seems reasonable to consider, as was done at the trial, their comparative cost to the consumer in terms of square area. . . . Cellophane costs two or three times as much, surface measure, as its chief competitors for the flexible wrapping market, glassine and greaseproof papers. Other forms of cellulose wrappings and those from other chemical or mineral substances, with the exception of aluminum foil, are more expensive. The uses of these materials, as can be observed by Finding 283 in Appendix A, are largely to wrap small packages for retail distribution. The wrapping is a relatively small proportion of the

---

[10] SCITOVSKY, WELFARE AND COMPETITION 396 (1951); BAIN, PRICING, DISTRIBUTION, AND EMPLOYMENT 52 (rev. ed. 1953).

entire costs of the article. [Footnote omitted.] Different producers need different qualities in wrappings and their need may
vary from time to time as their products undergo change. But
the necessity for flexible wrappings is the central and unchang-
ing demand. We cannot say that these differences in cost gave
du Pont monopoly power over prices in view of the findings of
fact on that subject. [Footnote omitted.]

"It is the variable characteristics of the different flexible wrappings and the energy and ability with which the manufacturers
push their wares that determine choice.

    * * *

"The facts above considered dispose also of any contention
that competitors have been excluded by du Pont from the packaging material market. That market has many producers and
there is no proof du Pont ever has possessed power to exclude
any of them from the rapidly expanding flexible packaging market. . . . Nor can we say that du Pont's profits, while liberal
(according to the Government 15.9% net after taxes on the 1937-
1947 average), demonstrate the existence of a monopoly without proof of lack of comparable profits during those years in
other prosperous industries. Cellophane was a leader, over 17%,
in the flexible packaging materials market. There is no showing
that du Pont's rate of return was greater or less than that of
other producers of flexible packaging materials. . . .

    * * *

"On the findings of the District Court, its judgment is affirmed.

Mr. JUSTICE CLARK and Mr. JUSTICE HARLAN took no
part in the consideration or decision of this case.

    * * *

"Mr. JUSTICE FRANKFURTER concurring.

    * * *

"Mr. CHIEF JUSTICE WARREN, with whom Mr. JUSTICE
BLACK and Mr. JUSTICE DOUGLAS join, dissenting.

"This case, like many under the Sherman Act, turns upon the
proper definition of the market. In defining the market in which
du Pont's economic power is to be measured, the majority virtually emasculate § 2 of the Sherman Act. They admit that 'cellophane combines the desirable elements of transparency,
strength and cheapness more definitely than any of' a host of
other packaging materials. Yet they hold that all of those materials are so indistinguishable from cellophane as to warrant their
inclusion in the market. We cannot agree that cellophane, in the
language of *Times-Picayune Publishing* Co. v. *United States,*
345 U.S. 594, 613, is 'the self-same product' as glassine, greaseproof and vegetable parchment papers, waxed papers, sulphite

papers, aluminum foil, cellulose acetate, and pliofilm and other films.[11]

* * *

"We cannot believe that buyers, practical businessmen, would have bought cellophane in increasing amounts over a quarter of a century if close substitutes were available at from one-seventh to one-half cellophane's price. That they did so is testimony to cellophane's distinctiveness.

"The inference yielded by the conduct of cellophane buyers is reinforced by the conduct of sellers other than du Pont. Finding 587 states that Sylvania, the only other cellophane producer, absolutely and immediately followed every du Pont price change, even dating back its price list to the effective date of du Pont's change. Producers of glassine and waxed paper, on the other hand, displayed apparent indifference to du Pont's repeated and substantial price cuts. . . . If 'shifts of business' due to 'price sensitivity' had been substantial, glassine and waxed paper producers who wanted to stay in business would have been compelled by market forces to meet du Pont's price challenge just as Sylvania was. . . .

* * *

"The trial court found that

'Du Pont has no power to set cellophane prices arbitrarily. If prices for cellophane increase in relation to prices of other flexible packaging materials it will lose business to manufacturers of such materials in varying amounts for each of du Pont's cellophane's major end uses.' Finding 712.

This further reveals its misconception of the antitrust laws. A monopolist seeking to maximize profits cannot raise prices 'arbitrarily.' Higher prices of course mean smaller sales, but they also mean higher per-unit profit. Lower prices will increase sales but reduce per-unit profit. Within these limits a monopolist has a considerable degree of latitude in determining which course to pursue in attempting to maximize profits. The trial judge thought that, if du Pont raised its price, the market would 'penalize' it with smaller profits as well as lower sales.[12] Du Pont proved him wrong. When 1947 operating earnings dropped below 26% for the first time in 10 years, it increased cellophane's price 7% and boosted its earnings in 1948. Du Pont's division manager then reported that 'If an operative return of 31% is

---

[11] In Times-Picayune Publishing Co. v. United States, 345 U.S. 594, 612, note 31, the Court said: "For every product, substitutes exist. But a relevant market cannot meaningfully encompass that infinite range. The circle must be drawn narrowly to exclude any other product to which, within reasonable variations in price, only a limited number of buyers will turn; in technical terms, products whose 'cross-elasticities of demand' are small."

[12] 118 F.Supp., at 206.

considered inadequate then an upward revision in prices will be necessary to improve the return.'[13] It is this latitude with respect to price, this broad power of choice, that the antitrust laws forbid.[14] Du Pont's independent pricing policy and the great profits consistently yielded by that policy leave no room for doubt that it had power to control the price of cellophane. The findings of fact cited by the majority cannot affect this conclusion.[15] For they merely demonstrate that, during the period covered by the complaint, du Pont was a 'good monopolist,' *i.e.*, that it did not engage in predatory practices and that it chose to maximize profits by lowering price and expanding sales. Proof of enlightened exercise of monopoly power certainly does not refute the existence of that power.

"The majority opinion purports to reject the theory of 'interindustry competition.' Brick, steel, wood, cement and stone, it says, are 'too different' to be placed in the same market. But cellophane, glassine, wax papers, sulphite papers, greaseproof and vegetable parchment papers, aluminum foil, cellulose acetate, Pliofilm and other films are not 'too different,' the opinion concludes. The majority approach would apparently enable a monopolist of motion picture exhibition to avoid Sherman Act consequences by showing that motion pictures compete in substantial measure with legitimate theater, television, radio, sporting events and other forms of entertainment. Here, too, 'shifts of business' undoubtedly accompany fluctuations in price and 'there are market alternatives that buyers may readily use for their purposes.' Yet, in *United States* v. *Paramount Pictures*, 334 U.S. 131, where the District Court had confined the relevant market to that for nationwide movie exhibition, this Court remanded the case to the District Court with directions to determine whether there was a monopoly on the part of the five major distributors 'in the *first-run* field for the entire country, in the *first-run* field in the 92 largest cities of the country, or in the *first-run* field in separate localities.' 334 U.S., at 172. Similarly, it is difficult to square the majority view with *United States* v. *Aluminum Co. of America*, 148 F.2d 416, a landmark § 2 case. There Judge Learned Hand, reversing a district court, held that the close competition which 'secondary' (used) aluminum offered to 'virgin' aluminum did not justify including the former within the relevant market for measuring Alcoa's economic power. Against these and other precedents, which the Court's opinion approves but does not follow, the formula of 'reasonable interchangeability,' as applied by the majority appears indistinguishable from the theory of 'interindustry competition.' The

---

[13] R. 4154-4155.

[14] See, *e.g.*, American Tobacco Co. v. United States, 328 U.S. 781, 805-806.

[15] See note 31, majority opinion.

danger in it is that, as demonstrated in this case, it is 'perfectly compatible with a fully monopolized economy.'[16]

The majority hold in effect that, because cellophane meets competition for many end uses, those buyers for other uses who need or want only cellophane are not entitled to the benfits of competition within the cellophane industry. . . .

The foregoing analysis of the record shows conclusively that cellophane is the relevant market. Since du Pont has the lion's share of that market, it must have monopoly power, as the majority concede. [Footnote omitted] This being so, we think it clear that, in the circumstances of this case, du Pont is guilty of 'monopolization.' The briefest sketch of du Pont's business history precludes it from falling within the 'exception to the Sherman Act prohibitions of monopoly power' (majority opinion, p. 13) by successfully asserting that monopoly was 'thrust upon' it. Du Pont was not 'the passive beneficiary of a monopoly' within the meaning of *United States* v. *Aluminum Co. of America, supra*, at 429-430. It sought and maintained dominance through illegal agreements dividing the world market, concealing and suppressing technological information, and restricting its licensee's production by prohibitive royalties, [Footnote omitted] and through numerous maneuvers which might have been 'honestly industrial' but whose necessary effect was nevertheless exclusionary.[17] Du Pont cannot bear 'the burden of proving that it owes its monopoly *solely* to superior skill. . . .' (Emphasis supplied.) *United States* v. *United Shoe Machinery Corp.*, 110 F.Supp. 295, 342, aff'd *per curiam*, 347 U.S. 521.

* * *

"If competition is at the core of the Sherman Act, we cannot agree that it was consistent with that Act for the enormously lucrative cellophane industry to have no more than two sellers from 1924 to 1951. The conduct of du Pont and Sylvania illustrates that a few sellers tend to act like one and that an industry which does not have a competitive structure will not have competitive behavior. The public should not be left to rely upon the dispensations of management in order to obtain the benefits which normally accompany competition. Such beneficence is of uncertain tenure. Only actual competition can assure long-run enjoyment of the goals of a free economy."

The *Cellophane* case has been widely discussed.[18] Today, it may be asked, whether the cross-elasticity of demand test as

----

16 Adams, *The "Rule of Reason": Workable Competition or Workable Monopoly?*, 63 Yale L.J. 348, 364.

17 See United States v. Aluminum Co. of America, 148 F.2d 416, 431.

18 See, *e.g.*, Turner, *Antitrust Policy and the Cellophane Case*, 70 HARV. L. REV. 281 (1956); Dirlam and Stelzer, *The Cellophane Labyrinth*, 1 ANTITRUST BULL. 633 (1956); Stocking and Mueller, *The Cellophane Case and the New Competition*, 45 AM.ECON.REV. 29 (1955); Chadwell,

applied in this case for determining the relevant market may be reconciled with the narrower test recently laid down in *du Pont-General Motors*,[19] decided under section 7 of the Clayton Act. In the latter case, the Court held that it suffices to show that there are enough peculiar characteristics and uses of the products to make them sufficiently distinct from all other similar products. "Thus, the bounds of the relevant market for the purposes of this case are not coextensive with the total market for finishes and fabrics, but are coextensive with the automobile industry, the relevant market for automotive finishes and fabrics."[20]

Hence, products which are "reasonably interchangeable by consumers for the same purpose"[21] within *Cellophane*, nevertheless may still have "sufficient peculiar characteristics and uses to constitute them products sufficiently distinct from all other" similar products "to make them a 'line of commerce' within the meaning of the Clayton Act."[22] However, the impact of *du Pont-General Motors* on *Cellophane* and future monopolization cases under section 2 remains to be seen. It is an open question whether, in determining the relevant market, the same test and the same standards should be applied to both monopoly and merger cases.

After *Cellophane* had been decided, attempts were made to bring other factual situations under its rule.[22a] In *Kansas City Star Co. v. United States*[23] the court of appeals rejected a newspaper company's contention that it did not monopolize the dissemination of news and advertising in the Kansas City area because it was

"in direct and vigorous competition with other mass media engaged in the dissemination of news and advertising and . . . could not exclude them from the market or control their prices.

Legal Tests for Violation of Section 2 of the Sherman Act and Section 7 of the Clayton Act in the Light of the Cellophane Opinion, 2 ANTITRUST BULL. 449 (1957); Gesell, *Legal Problems Involved in Proving Relevant Markets, id.*, 463; Stocking, *Economic Tests of Monopoly and the Concept of the Relevant Market, id.*, 479.

[19] United States v. E. I. du Pont de Nemours & Co., 353 U. S. 586 (1957), discussed in the next chapter.

[20] *Id.*, at 594-595.

[21] United States v. E. I. du Pont de Nemours & Co., 351 U. S. 377, at 395 (1956).

[22] United States v. E. I. du Pont de Nemours & Co., 353 U.S. 586, at 594 (1957).

[22a] A peculiar application of the relevant market concept is involved in United States v. Guerlain, Inc., 155 F.Supp. 77 (D.C. N.Y. 1957), *probable jurisdiction noted*, 78 S.Ct. 429 (1958).

[23] 240 F.2d 643 (8th Cir.1957), *cert. denied*, 354 U.S. 923 (1957).

"The indictment makes it clear that the appellants were charged with attempting to monopolize and monopolizing the dissemination of news and advertising in newspapers and on radio and television broadcasting stations in the four-county area referred to. In other words, the appellants were charged with attempting to monopolize and monopolizing trends in the media in which they did business. The Star refers to the other daily newspapers in the area and to the fact that in 1952 there were 78 weekly newspapers and suburban papers published in the four-county area which it claims disseminated news and advertising in competition with the appellant. The Star also claims that it received competition from radio and television stations, magazines, both monthly and weekly, newsreels, topical books, etc., from which it argues that the evidence was wholly insufficient to sustain the verdict that it had monopolized in the dissemination of news and advertising. What was the Star's market control and who were its competitors? In searching for the answer to that question the appellants rely strongly on the case of *United States* v. *E. I. du Pont de Nemours & Co.*, 1956, 351 U.S. 377.

* * *

"In this case we do not think that radio stations and television stations located outside the metropolitan area herein described, magazines, newsreel, topical books, specialty publications, etc., are 'market alternatives' or effective substitutes such as was meant by the Supreme Court in the *du Pont* case. In that case, the Supreme Court also made clear that the market which must be examined to determine the existence of monopoly power will vary with the part of commerce under study. The considerations that go to determine The Star's relevant market must be with due regard to the realities of newspaper advertising. That is what is meant when the Supreme Court speaks about narrowing the infinite range that market substitutes could encompass. *Times-Picayune* v. *United States*, *supra*, at page 612. In footnote 31, at page 612 of the *Times-Picayune* case, the Supreme Court makes specific reference to the kind of market with which we are here concerned:

'The advertising industry and its customers, for example, markedly differentiate between advertising in newspapers and other mass media. See, *e.g.*, Frey, Advertising (2d ed. 1953), cc. 12, 15; Duffy, Advertising Media and Markets (2d ed. 1951), cc. 3, 4; Hepner, Effective Advertising, c. 20 (1949); Borden, Taylor and Hoyde, National Advertising in Newspapers, *passim* (1946); Sandage, Advertising Theory and Practice (3d ed. 1948), cc. XX, XXI.'

The other media mentioned by appellants were not competitors in the real sense of the word and this is true in both advertising and news. Magazines are not effective alternatives for the daily newspapers and certainly the grocer who desires to advertise a specialty in some of his items and has only The Star publications for daily use would hardly find a monthly or weekly magazine an effective substitute. In view of the dominant position The Star enjoyed in the field of advertising and news, the court's instructions on this point were nevertheless eminently fair. The Court instructed the jurors that they could take into consideration the existence of a wide range of competing media to determine if The Star was in a monopolistic position, (although the relevant market was restricted to metropolitan Kansas City throughout the trial). While the court commented that weekly and neighborhood newspapers could scarcely be considered sizeable competitors, it nevertheless ended these expressions of opinion by cautioning the jurors that such statements did not imply guilt or innocence, and that the jurors would be the final judges as to what was or was not competition. From these instructions, it is quite clear that the jurors could have considered as sizeable competitors those which the Court thought were not, and that other media, with a small field of circulation compared to that of the Star, were actually a bar to monopoly."[24]

(b) *The extent of control necessary under section 2*

In *United States* v. *Swift & Co.*[25] Justice Cardozo said: "Mere size, according to the holding of this court, is not an offense against the Sherman Act unless magnified to the point at which it amounts to monopoly . . . but size carries with it an opportunity for abuse that is not to be ignored when the opportunity is proved to have been utilized in the past."

In the first *Alcoa* case Judge Learned Hand stated:[26] "[I]t is no excuse for 'monopolizing' a market that the monopoly has not been used to extract from the consumer more than a 'fair' profit. The Act has wider purposes. . . . [Congress] did not condone 'good trusts' and condemn 'bad' ones; it forbade all."[27]

The problem is, of course, *how much* market power is needed to constitute monopoly and how to measure the degree of this power. Again, a review of court decisions shows that there is no simple test or rule and that the result depends on the vary-

---

[24] 240 F.2d at 659-660.

[25] 286 U.S. 106, at 116 (1932).

[26] United States v. Aluminum Co. of America, 148 F.2d 416, at 427 (2d Cir.1945).

[27] See also the second Alcoa case, where the district court continues to follow this line: "[T]he mere existence of what is denominated 'monopoly power,' irrespective of its exercise may be the focal element that will resolve the outcome of a particular suit" and "is some indication of illegality." United States v. Aluminum Co. of America, 91 F.Supp. 333, at 341, 342 (S.D.N.Y. 1950).

ing facts of each case.[28] In *United States* v. *Paramount Pictures, Inc.* Justice Douglas stated that section 2 of the Sherman Act "condemns monopoly of 'any part' of trade or commerce. 'Any part' is construed to mean an appreciable part. . . ."[29] In the *Alcoa* case the court noted that ninety per cent of supply "is enough to constitute a monopoly; it is doubtful whether sixty or sixty-four per cent would be enough; and certainly thirty-three per cent is not."[30] However, in the *Lehigh Valley* case[31], the Supreme Court found unlawful monopolization where it was disclosed that the amount of anthracite coal transported by the railroad (which also controlled coal properties) exceeded one-fifth of the entire annual production of the country.

In addition, the courts look to "the strength of remaining competition, whether the action springs from business requirements or purpose to monopolize, the probable development of the industry, consumer demands, and other characteristics of the market."[32]

(c) *Monopoly acquired by lawful means*

An enterprise need not necessarily acquire a monopoly by anticompetitive activities. "It does not follow because 'Alcoa' had such a monopoly, that it 'monopolized' the ingot market; it may not have achieved monopoly; *monopoly may have been thrust upon it.*"[33]

In the *United Shoe Machinery* case[34] Judge Wyzanski had to deal with both this defense and the difficult problem of defining monopolization under section 2. United manufactured and distributed, through leases only, all the main types of machines used in making shoes. It dealt with approximately 90 per cent of all shoe factories, and supplied more than 75 per cent of the demand for shoe machinery. The district court said, *inter alia*:[35]

> "It will be recalled that Judge Hand said [in *Alcoa*] that one who has acquired an overwhelming share of the market 'monopolizes' whenever he does business, 148 F.2d at page 428, column 1, apparently even if there is no showing that his business involves any exclusionary practice. But, it will also be recalled

---

[28] United States v. Columbia Steel Co., 334 U.S. 495, 527 (1948).

[29] 334 U.S. 131, at 173 (1948).

[30] United States v. Aluminum Co. of America, 148 F.2d 416, at 424 (2d Cir. 1945).

[31] United States v. Lehigh Valley Railroad Co., 254 U.S. 255 (1920).

[32] United States v. Columbia Steel Co., 334 U.S. 495, 527 (1948).

[33] *Id.*, at 429. (Emphasis added.)

[34] United States v. United Shoe Machinery Corp., 110 F.Supp. 295 (D.Mass. 1953), *aff'd per curiam*, 347 U.S. 521 (1954).

[35] *Id.*, at 342-345.

that this doctrine is softened by Judge Hand's suggestion that the defendant may escape statutory liability if it bears the burden of proving that it owes its monopoly solely to superior skill, superior products, natural advantages, (including accessibility to raw materials or markets), economic or technological efficiency, (including scientific research), low margins of profit maintained permanently and without discrimination, or licenses conferred by, and used within, the limits of law, (including patents on one's own inventions, or franchises granted directly to the enterprise by a public authority).

* * *

"[T]aken as a whole, the evidence satisfies the tests laid down in both *Griffith* and *Aluminum*. The facts show that (1) defendant has, and exercises, such overwhelming strength in the shoe machinery market that it controls that market, (2) this strength excludes some potential, and limits some actual, competition, and (3) this strength is not attributable solely to defendant's ability, economies of scale, research, natural advantages, and adaptation to inevitable economic laws.

"In estimating defendant's strength, this Court gives some weight to the 75 plus percentage of the shoe machinery market which United serves.[36] But the Court considers other factors as well. In the relatively static shoe machinery market where there are no sudden changes in the styles of machines or in the volume of demand, United has a network of long-term, complicated leases with over 90% of the shoe factories. These leases assure closer and more frequent contacts between United and its customers than would exist if United were a seller and its customers were buyers. Beyond this general quality, these leases are so drawn and so applied as to strengthen United's power to exclude competitors. Moreover, United offers a long line of machine types, while no competitor offers more than a short line. Since in some parts of its line United faces no important competition, United has the power to discriminate, by wide differentials and over long periods of time, in the rate of return it procures from different machine types. Furthermore, being by far the largest company in the field, with by far the largest resources in dollars, in patents, in facilities, and in knowledge, United has a market capacity to attract offers of inventions, inventors' services, and shoe machinery businesses. And, finally, there is no substantial substitute competition from a vigorous secondhand market in shoe machinery.

* * *

---

[36] This is in accord with the ruling in United States v. Columbia Steel Co., 334 U.S. 495, 527-528 (though Mr. Justice Reed was addressing himself primarily to problems under § 1, not § 2, of the Sherman Act). This Court does not consider whether this high percentage, by itself, would warrant (but not compel) an inference that United has such overwhelming

"Not only does the evidence show United has control of the market, but also the evidence does not show that the control is due entirely to excusable causes. The three principal sources of United's power have been the original constitution of the company, the superiority of United's products and services, and the leasing system. The first two of these are plainly beyond reproach. The original constitution of United in 1899 was judicially approved in *United States* v. *United Shoe Machinery Company of New Jersey*, 247 U.S. 32. It is no longer open to question, and must be regarded as protected by the doctrine of *res judicata*, which is the equivalent of a legal license. Likewise beyond criticism is the high quality of United's products, its understanding of the techniques of shoemaking and the needs of shoe manufacturers, its efficient design and improvement of machines, and its prompt and knowledgeable service. These have illustrated in manifold ways that 'superior skill, foresight and industry' of which Judge Hand spoke in *Aluminum*, 148 F.2d at page 430.

"But United's control does not rest solely on its original constitution, its ability, its research, or its economies of scale. There are other barriers to competition, and these barriers were erected by United's own business policies. Much of United's market power is traceable to the magnetic ties inherent in its system of leasing, and not selling, its more important machines. The lease-only system of distributing complicated machines has many 'partnership' aspects, and it has exclusionary features such as the 10-year term, the full capacity clause, the return charges, and the failure to segregate service charges from Machine charges. Moreover, the leasing system has aided United in maintaining a pricing system which discriminates between machine types.

"In addition to the foregoing three principal sources of United's power, brief reference may be made to the fact that United has been somewhat aided in retaining control of the

---

strength that it could exclude competition. Nor does this Court consider whether, drawing upon United States v. Griffith, 334 U.S. 100, 107, footnote 10, and United States v. Aluminum Co. of America, 2d Cir., 148 F.2d 416, 428, 429, a bold, original court, mindful of what legal history teaches about the usual, if not invariable, relationship between overwhelming percentage of the market and control of the market, and desirous of enabling trial judges to escape the morass of economic data in which they are now plunged, might, on the basis of considerations of experience and judicial convenience, announce that an enterprise having an overwhelming percentage of the market, was presumed to have monopoly power, that a plaintiff bore its burden of proof under § 2 of the Sherman Act if it satisfied the trier of fact that defendant had the prohibited percentage, and that defendant, to escape liability, must bear the burden of proving that its share of the market was attributable to its ability, natural advantage, legal license, or, perhaps, to others' lack of interest in entering the market.

shoe machinery industry by its purchases in the secondhand market, by its acquisitions of patents, and, to a lesser extent, its activities in selling to shoe factories supplies which United and others manufacture.

* * *

"[These practices] are not practices which can be properly described as the inevitable consequences of ability, natural forces, or law. They represent something more than the use of accessible resources, the process of invention and innovation, and the employment of those techniques of employment, financing, production, and distribution, which a competitive society must foster. They are contracts, arrangements, and policies which, instead of encouraging competition based on pure merit, further the dominance of a particular firm. In this sense, they are unnatural barriers; they unnecessarily exclude actual and potential competition; they restrict a free market. While the law allows many enterprises to use such practices, the Sherman Act is now construed by superior courts to forbid the continuance of effective market control based in part upon such practices. Those courts hold that market control is inherently evil and constitutes a violation of § 2 unless economically inevitable, or specifically authorized and regulated by law. [Footnote omitted.]"[37]

The important enforcement aspect of the decision which also granted equitable relief, will be discussed in chapter 8. In this connection reference is also made to the discussion in chapter 8 of the consent decree entered in the monopoly case, *United States* v. *United Fruit Co.*[37a]

(2) Oligopoly under Section 2

Monopoly power must, in an economic sense, be in the hands of a single firm, but the same effects may result from the power *jointly* to dominate and control a certain industry or market. Consequently, section 2 of the Sherman Act also prohibits "monopolization" by a combination or conspiracy of a group of firms.[38]

But is it lawful, in the absence of agreement or conspiracy, when each of a small number of competitors, acting independently but closely watching his rivals, arrives at a pattern of parallel and non-competitive behavior? This is the case when an

---

[37] For a discussion, see, *e.g.*, KAYSEN, UNITED STATES V. UNITED SHOE MACHINERY CORPORATION: AN ECONOMIC ANALYSIS OF AN ANTITRUST CASE (1956).

[37a] Civil No. 4560, E.D.La., complaint filed July 2, 1954, final judgment filed February 4, 1958, 1958 CCH TRADE CASES Para. 68,941 (E.D. La. 1958).

[38] See, *e.g.*, American Tobacco Co. v. United States, 328 U.S. 781, at 809 (1946); United States v. Paramount Pictures, Inc., 334 U.S. 131 (1948), and 85 F.Supp. 881 (S.D. N.Y. 1949).

oligopoly exists: any industry where the suppliers or purchasers are few in number and relatively strong and where these persons base their production and marketing activities on close observation of their competitors' activities. Under certain market conditions, such sellers hesitate to reduce prices in order to increase sales because of the certainty that other sellers will almost immediately match the price reduction and thus all sellers will find themselves in a worse situation. Competition then tends to take the form of rivalry based on product differentiation, advertising, and service.[39]

Practically speaking, there is no explicit antitrust law on oligopolies. In the absence of agreement, price uniformity and other uniform business practices among competitors have been held not to violate the Sherman Act. In *Theatre Enterprises, Inc.* v. *Paramount Film Distributing Corp.*, the Supreme Court said:[40]

> "The crucial question is whether respondents' conduct . . . stemmed from independent decision or from an agreement, tacit or express. To be sure, business behavior is admissible circumstantial evidence from which the fact finder may infer agreement. . . . But this Court has never held that proof of parallel business behavior conclusively establishes agreement or phrased differently that such behavior itself constitutes a Sherman Act offense. Circumstantial evidence may have made heavy inroads into the traditional judicial attitude toward conspiracy, but 'conscious parallelism' has not yet read conspiracy out of the Sherman Act entirely."

While by no means solving all questions, this general rule is still the law.[41]

At present, the government is seeking to proceed under section 2 of the Sherman Act in a case involving a typical oligopolistic situation, *United States* v. *Procter & Gamble Co.*[42] The other defendants are Colgate-Palmolive-Peet Co., Lever Brothers

---

[39] For the views of economists, see, *e.g.*, A Study of the Antitrust Laws, *Hearings Before the Subcommittee on Antitrust and Monopoly of the Senate Committee on the Judiciary*, 84th Cong., 1st Sess., Part 1, 187 *et seq.* 238, 385 *et seq.*, 405 *et seq.*, 426 *et seq.*, Part 2, 627 *et seq.* (1955); MACHLUP, THE ECONOMICS OF SELLER'S COMPETITION cc. 11-16 (1952); FELLNER, COMPETITION AMONG THE FEW (1949).

[40] 346 U.S. 537, 540-541 (1954).

[41] See, *e.g.*, Morton Salt Co. v. United States, 235 F.2d 573 (10th Cir. 1956); United States v. Twentieth Century-Fox Film Corp., 137 F.Supp. 78 (S.D. Cal. 1956); Ford v. Hughes Tool Co., 215 F.2d 924 (10th Cir. 1954).

[42] Civil No. 1196-52 (D.N.J.).

Co., and the Association of American Soap and Glycerine Producers. Paragraph 2 of the prayer reads as follows:[43]

> "That the Court adjudge and decree that the defendants Procter, Colgate and Lever have monopolized interstate trade and commerce in the production and sale of household-soap and household-synthetic-detergents and in the purchase and sale of the principal materials used in soap and synthetic detergents in violation of Section 2 of the Sherman Act."

While other prayers assume coordination of the activities of the three soap firms, this prayer raises the question of the applicability of section 2 to oligopolistic situations.

The government does not allege that the defendants have maintained identical list prices pursuant to a written or an express oral agreement. Judge Barnes, at that time Assistant Attorney General in charge of the Antitrust Division, made the following comment on this case:[44]

> ". . . we have joined the large soap manufacturers on the question involving primarily whether their uniform prices changed day by day, week by week, month by month at almost the precise moment—I would say at the precise moment in probably 90 per cent of the cases; whether that is price leadership as they maintain or whether it is an attempt to monopolize by more than one large corporation within an industry.
>
>   * * *
>
> "I think that that may be considered as a case that may—and I am speaking only in possibilities—give us considerable enlightenment on that particular area of where you have what the economists like to call the oligopoly position in a particular market area.
>
>   * * *
>
> "Whether or not the laws are adequate, and the factual situation is such as to convince the courts that the oligopoly position constitutes the equivalent of a monopoly position, is something that to my knowledge, the Supreme Court has thus far not passed upon."

Among the remedies sought by the Government is the following:[45]

> "4. That each of the defendants Procter, Colgate and Lever be dissolved into separate and independent organizations. . . ."

Some appreciation of the nature of this antitrust action may be obtained from reading that part of the complaint concern-

---

[43] Complaint, p. 17.

[44] Statement in *Hearings Before the Subcommittee on Antitrust and Monopoly of the Senate Committee on the Judiciary,* 84th Cong., 1st Sess., Part 1, at 286, 287 (1955).

[45] Complaint, p. 18.

ing defendants' position in the household-soap and household-synthetic-detergent industry. Paragraphs 25-29 read as follows:[46]

"In 1951 total sales of household-soap by all producers in the United States were approximately $430,000,000. Defendants Procter, Colgate and Lever together have produced and sold at least three-fourths of the national sales of household-soap for each of the past twenty years. The following table shows for selected years the approximate percentages of dollar sales of household-soap in the United States by (1) Procter, (2) Colgate, (3) Lever and (4) Procter, Colgate and Lever combined:

Year	(1)Procter	(2)Colgate	(3)Lever	(4)Total
1925	30%	27%	9%	66%
1937	40%	18%	22%	80%
1947	37%	19%	19%	75%
1951	40%	14%	21%	75%

"In 1951 total sales of household-synthetic-detergents by all producers in the United States were approximately $280,000,000. The following table shows for each of the past three years the approximate percentages of dollar sales of household-synthetic-detergents in the United States by (1) Procter, (2) Colgate, (3) Lever and (4) Procter, Colgate and Lever combined:

Year	(1)Procter	(2)Colgate	(3)Lever	(4)Total
1949	66%	20%	6%	92%
1950	67%	15%	11%	93%
1951	69%	14%	10%	93%

"In 1951 there were, in addition to the defendants Procter, Colgate and Lever, not more than seven producers of household-soap which sold as much as one per cent of all household-soap sold in the United States and none of these seven sold as much as four per cent of the total. Each of these producers has been in the household-soap business since sometime prior to 1926. No producer who has entered the household-soap business since 1926 has been able to sell even one per cent of the total household-soap in any year. Of the producers of household-soap who were in business in 1926 who are not in business today, the soap businesses of eight were acquired by Procter, one by Colgate, and one by Lever.

"In 1926 there were no producers of household-synthetic-detergents. Today, in addition to Procter, Colgate and Lever, there are not more than two producers of household-synthetic-detergents who in 1951 sold as much as one per cent of the national total, and neither of these two sold as much as three per cent.

---

[46] *Id.*, pp. 8-10.

"The following table shows for 1951 the approximate amounts expended by Procter, Colgate and Lever for advertising and promotion of household-soap and household-synthetic-detergents.

Procter	....	$74,000,000
Colgate	....	26,000,000
Lever	....	27,000,000."

While oligopoly is of course not only a legal problem under section 2 of the Sherman Act,[47] oligopoly and monopoly are both related to the broader problem of bigness and concentration in American industry.[48] However, a consideration of the problems of bigness and economic concentration lies far beyond the scope of this book.

---

[47] See, e.g., Stewart and E. D. Turner, *The Significance of Oligopoly in Acquisition and Exclusive Dealing Situations Under the Clayton Act,* 25 U.CIN.L.REV. 427 (1956) and cases discussed therein.

[48] For discussion, see, e.g., MASON, ECONOMIC CONCENTRATION AND THE MONOPOLY PROBLEM (1957); EDWARDS, BIG BUSINESS AND THE POLICY OF COMPETITION (1956). In recent years, Congress has shown an increasing awareness of the problems of size and concentration. See report by Burns, *Problems of Size and Integration,* 2 ANTITRUST BULL. 584 (1957); *Antitrust and Monopoly,* Report of the Senate Committee on the Judiciary, S.REP. No. 128, 85th Cong., 1st Sess. (1957). For example, the Senate Subcommittee on Antitrust and Monopoly has undertaken an illustrative case study of the General Motors Corporation. See, A Study of the Antitrust Laws, *Hearings Before the Subcommittee on Antitrust and Monopoly of the Senate Committee on the Judiciary,* 84th Cong., 1st Sess., Parts 6-8 (1956); *Bigness and Concentration of Economic Power—A Case Study of General Motors Corporation,* Staff Report of the same Subcommittee, 84th Cong., 2d Sess. (1956). It has also recently published an important statistical report entitled *Concentration in American Industry.* See, Report of the same Subcommittee, S.REP. No. ...., 85th Cong., 1st Sess. (1957). Another valuable compilation of factual data is the FEDERAL TRADE COMMISSION'S REPORT ON INDUSTRIAL CONCENTRATION AND PRODUCT DIVERSIFICATION IN THE 1,000 LARGEST MANUFACTURING COMPANIES: 1950 (1957).

Chapter 3

MERGERS AND ACQUISITIONS*

One of the easiest ways of eliminating competition is to buy out competitors. For a long time corporations were able to evade the Sherman Act through this simple device, until they were restrained to some extent by section 7 of the Clayton Act of 1914.[1] Originally, this provision applied only to acquisitions of the *stock* of competitors. In 1950, Congress amended section 7[2] to make it also apply to acquisitions of the *assets* of *any* corporation, whether a competitor of the acquiring corporation or not, if damage to competition is reasonably probable as a result of the acquisition.

(1) Continued Growth of Mergers and Enforcement of Section 7

Corporate mergers and acquisitions continued to occur at a high rate despite the new legislation. Tabulations released by the Federal Trade Commission show a total of 703 acquisitions in 1951, 822 in 1952, 793 in 1953, 617 in 1954, 846 in 1955, and 905 in 1956.[3] During the first six months of 1957, 462 major business mergers have been reported.[4]

---

* The problem of *bank* acquisitions and mergers is discussed in chapter 9 of this book.

[1] 38 STAT. 730 (1914), 15 U.S.C. § 18 (1952).

[2] 64 STAT. 1125 (1950), 15 U.S.C. § 18 (1952). The text of section 7 may be found in the appendix.

[3] Federal Trade Commission, Press Releases of June 18, 1956, reported in 3 CCH TRADE REG. REP. Para. 23,365, at p. 33,228 (10th ed. 1956) and of February 14, 1957.

> "The tabulation also showed that a third of the mergers in manufacturing and mining in 1955 were by acquiring concerns whose assets were at least $50 million. Nearly 37 percent were by acquiring concerns with assets from $10 to $50 million."

More than 50 important mergers were recorded during 1955 in the following industries: non-electrical machinery (112); food and kindred products (87); mining (62); primary metals (59); fabricated metals (56); electrical machinery (53); and chemicals (52). 3 CCH TRADE REG. REP. *id.* See also FEDERAL TRADE COMMISSION, REPORT ON CORPORATE MERGERS AND ACQUISITIONS (1955).

[4] CCH TRADE REG. REPORTS No. 78 p. 3 (July 12, 1957), citing staff reports made to the Federal Trade Commission.

During this period the Antitrust Division of the Department of Justice and the Federal Trade Commission initiated cases against acquisitions under section 7 as follows: none in 1951, one in 1952, none in 1953, two in 1954, eight in 1955 and 18 in 1956.[5] Thus, twenty-nine mergers and acquisitions out of a reported total of 4,686 have been challenged from 1951 to 1956. "Four of these cases have been settled by consent. No case before the courts has yet been decided on the merits. Eighteen of the actions . . . were brought before the Federal Trade Commission. A decision on the issue has been made by the Commission in one case. No other case has yet reached the Commission for decision."[6]

Meanwhile, private corporations have successfully enjoined competing firms from voting the stock of the plaintiff corporation obtained by the competitor in violation of section 7.[7]

The numerical count of acquisitions can of course only serve to demonstrate the present trend of concentration through this means. It does not indicate the effects on competition nor the relative economic importance of the different mergers recorded. There is disagreement among economists as to the various economic aspects of the merger problem:[8]

"[E]conomic theory argues persuasively for limiting the growth of market power through merger but it provides us with no precise set of criteria by which we can identify the competitive consequences of its incremental growth. Yet incremental accretion of market power is the substance of which even the biggest of the current crop of mergers are made. Appraisal, therefore, forces us at some point to depart from neat predictive market

---

[5] Bock, *Economic Patterns in Merger Cases,* in ECONOMIC CONCENTRATION MEASURES: USES AND ABUSES 35, at 39 (National Industrial Conference Board ed. 1957). United States v. E. I. du Pont de Nemours & Co., 353 U.S. 586 (1957), was not included in these figures.

[6]*Corporate Mergers and Acquisitions,* Staff Report of the Subcommittee on Antitrust and Monopoly of the Senate Committee on the Judiciary, S.REP. No. 132, 85th Cong., 1st Sess. 4 (1957). The 29 complaints are briefly summarized *id.* at 4-19. *Cf.* Jacobs, *Consent Judgment in Merger Cases;* 43 A.B.A.J. 23 (1957). By now, two more cases have been settled, one more decided.

[7] American Crystal Sugar Co. v. Cuban-American Sugar Co., 152 F.Supp. 387 (S.D.N.Y. 1957); Hamilton Watch Co. v. Benrus Watch Co., 114 F.Supp. 307 (D.Conn. 1953), *affirmed,* 206 F.2d 738 (2d Cir. 1953).

[8] See, *e.g.,* survey in *Corporate Mergers and Acquisitions,* Staff Report of the Subcommittee on Antitrust and Monopoly of the Senate Committee on the Judiciary, S.REP. No. 132, 85th Cong., 1st Sess. 21-26 (1957). See also Burns, *Legal, Economic and Political Considerations Involved in Mergers,* 11 VAND. L.REV. 59 (1957).

models and enter the somewhat cloudy realm of value judgments. . . .

"As one distinguished economist has put it, 'a judgment concerning market power is the essence of merger policy.' . . . If market power can be identified at all it certainly must be identified with a particular firm's share of a relevant market and, less certainly, with the firm's absolute size."[9]

Writing in favor of the new section 7, Corwin D. Edwards has recently stated:[10]

"Growth by merger is an outstanding example of functionless and dangerous growth. When one competitor acquires another, there is little chance that the properties of the two, originally designed for separate operation, can be effectively coordinated as a single operating unit. But there is a probability that if either concern is large competition will be reduced by the acquisition. One of the big units becomes bigger; the number of competitors is reduced; and the merging corporation expands in a way that does not expand the industry. Though particular instances can doubtless be found in which such a merger is harmless, the typical result must be that efficiency is not well served and competition is ill served. Growth achieved by this means is not limited by a market struggle for public favor, as is the ordinary expansion of sales. Hence this kind of growth is peculiarly likely to outrun the growth of the economy."

Senator O'Mahoney, Chairman of the Subcommittee on Antitrust and Monopoly of the Senate Committee on the Judiciary, commented upon the merger development as follows:[11]

"The numerical count of mergers does not in itself demonstrate adverse effects on the competitive structure of the economy. At the same time, however, the subcommittee has recognized in the uninterrupted trend of corporate mergers in the last few years a danger signal of which it must take cognizance in view of the unmistakable intention of the Congress to establish a more stringent control over corporate growth by merger or acquisition than by internal expansion."

Similar concern has been expressed by Congressman Celler, Chairman of the Antitrust Subcommittee of the House Commit-

---

[9] Markham, *Merger Policy Under the New Section 7: A Six-Year Appraisal*, 43 VA.L. REV. 489, 521 (1957), quoting MASON, ECONOMIC CONCENTRATION AND THE MONOPOLY PROBLEM 400 (1957).

[10] BIG BUSINESS AND THE POLICY OF COMPETITION 123 (1956). *Cf.* also Stigler, *Mergers and Preventive Antitrust Policy*, 104 U.PA.L.REV. 176 (1955).

[11] *Corporate Mergers and Acquisitions*, Staff Report of the Subcommittee on Antitrust and Monopoly of the Senate Committee on the Judiciary, S.REP. No. 132, 85th Cong., 1st Sess. III (1957).

tee on the Judiciary.[12] This Subcommittee came to the following conclusions, *inter alia* on the present merger trend and the fight against it:[13]

"To a large extent this merger activity is due to large corporations buying up small businesses, not to small businesses consolidating in order to compete more effectively with larger concerns in the industry.

* * *

"[M]erger enforcement activity has been seriously hampered by lack of sufficient funds. . . . The merger movement is too widespread and too pervasive for anything less than a full-scale, concentrated enforcement effort to produce adequate results. . . .

"[I]n only one of the merger cases instituted thus far . . . has an effort been made to block consummation of the merger or acquisition by premerger injunctive proceedings. This means that the parties to the other mergers have gone ahead, true at their peril. But by the time any of these cases is ripe for a final order, the properties of the companies may have become so commingled as to make it difficult, if not impossible, to unscramble them.

"Failure to invoke premerger injunctive remedies cannot be justified on the basis that legal authority is lacking. The attorney General has ample authority to institute legal proceedings to prevent consummation of mergers pending a determination of their legality. The Federal Trade Commission, though seeming to lack similar legal authority, could easily turn the entire case over to the Department of Justice . . . ."

(2) Mergers and Acquisitions Brought Under the Probihition of Section 7

Turning to the "key interpretative question" under amended section 7, namely, what kind of evidence is necessary to satisfy the test that the merger effect "may be substantially to lessen competition," the Celler Subcommittee concluded:[14]

"[F]or example, a leading company in a market acquires another concern whose share of that market is *quantitatively* substantial. Proof of these facts, the subcommittee believes, is sufficient since it was not the intent of the Congress in enacting this legislation to require examination of all economic factors that are appropriate in Sherman Act cases."

---

[12] *The Merger Movement in the Textile Industry,* Staff Report to Subcommittee No. 5 of the House Committee on the Judiciary, 84th Cong., 1st Sess. III (1955).

[13] *Corporate and Bank Mergers,* Interim Report of the Antitrust Subcommittee (Subcommittee No. 5) of the House Committee on the Judiciary, 84th Cong., 1st Sess. 37-38 (1955).

[14] *Id.,* at 39. Emphasis added.

Another important question is how to determine whether a certain planned acquisition will be considered lawful by the enforcement agencies. The solution may be sought by examining the principal kinds of economic facts alleged in the cases heretofore initiated against mergers.

> "If one is to judge on the basis of the twenty-nine cases, . . . a merger is most vulnerable if the acquiring company's sales exceed $10 million or its assets exceed $50 million and if it is one of the first companies in its field; if the acquired unit is also one of the major organizations in its field; if the combined market shares of the two companies exceed 15%; and if a high percent of the output of the products or services in question is concentrated in relatively few companies. Vulnerability is greatest under such conditions if the merging companies operate in the same field. If they do not, vulnerability appears to depend on whether the acquisition can be said to enhance the market position of an already dominant company."[15]

(3) **The 1957 du Pont-General Motors Decision**

At the height of nation-wide discussion on various proposals for revision of amended section 7, the Supreme Court rendered its far-reaching decision in *United States* v. *E. I. du Pont de Nemours & Co.*[16] The Court disposed of the case by interpreting the applicability of section 7 of the Clayton Act to *vertical* acquisitions. In a 4 to 2 decision, it held that du Pont had violated section 7 by acquiring 23 per cent of General Motors stock in 1917, thereby securing and retaining a preferential sales position as a supplier of General Motors in the market for automotive finishes and fabrics.

Specifically, the Court established five principles governing the application of section 7 of the Clayton Act:

(1) Section 7 applies to *vertical* as well as to horizontal stock acquisitions.

(2) Section 7 is not only applicable to the acquisition of stock at or near the time of acquisition but rather "*at any time* when a threat of the prohibited effects is evident."[17]

---

[15] In ECONOMIC CONCENTRATION MEASURES: USES AND ABUSES 35-55 (National Industrial Conference Board ed. 1957). Very similar results were reached by Markham in *Merger Policy Under the New Section 7: A Six-Year Appraisal*, 43 VA.L.REV. 489, 513-521 (1957).

[16] 353 U.S. 586 (1957). See Bicks, *Mergers and Acquisitions: A Government Lawyer's View*, 11 ABA ANTITRUST SECTION REPORT 20 (July 1957); Dirlam and Stelzer, *The Du Pont-General Motors Decision: In The Antitrust Grain*, 58 COLUM. L.REV. 24 (1958); Manne, *The Perplexing Du Pont Case: Additional Confusion in the Law of Mergers*, 106 U.PA. L.REV. 385 (1958). Symposium, 46 GEO.L.J. No. 4 (1958).

[17] 353 U.S. at 598.

(3) The test for a section 7 violation with respect to vertical acquisitions is whether there is a *reasonable probability that the acquisition will result in the foreclosure of competitors of the acquiring corporation from a substantial share of the relevant market.* A showing of any abuse of the stock interest to gain the preferential treatment from the acquired corporation is not required.

(4) For determining the *relevant market* ("line of commerce") under section 7, it suffices to show that there are enough peculiar characteristics and uses of the products used in an industry to make them sufficiently distinct from all other products of the same type used in other industries. "Thus, the bounds of the relevant market for the purposes of this case are not coextensive with the total market for finishes and fabrics, but are coextensive with the automobile industry, the relevant market for automotive finishes and fabrics."[18]

(5) The relevant market must be *substantial* and "the government must prove a likelihood that competition may be 'foreclosed in a substantial share of . . . [that market]'".[19] It suffices to show that a considerable *dollar volume of sales* of the relevant products is involved. "Because the record clearly shows that quantitatively and percentagewise du Pont supplies the largest part of General Motors' requirements, we must conclude that du Pont has a substantial share of the relevant market."[20]

UNITED STATES v. E. I. DU PONT DE NEMOURS & CO.

Supreme Court of the United States 353 U.S. 586 (1957)

"Mr. JUSTICE BRENNAN delivered the opinion of the Court.

"This a direct appeal under § 2 of the Expediting Act[21] from a judgment of the District Court for the Northern District of Illinois,[22] dismissing the Government's action brought in 1949 under § 15 of the Clayton Act.[23] The complaint alleged a violation of § 7 of the Act[24] resulting from the purchase of E. I. du Pont de Nemours and Company in 1917-1919 of a 23% stock interest in General Motors Corporation. This appeal is from the dismissal of the action as to du Pont, General Motors and the

---

[18] 353 U.S. at 594-595.

[19] 353 U.S. at 595.

[20] 353 U.S. at 596.

[21] 32 STAT. 823, as amended, 15 U.S.C. § 29. The Court noted probable jurisdiction. 350 U.S. 815.

[22] 126 F.Supp. 235.

[23] 38 STAT. 736, 15 U.S.C. § 25 (1946).

[24] This action is governed by the Clayton Act as it was before the 1950 amendments, which by their terms are inapplicable to acquisitions prior to 1950. 64 STAT. 1125, 15 U.S.C. § 18.

corporate holders of large amounts of du Pont stock, Christiana Securities Corporation and Delaware Realty & Investment Company.[25]

"The primary issue is whether du Pont's commanding position as General Motors' supplier of automotive finishes and fabrics was achieved on competitive merit alone, or because its acquisition of the General Motors' stock, and the consequent close intercompany relationship, led to the insulation of most of the General Motors' market from free competition, with the resultant likelihood, at the time of suit of the creation of a monopoly of a line of commerce.

* * *

"Section 7 is designed to arrest in its incipiency not only the substantial lessening of competition from the acquisition by one corporation of the whole or any part of the stock of a competing corporation, but also to arrest in their incipiency restraints or monopolies in a relevant market which, as a reasonable probability, appear at the time of suit likely to result from the acquisition by one corporation of all or any part of the stock of any other corporation. The section is violated whether or not actual restraints or monopolies, or the substantial lessening of competition, have occurred or are intended. Acquisitions solely for investment are excepted, but only if, and so long as, the stock is not used by voting or otherwise to bring about, or in attempting to bring about, the substantial lessening of competition.

"We are met at the threshold with the argument that § 7, before its amendment in 1950, applied only to an acquisition of the stock of a competing corporation, and not to an acquisition by a supplier corporation of the stock of a customer corporation —in other words, that the statute applied only to horizontal and not to vertical acquisitions. This is the first case presenting the question in this Court. *International Shoe Co.* v. *Federal Trade Commission,* 280 U.S. 291, and *Thatcher Mfg. Co.* v. *Federal Trade Commission,* 272 U.S. 554, involved corporate acquisitions of stock of competitors.

"During the 35 years before this action was brought, the Government did not invoke § 7 against vertical acquisitions. The Federal Trade Commission has said that the section did not apply to vertical acquisitions. See F.T.C., Report on Corporate Mergers and Acquisitions, 168 (1955), H. R. Doc. No. 169, 84th Cong., 1st Sess. Also, the House Committee considering the 1950 revision of § 7 stated that ". . . it has been thought by some that this legislation [the 1914 Act] applies only to the so-

---

[25] The amended complaint also alleged violation of §§ 1 and 2 of the Sherman Act. 26 STAT. 209, as amended, 50 STAT. 693, 15 U.S.C. §§ 1, 2. In view of our determination of the case, we are not deciding the Government's appeal from the dismissal of the action under the Sherman Act.

called horizontal mergers. . . ." H.R. Rep. No. 1191, 81st Cong., 1st Sess. 11. The House Report adds, however, that the 1950 amendment was purposed '. . . to *make it clear* that the bill applies to all types of mergers and acquisitions, vertical and conglomerate as well as horizontal. . . .' (Emphasis added.)

"This Court has the duty to reconcile administrative interpretations with the broad antitrust policies laid down by Congress. *Cf. Automatic Canteen Co.* v. *Federal Trade Commission,* 346 U.S. 61, 74. The failure of the Commission to act is not a binding administrative interpretation that Congress did not intend vertical acquisitions to come within the purview of the Act. *Accord, Baltimore & Ohio R. Co.* v. *Jackson,* 353 U.S. 325, 331.

"The first paragraph of § 7, written in the disjunctive, plainly is framed to reach not only the corporate acquisition of stock of a competing corporation, where the effect may be substantially to lessen competition between them, but also the corporate acquisition of stock of any corporation, competitor or not, where the effect may be either (1) to restrain commerce in any section or community, or (2) tend to create a monopoly of any line of commerce. The amended complaint does not allege that the effect of du Pont's acquisition may be to restrain commerce in any section or community but alleges that the effect was '. . . to tend to create a monopoly in particular lines of commerce. . . .'

"Section 7 contains a second paragraph dealing with a holding company's acquisition of stock in two or more corporations. [Footnote omitted.] Much of the legislative history of the section deals with the alleged holding company evil. [Footnote omitted.] This history does not aid in interpretation because our concern here is with the first paragraph of the section. There is, however, pertinent legislative history which does aid and support our construction.

"Senator Chilton, one of the Senate managers of the bill, explained that the House conferees insisted that to prohibit just the acquisitions where the effect was 'substantially' to lessen competition would not accomplish the designed aim of the statute, because 'a corporation might acquire the stock of another corporation, and there would be no lessening of competition, but the tendency might be to create monopoly or to restrain trade or commerce.' 'Therefore,' said Senator Chilton, 'there was added . . . the following: "Or to restrain such commerce in any section or community or tend to create a monopoly of any line of commerce." '[26] This construction of the section, as embracing

---

[26] 51 Cong. Rec. 16002.

three separate and distinct effects of a stock acquisition, has also been recognized by a number of federal courts.[27]

"We hold that any acquisition by one corporation of all or any part of the stock of another corporation, competitor or not, is within the reach of the section whenever the reasonable likelihood appears that the acquisition will result in a restraint of commerce or in the creation of a monopoly of any line of commerce. Thus, although du Pont and General Motors are not competitors, a violation of the section has occurred if, as a result of the acquisition, there was at the time of suit a reasonable likelihood of a monopoly of any line of commerce. Judge Maris correctly stated in *Transamerica Corp.* v. *Board of Governors,* 206 F.2d 163, 169:

'A monopoly involves the power to . . . exclude competition when the monopolist desires to do so. Obviously, under Section 7 it was not necessary . . . to find that . . . [the defendant] has actually achieved monopoly power but merely that the stock acquisitions under attack have brought it measurably closer to that end. For it is the purpose of the Clayton Act to nip monopoly in the bud. Since by definition monopoly involves the power to eliminate competition a lessening of competition is clearly relevant in the determination of the existence of a tendency to monopolize. Accordingly in order to determine the existence of a tendency to monopoly in . . . any . . . line of business the area or areas of existing effective competition in which monopoly power might be exercised must first be determined. . . .'

"Appellees argue that there exists no basis for a finding of a probable restraint or monopoly within the meaning of § 7 because the total General Motors market for finishes and fabrics constituted only a negligible percentage of the total market for these materials for all uses, including automotive uses. It is stated in the General Motors brief that in 1947 du Pont's finish sales to General Motors constituted 3.5% of all sales of finishes to industrial users, and that its fabrics sales to General Motors comprised 1.6% of the total market for the type of fabric used by the automobile industry.

"Determination of the relevant market is a necessary predicate to a finding of a violation of the Clayton Act because the threatened monopoly must be one which will substantially lessen

---

[27] Aluminum Co. of America v. Federal Trade Commission, 284 F. 401; Ronald Fabrics Co. v. Verney Brunswick Mills, Inc., CCH TRADE CASES Para. 57,514 (D.C.S.D.N.Y. 1946); United States v. New England Fish Exchange, 258 F.2d 732; *cf.* Transamerica Corp. v. Board of Governors, 206 F.2d 163; Sidney Morris & Co. v. National Assn. of Stationers, 40 F.2d 620, 625.

competition 'within the area of effective competition.'[28] Substantiality can be determined only in terms of the market affected. The record shows that automobile finishes and fabrics have sufficient peculiar characteristics and uses to constitute them products sufficiently distinct from all other finishes and farbics [Footnote omitted.] to make them a 'line of commerce' within the meaning of the Clayton Act. *Cf. Van Camp & Sons Co.* v. *American Can Co.*, 278 U.S. 245. [Footnote omitted.] Thus, the bounds of the relevant market for the purposes of this case are not coextensive with the total market for finishes and fabrics, but are coextensive with the automobile industry, the relevant market for automotive finishes and fabrics. [Footnote omitted.]

"The market affected must be substantial. *Standard Fashion Co.* v. *Magrane-Houston Co.*, 258 U.S. 346, 357. Moreover, in order to establish a violation of § 7 the Government must prove a likelihood that competition may be 'foreclosed in a substantial share of . . . [that market]'.[29] Both requirements are satisfied in this case. The substantiality of a relevant market comprising the automobile industry is undisputed. The substantiality of General Motors' share of that market is fully established in the evidence.

"General Motors is the colossus of the giant automobile industry. It accounts annually for upwards of two-fifths of the total sales of automotive vehicles in the nation. [Footnote omitted.] In 1955 General Motors ranked first in sales and second in assets among all United States industrial corporations[30] and became the first corporation to earn over a billion dollars in annual net income.[31] In 1947 General Motors' total purchases of all products from du Pont were $26,628,274, of which $18,938,229 (71%) represented purchases from du Pont's Finishes Division. Of the latter amount purchases of "Duco"[32] and the thinner used to apply "Duco" totaled $12,224,798 (65%), and "Dulux"[33] purchases totaled $3,179,225. Purchases by General Motors of du Pont fabrics in 1948 amounted to $3,700,000, making it the

---

[28] Standard Oil Co. of California v. United States, 337 U.S. 293, 299, n.5. Section 3 of the Act, with which the Court was concerned in Standard Oil, makes unlawful certain agreements ". . . where the effect . . . may be to substantially lessen competition or tend to create a monopoly *in any line of commerce.*" 38 STAT. 731, 15 U.S.C. § 14 (1946). (Emphasis added.)

[29] Standard Oil Co. of California v. United States, 337 U.S. 293, at 314.

[30] Fortune Directory of the 500 Largest U.S. Industrial Corporations, July 1956, p. 2.

[31] New York Times, February 3, 1956, p. 1, col. 3.

[32] A finish developed specially by du Pont and General Motors for use as an automotive finish.

[33] A synthetic enamel developed by du Pont which is used on refrigerators, also manufactured by General Motors.

largest account of du Pont's Fabrics Division. Expressed in percentages, du Pont supplied 67% of General Motors' requirements for finishes in 1946 and 68% in 1947.[34] In fabrics du Pont supplied 52.3% of requirements in 1946, and 38.5% in 1947.[35] Because General Motors accounts for almost one-half of the automobile industry's annual sales, its requirements for automotive finishes and fabrics must represent approximately one-half of the relevant market for these materials. Because the record clearly shows that quantitatively and percentagewise du Pont supplies the largest part of General Motors' requirements, we must conclude that du Pont has a substantial share of the relevant market.

"The appellees argue that the Government could not maintain this action in 1949 because § 7 is applicable only to the acquisition of stock and not to the holding or subsequent use of the stock. This argument misconceives the objective toward which § 7 is directed. The Clayton Act was intended to supplement the Sherman Act.[36] Its aim was primarily to arrest apprehended consequences of inter-corporate relationships before those relationships could work their evil, which may be at or any time after the acquisition, depending upon the circumstances of the particular case. The Senate declared the objective of the Clayton Act to be as follows:

'. . . Broadly stated, the bill, in its treatment of unlawful restraints and monopolies, seeks to prohibit and make unlawful certain trade practices which, as a rule, singly and in themselves, are not covered by the Act of July 2, 1890 [the Sherman Act], or other existing antitrust acts, and thus, by making these practices illegal, to arrest the creation of trusts, conspiracies, and monopolies *in their incipiency and before consummation*. . . . ' S.Rep. No. 698, 63d Cong., 2d Sess. 1. (Emphasis added.)

" 'Incipiency' in this context denotes not the time the stock was acquired, but any time when the acquisition threatens to ripen into a prohibited effect. See *Transamerica Corp.* v. *Board of Governors*, 206 F.2d 163, 166. To accomplish the congressional aim, the Government may proceed at any time that an acquisition may be said with reasonable probability to contain a threat that it may lead to a restraint of commerce or tend to create a monopoly of a line of commerce.[37] Even when the purchase is solely for investment, the plain language of § 7 contemplates an action at any time the stock is used to bring about, or

---

[34] 126 F.Supp., at 295.

[35] *Id.*, at 300-301.

[36] Standard Fashion Co. v. Magrane-Houston Co., 258 U.S. 346.

[37] *Cf.* Corn Products Refining Co. v. Federal Trade Commission, 324 U.S. 726, 738.

in attempting to bring about, the substantial lessening of competition. [Footnote omitted.]

"Prior cases under §7 were brought at or near the time of acquisition. See, *e.g.*, *International Shoe Co.* v. *Federal Trade Commission*, 280 U.S. 291; *V. Vivaudou, Inc.* v. *Federal Trade Commission*, 54 F.2d 273; *Federal Trade Comm'n* v. *Thatcher Mfg. Co.*, 5 F.2d 615, *rev'd in part on other ground*, 272 U.S. 554; *United States* v. *Republic Steel Corp.*, 11 F.Supp. 117; *In re Vanadium-Alloys Steel Co.*, 18 F.T.C. 194. None of these cases holds, or even suggests, that the Government is foreclosed from bringing the action at any time when a threat of the prohibited effects is evident.

"Related to this argument is the District Court's conclusion that 30 years of nonrestraint negated 'any reasonable probability of such a restraint' at the time of the suit.[38] While it is, of course, true that proof of a mere *possibility* of a prohibited restraint or tendency to monopoly will not establish the statutory requirement that the effect of an acquisition 'may be' such restraint or tendency,[39] the basic facts found by the District Court demonstrate the error of its conclusion.[40]

"The du Pont Company's commanding position as a General Motors supplier was not achieved until shortly after its purchase of a sizable block of General Motors stock in 1917.[41] At that time its production for the automobile industry and its sales to General Motors were relatively insignificant.

* * *

"Thus, before the first block of General Motors stock was acquired, du Pont was seeking markets not only for its nitrocellulose, but also for the artificial leather, celluloid, rubber-coated goods, and paints and varnishes in demand by automobile companies. In that connection, the trial court expressly found that '. . . reports and other documents written at or near the time of the investment show that du Pont's representatives were well aware that General Motors was a large consumer of products of the kind offered by du Pont,' and that John J. Raskob, du Pont's treasurer and the principal promoter of the investment, 'for one, thought that du Pont would ultimately get all that business. . . .'[42]

---

[38] 126 F.Supp., at 335.

[39] Standard Fashion Co. v. Magrane-Houston Co., 258 U.S. 346, at 356-357.

[40] There is no significant dispute as to the basic facts pertinent to the decision. We are thus confronted here with the provision of Fed. Rules Civ. Proc., 52(a), that findings of fact shall not be set aside unless clearly erroneous.

[41] Before 1917, du Pont supplied General Motors with coated fabrics. 126 F.Supp., at 297.

[42] 126 F.Supp., at 243.

"The Company's interest in buying into General Motors was stimulated by Raskob and Pierre S. du Pont, then du Pont's president, who acquired personal holdings of General Motors stock in 1914.

* * *

"Finally, Raskob broached to Pierre S. du Pont the proposal that part of the fund earmarked for du Pont expansion be used in the purchase of General Motors stock. At this time about $50,000,000 of the $90,000,000 fund was still in hand. Raskob foresaw the success of the automobile industry and the opportunity for great profit in a substantial purchase of General Motors stock. On December 19, 1917, Raskob submitted a Treasurer's Report to the du Pont Finance Committee recommending a purchase of General Motors stock in the amount of $25,000,000. That report makes clear that more than just a profitable investment was contemplated. A major consideration was that an expanding General Motors would provide a substantial market needed by the burgeoning du Pont organization. Raskob's summary of reasons in support of the purchase includes this statement: 'Our interest in the General Motors Company will undoubtedly secure for us the entire Fabrikoid, Pyralin [celluloid], paint and varnish business of those companies, *which is a substantial factor.*' (Emphasis added.)[43]

"This thought, that the purchase would result in du Pont's obtaining a new and substantial market, was echoed in the Company's 1917 and 1918 annual reports to stockholders. In the 1917 report appears: 'Though this is a new line of activity, it is one of great promise and one that seems to be well suited to the character of our organization. *The motor companies are very large customers of our Fabrikoid and Pyralin as well as paints and varnishes.*' (Emphasis added.) The 1918 report says: 'The consumption of paints, varnishes and fabrikoid in the manufacture of automobiles gives another common interest.'

"This background of the acquisition, particularly the plain implications of the contemporaneous documents, destroys any basis for a conclusion that the purchase was made 'solely for investment.' Moreover, immediately after the acquisition, du Pont's influence growing out of it was brought to bear within General Motors to achieve primacy for du Pont as General Motors' supplier of automotive fabrics and finishes.

"Two years were to pass before du Pont's total purchases of General Motors stock brought its percentage to 23% of the outstanding stock and its aggregate outlay to $49,000,000. During that period, du Pont and Durant worked under an arrangement giving du Pont primary responsibility for finances and Durant the responsibility for operations. But J. A. Haskell, du Pont's

---

[43] 126 F.Supp., at 241.

former sales manager and vice president, became the General
Motors vice president in charge of the operations committee.
The trial judge said that Haskell '. . . was willing to undertake
the responsibility of keeping du Pont informed of General
Motors affairs during Durant's regime. . . .'[44]

"Haskell frankly and openly set about gaining the maximum
share of the General Motors market for du Pont. In a contemporaneous 1918 document, he reveals his intention to 'pave the
way for perhaps a more general adoption of our material,' and
that he was thinking 'how best to get cooperation [from the
several General Motors Divisions] whereby makers of such of
the low priced cars as it would seem possible and wise to get
transferred will be put in the frame of mind necessary for its
adoption [du Pont's artificial leather].'

"Haskell set up lines of communication within General Motors
to be in a position to know at all times what du Pont products
and what products of du Pont competitors were being used. It
is not pure imagination to suppose that such surveillance from
that source made an impressive impact upon purchasing offcials.
It would be understandably difficult for them not to interpret it
as meaning that a preference was to be given to du Pont products. Haskell also actively pushed the program to substitute
Fabrikoid artificial leathers for genuine leather and sponsored
use of du Pont's Pyralin sheeting through a liaison arrangement
set up between himself and the du Pont sales organization.

"Thus sprung from the barrier, du Pont quickly swept into a
commanding lead over its competitors, who were never after-
wards in serious contention. Indeed, General Motors' then principal paint supplier, Flint Varnish and Chemical Works, early in
1918 saw the handwriting on the wall. The Flint president came
to Durant asking to be bought out, telling Durant, as the trial
judge found, that he 'knew du Pont had bought a substantial
interest in General Motors and was interested in the paint industry; that . . . [he] felt he would lose a valuable customer, General Motors.'[45] The du Pont Company bought the Flint Works
and later dissolved it.

"In less than four years, by August 1921, Lammot du Pont,
then a du Pont vice president and later Chairman of the Board
of General Motors, in a response to a query from Pierre S. du
Pont, then Chairman of the Board of both du Pont and General
Motors, 'whether General Motors was taking its entire requirements of du Pont products from du Pont,' was able to reply that
four of General Motors' eight operating divisions bought from
du Pont their entire requirements of paints and varnishes, five
their entire requirements of Fabrikoid, four their entire requirements of rubber cloth, and seven their entire requirements of

---

[44] 126 F.Supp., at 245.
[45] 126 F.Supp., at 267.

Pyralin and celluloid. Lammot du Pont quoted du Pont's sales department as feeling that 'the condition is improving and that eventually satisfactory conditions will be established in every branch, but they wouldn't mind seeing things going a little faster.' Pierre S. du Pont responded that 'with the change of management at Cadillac, Oakland and Olds [Cadillac was taking very little paints and varnishes, and Oakland but 50%; Olds was taking only part of its requirements for fabrikoid], I believe that you should be able to sell substantially all of the paint, varnish and fabrikoid products needed.' He also suggested that 'a drive should be made for the Fisher Body business. Is there any reason why they have not dealt with us?'

"Fisher Body was stubbornly resistant to du Pont sales pressure. General Motors, in 1920, during Durant's time, acquired 60% stock control of Fisher Body Company. However, a voting trust was established giving the Fisher brothers broad powers of management. They insisted on running their own show and for years withstood efforts of highranking du Pont and General Motors executives to get them to switch to du Pont from their accustomed sources of supply. Even after General Motors obtained 100% stock control in 1926, the Fisher brothers retained sufficient power to hold out. By 1947 and 1948, however, Fisher resistance had collapsed, and the proportions of its requirements supplied by du Pont compared favorably with the purchases by other General Motors Divisions.

"In 1926, the du Pont officials felt that too much General Motors business was going to its competitors. When Pierre S. du Pont and Raskob expressed surprise, Lammot du Pont gave them a breakdown, by dollar amounts, of the purchases made from du Pont's competitors. This breakdown showed, however, that only Fisher Body of the General Motors divisions was obtaining any substantial proportion of its requirements from du Pont's competitors.

"Competitors did obtain higher percentages of the General Motors business in later years, although never high enough at any time substantially to affect the dollar amount of du Pont's sales. Indeed it appears likely that General Motors probably turned to outside sources of supply at least in part because its requirements outstripped du Pont's production, when General Motors' proportion of total automobile sales grew greater and the company took its place as the sales leader of the automobile industry. For example, an undisputed Government exhibit shows that General Motors took 93% of du Pont's automobile Duco production in 1941 and 83% in 1947.

"The fact that sticks out in this voluminous record is that the bulk of du Pont's production has always supplied the largest part of the requirements of the one customer in the automobile industry connected to du Pont by a stock interest. The inference is overwhelming that du Pont's commanding position was promoted by its stock interest and was not gained solely on competitive merit.

"We agree with the trial court that considerations of price, quality and service were not overlooked by either du Pont or General Motors. Pride in its products and its high financial stake in General Motors' success would naturally lead du Pont to try to supply the best. But the wisdom of this business judgment cannot obscure the fact, plainly revealed by the record, that du Pont purposely employed its stock to pry open the General Motors market to entrench itself as the primary supplier of General Motors' requirements for automotive finishes and fabrics. [Footnote omitted.]

"Similarly, the fact that all concerned in high executive posts in both companies acted honorably and fairly, each in the honest conviction that his actions were in the best interests of his own company and without any design to overreach anyone, including du Pont's competitors, does not defeat the Government's right to relief. It is not requisite to the proof of a violation of § 7 to show that restraint or monopoly was intended.

"The statutory policy of fostering free competition is obviously furthered when no supplier has an advantage over his competitors from an acquisition of his customer's stock likely to have the effects condemned by the statute. We repeat, that the test of a violation of § 7 is whether, at the time of suit, there is a reasonable probability that the acquisition is likely to result in the condemned restraints. The conclusion upon this record is inescapable that such likelihood was proved as to this acquisition. The fire that was kindled in 1917 continues to smolder. It burned briskly to forge the ties that bind the General Motors market to du Pont, and if it has quieted down, it remains hot, and, from past performance, is likely at any time to blaze and make the fusion complete.[46]

"The judgment must therefore be reversed and the cause remanded to the District Court for a determination after further hearing of the equitable relief necessary and appropriate in the public interest to eliminate the effects of the acquisition offensive to the statute. The District Courts, in the framing of equitable decrees, are clothed 'with large discretion to model their judgments to fit the exigencies of the particular case.' *International Salt Co.* v. *United States,* 332 U.S. 392, 400-401.

* * *

It is so ordered.

---

[46] The potency of the influence of du Pont's 23% stock interest is greater today because of the diffusion of the remaining shares which, in 1947, were held by 436,510 stockholders; 92% owned no more than 100 shares each, and 60% owned no more than 25 shares each. 126 F.Supp., at 244.

"Mr. JUSTICE CLARK, Mr. JUSTICE HARLAN and Mr. JUSTICE WHITTAKER took no part in the consideration or decision of this case.

* * *

"Mr. JUSTICE BURTON, whom Mr. JUSTICE FRANKFURTER joins, dissenting.

* * *

"The Government's basic contention in this Court is that du Pont violated §§ 1 and 2 of the Sherman Act in that, by means of its alleged control of General Motors, it obtained an unlawful preference with respect to General Motors' purchases of materials. In the closing pages of its brief, and for a few minutes in its oral argument, the Government added the assertion that du Pont had violated § 7 of the Clayton Act in that its stock interest in General Motors 'has been used to channel General Motors' purchases to du Pont.'

"This Court, ignoring the Sherman Act issues which have been the focal point of eight years of litigation, now holds that du Pont's acquisition of a 23% stock interest in General Motors during the years 1917-1919 violates § 7 of the Clayton Act because 'at the time of suit [in 1949] there [was] a reasonable probability that the acquisition [was] likely to result in the condemned restraints.'

* * *

"For the reasons given below, I believe that the Court has erred in (1) applying § 7 to a vertical acquisition; (2) holding that the time chosen by the Government in bringing the action is controlling rather than the time of the stock acquisition itself; and (3) concluding, in disregard of the findings of fact of the trial court, that the facts of this case fall within its theory of illegality.

* * *

"Section 7 never has been authoritatively interpreted as prohibiting the acquisition of stock in a corporation that is not engaged in the same line of business as the acquiring corporation. Although the language of the Act is ambiguous, the relevant legislative history, administrative practice, and judicial interpretation support the conclusion that § 7 does not apply to vertical acquisitions.

* * *

"The offense described by § 7 is the acquisition, not the holding or the use, of stock. When the acquisition has been made, the offense, if any, is complete. The statutory language is unequivocal. It makes the test the probable effect of the acquisition at the time of the actual acquisition, and not at some later date to be arbitrarily chosen by the Government in bringing suit.

* * *

"The Court ignores the all-important lawfulness or unlawfulness of the stock acquisition at or about the time it occurred, and limits its attention to the probable anti-competitive effects of the continued holding of the stock at the time of suit, some 30 years later. The result is to subject a good-faith stock acquisition, lawful when made, to the hazard that the continued holding of the stock may make the acquisition illegal through unforeseen developments. Such a view is not supported by the statutory language and violates elementary principles of fairness. Suits brought under the Clayton Act are not subject to any statute of limitations, and it is doubtful whether the doctrine of laches applies as against the Government. The result is that unexpected and unforeseeable developments occurring long after a stock acquisition can be used to challenge the legality of continued holding of the stock. In such an action, the Government need only prove that *probable* rather than *actual* anticompetitive effects exist as of the time of suit. The Government may thus set aside a transaction which was entirely lawful when made, merely by showing that it would have been unlawful had it occurred at the time of suit, many years later. The growth of the acquired corporation, a fortuitous decline in the number of its competitors, or the achievement of control by an accidental diffusion of other stock may result, under this test, in rendering the originally lawful acquisition unlawful *ab initio*. Strikingly enough, all of these factors are involved in this case. [Footnote omitted.]

❋ ❋ ❋

"The Court cites no authority in support of its new interpretation of this 40-year-old statute. On the other hand, examination of the dozen or more cases brought under § 7 reveals that in every case the inquiry heretofore has centered on the probable anticompetitive effects of the stock acquisition at or near the time it was made.

❋ ❋ ❋

"The remaining issues are factual: (1) whether the record establishes the existence of a reasonable probability that du Pont's competitors will be foreclosed from securing General Motors' trade, and (2) whether the record establishes that such foreclosure, if probable, involves a substantial share of the relevant market and significantly limits the competitive opportunities of others trading in that market. In discussing these factual issues, I meet the Court on its own ground, that is, I assume that the old § 7 applies to vertical acquisitions, and that the potential threat at the time of suit is controlling. Even on that basis the record does not support the Court's conclusion that § 7 was violated by this 1917-1919 stock acquisition.

❋ ❋ ❋

"The Court, disregarding the mass of evidence supporting the District Court's conclusion that General Motors purchased du Pont paint and fabrics solely because of their competitive merit, relies for its contrary conclusion on passages drawn from several documents written during the years 1918-1926, and on the logical fallacy that because du Pont over a long period supplied a substantial portion of General Motors' requirements of paint and fabrics, its position must have been obtained by misuse of its stock interest rather than competitive considerations.

＊　＊　＊

"[A]ll of the evidence after 1926 affirmatively establishes without essential contradiction that du Pont did not use its stock interest to receive any preferential treatment from General Motors.

"Nor can present illegality be presumed from the bare fact that du Pont has continued to make substantial sales of several products to General Motors. [Footnote omitted.] In the first place, the record affirmatively shows that the new products which du Pont has sold to General Motors since 1926 have made their way, at General Motors as elsewhere, on their merits. Sales of Duco, Dulux, Fabrilite and Teal are not attributable in any way to dealings in the earlier period. Secondly, the Court's presumption is based on the fact that du Pont does not sell to all other automobile manufacturers in the same proportion as it does to General Motors. But there is no reason why it should—the Government has not shown that sellers normally sell to all members of an industry in the same proportion. In any event, the record fully explains the disproportion. Since 1930, du Pont's sales to other members of the industry have proportionately declined, largely because Ford has chosen to make the major share of its requirements of paint and fabrics, and because Chrysler has followed the policy of selecting a single supplier to whom it can be the most important customer. The fact is that du Pont *has* continued to sell in substantial amounts to the smaller members of the automobile industry.

＊　＊　＊

"The Court holds that the relevant market in this case is the automotive market for finishes and fabrics, and not the total industrial market for these products. The Court reaches that conclusion because in its view 'automobile finishes and fabrics have sufficient peculiar characteristics and uses to constitute them products distinct from all other finishes and fabrics. . . .' *Ante,* pp. 593-594. We are not told what these 'peculiar characteristics' are. Nothing is said about finishes other than that Duco represented an important contribution to the process of manufacturing automobiles. Nothing is said about fabrics other than that sales to the automobile industry are made by means of bids rather than fixed price schedules. Dulux is included in the 'automobile' market even though it is used on refrigerators and other appliances, but not on automobiles. So are other finishes and fabrics used on diesel locomotives, engines, parts, appliances and other products which General Motors manufactures. Arbitrary conclusions are not an adequate substitute for analysis of the pertinent facts contained in the record.

"The record does not show that the fabrics and finishes used in the manufacture of automobiles have peculiar characteristics differentiating them from the finishes and fabrics used in other industries. What evidence there is in the record affirmatively indicates the contrary. The sales of the four products principally involved in this case—Duco, Dulux, imitation leather, and coated fabrics—support this conclusion.

      * * *

"The burden was on the Government to prove that a substantial share of the relevant market would, in all probability, be affected by du Pont's 23% stock interest in General Motors. The Government proved only that du Pont's sales of finishes and fabrics to General Motors were large in volume, and that General Motors was the leading manufacturer of automobiles during the later years covered by the record. The Government did not show that the identical products were not used on a large scale for many other purposes in many other industries. Nor did the Government show that the automobile industry in general, or General Motors in particular, comprised a large or substantial share of the total market. What evidence there is in the record affirmatively indicates that the products involved do have wide use in many industries, and that an insubstantial portion of this total market would be affected even if an unlawful preference existed or were probable.

      * * *

"I would affirm the judgment of the District Court."

By this decision, the Court broadened the scope of section 7 considerably. It has construed the relevant market restrictively and expressly referred to the so-called quantitative substantiality test as applied in the *Standard Stations* case under section 3 of the Clayton Act.[47] The decision makes it much easier to prove antitrust charges under section 7 of the Clayton Act.

At the same time, the *du Pont-General Motors* decision raises many as yet unanswered questions. Consequently its impact on the American business merger pattern may not yet be foreseen.

---

[47] 353 U.S., at 395. See Standard Oil Co. of California v. United States, 337 U.S. 293, at 314 (1956).

It is an open question not only what du Pont will be required to do about its General Motors stock,[47a] but also what will happen to numerous other corporations in a similar position.

The "retroactive" aspect of the decision may have a general effect on antitrust law enforcement by the administrative agencies. With respect to the oil industry, it has been said:[48]

> "[T]he recent opinion of the Supreme Court . . . has opened new vistas of antitrust enforcement. . . . This decision now makes perfectly clear that section 7 applies to stock acquisitions of many years standing if the result is a reasonable probability of substantial lessening of competition or tendency to monopoly in any line of commerce. . . . It would seem that much more potential danger to competition exists in the case of 100 percent ownership or control by major oil companies over pipelines where such control has been used to deny independent producers access to markets. This control also may create a reasonable probability that competition among refineries may be substantially lessened by denying them access to crude. It is strongly urged that the Department of Justice, in reviewing new enforcement possibilities under this recent decision, begin with an examination of the ownership and control by major oil companies over pipelines."

Following these and other charges, the Subcommittee recommended that the Department of Justice initiate an immediate investigation.[49]

The decision also raises the question as to whether its definition of the relevant market can be reconciled with the cross-elasticity of demand test applied in the *Cellophane* case[50] under the Sherman Act. The new doctrine may point to a changing attitude on the part of the federal courts.

Whatever answer the future may present to these questions, the preventive function of the decision as to planned mergers and acquisitions will perhaps become one of its most important effects.

[47a] The main provisions of the Government's proposed final judgment in the case are summarized in 2 ANTITRUST BULL. 715-718 (1957).

[48] Statement of Donald P. McHugh, Counsel of the Subcommittee on Antitrust and Monopoly of the Senate Committee on the Judiciary, in *Petroleum, The Antitrust Laws and Government Policies*, Report of same Committee, S.REP. No. ......, 85th Cong., 1st Sess. 32 (1957).

[49] *Id.*, at 7, 161.

[50] United States v. E. I. du Pont de Nemours & Co., 351 U.S. 377 (1956).

(4) Horizontal Acquisitions

In *Pillsbury Mills, Inc.*[51] the Federal Trade Commission interpreted section 7 with respect to horizontal acquisitions.[52]

"The trial examiner there dismissed the complaint without prejudice on grounds that its allegations were not supported *prima facie* by reliable evidence. The Commission reversed, finding that probative[53] evidence tended to show the acquisition of two substantial competitors by the second largest American miller. The Commission looked at Pillsbury's market position before and after the two challenged acquisitions, both in the national market and in the Southeast, the geographic area principally involved. Pillsbury's shares were substantial, and the increase in its share of some markets through the acquisitions was also substantial. In the mix market, for example, Pillsbury increased its leading share in the Southeast from 22.7 percent to 44.9 percent and moved ahead nationally from second to first place, increasing its share from 16 percent to approximately 23 percent.

"But market share was only one of several factors which the Commission considered in finding a *prima facie* case of illegality. Rejecting any automatic test of illegality, the Commission pointed out that 'competition cannot be directly measured; no single set of standards can be applied to the whole range of American industries. No single characteristic of an acquisition,' the Commission continued, would in all cases 'of itself be sufficient to determine its effect on competition. For this reason,' the Commission concluded, 'it would not be sufficient to show' that the two companies 'control a substantial' dollar volume of sales 'or that a substantial portion of commerce is affected.' Instead, the Commission viewed its task under section 7 as requiring 'a case-by-case examination of all relevant factors' in order to ascertain the probable economic consequences.[54]

"At the same time the[55] Commission made clear that its 'examination of all relevant factors' did not call for application of Sherman Act tests. It squarely recognized the Congressional intent that such tests are not meant for Section 7; the essential

---

[51] F.T.C. Dkt. No. 6000 (Dec. 28, 1952, remanding initial decision of May 1, 1953; pending).

[52] The following summary is quoted from REPORT OF THE ATTORNEY GENERAL'S NATIONAL COMMITTEE TO STUDY THE ANTITRUST LAWS 120-122 (1955). The Committee agreed with the Commission's handling of the Pillsbury case. *Ibid.*

[53] The disputed evidence consisted of letters from Pillsbury setting forth its own sales history, that of the two competing companies it was acquiring, and its best estimates of its competitors' market share. The letters allegedly were based on market reports by an outside company.

[54] F.T.C. Dkt. No. 6000, at p. 9.

[55] *Ibid.*

difference, in the Commission's view, seems to be that the Clayton Act requires a 'less stringent burden of proof.' [Footnote omitted.]

"Thus the Commission concluded that, though the Sherman Act was not transgressed, the facts nevertheless established a *prima facie* violation of Section 7.[56] Without stressing any factor particularly, and without indicating what might even be relevant in a different industry and a different market, the Commission, in reaching its conclusion, emphasized the following factors: a pattern of acquisitions in the industry and by Pillsbury particularly; a general increase in the major's percentage market shares; a decline in the number of mills; a lack of new entries and a movement in the direction of oligopoly in the urban markets."

The decision was criticized by the Antitrust Subcommittee of the House Committee on the Judiciary:[57]

"The subcommittee believes that the Commission, by its insistence upon elaborate economic evidence in merger cases of this kind, has in effect ignored the congressional intention and applicable judicial precedents as well. The subcommittee also believes that the principal effect of the Commission's decision in the *Pillsbury* case is to obliterate in large part the distinction between the Sherman Act and the Celler-Kefauver Act and to weaken the latter act as an effective weapon to deal with corporate mergers and acquisitions."

Whatever view one may take, the *Du Pont- General Motors* decision, *supra*, raises the following questions: Can the Commission's standards be reconciled with the Supreme Court's doctrine, particularly with respect to its definition of the relevant market? What are the differences between the two standards and the consequences as to enforcement? What are the differences with regard to the facts underlying the two cases? Do they justify or even require an application of different legal and economic tests? In particular, what conclusions follow from the distinction between horizontal and vertical acquisitions?

While the impact of the *du Pont-General Motors* decision on the *Pillsbury Mills* case remains to be seen, its influence became quite obvious in the Federal Trade Commission's recent decision in the matter of the *Crown Zellerbach Corp.*[57a] In this case, the Commission ordered respondent to divest itself of all acquisitions made as a result of the merger between Crown and one of its

---

[56] Mimeo opinion, pp. 13, 16.

[57] *Corporate and Bank Mergers,* Interim Report, 85th Cong., 1st Sess. 39 (1957).

[57a] F.T.C. Dkt. No. 6180 (Dec. 26, 1957).

competitors, the St. Helens Pulp and Paper Co., which took place
in 1953. Crown, a fully integrated firm, produces and distributes
pulp, paper and paper products. It is one of the largest producers
of paper and paper products in the United States and owns and
controls considerable timber reserves.

St. Helens, prior to the acquisition, was a fully integrated mill,
also owning and controlling its own timber reserves, producing
most of its pulp requirements, and manufacturing and selling
paper and paper products. The first question for determination
was whether the "line of commerce" was *trade* coarse paper
(classified into wrapping, bag, sack and other converting papers,
special industrial papers, sanitary tissue and other tissue papers,
and paperboard) or *Census* coarse paper (as defined by the
Bureau of the Census and including wrapping papers, bag and
sack paper and other converting papers).

The Commission, referring to the *du Pont-General Motors*
case, noted first that the clause "in any line of commerce" is
satisfied literally if the forbidden effect or tendency is produced
in one out of all the various lines of commerce. The Commission
then continued:[57b]

> "All such [Census coarse] papers are in a relatively allied line,
> particularly in respect to markets and end uses. They generally
> relate to the packaging and wrapping field where a flexible type
> packaging material is appropriate or desirable. Wrapping papers,
> as the name implies, are made and used primarily for wrapping;
> they are produced in many sizes, colors, finishes, weights and
> other specifications appropriate for this field. Similar considera-
> tions apply as to bag and sack papers and other converting
> papers. Such factors as physical characteristics, markets, prices,
> and uses, all or in part tend to distinguish these papers from
> other papers and paperboard.
>
> "Distinctions among individual types of paper or paperboard
> are readily apparent. As an example, one of the papers which
> respondent would include with the relevant product is container
> board, a separate category in the broad line of trade coarse
> papers. Container board is used in the manufacture of boxes,
> particularly the corrugated paper box. This is ordinarily a heavier
> paper than the usual run of wrapping and bag papers. Container
> board also utilizes a high proportion of waste paper as compared
> with the coarse wrapping and bag papers, resulting generally in
> a lower quality paper. In addition, these particular papers in-
> volve different markets. Container board is made into boxes and
> sold to manufacturers of products requiring strong, lightweight
> shipping containers. Wrapping papers and bags (the converted
> product) are generally sold in markets which include paper job-

---

[57b] *Id.*, at 3-7.

bers, wholesalers, such as grocery wholesalers, and large consumers, such as chain grocers, ultimately to be used in large part by retailers for packaging or wrapping at the point of sale to the consumer. Moreover, there is evidence of price variations as between such categories of paper or paperboard. These and other differentiating factors illustrate the distinctiveness of the competitive fields involved in the broad trade coarse paper line.

"It is argued by the respondent that some of the papers in the coarse wrapping, bag, sack, and converting paper field are substantially similar to some of the papers in other fields and that since they may be used interchangeably, the product line of commerce should not be so narrowly defined. The nature of many papers indicates that they are unsuitable generally for any purpose other than that for which they are made, such as toilet tissue. On the other hand, some papers such as certain container boards and certain wrapping papers might replace each other in use, but the evidence indicates that there is little such substitution in actual practice.

"It is our opinion, in view of the foregoing considerations, that the coarse paper line relating generally to coarse wrapping papers, bag and sack papers and converting papers is a sufficiently distinct product line to be a "line of commerce" within the meaning of Section 7. . . .

"Relative to respondent's contention as to the section of the country, we are satisfied that in this instance the Eleven Western States, as found by the hearing examiner, is an appropriate section. This area constitutes the greater natural market for the Western producers of the relevant product and it is the market in which both Crown and St. Helens made the majority of their sales of this product.

* * *

"The relevant market here is a substantial market. Papers in the coarse wrapping, bag, sack and converting paper field accounted for 437,384 tons of the production in the West in 1953, which was 36.3% of the total paper produced in the area exclusive of paperboard.

"In terms of the relevant market, a further question for consideration is whether the effect of the acquisition may be substantially to lessen competition or tend to create a monopoly. Both Crown and St. Helens were substantial producers of the coarse wrapping, bag, sack, and converting papers. About 84% of the production of St. Helens was in this line and, other than for newsprint and printing papers, over 50% of Crown's production. Such papers accounted for about 30% of all grades of paper and paperboard produced by Crown.

* * *

"Crown and St. Helens prior to the acquisition were competing in the sale of the relevant product in the West. At the time of the acquisition, there were only ten producers of such products in the West, and four of the ten manufactured only small quantities. In 1952, Crown, St. Helens, Longview Fibre Company, and St. Regis Paper Company, in combination, produced 94.2% of the total; in 1954, 93.9% of the total. Of the four, only Crown, St. Helens and Longview Fibre Company sold a relatively broad line of wrapping papers, bag papers and allied papers which was of particular importance to the jobbing trade. St. Regis sold only a limited selection of such papers. Its production was principally in bleached shipping sack paper. Longview Fibre Company, while it produced and sold a relatively broad line, converted a substantial portion of its production and sold jobbing papers to only three jobbers.

"Respondent produced 51.5% and St. Helens 11.0% of the relevant product in the West in 1953, for a total of 62.5% of the Western production. This clearly constituted a predominant share of the market considering its relative isolation. One immediate result of the acquisition was to remove from the Western supplier market an important, fully integrated competitor having its own timber reserves, pulp manufacturing and converting facilities and fully developed sales outlets to the trade. Another immediate result was to increase significantly the size of respondent in the relevant line of commerce in which it already had a commanding lead.

"Respondent, a company which produced in the West in 1953, 56.2% of all the paper produced in the area and 27.3% of the paper and paperboard production combined, was by far the leading producer in the relevant line of papers with 51.5% of the total. In 1954, the year following the acquisition, of the 455,934 tons of the relevant papers produced, Crown manufactured 242,-539 tons, or 53.2%, plus 49,317 tons, or 10.8% through St. Helens, for a total of 64%. Only two Western competitors produced any significant volumes of such papers in this year. These were Longview Fibre Company with 80,108 tons or 17.6% of the total and St. Regis Paper Company with 56,068 tons or 12.3%.

"Crown's position has been additionally enhanced as a result of the acquisition because through its jobber division, Zellerbach Paper Company, it is now competing with many more jobbers for which it has become a major supplier. The record demonstrates that jobbers must have a dependable source of supply of a wide range of papers in the relevant line to be competitive. Very few producers in the West supplied a substantially broad line of such papers, and suppliers outside the West were generally unreliable sources, particularly in times of paper shortages. Clearly, with the elimination of St. Helens, Western jobbers generally have been severely restricted as to sources from which the relevant papers may be purchased. It likewise appears that many converters which formerly could look to St. Helens for purchases of the relevant paper must now depend upon Crown as a primary source of supply, a company which is a major competitor since Crown converts a substantial share of its production.

* * *

"Considering all the factors, we conclude that the effect of this acquisition may be substantially to lessen competition or tend to create a monopoly in the relevant line of commerce and, as such, is in violation of Section 7 of the Clayton Act."

(5) A Summary on Procedures Under Section 7

One of the most important current merger problems is how to enforce section 7 in an efficient and timely way. Therefore, this procedural problem has been thoroughly studied by legislative and administrative bodies in recent years.

(a) *Acquisition clearance*

At present, the enforcement activity starts with the so-called "clearance" procedures

"which have been established in both the Department of Justice and the Federal Trade Commission to consider the legality of proposed mergers or acquisitions submitted *voluntarily* by the parties with a request for such review. Under these clearance procedures, the enforcement agency concerned, in effect, advises the parties by letter whether, based upon the facts presented, consummation of the proposed transition would subject the parties to the risk of adversary proceedings instituted by the agency. Clearances granted under the program are not legally binding from a technical standpoint, but obviously are of considerable practical importance in the decision of the parties as to whether or not to proceed with a proposed merger acquisition. Although merger clearance activities have gradually increased since the amendment of section 7, these activities are still of sharply limited dimension. . . . The Commission expressed its approval or denial of clearance by indicating whether or not a full investigation of the proposed transaction is contemplated if it is consummated. . . . The Department of Justice expresses its decision concerning a request for clearance in terms of whether or not it intends at that time to take action with respect to the proposed acquisition.[58]

"[P]resent clearance procedures . . . depend upon voluntary submission of merger and acquisition proposals by the companies involved. While designed to encourage parties to submit such proposals for advance legal review, relatively few such sub-

---

[58] *Corporate Mergers and Acquisitions*, Staff Report of the Subcommittee on Antitrust and Monopoly of the Senate Committee on the Judiciary, S.REP. No. 132, 85th Cong., 1st Sess. 19-20 (1957) (Emphasis added.) See also Jacobs, *Merger Clearance Problems*, 2 ANTITRUST BULL. 187 (1956).

missions have been made and the program as a whole suffers from defective legal authority.[59]

(b) *Length of litigation*

The present procedures necessarily produce expenses and result in a great loss of time. A striking example is the *Pillsbury Mills* case discussed *supra*.

"The Pillsbury merger took place in June of 1951. After a year of investigation, the Federal Trade Commission issued a complaint in June of 1952. Shortly thereafter hearings started before a Federal Trade Commission hearing examiner, and these hearings are still going on. In other words, the merger took place 4½ years ago, and the litigation has been going on for 3½ years, and the end of the litigation is nowhere in sight."[60]

Another time-consuming problem of enforcement arises from the non-final nature of cease and desist orders issued by the Commission under section 11 of the Clayton Act.[61]

(c) *Premerger injunction*[62]

"Although the Department of Justice and the Federal Trade Commission now have concurrent jurisdiction with respect to section 7 (as well as secs. 2, 3, and 8) of the Clayton Act, only the former agency is empowered to institute legal proceedings to prevent and restrain violations. This power derives from section 15 of the Clayton Act. . . .

"Under this provision the Department of Justice may apply to a court for an order staying the consummation of a proposed merger or acquisition either for a temporary period or pending its adjudication by the court. Private parties have also the right to petition a Federal district court to enjoin the consummation of a proposed merger or acquisition, as in the case of *Hamilton Watch Company* v. *Benrus Watch Company*.[63]

---

[59] *Id.*, at 63.

[60] Statement of Congressman Wright Patman, Amending Clayton Act By Requiring Prior Notification . . . *Hearings Before the Antitrust Subcommittee* (*Subcommittee No. 5*) *of the House Committee on the Judiciary*, 84th Cong., 2d Sess., ser. 15, at 12-13 (1956). Similar criticism has been expressed in *Hearings Before the Subcommittee on Antitrust and Monopoly of the Senate Committee on the Judiciary*, 84th Cong., 1st Sess., pt. 1, Corporate Mergers, at 139 *et seq.* (1955).

[61] See "Tentative Draft of Report of the Federal Trade Commission on Clayton Act Legislative Recommendations" as presented by Chairman John W. Gwynne in Hearings on Amending Clayton Act by Requiring Prior Notification of Certain Corporate Mergers and for Other Purposes, *Hearings Before the Antitrust Subcommittee* (*Subcommittee No. 5*) *of the House Committee on the Judiciary*, 84th Cong., 2d Sess. 27, at 31 (1956).

[62] The following is quoted from *Corporate Mergers and Acquisitions*, Staff Report of the Subcommittee on Antitrust and Monopoly of the Senate Committee on the Judiciary, S.REP. No. 132, 85th Cong., 1st Sess. 52-54 (1957).

[63] 114 F.Supp. 307 (D.Conn. 1953).

"It has been suggested that the Federal Trade Commission be provided with the same premerger injunction power as the Department of Justice with respect to corporations under the jurisdiction of the Commission. . . .

"Although the Federal Trade Commission now lacks the power to seek restraining action of a court to prevent consummation of a proposed merger or acquisition or to maintain the status quo, it does have the right to request the Attorney General to seek such action on its behalf. This right has never been exercised, even in the four cases in which, prior to consummation of the transaction, the companies involved had sought, and been denied, clearance by the Federal Trade Commission. These cases include the acquisition by Pillsbury Mills of two of its competitors, and the acquisition by International Paper Co. of Long-Bell Lumber Co., both of which were made the subject of complaints brought by the Federal Trade Commission subsequent to consummation. In the case of the International Paper acquisition, the Federal Trade Commission, immediately following announcement of the proposed transaction, moved under the all-writs statute to obtain a court injunction to restrain International Paper from taking any further steps to consummate the merger pending adjudication of its legality; . . ."

In this case, however, the court dismissed the petition.

FEDERAL TRADE COMMISSION v. INTERNATIONAL PAPER CO.

United States Court of Appeals for the Second Circuit
241 F.2d 372 (1956)

"PER CURIAM.

"When this petition came on for oral argument on December 14, 1956, it was dismissed from the bench for lack of jurisdiction, with the statement that a written opinion would be handed down later.

"The petition was filed November 27, 1956, and the respondent's answer on December 11. Without going into greater detail it will suffice to say that the petition alleges in substance that on November 5, 1956 the stockholders of International Paper Company, a New York corporation, and the stockholders of two Missouri corporations, Long-Bell Lumber Corporation and Long-Bell Lumber Company, voted upon and approved a plan of merger; that on November 6, 1956 the Federal Trade Commission filed a complaint charging that International by acquisition of the two Long-Bell companies had violated section 7 of the amended Clayton Act, 15 U.S.C.A. § 18, in that such acquisition may substantially lessen competition or tend to create a monopoly as more particularly specified in the complaint; and that if the Commission, after hearings, should find that section 7 has been violated and should order International to divest itself of stock and assets acquired, 'it will be impossible to separate the acquired assets from those which are the joint result of the combined operations and the assets of International,' if action contemplated by the respondent with respect to the acquired companies is allowed to occur. The prayer for injunctive relief in substance asks that the status quo be maintained until conclusion of the administrative proceeding.

"The Clayton Act contains a scheme of dual enforcement. *United States* v. *W. T. Grant Co.*, 345 U.S. 629, 632. Section 7 of the Act, and certain other sections not here relevant, may be enforced either by cease and desist orders of the Commission, 15 U.S.C.A. § 21, or by suits in equity instituted by the several district attorneys in their respective districts, under the direction of the Attorney General, 15 U.S.C.A. § 25. *U. S. Alkali Export Assn.* v. *United States*, 325 U.S. 196, 208. Individuals may also have injunctive relief against threatened loss or damage by a violation of the antitrust laws under the same conditions and principles as govern the granting of injunctions by courts of equity, that is to say, district courts, 15 U.S.C.A. § 26. These specific provisions as to who may seek injunctive relief, and in what courts, imply that the Commission itself is not authorized to do so. This implication is required by the statutory provisions of 15 U.S.C.A. § 21, under which a court of appeals acquires jurisdiction to review an order of the Commission only after the administrative proceeding has been concluded and a transcript of the record therein filed with the court.[64] The Commission's findings of fact, if supported by substantial evidence, are conclusive upon the court, and if either party shows grounds for adducing additional evidence, the court may order it to be taken before the Commission. The Clayton Act clearly recognizes that a court of appeals has no fact finding powers, and that if an injunction is to be obtained by a United States Attorney or a private litigant it must be sought in a U.S. District Court under sections 25 or 26 of Title 15, U.S.C.A. Nor did this legislation contemplate applications by the Commission for interlocutory relief by way of injunction to maintain the status quo during the pendency of a proceeding before the Commission."

With respect to the premerger injunction power of the *Department of Justice,* the Staff Report[65] comments as follows:

"The premerger injunctive remedy now available to the Department of Justice has not been used to any significant extent

---

[64] *Cf.* Federal Power Comm'n v. Metropolitan Edison Co., 304 U.S. 375; *In re* National Labor Relations Board, 304 U.S. 486.

[65] *Corporate Mergers and Acquisitions,* Staff Report of the Subcommittee on Antitrust and Monopoly of the Senate Committee on the Judiciary, S.REP. No. 132, 85th Cong., 1st Sess. 54-55 (1957).

to date, even with respect to proceedings initiated by that agency. In only two cases to date, one involving an acquisition by the Brown Shoe Co., and one by Continental Can Co., has the Attorney General employed this preliminary injunction power to attempt to prevent consummation of a proposed merger. In both cases the court refused to grant the relief sought by the Government.

"In the *Brown Shoe*[66] case, the restraining order issued by the court permitted the merger to be consummated under certain conditions before the Government complaint was decided. The court granted a temporary injunction under which the parties may proceed with the merger, pending final adjudication of the issues, provided that the stock earnings and profits of the acquired company are maintained in segregated form. In its opinion the court stated:

'The appellate court decisions and the affidavits of all parties in this case convince this court that the shoe industry is not simple in its operations and that many factors of a complex nature must be considered before it can be determined that a merger of the character presented in this case would violate section 7 * * *[67]

'There is no way to determine how long this case will take before the decree becomes final. The merger depends on economic and stock market factors. They are now favorable to consummation of the merger. On the day of final judgment they may be such as to make the merger impossible. If there is a final judgment in favor of defendants, and economic and market conditions at that time are such as to make the merger impossible, plaintiff would have the victory in fact but not on the record.'[68]

"In the *Continental Can*[69] case, the court refused to take any step whatever to prevent the consolidation of the operations of the two companies pending the adjudication of the legal issues."

(6) Legislative Efforts

For all these reasons and

"in view of the basic purpose of section 7 of the Clayton Act, as reaffirmed in the 1950 amendment, to retard increases in concentration resulting from external business growth, the near record number of mergers and acquisitions, together with the

---

[66] United States v. Brown Shoe Co., Inc., 1956 CCH TRADE CASES Para. 68,244 (D.C.Mo. 1956).

[67] *Id.*, at p. 71,115.

[68] *Id.*, at p. 71,116.

[69] United States v. Continental Can Co., Inc., 1956 CCH TRADE CASES Para. 68,479 (S.D.N.Y. 1956).

size, power, and growth history of many of the companies involved, has awakened a growing sentiment in Congress and elsewhere as to the need for prompt action to add further strength to the statute in order to help achieve its intended purpose."[70]

"Several bills were introduced in . . . Congress which embodied proposals for requiring all companies over a given size planning a merger or acquisition to file a notification of such plan with the enforcement agencies, in advance of the transaction, and to furnish supplementary information requested by these agencies. During a stipulated waiting period thereafter the merger or acquisition could not legally be consummated. Similar provisions were contained in bills considered by the Congress prior to the 1950 amendment, but apparently were omitted from the latter in the interest of facilitating its passage. The President recommended such legislation in his Economic Report transmitted to the Congress in January 1956.

"The principal advantages which have been cited for the advance notification requirement are that it would provide a more systematic stream of intelligence to the Department of Justice and the Federal Trade Commission concerning proposed mergers or acquisitions, and would assure these agencies of a timely opportunity to challenge the legality of a questionable transaction before it became accomplished fact. The notification requirement would enable the enforcement agencies to keep currently informed of such transactions and would allow them a reasonable period of time in which to study the competitive implications before deciding whether to seek preventive action."[71]

It may be fortuitous that the pending bills have not yet been enacted. A careful consideration of the implications of the *du Pont-General Motors* case,[72] especially as to the wisdom of complete reliance on a pre-certification procedure, seems to be necessary.

———————

[70] *Corporate Mergers and Acquisitions,* Staff Report of the Subcommittee on Antitrust and Monopoly of the Senate Committee on the Judiciary, S.REP. No. 132, 85th Cong., 1st Sess. 4 (1957).

[71] *Id.,* at 47. A summary and analysis of the provisions of the reported bills is presented *id.,* at 47 *et seq.* See also: Amending Clayton Act by Requiring Prior Notification . . . , *Hearings Before the Antitrust Subcommittee (Subcommittee No. 5) of the House Committee on the Judiciary,* 84th Cong., 2d Sess., ser. 15 (1956); Amending the Clayton Act . . . , H.R. REP. No. 1889, 84th Cong., 2d Sess. (1956); Legislation Affecting Corporate Mergers, *Hearings Before the Subcommittee on Antitrust and Monopoly of the Senate Committee on the Judiciary,* 84th Cong., 2d Sess. (1956).

[72] United States v. E. I. du Pont de Nemours & Co., 353 U.S. 586 (1957).

Chapter 4

EXCLUSIVE DEALING

Like price discrimination, exclusive dealing comprises a number of trade practices frequently abused to stifle competition in the distribution sector of the economy. If a manufacturer induces his dealer to abstain from offering competing products and to concentrate on sales promotion of his goods, his competitors are prevented from access to that market, dealers are denied the freedom to handle competing products, and the consumer is restricted in his choice among a number of competing products.[1] A variation of exclusive dealing consists of arrangements, known as requirements contracts, in which the buyer agrees to purchase from the supplier his requirements of a product for a certain length of time. A related business practice is the tying agreement, the essence of which is the "forced purchase of a second distinct commodity with the desired purchase of a dominant 'tying' product, resulting in economic harm to competition in the 'tied' market."[2] ,

Such arrangements may fall both within the scope of sections 1 and 2 of the Sherman Act as well as under the narrower provision of section 3 of the Clayton Act.[3] Section 3 was specifically enacted in 1914 to prevent those exclusive dealing and tying arrangements, the effect of which "may be to substantially lessen competition or tend to create a monopoly in any line of commerce."[4]

---

[1] *Cf.* Stewart & Turner, *Significance of Oligopoly in Acquisition and Exclusive Dealing Situations Under the Clayton Act,* 25 U.CIN.L.REV. 427, 435 (1956).

[2] Times-Picayune Publishing Co. v. United States, 345 U.S. 594, 614 (1953).

[3] *Cf.* Lockhart & Sacks, *The Relevance of Economic Factors in Determining Whether Exclusive Arrangements Violate Section 3 of the Clayton Act,* 65 HARV.L.REV. 913 (1952).

[4] 38 STAT. 731 (1914), 15 U.S.C. § 14 (1952). The text of section 3 appears in the appendix.

(1) Tying Agreements

The law on tying agreements was recently interpreted and restated by the Supreme Court in *Northern Pacific Railway Co. v. United States.*[5] In an important five to three decision (one Justice not participating), the Court held Northern Pacific's "preferential routing" clauses illegal *per se* under section 1 of the Sherman Act. These clauses require the grantees or lessees of land owned by Northern Pacific to ship over this railroad all commodities produced by or on the land, provided that Northern Pacific's rates or services are equal to those of competing carriers.

The decision is particularly noteworthy for its broad and strong language and its new construction of two prior opinions of the Court as to tying clauses, *International Salt Co. v. United States*[5a] and *Times-Picayune Publishing Co. v. United States.*[5b] In addition, the majority opinion contains a clear statement on the rationale underlying the Sherman Act in general and the so-called unreasonable *per se* antitrust violations in particular. A brief explanation of this rule may be necessary.

In early cases under section 1 the statutory language "[e]very contract, combination . . . or conspiracy . . . in restraint of trade . . . is hereby declared to be illegal" was taken literally.[5c] In *Standard Oil of New Jersey*[5d] and *American Tobacco,*[5e] however, decided in 1911, the Supreme Court by judicial construction of the Sherman Act introduced the famous Rule of Reason. This principle gives the courts some discretion in interpreting the word "every" in section 1 by permitting them to inquire whether and to what extent the particular practice reviewed actually constitutes a restraint of competition and whether it is significant enough to be held illegal. Hence, the issue is not whether the practice at bar is reasonable from the viewpoint of the parties involved. The Rule of Reason "makes obsolete once prevalent arguments, such as, whether monopoly arrangements would be socially preferable to competition in a particular industry, be-

---

[5] 78 S.Ct. 514 (1958).

[5a] 332 U.S. 392 (1947).

[5b] 345 U.S. 594 (1953).

[5c] United States v. Joint Traffic Ass'n., 171 U.S. 505 (1898); United States v. Trans-Missouri Freight Ass'n., 166 U.S. 290 (1897).

[5d] Standard Oil Co. of New Jersey v. United States, 221 U.S. 1 (1911); see Handler, *The Judicial Architects of the Rule of Reason,* 10 ABA ANTITRUST SECTION REPORT 21 (April 1957).

[5e] United States v. American Tobacco Co., 221 U.S. 106 (1911).

cause, for example, of high fixed costs or the risks of 'cut-throat' competition or other similar unusual conditions."[5f]

A part of this rule of reason is the so-called unreasonable *per se* rule. Under this rule certain types of anticompetitive agreements are held illegal in and of themselves. In other words, whenever such restraints of trade have been proved to exist in fact (by circumstantial or by direct evidence), the court will not permit the defendant to introduce evidence intended to show that no restraint of trade, or only a reasonable one actually resulted.[5g] Instead, by reason of their nature or their necessarily restrictive effects on competition, these activities are *conclusively presumed* to be unreasonable.[5h]

In the following case, the Supreme Court briefly summarizes the rationale of this *per se* rule and its scope, and then continues to discuss its relevance with respect to tying agreements.

NORTHERN PACIFIC RAILWAY CO. v. UNITED STATES
Supreme Court of the United States 78 S.Ct. 514 (1958).

"Mr. JUSTICE BLACK delivered the opinion of the Court.

"In 1864 and 1870 Congress granted the predecessor of the Northern Pacific Railway Company approximately forty million acres of land in several Northwestern States and Territories to facilitate its construction of a railroad line from Lake Superior to Puget Sound. [Footnote omitted.] In general terms, this grant consisted of every alternate section of land in a belt 20

[5f] REPORT OF THE ATTORNEY GENERAL'S NATIONAL COMMITTEE TO STUDY THE ANTITRUST LAWS 11 (1955).

[5g] For a comprehensive statement of the reasons for the unreasonable *per se* rule, see United States v. Trenton Potteries Co., 273 U.S. 392, 396-398 (1927); United States v. Socony-Vacuum Oil Co., 310 U.S. 150, 221-224 (1940).

[5h] "It has been held too often to require elaboration now that price fixing is contrary to the policy of competition underlying the Sherman Act, and that its illegality does not depend on a showing of unreasonableness, since it is conclusively presumed to be unreasonable." United States v. McKesson & Robbins, 351 U.S. 305, at 309-310 (1957), discussed in chapter 6.

For a different approach, see, *e.g.*, Oppenheim, *Federal Antitrust Legislation: Guideposts to a Revised National Anti-Trust Policy*, 50 MICH. L. REV. 1139 (1952). For a critical survey on history and recent discussions of the concept of "effective" or "workable" competition, see *e.g.*, Stocking, *On the Concept of Workable Competition as an Antitrust Guide*, 2 ANTITRUST BULL. 3 (1956). For the meaning of this economic concept and the factors bearing on its identification, see REPORT OF THE ATTORNEY GENERAL'S NATIONAL COMMITTEE TO STUDY THE ANTITRUST LAWS, chapter 7 (1955). For a critical review, see Brewster, *Enforceable Competition: Unruly Reason of Reasonable Rules?*, 46 AM. ECON. REV. No. 2, 482 (1956). *Cf.* also the writings cited in the Preface under n. 6.

miles wide on each side of the track through States and 40 miles wide through Territories. The granted lands were of various kinds; some contained great stands of timber, some iron ore or other valuable mineral deposits, some oil or natural gas, while still other sections were useful for agriculture, grazing or industrial purposes. By 1949 the Railroad had sold about 37,000,000 acres of its holdings, but had reserved mineral rights in 6,500,-000 of those acres. Most of the unsold land was leased for one purpose or another. In a large number of its sales contracts and most of its lease agreements the Railroad had inserted 'preferential routing' clauses which compelled the grantee or lessee to ship over its lines all commodities produced or manufactured on the land, provided that its rates (and in some instances its services) were equal to those of competing carriers. [Footnote omitted.] Since many of the goods produced on the lands subject to these 'preferential routing' provisions are shipped from one State to another the actual and potential amount of interstate commerce affected is substantial. Alternative means of transportation exist for a large portion of these shipments including the facilities of two other major railroad systems.

❋ ❋ ❋

"The Sherman Act was designed to be a comprehensive charter of economic liberty aimed at preserving free and unfettered competition as the rule of trade. It rests on the premise that the unrestrained interaction of competitive forces will yield the best allocation of our economic resources, the lowest prices, the highest quality and the greatest material progress, while at the same time providing an environment conducive to the preservation of our democratic political and social institutions. But even were that premise open to question, the policy unequivocally laid down by the Act is competition. And to this end it prohibits 'Every contract, combination . . . or conspiracy, in restraint of trade or commerce among the several States.' Although this prohibition is literally all encompassing, the courts have construed it as precluding only those contracts or combinations which 'unreasonably' restrain competition. *Standard Oil Co. of New Jersey* v. *United States,* 221 U.S. 1; *Chicago Board of Trade* v. *United States,* 246 U.S. 231.

"However, there are certain agreements or practices which because of their pernicious effect on competition and lack of any redeeming virtue are conclusively presumed to be unreasonable and therefore illegal without elaborate inquiry as to the precise harm they have caused or the business excuse for their use. This principle of *per se* unreasonableness not only makes the type of restraints which are proscribed by the Sherman Act more certain to the benefit of everyone concerned, but it also avoids the necessity for an incredibly complicated and prolonged economic investigation into the entire history of the industry involved, as well as related industries, in an effort to determine at large whether a particular restraint has been unreasonable—an inquiry so often wholly fruitless when undertaken. Among the practices which the courts have heretofore deemed to be unlawful in and of themselves are price fixing, *United States* v. *Socony Vacuum Oil Co.,* 310 U.S. 150, 210; division of markets, *United States* v. *Addyston Pipe & Steel Co.,* 85 F.271; *aff'd,* 175 U.S. 211; group boycotts, *Fashion Originators' Guild* v. *Federal Trade Commission,* 312 U.S. 457; and tying arrangements, *International Salt Co.* v. *United States,* 332 U.S. 392.

"For our purposes a tying arrangement may be defined as an agreement by a party to sell one product but only on the condition that the buyer also purchases a different (or tied) product, or at least agrees that he will not purchase that product from any other supplier. [Footnote omitted.] Where such conditions are successfully exacted competition on the merits with respect to the tied product is inevitably curbed. Indeed 'tying agreements serve hardly any purpose beyond the suppression of competition.' *Standard Oil Co. of California* v. *United States,* 337 U.S. 293, 305-306. [Footnote omitted.] They deny competitors free access to the market for the tied product, not because the party imposing the tying requirements has a better product or a lower price but because of his power or leverage in another market. At the same time buyers are forced to forego their free choice between competing products. For these reasons 'tying agreements fare harshly under the laws forbidding restraints of trade.' *Times-Picayune Publishing Co.* v. *United States,* 345 U.S. 594, 606. They are unreasonable in and of themselves whenever a party has sufficient economic power with respect to the tying product to appreciably restrain free competition in the market for the tied product and a 'not insubstantial' amount of interstate commerce is affected. *International Salt Co.* v. *United States,* 332 U.S. 392. *Cf. United States* v. *Paramount Pictures,* 334 U.S. 131, 156-159; *United States* v. *Griffith,* 334 U.S. 100. Of course where the seller has no control or dominance over the tying product so that it does not represent an effectual weapon to pressure buyers into taking the tied item any restraint of trade attributable to such tying arrangements would obviously be insignificant at most. As a simple example, if one of a dozen food stores in a community were to refuse to sell flour unless the buyer also took sugar it would hardly tend to restrain competition in sugar if its competitors were ready and able to sell flour by itself.

"In this case we believe the district judge was clearly correct in entering summary judgment declaring the defendant's 'preferential routing' clauses unlawful restraints of trade. We wholly agree that the undisputed facts established beyond any genuine question that the defendant possessed substantial economic power by virtue of its extensive landholdings which it used as leverage to induce large numbers of purchasers and lessees to give it preference, to the exclusion of its competitors, in carrying goods or produce from the land transferred to them. Nor can there be any real doubt that a 'not insubstantial' amount of interstate commerce was and is affected by these restrictive provisions.

"As pointed out before, the defendant was initially granted large acreages by Congress in the several Northwestern States through which its lines now run. This land was strategically located in checkerboard fashion amid private holdings and within economic distance of transportation facilities. Not only the testimony of various witnesses but common sense makes it evident that this particular land was often prized by those who purchased or leased it and was frequently essential to their business activities. In disposing of its holdings the defendant entered into contracts of sale or lease covering at least several million acres of land which included 'preferential routing' clauses. [Footnote omitted.] The very existence of this host of tying arrangements is itself compelling evidence of the defendant's great power, at least where, as here, no other explanation has been offered for the existence of these restraints. The 'preferential routing' clauses conferred no benefit on the purchasers or lessees. While they got the land they wanted by yielding their freedom to deal with competing carriers, the defendant makes no claim that it came any cheaper than if the restrictive clauses had been omitted. In fact any such price reduction in return for rail shipments would have quite plainly constituted an unlawful rebate to the shipper.[5i] So far as the Railroad was concerned its purpose obviously was to fence out competitors, to stifle competition. While this may have been exceedingly beneficial to its business, it is the very type of thing the Sherman Act condemns. In short, we are convinced that the essential prerequisites for treating the defendant's tying arrangements as unreasonable *'per se'* were conclusively established below and that the defendant has offered to prove nothing there or here which would alter this conclusion.

"In our view *International Salt Co.* v. *United States*, 332 U.S. 392, which has been unqualifiedly approved by subsequent decisions, is ample authority for affirming the judgment below. In that case the defendant refused to lease its salt-dispensing machines unless the lessee also agreed to purchase all the salt it used in the machines from the defendant. It was established that the defendant had made about 900 leases under such conditions and that in the year in question it had sold about $500,-000 worth of salt for use in the leased machines. On that basis we affirmed unanimously a summary judgment finding the defendant guilty of violating § 1 of the Sherman Act. The Court

---

[5i] 49 U.S.C. §§ 2, 6 (7), 41 (3).

ruled that it was 'unreasonable, *per se,* to foreclose competitors from any substantial market' by tying arrangements. As we later analyzed the decision, 'it was not established that equivalent machines were unobtainable, it was not indicated what proportion of the business of supplying such machines was controlled by defendant and it was deemed irrelevant that there was no evidence as to the actual effect of the tying clauses upon competition.' *Standard Oil Co. of California* v. *United States,* 337 U.S. 293, 305.

"The defendant attempts to evade the force of *International Salt* on the ground that the tying product there was patented while here it is not. But we do not believe this distinction has, or should have, any significance. In arriving at its decision in *International Salt* the Court placed no reliance on the fact that a patent was involved nor did it give the slightest intimation that the outcome would have been any different if that had not been the case. If anything, the Court held the challenged tying arrangements unlawful *despite* the fact that the tying item was patented, not because of it. 'By contracting to close this market for salt against competition, International has engaged in a restraint of trade for which its patents afford no immunity from the antitrust laws.' 332 U.S., at 396. Nor have subsequent cases confined the rule of *per se* unreasonableness laid down in *International Salt* to situations involving patents. *Cf. United States* v. *Griffith,* 334 U.S. 100; *United States* v. *Paramount Pictures, Inc.,* 334 U.S. 131, 156; *Times-Picayune Publishing Co.* v. *United States,* 345 U.S. 594. [Footnote omitted.]

"The defendant argues that the holding in *International Salt* was limited by the decision in *Times-Picayune Publishing Co.* v. *United States,* 345 U.S. 594. There the Court held that a unit system of advertising in two local newspapers did not violate § 1 of the Sherman Act. On the facts before it the majority found there was no tying problem at all since only one product was involved and that, in any event, the defendant did not possess sufficient economic power in the advertising market to bring its unit rule within the principle of *per se* unreasonableness. But the Court was extremely careful to confine its decision to the narrow record before it. *Id.,* at 627-628. And far from repudiating any of the principles set forth in *International Salt* it vigorously reasserted them by broadly condemning tying arrangements as wholly inconsistent with the fundamental principles of the antitrust laws. In the Court's forceful terms, 'Tying arrangements . . . flout the Sherman Act's policy that competition rule the marts of trade. . . . By conditioning his sale of one commodity on the purchase of another, a seller coerces the abdication of buyers' independent judgment as to the "tied" product's merits and insulates it from the competitive stresses of the open market. But any intrinsic superiority of the "tied" product would convince freely choosing buyers to select it over others, anyway.' *Id.*, at 605.

"While there is some language in the *Times-Picayune* opinion which speaks of 'monopoly power' or 'dominance' over the tying product as a necessary precondition for application of the rule of *per se* unreasonableness to tying arrangements, we do not construe this general language as requiring anything more than sufficient economic power to impose an appreciable restraint on free competition in the tied product (assuming all the time, of course, that a 'not insubstantial' amount of interstate commerce is affected). To give it any other construction would be wholly out of accord with the opinion's cogent analysis of the nature and baneful effects of tying arrangements and their incompatibility with the policies underlying the Sherman Act. *Times-Picayune*, of course, must be viewed in context with *International Salt* and our other decisions concerning tying agreements. There is no warrant for treating it as a departure from those cases. Nor did it purport to be any such thing; rather it simply made an effort to restate the governing considerations in this area as set forth in the prior cases. And in so doing it makes clear, as do those cases, that the vice of tying arrangements lies in the use of economic power in one market to restrict competition on the merits in another, regardless of the source from which the power is derived and whether the power takes the form of a monopoly or not.

"The defendant contends that its 'preferential routing' clauses are subject to so many exceptions and have been administered so leniently that they do not significantly restrain competition. It points out that these clauses permit the vendee or lessee to ship by competing carrier if its rates are lower (or in some instances if its service is better) than the defendant's. [Footnote omitted.] Of course if these restrictive provisions are merely harmless sieves with no tendency to restrain competition, as the defendant's argument seems to imply, it is hard to understand why it has expended so much effort in obtaining them in vast numbers and upholding their validity, or how they are of any benefit to anyone, even the defendant. But however that may be, the essential fact remains that these agreements are binding obligations held over the heads of vendees which deny defendant's competitors access to the fenced-off market on the same terms as the defendant. In *International Salt* the defendants similarly argued that their tying arrangements were inoffensive restraints because they allowed lessees to buy salt from other suppliers when they offered a lower price than International. The Court's answer there is equally apt here.

'[This exception] does, of course, afford a measure of protection to the lessee, but it does not avoid the stifling effect of the agreement on competition. The appellant had at all times a priority on the business at equal prices. A competitor would have to undercut appellant's price to have any hope of capturing the market, while appellant could hold that market by merely meeting competition. We do not think this concession relieves the contract of being a restraint of trade, albeit a less harsh one than would result in the absence of such a provision.' 332 U.S., at 397.

"All of this is only aggravated, of course, here in the regulated transportation industry where there is frequently no real rate competition at all and such effective competition as actually thrives takes other forms.

"*Affirmed.*

"Mr. JUSTICE CLARK took no part in the consideration or decision of this case.

"Mr. JUSTICE HARLAN, whom Mr. JUSTICE FRANKFURTER and Mr. JUSTICE WHITTAKER join, dissenting.

"The Court affirms summary judgment for the Government by concluding that 'the essential prerequisites for treating the defendant's tying arrangements as unreasonable "*per se*" were conclusively established below. . . .' In my view, these prerequisites were not established, and this case should be remanded to the District Court for a trial on the issue whether appellants' land-holdings gave them that amount of control over the relevant market for land necessary under this Court's past decisions to make the challenged tying clauses violative *per se* of the Sherman Act. Further, in light of the Court's disposition of the case and the nature of the findings made below, I think that the Court's discussion of *International Salt Co.* v. *United States,* 332 U.S. 392, is apt to produce confusion as to what proof is necessary to show *per se* illegality of tying clauses in future Sherman Act cases.

". . . *Times-Picayune Publishing Co.* v. *United States,* 345 U.S. 594, has made it clear beyond dispute that both *proof* of dominance in the market for the tying product *and* a showing that an appreciable volume of business in the tied product is restrained are essential conditions to judicial condemnation of a tying clause as a *per se* violation of the Sherman Act. [Footnote omitted.] 345 U.S., at 608-611. . . .

"My primary difficulty with the Court's affirmance of the judgment below is that the District Court made no findings that the appellants had a 'dominant position' or, as this Court now puts it, 'sufficient economic power,' in the relevant land market.

      *   *   *

". . . The District Court should have taken evidence of the relative strength of appellants' landholdings vis-a-vis that of others on the appropriate market for land of the types now or formerly possessed by appellants, [Footnote omitted.] of the 'uniqueness' of appellants' landholdings in terms of quality or use to which they may have been put, and of the extent to which the location of the lands on or near the Northern Pacific's railroad line, or any other circumstances, put the appellants in a strategic position as against other sellers and lessors of land. Short of such an inquiry I do not see how it can be determined whether the appellants occupied such a dominant position in the relevant land market, *cf. United States* v. *E. I. du Pont de Nemours & Co.*, 351 U.S. 377, as to make these tying clauses illegal *per se* under the Sherman Act.

❋ ❋ ❋

"Finally, the Court leaves in unsettling doubt the future effect of its statement that the use of the word 'dominance' in *Times-Picayune* implies no more of a showing of market dominance than 'sufficient economic power to impose an appreciable restraint on free competition in the tied product.' . . . As already indicated, I should think that a showing of 'sufficient economic power' in cases of this kind could be based upon a variety of factors, such as significant percentage control of the relevant market, desirability of the product to the purchaser, use of tying clauses which would be likely to result in economic detriment to vendees or lessees, and such uniqueness of the tying product as to suggest comparison with a monopoly by patent. But I venture to predict that the language of the Court, taken in conjunction with its approval of the summary disposition of this case, will leave courts and lawyers in confusion as to what the proper standards now are for judging tying clauses under the Sherman Act."

(2) Exclusive Dealing Agreements

The law of exclusive dealing contracts continues to be very controversial. Despite considerable litigation, the courts and the Federal Trade Commission have not laid to rest the dispute over the nature of proof required to show a violation of section 3 of the Clayton Act.

(a) *The Judicial Interpretation of the Standard Stations Case*

In the *Standard Stations* case,[6] the Supreme Court dealt with the question "whether the requirement of showing that the effect of the agreement 'may be to substantially lessen competition' may be met simply by proof that a substantial portion of commerce is affected or whether it must also be demonstrated that competitive activity has actually diminished."[7] While the Supreme Court chose the first alternative, the meaning of this so-called "quantitative substantiality" test has remained as controversial as the decision itself. This is vividly demonstrated by the following case.

---

[6] Standard Oil of California v. United States, 337 U.S. 293 (1949). See also Richfield Oil Corp. v. United States, 343 U.S. 922 (1952).

[7] 337 U.S. at 299.

DICTOGRAPH PRODUCTS, INC. v. FEDERAL TRADE COMMISSION

United States Court of Appeals for the Second Circuit
217 F.2d 821 (1954)[8]

"MEDINA, Circuit Judge.

"This is a proceeding to review an order of the Federal Trade Commission directing petitioner to eliminate from its contract with independent distributors certain restrictive, exclusive-dealing clauses and to cease and desist from certain practices connected therewith, in alleged violation of Section 3 of the Clayton Act, 15 U.S.C.A. § 14, and Section 5 of the Federal Trade Commission Act, 15 U.S.C.A. § 45(a) (c).

"For many years petitioner and its predecessor company have manufactured and distributed hearing aids under its trade name 'Acousticon.' Due to the fact that there are said to be from 25,-000,000 to 55,000,000 persons in the United States who are hard of hearing and to the rapid development in recent years of electronics and allied areas of scientific knowledge, the industry has had phenomenal growth, especially since 1940 or thereabouts. Since long prior to that date petitioner has been one of the largest manufacturers of hearing aids, although there is nothing in the voluminous record now before us to indicate that petitioner now or at any time had a 'dominant' position in the hearing aid business.

   * * *

"While some makes of hearing aids are sold by at least one mail order house and in department, optical and drug stores over the counter, the best market for the manufacturers of hearing aids is the independently established retail distributor, whose business is devoted entirely to the fitting and sale of hearing aids to the hard of hearing public, and these distributors also serve as the best market for parts and accessories.

"There is a substantial evidence to sustain the findings below that there are only approximately 1,000 established responsible distributors specializing in the sale of hearing aids in the United States and, of these, 220 are distributors of the 'Acousticon,' operating generally under 'franchise' from petitioner for designated territories and always pursuant to the terms of the restrictive, exclusive-dealing agreements which, together with the arrangements which commonly accompany them, forbid dealing in the products of competitors and in the sale or distribution of used instruments which are traded in or may be otherwise procured or obtained; and the strict enforcement of such agreements has had the effect of establishing and maintaining an area or

---

[8] *Cert. denied,* 349 U.S. 940 (1955). *Cf.* Anchor Serum Co. v. Federal Trade Commission, 217 F.2d 867 (7th Cir. 1954).

segment of the hearing aid business in which the independent distributors of the 'Acousticon' will not undertake to sell the hearing aids of competing manufacturers but deal only in 'Acousticon,' despite requests by competent manufacturers that they handle their products, and despite the fact that many independent distributors handle more than one make of hearing aids. Accordingly, it was found by the hearing examiner and by the Commission:

> 'Respondent's distributors constitute a substantial segment of the outlets for sale of hearing aids and supply coverage for the more important trade areas of the United States. In such segment the respondent has effectively established a monopoly. Competing manufacturers of hearing aids have suffered substantial injury in the form of loss of sales and inadequate distribution of their competing products as a result of the respondent's requirements that its distributors and dealers handle only the products manufactured and sold by the respondent, and such competing manufacturers have been forced to sell less desirable outlets for their products such as optical stores, department stores and drug stores.'
> * * *

"These findings are supported by substantial evidence and we see no reason to review the evidence in detail.

"It is claimed that, as a matter of law, the proofs fall short of the basic requirement of Section 3 that the effect of the use of these restrictive, exclusive-dealing agreements, 'may be to substantially lessen competition or tend to create a monopoly.' It is asserted that 'competition in the industry has in fact increased,' and this assertion is based upon the fact that from less than twenty in the years 1938 to 1940 the number of manufacturers of hearing aids has increased to over eighty, that competition at all times was and is keen and active, that newcomers to the industry have been able to establish themselves and increase the sale of their products from year to year and that 'there is plenty of business for everyone.' But the fact remains that petitioner has maintained its position, during all this period of growth of the industry, as one of the top three in the business, and at least two other leading manufacturers maintain effective control of a substantial number of established distributors by means of similar restrictive, exclusive-dealing agreements.

"Thus, it is apparent that the first question presented for our resolution relates to the necessary evidence required to bring this case within the qualification to the otherwise general proscriptive language of Section 3 of the Clayton Act. Specifically, we are required to decide whether the phrase 'may be to substantially lessen competition or tend to create a monopoly' precludes a finding of unlawful conduct under Section 3, in the absence of a showing that as a result of the use of these exclusive-dealing arrangements there has, in fact been or probably will be a diminution in competitive activity, or in the face of evidence tending to indicate that the number of competitors in a particular line of commerce has increased.

"Closely related to this question of the sufficiency of the government's evidence to establish a violation of Section 3 of the Clayton Act is the problem of what proof, if any, may be introduced to refute the inferences to be drawn from the proof of the employment of these restrictive devices by the petitioner or to establish a justification for their use. It is to this latter problem that the other main contention of petitioner principally relates. Specifically, petitioner has gone to great pains to trace the development and improvement of its products, emphasizing the large expense over the years for research and engineering, demonstrating its solicitude for the hard of hearing and its efforts to use the most effective psychological and 'philosophical' approach to those who hate the very thought of wearing a hearing aid, and for the employment of the most up-to-date apparatus and techniques to determine precisely the needs of each individual prospective customer. As a result of these unceasing efforts to improve its product and the training programs which it has furnished to the independent retailers with whom it deals, petitioner asserts that it has an established good will and a reputation for the excellence of its product and that these exclusive-dealing contracts are indispensable to the maintenance of its status and are necessary to prevent the almost certain diminution in the quality of its service to the public which would occur if its distributors were permitted to sell other makes of hearing aids in addition to "Acousticon." Petitioner thus offers a two-pronged justification for its use of exclusive-dealing arrangements, one cast in terms of economic necessity and the other in terms of the public interest.

"The opinion of the Supreme Court in *Standard Oil Co.* v. *United States,* 1949, 337 U.S. 293, appears in large measure to be dispositive of the first of these issues and offers much assistance in the resolution of the second. . . . In affirming the District Court's decree granting the injunction, its exclusion of testimony concerning the economic merits of the system used as contrasted to other possible systems and its determination that it was unnecessary to make findings concerning the comparative economic status of Standard and its competitors before and after the adoption of that system, the Supreme Court addressed itself to the proscriptive effect of Section 3 of the Clayton Act and found it necessary to construe the very same qualifying phrase with which we are now concerned.

"After reviewing its previous decisions which had indicated that proof of the use of exclusive-dealing agreements by a dominant power in an industry was all that was necessary to establish a violation of Section 3 of the Clayton Act and the extension of that doctrine in the case of contracts tying the sale of non-patented to patented products to situations where it is shown merely that the volume of business affected was not insubstantial and that competitors were preempted from a substantial market, the Court concluded that 'the qualifying clause of Section 3 is satisfied by proof that competition has been foreclosed in a substantial share of the line of commerce affected.' This disposed of an assertion virtually identical with the first contention of the petitioner in the instant case.

* * *

"Thus it appears clear that unless the petitioner's second contention seeking to justify the employment of these exclusive-dealing arrangements upon economic grounds or because their use is in the public interest, is sustained, the proof adduced herein, indicating that the petitioner has been doing business amounting to $2,000,000 a year and has, through these contracts, foreclosed competitors from dealing with more than 22% of the nation's choicest retail outlets for hearing aids, would seem not only to support but virtually to compel a finding that Section 3 has been violated.

"Preliminarily, it should be noted that potential or even probable adverse effects upon petitioner's business alone is not a sufficient basis for withholding injunctive relief. Were we to hold otherwise, we would quite effectually draw the teeth of Section 3 and of the antitrust laws generally. It appears self-evident that any prohibition upon behavior which stifles competition will necessarily enure to the immediate economic disadvantage of the individual or business organization engaging in that behavior. The more efficacious these clauses are in the maintenance of petitioner's competitive position, the clearer is the case against permitting their continued use. We are thus constrained to conclude that it is only when the factors relating to economic necessity and public interest take the case outside the scope of the purpose for which the particular prohibition was imposed that they become relevant. Whether organizations situated as is the petitioner can ever successfully avail themselves of any opportunity to introduce evidence of economic data to remove themselves from the proscriptive effect of Section 3 is a question which underlies both of petitioner's main contentions. On the other hand, petitioner sought to accomplish this by demonstrating that competition had not diminished because of the use of these devices and on the other, by asserting that the purpose of their use was not to suppress competition but to attain legitimate economic ends. Assuming the appropriateness of allegations of this nature in a suit brought under the Sherman Act, we still must examine the extent of their efficacy under Section 3 of the Clayton Act.

* * *

[Having reviewed the legislative history of Section 3 of the Clayton Act, the court concluded:] ". . . [I]t is hard to believe that the Congress envisioned a full dress inquiry into economic motives or effects of such contracts in all cases, including those involving the use of these devices by established leaders or prominent businesses in an industry. Certainly such a view is more in consonance with the evident congressional purpose in passing the Clayton Act than is a view which could conceivably obliterate any distinction between the test applicable here and the tests previously applied.

"The cases in which the Supreme Court has dealt with the problem of exclusive-dealing arrangements evince a recognition of the legislative intention outlined above. Where the alleged violator dominated or was a leader in the industry, proof of such fact was, at an early stage, determined to be a sufficient predicate from which to conclude that the use of exclusive-dealing contracts was violative of Section 3 and other factors appear to have been largely ignored. *Standard Fashion Co.* v. *Magrane-Houston Co., supra; Fashion Originator's Guild* v. *Federal Trade Commission,* 1941, 312 U.S. 457; *Cf. United Shoe Machinery Corp.* v. *United States,* 1922, 258 U.S. 451; *International Business Machine Corp.* v. *United States,* 1936, 298 U.S. 131. More recently, the Supreme Court extended the rule to business organizations enjoying a powerful, though clearly not dominant, position in the trade and doing a substantial share of the industry's business by means of these contractual provisions and tacitly approved the trial court's refusal to consider other economic effects or merits of the system employed.

* * *

"In light of the foregoing, it seems clear that whatever utility the elaborate economic inquiry contended for by petitioner may still have under Section 3 of the Clayton Act when applied to organizations not doing a substantial share of the business or not yet firmly established in a particular line of commerce, it has no place in a case such as this where the condemned contracts are being employed by a corporation which does almost $2,000,000 worth of business each year, is one of the industry's three leaders, all or some of whom use this restrictive device, and which alone controls by such means over one-fifth of the nation's prime retail outlets for products of this kind. Accordingly, we need not weigh the claims of petitioner that its Acousticon hearing aid is the best in the market; it may be assumed that it has market superiority over some of the many others available. We are not concerned with the merits of petitioner's product but only with the probable effect on competition of the use of these restrictive, exclusive-dealing covenants.

* * *

Affirmed."

(b) *The Approach of the Federal Trade Commission*

In a recent address, the General Counsel of the Federal Trade Commission referred to the above decision in these words:[9]

> "On appeal, Dictograph was affirmed by the Second Circuit in what I have elsewhere labeled 'a curiously dated opinion,' and what the Attorney General's Committee bemoaned as 'reverting to a rigid *per se* rule.' "[10]

The General Counsel, as well as the majority of the Attorney General's Committee,[11] favors the actual foreclosure test with its connected requirements for economic proof:

> "Yet the court's reasoning is less than totally compelling. It is uncertain from the shifting language whether the decision rules out *any* economic inquiry into market effects or simply '*elaborate* economic inquiry' in the case of a dominant producer, or merely a 'Sherman Act type of inquiry into all economic factors in *every* Clayton Act Section 3 case,' [Emphasis added.] It is my own feeling that *Dictograph* need only be read as a verbally intricate affirmance of the proof standard there used by the Commission. And certainly neither that decision nor *Anchor-Serum*, which is also capable of *per se* implications, can be read to repudiate the Commission's own standard of proof. So construed, discretion as to the extent of economic inquiry properly remains with the Commission."[12]

And, referring to the Supreme Court's decisions, Mr. Kintner said:[13]

> "[N]ote, if you will, the dissent of Justice Frankfurter [in *Federal Trade Commission* v. *Motion Picture Advertising Service*, 344 U.S. 392 (1953)] in which he discoursed at length on his *Standard Stations'* opinion. *Standard Stations'* emphasis on business volume was unique to that case, he said, because of Standard's 'obvious bargaining power' over service stations; and he stressed the need in the ordinary case for economic analysis into the question of market foreclosure. Is this the hallmark of quantitative substantiality? I doubt it. To me, *Standard Stations* and *Motion Picture Advertising Service*, read together, frame

---

[9] Kintner, *Exclusive Dealing*, Remarks Before the Association of the Bar of the City of New York, April 11, 1956, mimeographed text, p. 6, reprinted in 3 PRACTICAL LAWYER 69, 76 (1957).

[10] REPORT OF THE ATTORNEY GENERAL'S NATIONAL COMMITTEE TO STUDY THE ANTITRUST LAWS 143, footnote 58 (1955).

[11] *Id.*, at 146-148.

[12] Kintner, *Exclusive Dealing*, Remarks Before the Association of the Bar of the City of New York, April 11, 1956, mimeographed text, p. 6, reprinted in 3 PRACTICAL LAWYER 69, 76 (1957).

[13] *Id.*, at 5.

Section 3's competitive injury test in realistic terms of substantial market foreclosure."

Whatever one may think about this interpretation of recent court decisions, the Federal Trade Commission has refrained from a strict quantitative substantiality test. Instead, it has invalidated exclusive dealerships only if it found—on the basis of a full analysis of all economic data—actual foreclosure of competitors from access to the market.[14] Since no one can bring a failure to act by the Federal Trade Commission before the courts, the difference of opinion between the Commission and the courts as to the standard of proof required under section 3 cannot be resolved by that method.

(c) *Protection of Gasoline Dealers*

The Government's action in *United States* v. *Sun Oil Company*, Civil No. 10-483, before the United States District Court in Philadelphia, involves an interesting attempted application of section 3 of the Clayton Act. Sun Oil abandoned the use of exclusive dealing clauses in contracts for service stations about 1936 because of the decision of the Supreme Court in *Gulf Refining Co.* v. *Fox*,[15] that oil companies may be subject to the chain store tax for each service station with which an exclusive dealing contract exists. After some developments in the contractual relations between Sun and the service stations, the contracts were freed from any exclusive dealing or requirement clause. However, the contracts were entered thereafter for only a very short period, such as one year.

The Department of Justice is attempting to prove that the abolition of such clauses was accompanied by a policy of Sun to refuse an extension of a contract, unless the service station remained loyal to company-supplied oil products as well as tires and batteries.

The Government interprets the *Standard Stations* rule to cover the facts of this case. The Government also relies on section 1 of the Sherman Act.

---

[14] See Dictograph Products, Inc., F.T.C. Dkt. No. 5655 (October 8, 1953), *aff'd.* 217 F.2d 821 (2d Cir. 1954), *cert. denied*, 349 U.S. 940 (1955); Anchor Serum Co., F.T.C. Dkt. No. 5965 (February 16, 1954), *aff'd.* 217 F.2d 867 (7th Cir. 1954); The Maico Co., Inc., F.T.C. Dkt. No. 5822 (December 2, 1953); Beltone Hearing Aid Co., F.T.C. Dkt. No. 5825 (February 18, 1954); Harley Davidson Motor Co., F.T.C. Dkt. No. 5698 (July 7, 1954); Revlon Products Corp., F.T.C. Dkt. No. 5685 (October 5, 1954). *Cf.* Note, *Tying Agreements and Exclusive Dealing Arrangements Before the Courts and the FTC*, 55 COLUM.L.REV. 561 (1955).

[15] 297 U.S. 381 (1936).

With respect to the general situation in the distribution of gasoline, Subcommittee No. 5 of the Select House Committee on Small Business, on the basis of the testimony received, came to the following conclusions:[16]

"(1) A substantial proportion of all sales of refined gasoline of major oil companies to the general public is made through retail outlets where the dealer has a short-term lease from the oil company supplier, usually for 1 year. The importance and the proportion of the total retail market serviced by such short-term lessee dealers has been increasing.

"(2) The dealer operating his station under a short-term lease with the oil company supplier frequently is not in fact independent and is subject to control by the oil company supplier. The freedom of choice of the dealer with respect to the manner in which he operates his station is circumscribed by the economic power of his oil company supplier, whether or not such power is specifically exercised against him.[17]

"(3) The short-term leases and sales practices of major oil companies in relation to sponsored products have had the effect of operating against a dealer's freedom of choice in using or dealing in competitive products, and operate to substantially lessen competition and tend to eliminate price competition.

✶ ✶ ✶

"(5) The lessee dealer needs immediate and permanent relief to enable him to fulfill his role as an independent businessman. The present laws, procedures and enforcement policies are inadequate to achieve effective and permanent relief."

The Subcommittee, therefore, recommended strengthening the antitrust laws "designed to protect and preserve small and independent business enterprises," and approved "the purposes and the principles embraced in H.R. 7096, for freedom of choice in trade, and H.R. 11, to secure equality of opportunity of all

---

16 *Alleged Coercive and Discriminatory Practices against Retail Gasoline Operators by Oil Company Suppliers,* Interim Report of Subcommittee No. 5 on Distribution Problems to the Select House Committee on Small Business, H.REP. No. 1423, 84th Cong., 1st Sess. 2-3 (1955); *cf.* also *Gasoline Price War in New Jersey,* Report of the Select Senate Committee on Small Business, S.REP. No. 2810, 84th Cong., 2d Sess. 12-13 (1956); Distribution Practices in the Petroleum Industry, *Hearings Before Subcommittee No. 5 of the Select House Committee on Small Business,* 85th Cong., 1st Sess., Parts I-IV (1957).

17 Representatives of some of the oil companies testified that such control is necessary in order that the oil companies may protect their substantial investments. Other witnesses testified that many retail stations have been maintained at locations long after economic reasons for the substantial investment therein and their operation had disappeared.

persons to compete in trade or business."[18] In addition, the Sub-committee recommended that all oil companies consider, *inter alia,* conversion of most short-term leases with a minimum term of three years.[19] To strengthen the position of the small independent dealer, H.R. 8395, another freedom of choice in trade bill, was introduced in the 84th Congress to amend sections 3 and 4 of the Clayton Act.[20]

In the 85th Congress, various bills dealing with marketing in the oil industry have been introduced. H.R. 426 would prohibit producers from selling at both wholesale and retail level. H.R. 428 would preclude gasoline dealers from acting as agents for, or receiving compensation from, manufacturers for sale of tires, batteries, and accessories. Under H.R. 425, gasoline retailers would have a right to sue in the federal courts to recover damages for the producer's failure to act in "good faith" in complying with, terminating or renewing franchises or leases with his dealers.

(d) *Statutory Protection of Automobile Dealers*

Similar problems exist in the relationship between the car manufacturers and their dealers.[21] It is common knowledge that most automobile dealers handling new American-made cars sell exclusively the product of one manufacturer. Under an elaborate franchise system, the automobiles are distributed through the manufacturer's own sales organization directly to carefully selected retailers. This system "may be defined as an agreement by which the manufacturer appoints the dealer to handle his line, and the dealer, in return for this privilege agrees to conduct his business according to the standards and desires of the manufacturer."[22] The franchise system and his vast economic power

---

[18] Interim Report, *id.,* at 3.

[19] *Ibid.*

[20] See, To Amend Sections 2 and 3 of the Clayton Act, *Hearings Before the Antitrust Subcommittee (Subcommittee No. 5) of the House Committee on the Judiciary,* 84th Cong., 2d Sess., ser. No. 21, at 81-132, 178-181, 202-205, 217-222, 260-261, 292-311, 374-379 (1956).

[21] *Cf.* Schwing Motor Co. v. Hudson Sales Corp., 239 F.2d 176 (4th Cir. 1956), *cert. denied,* 355 U.S. 823 (1957); Packard Motor Car Co. v. Webster Motor Car Co., 243 F.2d 418 (D.C. Cir. 1957), *cert. denied,* 355 U.S. 822 (1957). See Handler, *Annual Review of Recent Antitrust Developments,* 2 ANTITRUST BULL. 647 (1957).

[22] *A Case Study of General Motors Corporation,* Staff Report of the Subcommittee on Antitrust and Monopoly of the Senate Committee on the Judiciary, 84th Cong., 2d Sess. 79 (1956). See also *id.,* at 76-97.

"enables the manufacturer to wield great 'vertical power' in the form of supervisory control over retail operations."[23]

"To supplement the antitrust laws of the United States, in order to balance the power now heavily weighted in favor of automobile manufacturers," Congress, after an extensive investigation,[24] in 1956, passed the Automobile Dealer Franchise Act. Under its main provision,

> "An automobile dealer may bring suit against any automobile manufacturer engaged in commerce . . . and shall recover the damages by him sustained and the cost of suit by reason of the failure of said automobile manufacturer . . . to act in good faith in performing or complying with any of the terms or provisions of the franchise, or in terminating, cancelling, or not renewing the franchise with said dealer . . ."[25]

The term 'good faith' is defined to mean

> "the duty of each party to any franchise, and all officers, employees, or agents thereof to act in a fair and equitable manner toward each other so as to guarantee the one party freedom from coercion, intimidation, or threats of coercion or intimidation from the other party: *Provided,* That recommendation, endorsement, exposition, persuasion, urging or argument shall not be deemed to constitute a lack of good faith."

The other important provision of the Act is an antitrust saving clause. It reads:

> "No provision of this Act shall repeal, modify, or supersede, directly or indirectly, any provision of the antitrust laws of the United States."[26]

The reasons for this legislation were summarized in the Senate Report accompanying the bill.[27]

> "During the hearings before the Subcommittee on Antitrust and Monopoly, which began in November 1955, considerable

---

[23] Kessler & Brenner, *Automobile Dealer Franchise: Vertical Integration by Contract,* 66 YALE L.J. 1135, 1138 (1957), quoting PALAMOUNTAIN, THE POLITICS OF DISTRIBUTION 107 (1955).

[24] Automobile Dealer Franchises, *Hearings Before the Antitrust Subcommittee (Subcommittee No. 5) of the House Committee on the Judiciary,* 84th Cong., 2d Sess., ser. No. 26 (1956); Automobile Marketing Practices, *Hearings Before a Subcommittee of the Senate Committee on Interstate and Foreign Commerce,* 84th Cong., 2d Sess., parts I and II (1956); *Hearings Before the Subcommittee on Antitrust and Monopoly of the Senate Committee on the Judiciary,* 84th Cong., 1st Sess., pts. 6-8 (General Motors) (1956).

[25] 70 STAT. 1125, 15 U.S.C. § 1222 (Supp. 1956). See Note, *Statutory Regulation of Manufacturer-Dealer Relationships in the Automobile Industry,* 70 HARV.L.REV. 1239 (1957).

[26] 70 STAT. 1125, 15 U.S.C. § 1224 (Supp. 1956).

[27] S.REP. No. 2073, 84th Cong., 2d Sess., at 2, 3 and 5 (1956).

testimony was presented by automobile dealers holding franchises with the General Motors Corp. In addition, information was obtained from other sources bearing upon the relationship between automobile manufacturers and their dealers. The evidence obtained indicated that great pressure had been exerted, at least by the dominant automobile manufacturers, upon dealers to accept automobiles, parts, accessories, and supplies which they did not need, did not want, or did not feel their market was able to absorb. Many dealer witnesses asserted that while they were ostensibly independent businessmen, the factory dominated and controlled almost every phase of their operations at all times. The conflict in interest between factory and dealer is a conflict between parties of totally unequal economic power. Automobile production is one of the most highly concentrated industries in the United States, a matter of grave concern to officers of the Government charged with enforcement of the antitrust laws. Today there exist only 5 passenger-car manufacturers, 3 of which produce in excess of 95 percent of all passenger cars sold in the United States. There are approximately 40,000 franchised automobile dealers distributing to the public cars produced by these manufacturers. Dealers have an average investment of about $100,000. This vast disparity in economic power and bargaining strength has enabled the factory to determine arbitrarily the rules by which the two parties conduct their business affairs. These rules are incorporated in the sales agreement or franchise which the manufacturer has prepared for the dealer's signature.

"Dealers are with few exceptions completely dependent on the manufacturer for their supply of cars. When the dealer has invested to the extent required to secure a franchise, he becomes in a real sense the economic captive of his manufacturer. The substantial investment of his own personal funds by the dealer in the business, the inability to convert easily the facilities to other uses, the dependence upon a single manufacturer for supply of automobiles, and the difficulty of obtaining a franchise from another manufacturer all contribute toward making the dealer an easy prey for domination by the factory. On the other hand, from the standpoint of the automobile manufacturer, any single dealer is expendable. The faults of the factory-dealer system are directly attributable to the superior market position of the manufacturer. This economic strength manifests itself in two principal ways:

(1) Control and supervision of the dealer's business.

(2) Power to terminate or to refuse to renew the dealer's franchise.

"The threat of termination which the manufacturer holds over the dealer once the dealer commits himself to the requirements for entry into the industry permits the manufacturer to control the dealer and his operation. The dealer accepts this relationship in the expectation that it will be profitable. He later can reconsider his decision only with the knowledge that his business is specialized in nature and his capital not readily transferable to alternative uses. The threat of termination, therefore, makes him a pliable tool.

* * *

"While franchises among manufacturers differ and have been the subject of various changes over the years, they have generally provided for termination by either party without cause, or at will, or for causes determinable solely by the manufacturer. In other instances, as in the recent case of General Motors, the franchise existed for a very brief period of time. These short-term franchises left the dealers completely dependent upon the whim of the manufacturer for renewal. Dealers seeking redress for grievances under these franchises found themselves effectively foreclosed in attempting to bring suit upon the franchises. The terms of this one-sided document compelled the courts to conclude that, however inequitable the consequences, the dealer executing such a franchise had, for all practical purposes, surrendered his right to litigate his grievance. This has been the prevailing view of courts, both Federal and State, in passing suits filed by dealers under the franchises. Representative of the thinking of the courts is the decision in *Ford Motor Co.* v. *Kirkmeyer Motor Co.*, 65 F.2d 1001 (C.C.A. 4, 1933), . . .

* * *

"This bill does not prohibit the manufacturer from terminating or refusing to renew the franchise of a dealer who is not providing the manufacturer with adequate representation. It simply provides that . . . a dealer will be able to request a court to review the reasons for such termination or nonrenewal and to try the issue whether the factory acted in good faith."

The main purpose of the antitrust saving clause seems to be to make sure that a franchise cannot be terminated for the reason that the franchise dealer sold new automobiles to used car dealers for resale to consumers (new car bootlegging). In this connection, the Report of the House stated:[28]

"Any restriction on a dealer's right to sue based on the fact that he is selling to another dealer, franchised or not, for resale to the public . . . or sells at cut rates would contravene the congressional purposes underlying Section 4 of this bill. . . ."

The Chief Counsel of the Senate Subcommittee on Antitrust and Monopoly[29] called the Act

---

[28] H.R.REP. No. 2850, 84th Cong., 2d Sess. 10 (1956). See McHugh, *The Automobile Dealer Act of 1956*, 2 ANTITRUST BULL. 353, 357-359 (1957).

[29] McHugh, *id.*, at 362 and 363.

"an antitrust law in the sense that it arose out of the failure of the antitrust laws to deal with the problem of bigness and concentration. . . .

"Unlike the principal body of antitrust law, its immediate thrust is not upon competition in the market place. The prime objective of the law is to permit dealers to obtain an impartial forum for settlement of disputes with the factory. Undoubtedly Congress hoped that if dealers were enabled to litigate disputes in Federal courts, manufacturers would exercise greater restraint in policies which have immediate consequences in the market place."

While the purpose of the statute seems clear, its broad language raises difficult questions. The Department of Justice criticized the bill. The President, in signing it, approved it only with reservations and, at the same time, directed the enforcement agencies

"to review the conditions in the industry which brought about the demand for the legislation, to determine whether they continue to exist, to study alternative or different solutions to the problem, and to make recommendations for appropriate action by the next Congress."[30]

The statute has been attacked on the ground that it is unnecessary and unworkable, vague and uncertain, and that it constitutes class legislation and undue interference with the freedom of contract.[31] And it has been said that "in so far as the bill provides a means of lessening competition in the chain of distribution, it deserves all the criticism applied to fair trade laws."[32]

---

[30] Statement of President Eisenhower, reported in CCH TRADE REG. REPORTER, No. 55, at 6 (Aug. 23, 1956).

[31] See Brown and Conwill, *Automobile Manufacturer-Dealer Legislation,* 57 COLUM.L.REV. 219 (1957); Fulda, *The Automobile Dealer Franchise Act of 1956: A Dissent,* 2 ANTITRUST BULL. 367 (1957). The opposite view has been taken by McHugh, *The Automobile Dealer Franchise Act of 1956, id.,* at 353.

[32] Kessler and Brenner, *Automobile Dealer Franchises: Vertical Integration by Contract,* 66 YALE L.J. 1135, 1189 (1957).

Chapter 5

PRICE DISCRIMINATION

(1) Purpose of the Robinson-Patman Act

Discrimination in price or terms of sale among competitors[1] may restrict competition. The conditions under which discriminatory practices amount to a violation of the antitrust laws are set forth in section 2 of the Clayton Act as amended by the Robinson-Patman Act of 1936.[2]

Section 2(a), the key provision, reads:

> "That it shall be unlawful for any person engaged in commerce, in the course of such commerce, either directly or indirectly, to discriminate in price between different purchasers of commodities of like grade and quality . . . where the effect of such discrimination may be substantially to lessen competition or tend to create a monopoly in any line of commerce, or to injure, destroy, or prevent competition with any person who either grants or knowingly receives the benefit of such discrimination, or with customers of either of them . . ."

Two major exculpatory clauses condition this general prohibition: the "cost justification" proviso of section 2(a) and the "meeting of competition in good faith" proviso of section 2(b).

----

[1] See Machlup, *Characteristics and Types of Price Discrimination*, in BUSINESS CONCENTRATION AND PRICE POLICY 397 (National Bureau of Economic Research ed. 1955). Discrimination in the economic sense "means non-correspondence between cost differentials, so that the seller receives a greater net revenue from one or from some customers than from others." Adelman, *The Consistency of the Robinson-Patman Act*, 6 STAN.L.REV. 3, at 4 (1953).

[2] 38 STAT. 730 (1914), 49 STAT. 1526 (1936), 15 U.S.C. § 13(a)–(f) (1952). The full text of these statutes, as subsequently amended, is set out in the appendix.

Subsections (c), (d) and (e) of section 2 forbid certain ancillary discriminatory practices.[3] Finally, section 2(f) makes it illegal "knowingly to induce or receive a discrimination in price" prohibited under section 2(a), and seeks thus to reach directly the large buyer exerting bargaining pressure on small sellers.

Like the Miller-Tydings Amendment to the Sherman Act,[4] the Robinson Patman Act resulted from serious conflicts between small independent wholesalers and retailers and new-type distributors such as chain stores and mail-order houses. These mass distributors were deemed to endanger the survival of the small independent buyers, because of their power to command discriminatory discounts from sellers.[5] This was particularly true during the depression years of the Thirties. The Act was, therefore, "directed at mitigating the business hazards of aggressive competition during a period of declining consumer demand" by facilitating "proof of the substantive violation while narrowing the availability of statutory exceptions for justifying price differentials challenged under the Act."[6]

Since "precision of expression is not an outstanding characteristic of the Robinson-Patman Act",[7] numerous difficult and controversial questions as to the interpretation and policy of the Act continue to arise, both intrinsically and in its relation to the Sherman Act.[8]

The cases here presented by no means cover the whole range of these problems. They have been selected to illustrate the

---

[3] Section 2(c) relates to brokerage commission; section 2(d) to such matters as advertising allowances; and section 2(e) to offering special additional services or facilities in connection with a sale. See Rowe, *How to Comply with Sections* 2(c)-(f), in HOW TO COMPLY WITH ROBINSON PATMAN ACT, 1957 CCH ANTITRUST LAW SYMPOSIUM 124 (1957).

[4] 26 STAT. 209 (1890), 50 STAT. 693 (1937), 15 U.S.C. § 1 (1952).

[5] For a recent discussion of the economic conflicts underlying the Act, see PALAMOUNTAIN, THE POLITICS OF DISTRIBUTION 188-234 (1955).

[6] REPORT OF THE ATTORNEY GENERAL'S NATIONAL COMMITTEE TO STUDY THE ANTITRUST LAWS 129 and 156 (1955).

[7] Automatic Canteen Co. v. Federal Trade Commission, 346 U.S. 61, at 65 (1953).

[8] See, *e.g.*, Rowe, *The Evolution of the Robinson-Patman Act: A Twenty-Year Perspective*, 57 COLUM. L.REV. 1059 (1957). Rowe. *Price Differentials and Product Differentiation: The Issues Under the Robinson-Patman Act*, 66 YALE L.J. 1 (1956), with comprehensive survey on cases and authorities. See also Loevinger, *Enforcement of Robinson-Patman Act by Private Parties*, in HOW TO COMPLY WITH ROBINSON-PATMAN ACT, 1957 CCH ANTITRUST LAW SYMPOSIUM 145 (1957).

more important recent controversies and the present, sometimes confused, general state of the law.

The legality of charging different prices to different purchasers centers on the interpretation of certain phrases and clauses in the statutory text. The headings which follow represent the principal ones. The interpretations of the Act by the courts and the Federal Trade Commission, which enforces the Act in the first instance, are discussed under the pertinent provisions.

(2) Goods of Like Grade and Quality

With respect to this first prerequisite under section 2(a) "designed to serve as one of the necessary rough guides for separating out those commercial transactions insufficiently comparable for price regulation by the statute,"[9] no important recent developments can be reported. In this connection, it has been said:[10]

> "Despite the crucial status of 'like grade and quality' as a threshold control over the application of the act, twenty years of Robinson-Patman have left the law in flux. Precedent declares only the obvious with certainty: products made from inferior components are not of 'like grade and quality' with better goods; and inconsequential variations in labeling will not dispel otherwise 'like grade and quality.' Beyond this the contours of the law recede into confusion."

(3) Injury to Competition[11]

It is now well settled that section 2(a) does not require a finding that the price discriminations have in fact adversely affected competition. The language of section 2(a) is "may be substantially to lessen competition . . . or to injure, destroy, or prevent competition with any person who either grants or knowingly receives the benefit of such discrimination, or with customers of either of them." "The statute is designed to reach such discriminations 'in their incipiency,' before the harm to competition is effected. It is enough that they 'may' have the prescribed effect."[12]

---

[9] REPORT OF THE ATTORNEY GENERAL'S NATIONAL COMMITTEE TO STUDY THE ANTITRUST LAWS 157 (1955).

[10] Rowe, *Price Differentials and Product Differentiation: The Issues Under the Robinson-Patman Act,* 66 YALE L.J. 1, 15 [Footnotes omitted.] (1956); see also REPORT, *id.,* at 156-159 (1955).

[11] For a critical review, see Rowe, *Borderland Issues in Court and Commission Cases Under Sections 2 and 3 of the Clayton Act,* in 8 ABA ANTITRUST SECTION REPORT 60, 65-72 (April 1956).

[12] Corn Products Refining Co. v. Federal Trade Commission, 324 U.S. 726, 738, 742 (1945); Federal Trade Commission v. Morton Salt Co., 334 U.S. 37, 46 (1948); *cf.* Standard Fashion Co. v. Magrane-Houston Co., 258 U.S. 346, 356, 357 (1922); Moog Industries, Inc. v. Federal Trade

The meaning of the word "may" has been phrased in various ways. In the *Corn Products* case, the Supreme Court stated: ". . . [T]he use of the word 'may' was not to prohibit discriminations having 'the mere possibility' of those consequences, but to reach those which would *probably* have the defined effect on competition."[13] [Emphasis added.] Later in the same case, the Court declared:[14] "As we have said, the statute does not require that the discrimination must in fact have harmed competition, but only that there is a reasonable *possibility* that they 'may' have such an effect." [Emphasis supplied.] This statement was repeated in the *Morton Salt* case[15] with the qualification that it "is to be read also in the light of the *Corn Products* case."[16]

A key question under section 2(a) is: What test is to be applied, and, correlatively, what kind of proof is required in determining whether a discrimination in price injures or may reasonably tend to injure competition? In other words, was section 2(a) intended to reach discriminatory practices resulting merely in injury to one or several competitors, and is it enough to prove such individual injury, or must there be a showing of injury to *competition* in a particular market? Under what circumstances may injury to a competitor constitute a substantial lessening of competition in the relevant market?[17]

In *Samuel H. Moss, Inc.* v. *Federal Trade Commission*[18] the Second Circuit had held that proof of the bare fact of price differentials established a *prima facie* case of a violation of section 2(a) and that respondent had the burden of proving absence of injury under section 2(b).[19] This decision was contrary to earlier findings that the Federal Trade Commission had the burden of proving that there was competitive injury as required by

---

Commission, 238 F.2d 43, 51 (8th Cir. 1956); Whitaker Cable Corp. v. Federal Trade Commission, 239 F.2d 253, 254 (7th Cir. 1956).

[13] 324 U.S. at 738.

[14] *Id.*, at 742.

[15] 334 U.S. at 46.

[16] *Ibid.*, footnote 14.

[17] For a discussion, see Burns, *A Summary of a Study of the Antitrust Laws,* 1 ANTITRUST BULL. 695, 707-712 (1956).

[18] 148 F.2d 378 (2d Cir. 1945).

[19] Section 2(b) provides that

"Upon proof being made . . . that there has been discrimination . . . , the burden of rebutting the *prima facie* case thus made by showing justification shall be upon the person charged with a violation of this section. . . ."

section 2(a), whereupon the respondent could invoke the defenses allowed under section 2.[20]

However, in 1954, the widely disputed *Moss* doctrine was clearly rejected in the first *General Foods Corp.* case[21] which also stated a new Commission position as to the test for determining competitive injury under section 2(a). Under this decision, the burden of proof to establish injury to competition is with the complainant. A *prima facie* case of violation of the law requires proof of all three of the following elements: (1) discrimination in price between different purchasers of commodities of like grade and quality; (2) certain jurisdictional facts; and (3) competitive injury. Differences in price without competitive injury are not illegal. "The standard for determining the unlawfulness of an unjustified price discrimination, namely, the substantiality of the effects reasonably probable, is the same whether the competitive injury occurs at the seller level or at the customer level. The fact of injury is to be determined in all cases by a consideration of all the competent and relevant evidence and inferences which may be reasonably drawn therefrom."[22]

In a dissent, F.T.C. Commissioner Meade insisted upon giving a greater weight to the injury sustained by "competitors" as contrasted with injury to "competition."

---

[20] In A. E. Staley Mfg. Co. v. Federal Trade Commission, 135 F.2d 453, 455 (7th Cir. 1943), the court held: "There must be . . . a finding . . . that the discrimination had the effect substantially to lessen competition or tend to create a monopoly. Clearly, Congress meant something besides the mere showing of discrimination itself."

[21] F.T.C. Dkt. No. 5675 (April 27, 1954). The view expressed in this case accords to Purex Corp., Ltd., F.T.C. Dkt. No. 6008, at 7-16 (initial decision April 16, 1954, adopted by the Commission Sept. 15, 1954). See also The Yale and Towne Mfg. Co., F.T.C. Dkt. No. 6232, at 3-5 (June 28, 1956).

[22] *Id.*, at 2. See Federal Trade Commission v. Morton Salt Co., 334 U.S. 37 (1947). The Attorney General's Committee approved the rationale of the first General Foods decision and recommended "that analysis of the statutory 'injury' center on the *vigor of competition in the market rather than hardship to individual businessmen*. For the essence of competition is a contest for trade among business rivals in which some must gain while others lose, to the ultimate benefit of the consuming public. See, *e.g.*, Balian Ice Cream Co. v. Ardens Farms Co., 104 F.Supp. 796, 801 (S.D. Cal. 1952). Incidental hardships on individual businessmen in the normal course of commercial events can be checked by a price discrimination statute only at the serious risk of stifling the competitive process itself. [Emphasis supplied.] . . .

"In some circumstances, to be sure, injury to even a single competitor should bring the Act into play. Predatory price cutting designed to elimi-

The following decision by the Commission might be considered as support for the position that more emphasis should be given to injury to *competitors.*

(a) *Competitive injury on the seller's level*

IN THE MATTER OF ANHEUSER-BUSCH, INC.

Federal Trade Commission, Dkt. No. 6331 (Sept. 10, 1957)[23]

"By TAIT, Commissioner.

"The respondent in this proceeding is charged by the complaint with price discrimination in violation of Section 2(a) of the Clayton Act, as amended. . . . Specifically, it is alleged that respondent in connection with the sale of beer made two successive price reductions in the area of St. Louis County, Missouri, from its previously established regular premium price for that area, and that it made no similar price reductions in any other area. It is charged that by so doing respondent discriminated in price between different purchasers of its beer of like grade and quality with the effect, among other things, of diverting substantial business from respondent's competitors to the respondent.

* * *

"In the St. Louis area, respondent's principal competitors are three regional brewers: Falstaff Brewing Corporation, Griesedieck Western Brewing Company, and Griesedieck Brothers Brewery Company (hereinafter referred to as Falstaff, G.W. and G.B., respectively). Prior to 1954, these competitors sold beer in the St. Louis area at prices substantially less than the price of Budweiser. The prices of the regional competing beers were in each instance $2.35 per case.[24] Respondent's price was $2.93 per case, a differential of $.58. Respondent first reduced its price on January 4, 1954, to $2.68 per case, leaving a new differential of $.33. Thereafter, on June 21, 1954, respondent again reduced its price, this time to $2.35 per case, at which price it was exactly matching the prices of its regional competitors.

* * *

"Respondent, however, made no price reductions anywhere else in the United States similar to those in the St. Louis area.

---

nate a smaller business rival, for example, is a practice which inevitably frustrates competition by excluding competitors from the market or deliberately impairing their competitive strength." REPORT OF THE ATTORNEY GENERAL'S NATIONAL COMMITTEE TO STUDY THE ANTITRUST LAWS 164-165 (1955).

[23] See also Maryland Baking Co., F.T.C. Dkt. No. 6327, at 4 (June 29, 1956), *affirmed per curiam,* The Maryland Baking Co. v. Federal Trade Commission, 243 F.2d 716, 718 (4th Cir. 1957).

[24] Case, as used herein unless otherwise indicated, refers to the standard case of 24-12 ounce regular returnable bottles.

As a result of maintaining higher prices to all purchasers outside of the St. Louis area and charging the lower prices, as reduced in 1954, to only those customers in the St. Louis area, respondent discriminated in price as between purchasers differently located.

"The price reductions of 1954 remained in effect until March, 1955, at which time respondent increased its price 45¢ per case. Its new higher price was then $2.80 per case. Falstaff, G.B. and G.W. almost immediately increased prices to $2.50, or 15¢ over their prior prices. This resulted in a new differential of 30¢ per case.

"One of the principal issues raised on this appeal is whether or not respondent's price reductions in 1954, resulting in discriminations in price between purchasers, were such as to have an injurious effect on competition within the meaning of Section 2(a). The hearing examiner found that respondent's price discriminations had the effect of diverting substantial business to Anheuser-Busch from its competitors in the St. Louis market; the effect of substantially lessening competition in the line of commerce in which Anheuser-Busch and its local competitors are engaged; and the further effect of tending to create a monopoly and having the potentialities to continue to do so.

"Prior to the price reduction by respondent in January, 1954, G.W. was the leading seller in the St. Louis market followed by Falstaff, G.B. and Anheuser-Busch. Immediately thereafter, respondent rose to third in volume of sales and G.B. dropped fourth. Following the June, 1954, price reduction, Anheuser-Busch became the leading seller in the area with Falstaff second, G.W. third and G.B. fourth. Respondent held its first place position in the market throughout the eight months of the full price reduction, from July, 1954, through February, 1955. During this period, the total market sales increased only about 9.2% as against the same period for 1953-54, while respondent, comparing its sales for the same periods, enjoyed an increase of 201.5%, a tripling of sales. On the other hand, Falstaff, G.B. and G.W. during the period of the price reductions lost in their volumes of sale as well as their respective shares of the total market in the St. Louis area. The losses of G.B. and G.W. were particularly large. Comparing the eight months of the full reduction with the same prior period, G.B.'s sales were cut by about 41% and G.W.'s about one-third. . . .

"The relative positions of the various competitors in the St. Louis market around the time of respondent's price reductions in 1954, as expressed in shares of the total market, may be shown as follows:

	Dec. 31 1953	June 30 1954	March 1 1955	July 31 1955
A.B.	12.5	16.55	39.3	21.03
G.B.	14.4	12.58	4.8	7.36
Falstaff	29.4	32.05	29.1	36.62
G.W.	38.9	33.	23.1	27.78
All Others	4.8	5.82	3.94	7.21

"G.B. and G.W. had been having progressively less sales volume in the St. Louis market for several years prior to the price reductions by respondent, and thus it is reasonable to expect that their sales under ordinary circumstances would have continued downward at about the same rates. The trends of their losses, however, do not indicate that their sales reverses in the 1954-55 period would have been anywhere nearly as severe if respondent had not so sharply reduced its prices. Falstaff, on the other hand, had been showing progressive gains in sales prior to the period of the price reductions, and according to this trend but for the reductions, Falstaff would not have lost sales, as it did, but would have shown a substantial increase.

"Taking into account all of the factors which may have affected the sales of the various competitors in the St. Louis market, it is evident that only respondent's price reductions could have had such a general adverse effect on the market. No other circumstance will account for the fact that, while respondent more than tripled its sales, most of its competition suffered such serious declines. This almost speaks for itself. Respondent's gains could only have been made at the expense of competition since the total sales in the St. Louis market did not increase by any such substantial amount as the sales of respondent and the small combined increase in sales by all of the other competitors could not begin to account for the losses experienced by Falstaff, G.B. and G.W. Respondent's price discriminations manifestly resulted in a substantial diversion of sales from competitors to itself. The gravity of the effect of the sales losses on these competitors is readily apparent from the showing that the St. Louis market accounted for 14% of Falstaff's sales, 24% of G.B.'s and 25% of G.W.'s. Moreover, in connection with the effect on competition, respondent's relative size in the beer industry cannot be disregarded. In 1953, the total sales of Budweiser of 6,711,222 barrels was in excess of even the combined total sales of its three leading St. Louis competitors. Their total sales in 1953 were as follows: Falstaff 2,911,393 barrels, G.W. 1,483,631 barrels, G.B. 778,142 barrels. Clearly respondent's discriminations in price had the effect of substantially lessening competition in the line of commerce in which Anheuser-Busch, Falstaff, G.B. and G.W. are engaged. We believe that the hearing examiner's findings in respect to competitive injury are amply supported by the record and free of error."

(b) *Competitive injury on the customers' level*

In recent cases involving impairment of competition on the customers' level rather than among the seller and its rivals, the test has been the same as the one stated in the *Anheuser-Busch* case with respect to competitive injury among the seller's competitors.

The leading case is *Moog Industries, Inc.*[25] Respondent, a manufacturer of automobile spare and repair parts, granted to its customers, at the end of each annual period, a retroactive volume rebate consisting of a flat, graded percentage of the aggregate dollar volume of their respective purchases in the preceding year. This rebate plan resulted in price differentials among its customers, which were held unlawful under section 2 of the Robinson-Patman Act.

The Federal Trade Commission stated:[26]

"The substantiality of respondent's price differences and the probability of injury to competition can best be shown by comparing it with the competitive effect of the amount represented by respondent's standard 2% discount for cash given to all customers. Distributors of respondent testified that they invariably took advantage of this 2% cash discount and that this discount was essential to the conduct of their respective businesses. Testimony in the record also indicates that the market in which these distributors compete is highly competitive with many dealers handling from 15 to 75 different lines of automotive products consisting of thousands of items, many of which sell for only a few cents. The dealers' financial life depends on the aggregate of small margins of profits made on a number of individual automotive items. One jobber in Dallas, Texas, ranking third or fourth in that area, testified that his overall net profit on automotive items ran less than 4%. With overall net profit so low, discounts to favored customers, ranging up to 19%, could well mean the difference between commercial life and death if these discounts were extended to a sufficient number of items purchased by a distributor. Nor is it controlling that the items herein considered may constitute only a very small part of the dealers' total sales. [Quotation from the *Morton Salt* case omitted.] Respondent contends that the evidence in the record does not support the hearing examiner's finding that 'the effect of such discriminations may be to substantially lessen, injure,

---

[25] F.T.C. Dkt. No. 5723 (April 29, 1955), *affirmed,* Moog Industries, Inc. v. Federal Trade Commission, 238 F.2d 43 (8th Cir. 1956). On the issue as to stay of the court's order supporting the Commission until petitioner's competitors are similarly restrained from offering the unlawful price discriminations, see chapter 7.

[26] F.T.C. Dkt. No. 5723, at 6-8.

destroy or prevent competition between customers receiving the benefit of said discriminations and customers who do not receive the benefit of such discriminations.' This contention appears to be based largely on the fact that respondent's customers testified generally that they had not been injured by reason of the higher prices paid by them as compared with prices paid by their competitors in the same trading area. On cross examination, however, these same witnesses admitted that their reasons for so testifying were due to the fact that both they and their competitors followed the suggested resale prices of the respondent and that there was no price competition in their particular trade areas. The adherence by respondent's customers to its suggested resale prices does not eliminate the question of injury to competition. As the Supreme Court said in the *Corn Products* case:[27]

> 'But it is asserted that there is no evidence that the allowances ever were reflected in the purchasers' resale prices. This argument loses sight of the statutory command. As we have said, the statute does not require that the discriminations must in fact have harmed competition, but only that there is a reasonable possibility that they 'may' have such effect. We think that it was permissible for the Commission to infer that these discriminatory allowances were a substantial threat to competition.'

The hearing examiner in his initial decision found that:

> "Any saving or advantage in price obtained by one competitor as against another increases his margin of profit, permits additional services to be extended to customers, the use of additional salesmen, the carrying of larger and more varied stocks, and the establishment of branch houses for expansion of the business. While price competition among customers was more or less non-existent, except in isolated instances, in the areas where testimony was taken, the possibility of price competition is ever present where lower prices to certain competing customers exist.' [Citation omitted.]

> "In support of the hearing examiner's finding of the requisite statutory injury, there is in the record reliable respectable probative evidence in the form of testimony that respondent's 2% discounts for cash were invariably taken by respondent's customers and that these customers considered this discount essential to the conduct of their business. Additionally, some witnesses testified that in order to expand their business, it would be necessary to hire additional salesmen, handle more lines, and provide additional services to customers which could only be effected through increased profits. We believe that the hearing examiner was justified in concluding that respondent's annual volume

---

[27] Corn Products Refining Co. v. Federal Trade Commission, 324 U.S. 726, 742 (1945).

rebate plan resulted in price discriminations violative of the Robinson-Patman Act."

A number of parallel cases have confirmed this approach.[28] In *Fruitvale Canning Co.,*[29] the Commission clearly indicated its present view on the rationale underlying the Robinson-Patman Act in such cases:[30]

> "The pattern of respondent's pricing practices as established in this proceeding closely parallels those pricing practices uncovered by the Commission Chain Store Investigation of 1934.[31] Even casual reference to the legislative history makes it clear that these and similar harmful competitive practices provided the major impetus for the passage of the Robinson-Patman Act of 1936. Indeed, as we view it, the *main thrust of the Robinson-Patman Act was to curb the predatory use of monopoly power by chain stores and mass buyers and to preserve the place of small business as well as to protect its competitive position.* This record discloses substantial price differentials favoring large chain groups and large wholesalers of a type and character identical to those we conceive the Robinson-Patman Act was enacted to curb. The testimony of many witnesses called in support of the complaint as above outlined demonstrates the injurious competitive effect of such price differentials. Having concluded that respondent's special defenses were not sustained on the record, there exists no sound basis for overturning the initial decision of the hearing examiner." [Emphasis supplied.]

And in *E. Edelmann & Co.* v. *Federal Trade Commission,* a court of appeals stated:[32]

> "But it must be remembered that in enacting the Robinson-Patman Act . . . , Congress undertook to strengthen this phase of the Clayton Act which it thought had been too restrictive in

---

28 P. Sorenson Mfg. Co., Inc., F.T.C. Dkt. No. 6052, at 5-7 (June 29, 1956), *affirmed per curiam,* P. Sorenson Mfg. Co., Inc. v. Federal Trade Commission, 246 F.2d 687 (D.C.Cir. 1957); P. & D. Mfg. Co., F.T.C. Dkt. No. 5913, at 7-12 (April 26, 1956), *affirmed,* P. & D. Mfg. Co. v. Federal Trade Commission, 245 F.2d 281 (7th Cir. 1957), *cert. denied,* 355 U.S. 884 (1957); General Foods Corp. (second case), F.T.C. Dkt. No. 6018, at 3-4 (Feb. 15, 1956); E. Edelmann & Co., F.T.C. Dkt. No. 5770, at 3-6 (April 29, 1955), *affirmed,* E. Edelmann & Co. v. Federal Trade Commission, 239 F.2d 152 (7th Cir. 1956), *cert. denied,* 78 S.Ct. 426 (1958); Whitaker Cable Corp., F.T.C. Dkt. No. 5722, at 9-10 (April 29, 1955), *affirmed,* Whitaker Cable Corp. v. Federal Trade Commission, 239 F.2d 253 (7th Cir. 1956).

29 F.T.C. Dkt. No. 5989 (June 15, 1956).

30 *Id.,* at 4.

31 Sen. Doc. No. 4, 74th Cong., 1st Sess.

32 239 F.2d 152, at 155 (7th Cir. 1957), *cert. denied,* 78 S.Ct. 426 (1958).

practice by directing *emphasis to individual competitive situations rather than competition in general.*" [Emphasis supplied.]

From this recent trend, it has been concluded[33] that

"the tests of competitive injury have hardened into rigidity. The 'injury' requirement has evolved into an almost automatic inference from the differential itself. . . .

* * *

"The most recent Commission decisions . . . have abandoned . . . market analysis and instead projected *Morton Salt* so as to condemn almost any price differential among rival customers as 'injurious' *per se.*"

(4) Cost Justification

The ability to grant price favors to selected buyers is a powerful competitive weapon. This ability sometimes springs from cost savings arising from large volume sales. In such instances, there arises a conflict between the interests of the small volume purchaser who is unable to command the lower price and therefore is placed at a disadvantage in competing with those who are able to obtain their supplies at the lower price and the ultimate consumer who is interested in receiving the benefit of distribution economies in the form of lower prices. Congress attempted to accommodate these conflicting interests in the Robinson-Patman Act.

Price discrimination can be justified under the Robinson-Patman Act if it makes no more than "due allowance" for cost differences in sales to different buyers.[34]

There is little case law on this cost defense. Justification of price differentials on the basis of costs has been seriously at-

---

[33] Rowe, *Price Differentials and Product Differentiation: The Issues Under the Robinson-Patman Act*, 66 YALE L.J. 1, 18, 20 (1956).

[34] The express proviso in section 2(a) reads:

"That nothing herein contained shall prevent differentials which make only due allowance for differences in the cost of manufacture, sale, or delivery resulting from the differing methods or quantities in which such commodities are to such purchasers sold or delivered."

This exception was deemed to be "of greatest importance, for while it leaves trade and industry free from any restriction or impediment to the adoption and use of more economic processes, and to the translation of appropriate shares of any savings so effected up and down the stream of distribution to the original producers and to the ultimate consumer, it also strictly limits the use of quantity price differences to that sphere, since beyond it they become instruments of favor and privilege and weapons of competitive oppression. . . ." S. REP. No. 1502, 74th Cong., 2d Sess. 5 (1936).

tempted in relatively few cases.[35] "After one successful cost defense before the Commission in 1937,[36] not until the *B. F. Goodrich* case seventeen years later did an accused seller in a fully contested proceeding succeed in establishing a complete cost defense to defeat every element in a discrimination charge.[37] While in other litigated and finally adjudicated proceedings a cost defense partially prevailed, the Federal Trade Commission in . . . [at least eleven] recorded instances rejected cost justification out of hand."[38]

The neglect of cost justification as a defense to a charge of unlawful price discrimination stems from at least two causes: (1) businessmen normally do not keep accurate distribution cost information of a sort useful in a section 2(a) case,[39] and (2) standards of proof do not exist which are sufficiently precise to guide the respondent or defendant in preparing this defense and to give him assurance that he can meet the requirements of the statute.[40] The Supreme Court commented upon this last problem in *Automatic Canteen Co.* v. *Federal Trade Commission*[41] as follows:

> "We have been invited to consider in this connection some of the intricacies inherent in the attempt to show costs in a Robinson-Patman Act proceeding. The elusiveness of cost data, which apparently cannot be obtained from ordinary business records, is reflected in proceedings against sellers.[42] Such proceedings

---

[35] See Fuchs, *The Requirement of Exactness in the Justification of Price and Service Differentials under the Robinson-Patman Act*, 30 TEXAS L.REV. 1, 14 (1951).

[36] Bird & Son, 25 F.T.C. 58 (1937).

[37] B. F. Goodrich Co., F.T.C. Dkt. No. 5677 (Jan. 22, 1954), adopting Initial Decision (Dec. 10, 1953); and Sylvania Elec. Products Co., F.T.C. Dkt. No. 5728 (Sep. 23, 1954).

[38] REPORT OF THE ATTORNEY GENERAL'S NATIONAL COMMITTEE TO STUDY THE ANTITRUST LAWS 171 (1955). Rejected in full were, *inter alia,* Fruitvale Canning Co., F.T.C. Dkt. No. 5989 (June 15, 1956); C. E. Niehoff & Co., F.T.C. Dkt. No. 5768 (May 17, 1955); Champion Spark Plug Co., F.T.C. Dkt. No. 3977 (July 10, 1953).

[39] Warmack, *Cost Accounting Problems under the Robinson-Patman Act,* CCH ROBINSON-PATMAN ACT SYMPOSIUM 105, 106 (1947).

[40] *Cf.* Note, 65 HARV. L.REV. 1011 (1952).

[41] 346 U.S. 61, 68-69, 79 (1953).

[42] For a collection of relevant authorities and secondary material available on cost showings under the Act, see Note, 65 HARV. L.REV. 1011. See also Fuchs, *The Requirement of Exactness in the Justification of Price and Service Differentials under the Robinson Patman Act,* 30 TEX. L.REV. 1; Haslett, *Price Discriminations and their Justifications under the Robinson-Patman Act of 1936,* 46 MICH. L.REV. 450, 472; Sawyer, *Accounting and Statistical Proof in Price Discrimination Cases,* 36 IOWA L.REV. 244. For discussion of specific cost cases under the Act, see Aronson, *Defenses*

make us aware of how difficult these problems are, but this record happily does not require us to examine cost problems in detail. It is sufficient to note that, whenever costs have been in issue, the Commission has not been content with accounting estimates; a study seems to be required, involving perhaps stop-watch studies of time spent by some personnel such as salesmen and truck drivers, numerical counts of invoices or bills and in some instances of the number of items or entries on such records, or other such quantitative measurement of the operation of a business.[43]

"What kind of proof would be required of a buyer we do not know. The Commission argues that knowledge generally available to the buyer from published data or experience in the trade could be used by petitioner [a buyer] to make a reasonable showing of his sellers' costs. There was no suggestion in the Commission's opinion, however, that it would take a different attitude toward cost showings by a buyer than it has taken with respect to sellers, and 'general knowledge of the trade,' to use the Commission's phrase, unsupported by factual analysis has as yet been far from acceptable, and indeed has been strongly reproved by Commission accountants, as the basis for cost showings in other proceedings before the Commission.[44]

"No doubt the burden placed on petitioner to show his sellers' costs, under present Commission standards, is heavy. . . . It is not a matter of obtaining information in the seller's hands. [Footnote omitted.] It is a matter of studying the seller's business afresh.

❋ ❋ ❋

". . . Proof of a cost justification being what it is, too often no one can ascertain whether a price is cost-justified."

---

under the Robinson-Patman Act, in BUSINESS AND THE ROBINSON-PATMAN LAW (Werne ed.), 212, 227; Taggart, *The Cost Principle in Minimum Price Regulation,* 110.8 MICH. BUS. STUDIES 151, 260 (1938); Warmack, *Cost Accounting Problems under the Robinson-Patman Act,* CCH ROBINSON-PATMAN ACT SYMPOSIUM (1947) 105; Comment, 35 ILL. L.REV. 60.

[43] Federal Trade Commission rulings in some cost cases "demonstrate that expert testimony and other evidence extrinsic to an actual cost analysis will be given little weight by the Commission. The FTC apparently believes that such materials lack the objectivity and relevance of the approved method of analysis." Note, 65 HARV. L.REV. 1011, 1013-1014. See also Warmack, *supra,* note 42. Compare *In re* Minneapolis-Honeywell Regulator Co., 44 F.T.C. 351, 394, a case in which "an extensive cost study" resulting from "sincere and extensive efforts" was in part accepted.

[44] See, *e.g.,* Warmack, *supra,* note 42, at 107, 110.

There have been considerable discussion and criticism of the Commission's attitude as well as proposals for reform.[45] A detailed study of the technical problems involved has been published recently by the Advisory Committee on Cost Justification to the Federal Trade Commission.[46] It proposed that the Federal Trade Commission "refrain as far as possible from adopting specific rules of accounting analysis exclusive of others," and that the Commission "encourage the application of ingenuity and imagination in this complex area."[47] Similarly, the Attorney General's Committee proposed:[48]

> "That the Commission adopt realistic standards acknowledging the inadequacies inherent in accounting measurements of price. . . .
>
> "As a legal framework, we recommend recognition that a Robinson-Patman cost defense is not susceptible to testing by precise or mechanical rules. We advise a liberal interpretation of the statute's 'due allowance' criterion as enacting a reasonable *de minimis* concept to exonerate a challenged price even if an attempted cost defense falls short of 'justifying' it by a fractional amount."

Based on such views, a court of appeals recently upheld a cost savings defense in *Reich* v. *Harper & Brothers*:[49]

> "Since Harper had no relevant cost records for the period of 1941 to 1950, the accountant hired to prepare the study used figures for 1951, adjusted backwards on the basis of general salary rates published by the Commerce and Industry Association of New York. Although such an accounting method obviously lacks the full measure of desired precision it appears to have been undertaken in good faith and to accord with the minimal requirements of sound accounting principles."

---

[45] See, *e.g.*, Rowe, *Price Differentials and Product Differentiation: The Issues under the Robinson-Patman Act*, 66 YALE L.J. 1, 21-23 and 41-45 (1956); Edwards, *Cost Justification and the Federal Trade Commission*, 1 ANTITRUST BULL. 563 (1956); Sawyer, *Cost Justifications and Quantity Differentials*, id., 573; Kintner, *Revitalized Federal Trade Commission: A Two-Year Evaluation*, 30 N.Y.U. L.REV. 1143, 1162-1165 (1955).

[46] ADVISORY COMMITTEE TO THE FEDERAL TRADE COMMISSION, REPORT ON COST JUSTIFICATION (1956). See Shnidermann, *Cost Justification Under the Robinson-Patman Act—The F.T.C. Advisory Committee's Report*, 25 U. CIN. L.REV. 389 (1956).

[47] *Id.*, at 10.

[48] REPORT OF THE ATTORNEY GENERAL'S NATIONAL COMMITTEE TO STUDY THE ANTITRUST LAWS 174 (1955).

[49] 235 F.2d 420, at 422 (2d Cir. 1956).

(5) Quantity Limits

The cost justification defense in section 2(a) is qualified by a further clause which authorizes the Federal Trade Commission to

> "fix and establish quantity limits . . . as to particular com- modities or classes of commodities, where it finds that available purchasers in greater quantities are so few as to render differen- tials on account thereof unjustly discriminatory or promotive of monopoly in any line of commerce. . . ."

There is only one case to date in which the Federal Trade Commission has attempted to limit quantity discounts under this proviso.[50] Its action was unsuccessful. In *Federal Trade Commis- sion v. B. F. Goodrich Co.*[51] a court of appeals affirmed the de- cision of the court below,[52] that the Federal Trade Commission's quantity-limit rule for tires and tubes, which fixed the maximum discount limit on sales at 20,000 pounds ordered at one time for delivery at one time, was invalid because the Commission failed to find that available purchasers in quantities greater than a 20,000-pound carload are so few as to render differentials on account thereof unjustly discriminatory or promotive of monop- oly. The court held that the Commission's finding as to the few- ness of available purchasers in annual dollar volumes greater than $600,000 did not support a rule fixing a quantity limit of one 20,000-pound carload and that a "Statement of Basis and Purpose" appended to the quantity limit rule could not be used to supplement the formal findings. No appeal from this decision has been taken.

(6) Meeting Competition in Good Faith

The second major defense to a price discrimination charge under section 2(a) is contained in section 2(b) of the amended Clayton Act,[53] and is based on meeting competition in good faith.

---

[50] *Cf.* McGee, *The Decline and Fall of Quantity Discounts: The Quan- tity Limit Rule in Rubber Tires and Tubes*, 25 J.BUS. U. CHI. 225 (1954).

[51] 242 F.2d 31 (D.C. Cir. 1957).

[52] 134 F.Supp. 39 (D.C. 1955).

[53] It reads:

> "That nothing herein contained shall prevent a seller rebutting the *prima facie* case thus made by showing that his lower price or the furnishing of services or facilities to any purchaser or purchasers was made in good faith *to meet an equally low price* of a competitor, or the services or facilities furnished by a competitor." [Emphasis sup- plied.]

The scope and legal effect of this defense were construed by the Supreme Court in *Standard Oil Co. of Indiana* v. *Federal Trade Commission.*[54] In its original decision, the Federal Trade Commission had held that the defense was available only to rebut a *prima facie* case established by a showing of price differentials without additional proof of competitive injury.[55] The Supreme Court, however, rejected this interpretation and construed the proviso as authorizing an "absolute" or complete defense irrespective of Commission findings as to competitive injury.[56]

Despite this controversial holding, the defense has not been successful in a single case to date.[57] The subsequent history of the *Standard Oil (Indiana)* case and certain problems arising therefrom have been recently considered in *Standard Oil Co.* v. *Brown:*[58]

> "The Supreme Court returned the case to the Federal Trade Commission to make its findings as to whether the Standard Oil Company had proven itself to come within § 2(b). The Commission reviewed the matter and failed to give full effect to the Supreme Court's opinion as to the availability of § 2(b) relief,[59] and the case was again appealed to the Court of Appeals for the 7th Circuit. That Court reversed the decision of the Commission[60] and there, for the first time, discussed the use of the word 'lawful' in connection with 'equally lower prices.' As to this matter the court said:
>
> > 'It is interesting and highly significant that the statute employs the language 'made in good faith to meet an equally low price of a competitor,' but that the Supreme Court in the instant case adds the word 'lawful,' so that it reads, 'made in good faith to meet a lawful and equally low price of a competitor,' 340 U.S., at pages 238 and 246. We do not know, of course, why the Supreme Court added the word 'lawful,' but we strongly suspect that it was for the purpose of giving emphasis to its previous decisions that a 'good faith' defense was not available to a seller who had met an unlawful price. In this connection, it is also pertinent to note that in the in-

---

[54] 340 U.S. 231 (1951). See also Federal Trade Commission v. A. E. Staley Mfg. Co., 324 U.S. 746 (1945).

[55] 41 F.T.C. 263 (1945).

[56] 340 U.S. 231, 247, 251 (1951). *Cf.* McGee, *Price Discrimination and Competitive Effect: The Standard Oil of Indiana Case,* 23 U. CHI. L.REV. 398 (1956).

[57] *Cf.* Kintner, *Revitalized Federal Trade Commission: A Two-Year Evaluation,* 30 N.Y.U. L.REV. 1143, 1165-1168 (1955).

[58] 238 F.2d 54, at 57-58 (5th Cir. 1956).

[59] 49 F.T.C. 923, 953-955 (1953).

[60] 233 F.2d 649 (7th Cir. 1956), *affirmed,* 78 S.Ct. 369 (1958).

stant situation there is no finding, no contention and not even a suspicion but that the competing prices which petitioner met were lawful. . . .' 233 F.2d 649, 653.

"However, to us it appears that the Supreme Court may have used the word 'lawful' merely because it was dealing with a case in which the facts showed that an equally low price had been met and the record was silent as to whether such competitor's price was illegal; the Court, under these circumstances, merely took the case as it stood and referred to the competitor's equally low prices as 'lawful' because there was nothing in the record to indicate that they were not lawful. The use of the word was not to establish a standard that must be met; it was rather a description of the facts presented in that case.

"Here, as in the *Standard Oil* case quoted from above, there is 'no finding, no contention, and not even a suspicion (in the record) but that the competing prices which petitioner met were lawful.' Appellee here contends that there is a burden on the seller to prove that the competing price was lawful. There is certainly no authority for this in either the Supreme Court or later Court of Appeals opinions in the case referred to at such length. The most, it seems to us, that could be made out of the use by the Supreme Court of the word 'lawful' is that if the seller discriminates in price to meet prices that he knows to be illegal or that are of such a nature as are inherently illegal, as was the basing point pricing system in the *Staley* case, *supra,* there is a failure to prove the 'good faith' requirement in § 2(b). There is nowhere a suggestion that the seller must carry the burden of proving the actual legality of the sales of its competitors in order to come within the protection of the proviso."

The Attorney General's Committee approved the result of the *Standard Oil (Indiana)* decision:[61]

"Whatever the interpretation of the substantive price discrimination offense, we think that a seller's right to meet a competitor's prices by granting price differentials to some customers without reducing his prices to all must remain an essential qualification to any anti-price discrimination law. For a seller constrained by law to reduce prices to *some* only at the cost of reducing prices to *all* may well end by reducing them to *none*. . . . The *Standard Oil* decision accordingly goes far toward harmonizing the Robinson-Patman Act with the basic tenor of antitrust policy."

---

[61] REPORT OF THE ATTORNEY GENERAL'S NATIONAL COMMITTEE TO STUDY THE ANTITRUST LAWS 181 (1955). *Cf.* also Burns, *A Summary of a Study of the Antitrust Laws,* 1 ANTITRUST BULL. 695, 712-717 (1956), for the consequences of an "absolute" good faith defense in oligopolistic markets.

The rationale of *Standard Oil* (*Indiana*) has been followed in *Balian Ice Cream Co., Inc.* v. *Arden Farms Co.*[62] The reaction of the Federal Trade Commission was stated by Commissioner Kern before the Senate Subcommittee on Antitrust and Monopoly as follows:[63]

"Mr. Kern: . . . In the *Balian* case, a number of independent local ice cream manufacturers in the Los Angeles market sued Arden Farms Co., a corporation operating in Arizona and the Pacific Northwest, for treble damages based on an injury allegedly resulting from Arden's lowering its prices in the Los Angeles market for a substantial length of time while maintaining them elsewhere.

"The trial court, with the subsequent approval of the Ninth Circuit Court of Appeals, accepted a good-faith defense that was based on a showing that there had been active price competition generally in the Los Angeles ice cream market and that defendants' lower prices were necessitated by 'competitive conditions.'

"Thus the courts held legal a harmful territorial price discrimination by Arden that lasted for months on the ground that Arden was 'meeting competition,' although the meeting of a particular price of a particular competitor, as the wording of the good-faith proviso of Section 2(b) of the Clayton Act seems plainly to contemplate, was not involved. In brief, Arden was permitted to plead a highly competitive market as a basis for 'meeting competition' through ruinous price discrimination.

"The Commission majority for which I speak feels strongly that these two decisions [*Standard Oil Co.* (*Indiana*) and *Balian*] dramatically illustrate the danger inherent in providing a complete good-faith defense to the charge of price discrimination.

"In fact, it is believed that if the defense can be successfully interposed in cases like *Standard Oil* and *Balian Ice Cream,* where there was no question that severe injury was suffered by small business concerns as a result of unfair pricing policies, then Section 2(a) of the Clayton Act is pretty much of a dead letter.

"In our judgment, in the light of these decisions it is hard to conceive of a situation where the absolute defense to a price discrimination charge cannot be arranged and thereafter raised. We cannot help concluding that the most important section of the Robinson-Patman Act has thus been emasculated. Indeed,

---

[62] 231 F.2d 356 (9th Cir. 1955), *cert. denied,* 350 U.S. 991 (1956). The defense of meeting competition in good faith is so strong that it "is read into every Commission order." Federal Trade Commission v. National Lead Co., 352 U.S. 419, 426 (1957).

[63] To Amend Section 2 of the Clayton Act, *Hearings Before the Subcommittee on Antitrust and Monopoly of the Senate Committee on the Judiciary,* 84th Cong., 2d Sess., 227-228 (1956).

the language of the minority of the Supreme Court in their 1951 *Standard Oil* decision appears to have been prophetic. They said this, speaking through Mr. Justice Reed:

'The Court's interpretation leaves what the seller can do almost as wide open as before [i.e., before the Robinson-Patman amendment]. * * * It seems clear to us that the interpretation put upon the clause of the Robinson-Patman Act by the Court means that no real change has been brought about by the amendment.' [340 U.S. at 235.]

"As we see it, large businesses will be free to 'meet' one another's competition through discriminatory price concessions to select customers, regardless of the competitive havoc thus inflicted on the small businesses required to pay higher prices while trying to compete with the favored accounts.

"And not only will the favored dealers be enabled to divert trade from those not in a position to meet their prices; the large companies utilizing price discrimination for the purpose of eliminating their smaller competitors will find it possible, because of their superior financial staying power, to subsidize less profitable or even unprofitable sales for long periods of time in order to achieve their ends.

"The need for strong anti-price discrimination laws is especially acute in the current buyer's market, when producers compete sharply and make price concessions to certain customers but not to all."

Along these lines, the Federal Trade Commission recently rejected the "good faith" defense in *Anheuser-Busch, Inc.*[64] Respondent had reduced its established premium price on Budweiser beer in the St. Louis area *to match exactly* the lower established price charged for beer by its local competitors. In all other areas, respondent, in accordance with its customary practice, had maintained the so-called differential in price between premium-priced Budweiser and the normally lower priced regional or local beers.

The Commission rejected respondent's contention that its practices did not result in competitive injury as provided in section 2(a) and then continued:[65]

"In this instance, respondent's purpose could not have been to protect its sales volume in the St. Louis market against an invasion by competitors. Its sales and share of the total market had been steadily increasing. None of the competitors consti-

---

[64] F.T.C. Dkt. No. 6331 (Sept. 10, 1957), reproduced in part *supra*.

[65] *Id.*, at 6. [Emphasis added.] *Cf.* also C. E. Niehoff & Co., F.T.C. Dkt. No. 5768, at 6-7 (May 17, 1955); Whitaker Cable Corp., F.T.C. Dkt. No. 5722, at 9 (April 29, 1955); E. Edelmann & Co., F.T.C. Dkt. No. 5770, at 8-10 (April 29, 1955).

tuted any threat at that time to respondent's relative position in the St. Louis market. In fact, the sales of two of its major competitors had been on the down grade for some time. Respondent argues that, while not losing sales in the St. Louis area, it had been having decreases in sales volume in other markets served by its St. Louis plant. This, however, would not justify the lowering of prices in the one market in which respondent had experienced no losses. *The emphasis of Section 2(b) is on individual competitive situations rather than upon a general system of competition.* F.T.C. v. A. E. Staley Mfg. Co., 324 U.S. 746. If respondent was faced with an individual competitive situation which it had to meet, it clearly was not in the St. Louis area. However more advantageous it may have been for respondent to lower its prices there, by so doing it has no defense under 2(b).

"Prior to the price reductions of 1954, Budweiser was sold at a considerably higher price in St. Louis than most of its competition and not only retained but steadily improved its sales volume in that market. After the price increases of March 1955, when there was again a differential in price between Budweiser and the regional beers in St. Louis, respondent's product continued to sell at a volume greater than that in the years prior to the price reductions. It is evident that Budweiser could and did successfully command a premium price in the St. Louis market as it has in most of the other markets in the nation. *The test in such a case is not necessarily a difference in quality but the fact that the public is willing to buy the product at a higher price in a normal market.* Clearly, therefore, respondent's reduction from the premium price to match the prices of the regional beers on the market was not a meeting of competition. The effect was to undercut competition. The huge gains which respondent made at the lower prices testifies to that fact. Under the circumstances, respondent cannot justly claim that it was meeting competition.

In *Enterprise Industries* v. *The Texas Co.*[66] a district court read into the "good faith" defense another restriction "which promises to be of considerable importance in future litigation"[67] and which seems to be at odds with the view taken in *Standard Oil (Indiana)*.

"Plaintiff was a gas station operator, whose purchases from defendant were in commerce. [Case cited.] It was established that in a gas war situation price allowances were made by de-

---

[66] 136 F.Supp. 420 (D.Conn. 1955), *revised on other grounds*, 240 F.2d 457 (2d Cir. 1957), *cert. denied*, 353 U.S. 965 (1957).

[67] Note, *The Good Faith Defense of the Robinson-Patman Act: A New Restriction Appraised*, 66 YALE L.J. 935, 937 (1957).

fendant to its dealers in the Hartford area, competing with one another in the sale of defendant's Fire Chief and Sky Chief brands of gasoline, on condition that the dealers drop their retail prices to a level competitive with neighboring dealers in rival brands. By 'competitive' was meant equal. During one period, plaintiff, declining to drop its retail prices, neither requested nor received the so-called allowances while competing Texaco dealers received them. At other periods some of the Texaco dealers competing with plaintiff received allowances which were greater than plaintiff's." [The amount of the price cut offered each dealer was based on the prevailing neighborhood price. Since the prevailing prices in the city were lower than on the highway, Texaco sold gasoline to the dealers in the city at a lower price than it charged plaintiff.]"[68]

The court held that this price discrimination between competing purchasers violated section 2(a).[69] Turning to defendant's "good faith" defense based on section 2(b), the court said:[70]

". . . Texas could justify discrimination only by a showing that it dropped its price to the other stations to meet an equally low price made available to those other stations by a competing oil company. In view of the short-term station and equipment leases in effect with some stations, perhaps it is a fiction to speak of price competition at the oil company sale to the station level. That is the competitive level at which the justification is provided for defendant in the Robinson-Patman Act, however. The Act does not go so far as to allow discriminatory price cutting to enable a *buyer* to meet competition, but only to enable the seller to meet a lawful price of the seller's competitor. The end effect is the same, perhaps, but the scheme adopted by Texas allows it, without first determining the price offered by its competitor, a flexibility that could result in undesirable discrimination between purchasers from Texas."

The Federal Trade Commission[71] and the Senate Subcommittee on Retailing, Distribution, and Fair Trade[72] have endorsed this decision, but it has also been subject to serious criticism.[73]

---

[68] 136 F.Supp. at 421.

[69] *Id.*, at 422.

[70] *Id.*, at 421.

[71] *Hearings Before the Subcommittee on Retailing, Distribution, and Fair Trade of the Senate Committee on Small Business*, 84th Cong., 1st Sess. and 2d Sess. pt. 3, at 450, 458 (1956). See also Pure Oil Co., F.T.C. Dkt. No. 6640 (complaint filed September 26, 1956).

[72] S. REP. No. 2810, 84th Cong., 2d Sess. 20, 28-29 (1956).

[73] Note, *The Good Faith Defense of the Robinson-Patman Act: A New Restriction Appraised*, 66 YALE L.J. 935, 938-945 (1957).

On January 27, 1958, the Supreme Court decided the 17-year old *Standard Oil (Indiana)* case for the second time.[73a] In a five to four decision, the Court held that the Seventh Circuit made a fair assessment of the record when it found that Standard's price reductions were not made pursuant to a price system. The Court, speaking through Justice Clark, said:

"Both parties acknowledge that discrimination pursuant to a price system would preclude a finding of 'good faith.' [Citations omitted.] The sole question then is one of fact: were Standard's reduced prices to four 'jobber' buyers—Citrin-Kolb, Stikeman, Wayne, and Ned's—made pursuant to a pricing system rather than to meet individual competitive situations.

"We have examined the findings of the Commission, which relies most heavily on the fact that no competitors' offers were shown to have been made to Citrin-Kolb, Stikeman, or Wayne prior to the time Standard initially granted them the reduced tank-car price. [Footnote omitted.] All three of these 'jobbers', however, were granted the tank-car price before the passage of the Robinson-Patman Act in 1936, and the trial examiner excluded proof of pre-1936 offers on the ground of irrelevancy. The Commission approved this ruling, and on remand failed to reopen the record to take any further proof. In our former opinion in this case, we said, '[T]here is no doubt that under the Clayton Act, before its amendment by the Robinson-Patman Act, [such] evidence would have been material and, if accepted, would have established a complete defense to the charge of unlawful discrimination.' 340 U.S. at pages 239-240. The proof should have been admitted; its absence can hardly be relied on by the Commission now as a ground for reversal. In any event, the findings that were made are sufficient for our disposition of the case.

"It appears to us that the crucial inquiry is not why reduced prices were first granted to Citrin-Kolb, Stikeman, and Wayne, but rather why the reduced price was continued subsequent to passage of the Act in 1936. The findings show that both major and local suppliers made numerous attempts in the 1936-1941 period to lure these 'jobbers' away from Standard with cut-rate prices, oftentimes much lower than the one and one-half cent reduction Standard was giving them. It is uncontradicted, as pointed out in one of the Commission dissents, that Standard lost three of its seven 'jobbers' by not meeting competitors' pirating offers in 1933-1934. . . .

"The findings as to Ned's, the only one of the 'jobbers' initially to receive the tank-car price *post* Robinson-Patman, are highly significant. After a prolonged period of haggling, during which

---

[73a] Federal Trade Commission v. Standard Oil Co. of Indiana, 78 S.Ct. 369 (1958), *affirming* 233 F.2d 649 (7th Cir. 1956).

Ned's pressured Standard with information as to numerous more attractive price offers made by other suppliers, Standard responded to an ultimatum from Ned's in 1936 with a half-cent per gallon reduction from the tank-wagon price. The Commission concedes that this first reduction occurred at a time when Ned's did not meet the criteria normally insisted upon by Standard before giving any reduction. Two years later, after a still further period of haggling [Footnote omitted.] and another Ned's ultimatum, Standard gave a second reduction of still another cent.

"In determining that Standard's prices to these four 'jobbers' were reduced as a response to individual competitive situations rather than pursuant to a pricing system, the Court of Appeals considered the factors just mentioned, all of which weigh heavily against the Commission's position. The Commission's own findings thus afford ample witness that a 'fair assessment' of the record has been made. Standard's use here of two prices, the lower of which could be obtained under the spur of threats to switch to pirating competitors, is a competitive deterrent far short of the discriminatory pricing of *Staley Cement*, and *National Lead*, *supra*, and one which we believe within the sanction of § 2(b) of the Robinson-Patman Act.

"*Affirmed.*

"Mr. Justice DOUGLAS, with whom THE CHIEF JUSTICE, Mr. Justice BLACK and Mr. Justice BRENNAN concur, dissenting.

"The Court today cripples the enforcement of the Robinson-Patman Act . . . in an important area. . . .

"Standard admitted that it gave reduced prices to some retailers and refused those reduced prices to other retailers. Before granting these retailers the reduced prices, Standard classified them as 'jobbers.' Standard's definition of a 'jobber' took into account the volume of sales of the 'jobber,' his bulk storage facilities, his delivery equipment, and his credit rating. If Standard's tests were met, the 'retailer' became a 'jobber' even though he continued to sell at retail. Moreover, Standard's tests of who was a 'jobber' did not take into account the cost to Standard of making these sales. So Standard's definition of 'jobber' was arbitrary, both as respects the matter of *costs* and the matter of *function*. It comes down to this: a big retailer gets one price; a small retailer gets another price. And this occurs at the *ipse dixit* of Standard, not because the cost of serving the big retailer is less or because the big retailer, as respects the sales in question, performs a function different from any other retailer.

* * *

". . . The Commission found 'the discriminations in price involved in this proceeding were made pursuant to respondent's established method of pricing.' The record amply supports this finding. [Footnote omitted.]

"If a seller offers a reduced price for no other reason than to meet the lawful low price of a competitor, then the seller's otherwise unlawful price falls within the protection of § 2(b). But where, as here, a seller establishes a discriminatory pricing *system*, this system does not acquire the protection of § 2(b) simply because in fact use of the system holds a customer against a competitive offer. . . .

"The mere fact that a competitor offered the lower price does not mean that Standard can lawfully meet it. Standard's system of price discrimination, shown not to be in 'good faith,' cannot be justified by showing that competitors were using the same system. . . .

      * * *

". . . It is only a *lawful* lower price that may be met. Were it otherwise then the law to govern is not the Robinson-Patman Act but the law of the jungle."

(7) Functional Discounts

Functional discounts are price differentials granted by a seller as a result of the buyer's role in the distribution process. Such discounts may be granted solely because of a purchaser's position in the distribution chain or they may depend on the services performed by the distributor receiving the discount, *e.g.*, warehousing, delivery, or advertising.

Although there was much discussion on functional discounts in Congress, the Robinson-Patman Act makes no reference to their legal status. In recent years,[74] two major decisions of the Federal Trade Commission have dealt with the difficult problems arising from functional discounts granted to integrated or multiple function and new type distributors: *Doubleday & Co., Inc.*[75] and *General Foods Corp.*[76]

IN THE MATTER OF DOUBLEDAY & CO., INC.
Federal Trade Commission Dkt. No. 5897 (August 31, 1955)

"Chairman HOWREY delivered the opinion of the Commission.

      * * *

". . . Count IV charged respondent with violating Section 2(a) of the amended Clayton Act by discriminating in favor of

---

[74] For an analysis of somewhat earlier developments, see Note, *Functional Discounts Under the Robinson-Patman Act: The Standard Oil Litigation*, 67 HARV. L.REV. 294 (1953).

[75] F.T.C. Dkt. No. 5897 (August 31, 1955).

[76] F.T.C. Dkt. No. 6018 (Feb. 15, 1956) (Second General Foods case).

certain jobbers or wholesalers to the injury of others competing with them and to the injury of respondent's competitors. [Respondent had sold the same books at different prices to different purchasers competing with each other in the resale of books.]

* * *

". . . [R]espondent attempted to show that the discounts allowed the so-called 'Big Three' jobbers were in reality functional discounts by which respondent compensated integrated jobbers for services rendered. The evidence on this issue is in the record on tender only, the hearing examiner having ruled that the asserted defense was unavailable on the ground that the law does not permit price differentials on the basis of what a customer does to resell his own merchandise; in other words that the character of the selling of the purchaser and not the buying determines functional classification.

"This principle is not without limitation or qualification.

"Inasmuch as the functional discount, as applied to our present dynamic economy and constantly changing methods of marketing, presents a difficult and perplexing problem, a brief historical discussion is in order.

"Functional discounts long have been a traditional pricing technique by which sellers compensated buyers for expenses incurred by the latter in assuming certain distributive functions. The typical functional discount system provided for graduated discounts to customers classified in accordance with their place in the distribution chain, namely, wholesaler, retailer and consumer in diminishing amounts. They were intended to reflect, at least from an economic viewpoint, the seller's estimates of the value of the marketing functions performed by the various classes of customers.

"Inasmuch as traditional discounts of this type, as any other price differential, remained lawful under the Robinson-Patman Act unless engendering adverse effects on competition, the ordinary discounts to wholesalers and retailers were considered entirely legal. The single function middleman presented no problem of classification, for he bought as well as sold in one distributive role, that is, strictly as a wholesaler or strictly as a retailer. A discount granted to such wholesalers did not injure retailers who received no equivalent price reduction, since they did not compete for the consumer's business. By virtue of the 'injury' prerequisite in Section 2(a) of the Act, therefore, functional discounts to single-function distributors were considered above legal reproach. The controversy, rather, centered on the more complex types of distributors who were beginning to dominate our market structure—distributors whose functions ranged from only partial performance of the wholesale function to those who were almost wholly integrated, that is, who were both wholesalers and retailers and often consumers as well.

"Under these conditions classification of buyers became unprecise and shifting in meaning. Wholesalers and retailers no longer comprised clear-cut separate links between the producer and the ultimate consumer, each responsible for a clearly defined set of duties. Marketing functions became scrambled, with many permutations and combinations. Many jobbers and brokers contributed genuine and important services, though assuming only a part of the traditional full-time wholesaler's job. More often there was the contrary trend toward integration of distributive functions. Manufacturers created their own outlets. Retailers integrated into wholesaling, and wholesaling into retailing, either by outright ownership or by cooperative arrangements. The number of patterns was legion and divers.

"This proliferation of modern marketing methods defies definition, neat nomenclature or descriptive labels.

"No useful purpose would be served, therefore, by reviewing past proceedings in this area of multiple-function distributors, involving for the most part agricultural supplies, where the Commission turned the discount on the selling functions of the purchaser and not his buying functions.[77] It is enough to say that functional discounts to dual distributors under present marketing methods remain in a suspended state of confusion. The stormy and still undetermined *Standard Oil* decision, which has been characterized by some critics as holding not only that the purchaser's resale activities determine his eligibility for a functional discount but also that the supplier must police resale prices, has, insofar, as this issue is concerned, settled nothing. [Citation omitted.]

"In our view, to relate functional discounts solely to the purchaser's method of resale without recognition of his buying function thwarts competition and efficiency in marketing, and inevitably leads to higher consumer prices. It is possible, for example, for a seller to shift to customers a number of distributional functions which the seller himself ordinarily performs. Such functions should, in our opinion, be recognized and reimbursed. Where a businessman performs various wholesale functions, such as providing storage, traveling salesmen and distribution of catalogues, the law should not forbid his supplier from compensating him for such services. Such a legal disqualification might compel him to render these functions free of charge. The value of the service would then be pocketed by the seller who did not earn it. Such a rule, incorrectly, we think, proclaims as a matter of law that the integrated wholesaler cannot pos-

---

[77] See Agricultural Laboratories, Inc., 26 F.T.C. 296 (1938); Hansen Inoculator Co., 26 F.T.C. 303 (1938); Albert L. Whiting, 26 F.T.C. 312 (1938); Nitragin Co., 26 F.T.C. 320 (1938); Sherwin-Williams Co., 36 F.T.C. 25, 40-41 (1943)—this element was subsequently dismissed without prejudice.

sibly perform the wholesaling function; it forbids the matter to be put to proof.

"On the other hand, the Commission should tolerate no subterfuge. Only to the extent that a buyer actually performs certain functions, assuming all the risks and costs involved, should he qualify for a compensating discount. The amount of the discount should be reasonably related to the expenses assumed by the buyer. It should not exceed the cost of that part of the function he actually performs on that part of the goods for which he performs it.

"We believe, therefore, that the evidence offered by respondent on this point was relevant and should have been admitted.

"However, respondent was not prejudiced by the examiner's ruling in this instance. We have treated all the evidence tendered on this point as being in the record and find it insufficient. It failed to establish any reasonable relation between the amount of discounts allowed and the value of services or facilities furnished by the Big Three.[78] Furthermore, the preferential discounts allowed the Big Three were enjoyed by them for as long as twenty-five years without any effort on respondent's part to determine what services were in fact rendered or how the benefit or savings, if any, inured to the respondent. From the record, it appears that the Big Three as well as respondent treated the higher discounts as price reductions and not payments or allowances for services rendered.

* * *

"Commissioner Gwynne concurs in the result. Commissioner Mead and Secrest concur in the result with separate opinions. . . ."

This opinion draws heavily on the language of the Report of the Attorney General's Committee[79] and seems to follow the Committee's recommendation that the legality of functional discounts should no longer solely depend on the *resale* function performed by a distributor, but also on the services or marketing functions actually rendered by the distributor as a *buyer*.[80]

In 1956, the Commissioner seriously restricted the scope of this rule in the second *General Foods Corp. case*,[81] involving, unlike *Doubleday*, discounts for entirely new distribution methods.

---

[78] In view of our ruling we do not consider, as did the examiner, the Southgate Brokerage case, 150 F.2d 607, which arose under the brokerage section of the Robinson-Patman Act, as controlling. Further, we do not agree with the examiner's statement in finding No. 95 to the effect that only the seller's costs may be shown "defensively" under the law.

[79] REPORT OF THE ATTORNEY GENERAL'S NATIONAL COMMITTEE TO STUDY THE ANTITRUST LAWS 202-208 (1955).

[80] *Id.*, at 208.

[81] F.T.C. Dkt. No. 6018 (Feb. 15, 1956).

General Foods distributed some of its products through numerous small Institutional Contract Wagon Distributors (so-called ICWD's) who competed with traditional wholesalers for the business from restaurants and similar establishments. General Foods agreed to grant ICWD's a 2.4 to 4 percent discount from its wholesale list price for coffee and a 10 percent reduction on other groceries in exchange for their undertaking to perform services not ordinarily performed by wholesalers: selling aggressively; providing door to store delivery; offering services generally offered by competitors; maintaining adequate stocks; arranging to dispose of older stocks first; handling damaged merchandise in accordance with General Foods policy; arranging for distribution and proper use of display and promotional material provided; and making deliveries of General Foods sales to multiple food operators for extra pay.[82]

The Commission held that the discounts violated section 2(a) of the amended Clayton Act, and that they were not within the exception of section 2(d).[83] Having held that respondent's practice injured competition,[84] the Commission stated with respect to the legality of functional discounts under section 2(a):[85]

> "Respondent next claims that the ICWDs constitute a class that is functionally distinct from respondent's other customers, and that because they perform their selling in a different manner than the conventional wholesaler, the lower prices to them are justified.
>
> "Over the years in the chain of distribution from the producer to the ultimate consumer, various groups have come into being, each having a particular status and performing its particular function. Familiar examples are wholesalers and retailers. Prices to these groups take into account their status and the part they play in distribution by virtue of that status. Characteristically, the members of each group compete with each other but not with the members of a different group.

---

[82] *Id.*, at 1-2.

[83] Section 2(d) reads:

"That it shall be unlawful for any person engaged in commerce to pay or contract for the payment of anything of value to or for the benefit of a customer of such person in the course of such commerce as compensation or in consideration for any services or facilities furnished by or through such customer in connection with the processing, handling, sale, or offering for sale of any products or commodities manufactured, sold, or offered for sale by such person, unless such payment or consideration is available on proportionately equal terms to all other customers competing in the distribution of such products or commodities."

[84] F.T.C. Dkt. No. 6018, at 3-4.

[85] *Id.*, at 6-7.

"While the Robinson-Patman Act does not mention functional pricing, it was written nevertheless against the background of the distribution system then in effect. As pointed out by respondent, a seller is not forbidden to sell at different prices to buyers in different functional classes and orders have been issued permitting lower prices to one functional class as against another, provided that injury to commerce as contemplated in the law does not result. For example, in the Matter of *Albert L. Whiting and Lucille D. Whiting,* trading as *Urbana Laboratories,* 26 F.T.C. 312, the Commission found that the functional classification made by the seller resulted in differences in prices to various customers all engaged competitively in the selling to consumers and entered an order against the practice. In *FTC* v. *Ruberoid Company* (1951) 343 U.S. 470, the Supreme Court said:

'The roofing material customers of Ruberoid may be classified as wholesalers, retailers, and roofing contractors or applicators. The discriminations found by the Commission were in sales to retailers and applicators. The Commission held that there was insufficient evidence in the record to establish discriminations among wholesalers, as such. Ruberoid contends that the order should have been similarly limited to sales to retailers and applicators. But there was ample evidence that Ruberoid's classification of its customers did not follow real functional differences. Thus some purchasers which Ruberoid designated as "wholesalers" and to which Ruberoid allowed extra discounts in fact competed with other purchasers as applicators. And the Commission found that some purchasers operated as both wholesalers and applicators. So finding, the Commission disregarded these ambiguous labels, which might be used to cloak discriminatory discounts to favored customers, and stated its order in terms of "purchasers who in fact compete." '

"The ICWD and the conventional grocer both sell to the feeding institutions. They are in competition with each other. As already pointed out, the special discounts to the ICWDs cause injury to that competition. It is true that by virtue of the contract with respondent, the ICWD performs his function of reselling in a different manner than most of the conventional wholesalers. He furnishes certain services specified in the contract. The law permits the seller to pay for services or facilities furnished in the resale of goods. If he elects to do so, however, the payments must be in accordance with the terms and conditions laid down in Section 2(d). To hold that the rendering of special services *ipso facto* gives him a separate functional classification would be to read Section 2(d) out of the Act."

With respect to the legality of General Foods' functional discounts under section 2(d) of the amended Clayton Act, the Commission said:[86]

"Respondent argues that the discounts allowed their ICWDs were payments for substantial services actually rendered; that instead of a discrimination prohibited by Section 2(a), they are payments properly made under Section 2(d).

"In construing Section 2(d), consideration must be given to (1) the evil which it was designed to eliminate, and (2) its specific place in the overall purpose of the Robinson-Patman Act.

"Legislative history indicates that the purpose of Section 2(d) was to reach the evil of granting discriminations in the form of special allowances in purported payment of advertising and other sales promotional services (See Senate Report No. 1502 and House Report No. 2287, 74th Congress, 2nd Sess.). Congressman Utterback, in explaining Sections 2(d) and 2(e), said:

'The existing evil at which this part of the bill is aimed is, of course, the grant of discriminations under the guise of payments for advertising and promotional services which, whether or not the services are actually rendered as agreed, results in an advantage to the customer so favored as compared with others who have to bear the cost of such services themselves. The prohibitions of the bill, however, are made intentionally broader than this one sphere, in order to prevent evasion in resort to others by which the same purpose might be accomplished, and it prohibits payment for such services or facilities, whether furnished "in connection with the processing, handling, sale or offering for sale of the products concerned."' (80 Cong. Rec. 9418).

The services for which payment may be made under section 2(d) must be of such a character that they can be made available on proportionally equal terms to all customers. The whole purpose was to bring about substantial equality of treatment based on services actually rendered rather than on the mere willingness or potentiality of rendering the services. As was said by Professor S. Chesterfield Oppenheim in *Price and Service Discriminations Under the Robinson-Patman Act*:

'Proof of performance of specified services should be required before payments are made; payments should not be made if buyers have not actually rendered services.'

"In the past failure to furnish the services, or the pretended furnishing, was one of the principal reasons for adopting Section 2(d). Thus in the matter of *Colgate-Palmolive Peet Company, et al.*, Dockets 5585, 5586 and 5587, the Commission said:

---

[86] *Id.*, at 4-6.

'Section 2(d) permits payments for services or facilities actually furnished. Certainly payments for services or facilities not furnished are not authorized.'

"The same thought was expressed in the rules promulgated for the Corset, Brassiere and Allied Products Industry:

'*Note* 1: Industry members giving advertising allowances to competing customers must exercise precaution and diligence in seeing that all of such allowances are used in accordance with the terms of their offers.'

'*Note* 2: When an industry member gives allowances to competing customers for advertising in a newspaper or periodical, the fact that a lower advertising rate for equivalent space is available to one or more, but not all, such customers, is not to be regarded by the industry member as warranting the retention by such customer or customers of any portion of the allowance for his or their personal use or benefit.'

"There must be a discernible relationship between the amounts paid and the cost or reasonable value of the services rendered. In other words, each type of service must be capable of having a price or value tag put on it.

"The discounts given to ICWDs do not meet the requirements of Section 2(d). In the first place, payments were not made for services actually rendered. The contract required the ICWD to perform certain enumerated services. It is obvious that all would not perform the same services, nor in the same amount, nor of the same quality. Some of the services could not be rendered unless the customer elected to receive them. Nevertheless, each ICWD received the same allowances whether he actually furnished all the services, none of them, or only a part. In the second place, some of the services required were of such a character that even if rendered in accordance with the contract, a price tag could not be put on them. This applies particularly to '(1) aggressively selling customers General Foods Sales Division Institution Products,' and '(3) offer services generally offered by competitors in the Designated Territory.'

"The hearing examiner found that 'the record showed generally, and it may be assumed, that these services have been performed conscientiously by each ICWD.'

"From none of these findings, or any others, can it be concluded that the requirement of payment for services actually rendered was observed as required by law. Respondent was really contracting for willingness and potentiality to perform certain services. It was paying for a certain method of doing business rather than for specific services actually rendered.

"The policing done by respondent was directed toward the general operation of a plan rather than toward checking services actually rendered as is usually done, for example, in advertising allowances. The contract with the ICWD provided that in case of 'the substantial failure of a distributor to perform any one or more of the distributor's obligations under this agreement,' respondent may terminate the agreement on five day's notice. Furthermore, the time and method of payments to the ICWDs are not related to actual services rendered and paid only after an accounting thereof. For example, the coffee allowance is paid by deducting the amount from the face of each invoice and remitting the balance subject to other allowances, such as cash discounts.

"The payments involved here were not of a character intended by Section 2(d). See in the Matter of *Champion Spark Plug Company* (1953), Docket 3977."

The cases demonstrate that there is an interdependency between the legality of functional discounts and the development of new methods in distribution. As a result, there is a controversy as to whether the second *General Foods* decision came out too much in favor of the traditional independent wholesalers, thereby hindering innovations in distribution and competition among oligopolistic producers.[87]

(8) The Liability of the Buyer

While section 2(a) forbids seller-induced discriminations, section 2(f) prevents buyer-induced discriminations, Congress' chief concern in 1936.[88]

This provision has been rarely invoked by the Commission. The Supreme Court's landmark decision in *Automatic Canteen Co.* v. *Federal Trade Commission*[89] provided the first authoritative construction of section 2(f). Since the decision is equally important with respect to its antitrust rationale, extensive extracts of the opinion follow.

AUTOMATIC CANTEEN CO. v. FEDERAL TRADE COMMISSION

Supreme Court of the United States 346 U.S. 61 (1953)

"Mr. JUSTICE FRANKFURTER delivered the opinion of the Court.

---

[87] See, *e.g.*, Note, *Robinson-Patman Curtailments on Distribution Innovation: A Status Sought for Functional Discounts,* 66 YALE L.J. 243, 248-256 (1956), and authorities cited therein.

[88] Section 2(f) reads:

"That it shall be unlawful for any person engaged in commerce, in the course of such commerce, knowingly to induce or receive a discrimination in price which is prohibited by this section."

[89] 346 U.S. 61 (1953), *reversing* 194 F.2d 433 (7th Cir. 1951), which had affirmed the decision of the Commission, 46 F.T.C. 861 (1950).

". . . [P]etitioner, a large buyer of candy and other confectionary products for resale through 230,000 odd automatic vending machines operated in 33 States and the District of Columbia . . .

"The Commission introduced evidence that petitioner received, and in some instances solicited, prices it knew were as much as 33% lower than prices quoted other purchasers . . . [T]he Commission stated that a prima facie case of violation had been established by proof that the buyer received lower prices on like goods than other buyers, 'well knowing that it was being favored over competing purchasers,' under circumstances where the requisite effect on competition had been shown. . . . On petitioner's failure to introduce evidence, the Commission made findings that petitioner knew the prices it induced were below list prices and that it induced them without inquiry of the seller, or assurance from the seller, as to cost differentials which might justify the price differentials. The Commission thereupon entered a cease and desist order. . . .

"Section 2(f) . . . , roughly the counterpart, as to buyers, of sections of the Act dealing with discrimination by sellers, is a vital prohibition in the enforcement scheme of the Act. In situations where buyers may have difficulty in proving their sellers' costs, § 2(f) could, if the Commission's view in this case prevails, become a major reliance for simplified enforcement of the Act not only by the Commission but by plaintiffs suing for treble damages. Such enforcement, however, might readily extend beyond the prohibitions of the Act and, in doing so, *help give rise to a price uniformity and rigidity in open conflict with the purposes of other antitrust legislation.* [Emphasis supplied.] . . .

✻ ✻ ✻

"We are here asked to settle a controversy involving simply the burden of coming forward with evidence and § 2(f) of the Act. The record . . . may be taken as presenting varying degrees of bargaining pressure exerted by a buyer on a seller to obtain prices below those quoted other purchasers. . . .

"The Commission made no finding negativing the existence of cost savings or stating that whatever cost savings there were did not at least equal price differentials petitioner may have received. It did not make any findings as to petitioner's knowledge of actual cost savings of particular sellers and found only, as to knowledge, that petitioner knew what the list prices to other buyers were. . . .

"Petitioner claims that the Commission has not, on this record, made a *prima facie* case of knowing inducement of prices that 'made more "than due allowance for" ' cost differences, while the Commission contends that it has established a *prima facie* case . . . where the buyer fails to introduce evidence. . . .

✻ ✻ ✻

"No doubt the burden placed on petitioner to show his seller's costs, under present Commission standards, is heavy. . . . It is not a question of obtaining information in the seller's hands. [Footnote omitted.] It is a matter of studying the seller's business afresh. *Insistence on proof of costs by the buyer . . . would almost inevitably require a degree of cooperation between buyer and seller, as against other buyers, that may offend other antitrust policies . . .* [Emphasis supplied.]

"It is against this background that the present dispute arises. . . . It is . . . apparent that the discriminatory price that buyers are forbidden by § 2(f) to induce cannot include price differentials that are not forbidden to sellers in other sections of the Act, and, what is pertinent in this case, a buyer is not precluded from inducing a lower price based on cost differences that would provide the seller with a defense. . . .

"It is not to say, however, that the converse follows, for § 2(f) does not reach all cases of buyer receipt of a prohibited discrimination in price. It limits itself to cases of knowing receipt of such prices. The Commission seems to argue, in part, that the substantive violation occurs if the buyer knows only that the prices are lower than those offered other buyers. Such a reading not only distorts the language but would leave the word 'knowingly' almost entirely without significance in § 2(f). A buyer with no knowledge whatsoever of facts indicating the possibility that price differences were not based on cost differences would be liable if in fact they were not. . . .

". . . The Commission argues that Congress was attempting to reach buyers who through their own activities obtain a special price and that 'knowingly to induce or receive' can be read as charging such buyers with responsibility for whatever unlawful prices result. But that argument would comprehend any buyer who engages in bargaining over price. If the Commission means buyers who exert undue pressure, the argument might find greater support in the legislative background but less in the language Congress has employed. Such a reading not only ignores the word 'receive' but opens up even more entangling difficulties with interpretation of what is undue pressure. [Footnote omitted.]

* * *

". . . § 2(f) was explained in Congress as a provision under which a seller, by informing the buyer that a proposed discount was unlawful under the Act, could discourage undue pressure from the buyer. . . . [B]*ut we are unable, in the light of congressional policy as expressed in other antitrust legislation, to read this ambiguous language as putting the buyer at his peril whenever he engages in price bargaining. Such a view must be rejected in view of the effect it might have on that sturdy bargaining between buyer and seller for which scope was presum-*

ably left in the areas of our economy not otherwise regulated.[90]
Although due consideration is to be accorded to administrative
construction where alternative interpretation is fairly open, *it is
our duty to reconcile such interpretation,* except where Congress
has told us not to do so, *with the broader antitrust policies that
have been laid down by Congress.* [Emphasis supplied.] Even if
the Commission has, by virtue of the Robinson-Patman Act, been
given some authority to develop policies in conflict with those of
the Sherman Act in order to meet the special problems created
by price discrimination, we cannot say that the Commission here
has adequately made manifest reasons for engendering such a
conflict so as to enable us to accept its conclusion. [Case cited.]

"We therefore conclude that a buyer is not liable under § 2(f)
if the lower prices he induces are either within one of the seller's
defenses such as the cost justification or not known by him not
to be within one of those defenses. This conclusion is of course
only a necessary preliminary in this case. . . . [W]e must in
this case determine whether proof that the buyer knew that the
price was lower is sufficient to shift the burden of introducing
evidence to the buyer.

* * *

"We need not concern ourselves with the Commission's interpretation of the words '*prima facie* case thus made' in § 2(b)
and the resulting conclusion that if § 2(a) and § 2(f) are to be
read as counterparts, the elements necessary for a *prima facie*
case under § 2(a) are sufficient for a *prima facie* showing of the
'discrimination in price which is prohibited by this section' in
§ 2(f). However that may be, the Commission recognizes that
there is an 'additional' element resulting from the word 'knowingly' in § 2(f), and, of course, it is that element about which
the controversy here centers and to which we must address ourselves. . . .

". . . The Commission's main reliance in this argument is
§ 2(b), which . . . we interpreted in the *Morton Salt* case as
putting the burden of coming forward with evidence of a cost
justification on the seller, on the one, that is, who claimed the
benefits of the justification.

"To this it is answered that although § 2(b) does speak not
of the seller but of the 'person charged with a violation of this
section,' other language in § 2(b) and its proviso seems directed
mainly to sellers, [Footnote omitted.] that the legislative chro-
nology of the various provisions ultimately resulting in the Robinson-Patman Act indicates that § 2(b) was drafted with sellers in
mind and that the few cases so far decided have dealt only with
sellers.

---

[90] *Cf.* Adelman, *Effective Competition and the Antitrust Laws,* 61 HARV.
L. REV. 1289, 1331 (1948); EDWARDS, MAINTAINING COMPETI-
TION 161 (1949).

"A confident answer cannot be given; some answer must be given. We think we must read the infelicitous language of § 2(b) as enacting what we take to be its purpose, that of making it clear that ordinary rules of evidence were to apply in Robinson-Patman Act proceedings. [Footnote omitted.] If § 2(b) is to apply to § 2(f), although we do not decide that it does because we reach the same result without it, we think it must so be read. *Considerations of fairness and convenience operative in other proceedings must, we think, have been controlling in the drafting of § 2(b)*, for it would require far clearer language than we have here to reach a contrary result. [Case cited. Emphasis supplied.] If that is so, however, decisions striking the balance of convenience for Commission proceedings *against sellers* are beside the point. [Footnote omitted. Emphasis supplied.] And we think the fact that the buyer does not have the required information, and for good reason should not be required to obtain it, has controlling importance in striking the balance in this case. This result most nearly accommodates this case to the reasons that have been given by judges and legislators for the rule of § 2(b), that is, that the burden of justifying a price differential ought to be on the one who 'has at his peculiar command the cost and other record data by which to justify such discriminations.'[91] Where, as here, such considerations are inapplicable, we think we must disregard whatever contrary indications may be drawn from a merely literal reading of the language Congress has used. It would not give fair effect to § 2(b) to say that the burden of coming forward with evidence as to costs [Footnote omitted.] and the buyer's knowledge thereof shifts to the buyer as soon as it is shown that the buyer knew the prices differed. Certainly the Commission with its broad power of investigation and subpoena, prior to the filing of a complaint, is on a better footing to obtain this information than the buyer. . . .

". . . Enforcement of the provisions of § 2(f) against . . . a buyer should not be difficult. Proof of a cost justification being what it is, too often no one can ascertain whether a price is cost-justified. But trade experience in a particular situation can afford a sufficient degree of knowledge to provide a basis for prosecution. By way of example, a buyer who knows that he buys in the same quantities as his competitor and is served by the seller in the same manner or with the same amount of exertion as the other buyer, can fairly be charged with notice that a substantial price differential cannot be justified. The Commission need only to show, to establish its *prima facie* case, that the buyer knew that the methods by which he was served and quantities in

---

[91] 80 CONG. REC. 3599 (1936). Samuel H. Moss, Inc. v. Federal Trade Commission, 148 F.2d 378, 379 (2d Cir. 1945); 80 CONG. REC. 8241 (1936).

which he purchased were the same as in the case of his competitor. If the methods or quantities differ, the Commission must only show that such differences could not give rise to sufficient savings in the cost of manufacture, sale or delivery to justify the price differential, and that the buyer, knowing these were the only differences, should have known that they could not give rise to sufficient cost savings. The showing of knowledge, of course, will depend to some extent on the size of the discrepancy between cost differential and price differential, so that the two questions are not isolated. A showing that the cost differences are very small compared with the price differential and could not reasonably have been thought to justify the price difference should be sufficient.

". . . *Certainly we should have a more solid basis than an unexplained conclusion before we sanction a rule of evidence that contradicts antitrust policy and the ordinary requirements of fairness*. [Emphasis supplied.] . . .

 ⊛ ⊛ ⊛

"Mr. JUSTICE DOUGLAS, with whom Mr. JUSTICE BLACK and Mr. JUSTICE REED concur, dissenting.

"This decision is a graphic illustration of the way in which a statute can be read with enervating effect.

 ⊛ ⊛ ⊛

"The record shows persistent and continuous efforts of this large buyer in wheedling and coercing suppliers into granting its discriminatory prices. . . .

 ⊛ ⊛ ⊛

"The Court disregards this history. The Court's construction not only requires the Commission to show that the price discriminations were not justified; it also makes the Commission prove what lay in the buyer's mind. I would let the acts of the buyer speak for themselves. Where, as here, the buyer undertakes to bludgeon sellers into prices that give him a competitive advantage, there is no unfairness in making him show that the privileges he demanded had cost justifications. This buyer over and again held itself out as a cost expert. I would hold it to its professions. Since it was the coercive influence, there is no unfairness in making it go forward with evidence to rebut the Commission's *prima facie* case."

(9) **Price Discrimination Under Section 3 of the Robinson-Patman Act**

In part overlapping the civil prohibitions of subsections 2(a) through 2(f) with their civil sanctions, section 3 imposes criminal penalties.[92] However, the Department of Justice appears to

---

[92] 49 STAT. 1528 (1936), 15 U.S.C. § 13 (a) (1952). The text of section 3 is set out in the appendix.

have brought no proceeding so far under this provision of the statute.[93]

Sections 4 and 16 of the Clayton Act, as amended,[94] permit private actions for treble damages and injunctive relief only in cases of injury resulting from practices forbidden by the "antitrust laws" as defined in section 1 of the Clayton Act.[94a] In a number of recent cases the controversial issue was raised whether section 3 of the Robinson-Patman Act is one of these "antitrust laws." The issue is important because section 3 includes a provision which is not found in section 2 of the Clayton Act, as amended, and which could be interpreted as an additional, broad cause of private action. This clause makes it unlawful to sell "goods at unreasonably low prices for the purpose of destroying competition or eliminating a competitor."

While a number of district courts and the Tenth Circuit had held that a private action could be founded on section 3,[94b] the Seventh Circuit reached the opposite conclusion and was recently affirmed by the Supreme Court in *Nashville Milk Co.* v. *Carnation Co.*[94c] In a 5 to 4 decision, the Court held that "the definition contained in section 1 of the Clayton Act is exclusive. Therefore it is of no moment here that the Robinson-Patman Act may be colloquially described as an 'antitrust' statute."[94d] In the opinion of the Court, Congress did not make section 3 of the Robinson-Patman Act a part of the Clayton Act, and, therefore, did not make it one of the "antitrust laws".

> "The Robinson-Patman Act, consisting of four sections, convincingly shows on its face that § 3 does not amend the Clayton Act, but stands on its own footing and carries its own sanctions.
>
> ⁕ ⁕ ⁕
>
> "What appears from the face of the Robinson-Patman Act finds full support in its legislative history. The fair conclusions to be drawn from that history are (a) that § 3 of the Robinson-Patman Act was not intended to become part of the Clayton Act, and (b) that the section was intended to carry only criminal sanctions, except that price discriminations, to the extent that they were common to both that section and § 2 of the Clayton

---

[93] Nashville Milk Co. v. Carnation Co., 78 S.Ct. 352, at 355, note 7, and at 361 (1958).

[94] 38 STAT. 730 (1914), 15 U.S.C. §§ 15, 26 (1952).

[94a] For the text of these provisions, see the appendix.

[94b] Vance v. Safeway Stores, Inc., 239 F.2d 144 (10th Cir. 1956), *vacated and remanded*, 78 S.Ct. 358 (1958).

[94c] 238 F.2d 86 (7th Cir. 1956), *affirmed*, 78 S.Ct. 352 (1958). See also Mackey v. Sears, Roebuck & Co., 237 F.2d 869 (7th Cir. 1956). See Note, 70 HARV. L.REV. 1490 (1957).

[94d] 78 S.Ct. at 354.

Act, were also understood to carry, *under the independent force of the Clayton Act*, the private remedies provided in §§ 4 and 16 of the Clayton Act. In other words, although price discriminations are both criminally punishable (under § 3 of the Robinson-Patman Act) and subject to civil redress (under § 2 of the Clayton Act), selling at 'unreasonably low prices' is subject only to the criminal penalties provided in § 3 of the Robinson-Patman Act.

* * *

"For the foregoing reasons, we hold that a private cause of action does not lie for practices forbidden only by § 3 of the Robinson-Patman Act. To the extent that such practices also constitute a violation of § 2 of the Clayton Act, as amended, they are actionable by one injured thereby solely under that Act."[94e]

In the dissent, concurred in by the Chief Justice and Justices Black and Brennan, Justice Douglas stated:[94f]

"In resolving all ambiguities against the grant of vitality to § 3, we forget that the treble damage technique for law enforcement was designed as an effective, if not the most effective, method of deterring violators of the Act.

* * *

". . . Because of the Court's holding that § 3 is not available in civil actions to private parties, the statute has in effect been repealed. It is apparent that the opponents of the Robinson-Patman Act have eventually managed to achieve in this Court what they could not do in Congress."

(10) Legislative Efforts

There has been considerable discussion in Congress on the Robinson-Patman Act in the past few years.[95] The basic controversy continues to exist: Is there a collision between the small business policy underlying the Robinson-Patman Act and the philosophy of the Sherman and Clayton Acts?[96]

[94e] *Id.*, at 354, 356-357.

[94f] *Id.*, at 361.

[95] See, *e.g.*, *Hearings Before the Select House Committee on Small Business on Price Discrimination*, 3 Parts, 84th Cong., 1st Sess. (1956); *Hearings Before the Subcommittee on Antitrust and Monopoly of the Senate Committee on the Judiciary*, Part 3, Distribution Practices, 84th Cong., 1st Sess. (1955).

[96] See, *e.g.*, Adelman, *The Consistency of the Robinson-Patman Act*, 6 STAN. L.REV. 3 (1953); Levi, in Symposium, *The Robinson-Patman Act —Is it in the Public Interest?*, 1 ABA ANTITRUST SECTION REPORT 60 (August 1952); Oppenheim, *Federal Antitrust Legislation: Guideposts to a Revised National Antitrust Policy*, 50 MICH. L.REV. 1139, 1198-1210 (1952).

The Supreme Court has recognized this problem:[97]

"We need not now reconcile, in its entirety, the economic theory which underlies the Robinson-Patman Act with that of the Sherman and Clayton Acts. [Footnote omitted.] It is enough to say that Congress did not seek by the Robinson-Patman Act either to abolish competition or so radically to curtail it that a seller would have no substantial right of self-defense against a price raid by a competitor."

And in the *Automatic Canteen* case the Court emphasized its "duty to reconcile" the interpretation of the Act "with the broader antitrust policies that have been laid down by Congress."[98]

Most economists have characterized the Robinson-Patman Act as anticompetitive and antithetical to the overall antitrust policy, either in basic conception or specific application.[99] One of the main arguments is that the Act necessarily fosters price uniformity and economic discrimination[100] and that it hinders product innovation and progress in the distributive sector of our economy. On the other hand, Walton Hamilton has attacked such views[101] and said that "the dominant purpose of the statute is in strict accord with the Sherman Act."[102]

The majority of the Attorney General's Committee took a rather critical view of the Act.[103] However, its report and recommendations were subject to sharp criticism in Congress. For example, the Select House Committee on Small Business stated in a lengthy report:[104]

"The [Attorney General's] committee declined to acknowledge a half-century of progress in the development of effective antitrust philosophy. Focusing instead on the Sherman Act 'approach,' the analysis of chapter IV, Antitrust Policy in Distribution, wears a pair of high-buttoned shoes. While it purports to

---

[97] Standard Oil Co. of Indiana v. Federal Trade Commission, 340 U.S. 231, 249 (1951).

[98] Automatic Canteen Co. v. Federal Trade Commission, 346 U.S. 61, 74 (1953).

[99] See Rowe, *Price Differentials and Product Differentiation: The Issues Under the Robinson-Patman Act*, 66 YALE L.J. 1, 34 at footnote 141 with survey on pertinent writings.

[100] See *id.*, at 26 *et seq.*

[101] HAMILTON, THE POLITICS OF INDUSTRY 147-149 (1957).

[102] *Id.*, at 148.

[103] REPORT OF THE ATTORNEY GENERAL'S NATIONAL COMMITTEE TO STUDY THE ANTITRUST LAWS 155-209 (1955).

[104] *Price Discrimination, The Robinson-Patman Act, and the Attorney General's National Committee to Study the Antitrust Laws*, H.R. REP. No. 2966, 84th Cong., 2d Sess. 73, 74, 76, 77-78 (1957); see also Final Report, same Committee, H.R. REP. No. 2970, 84th Cong., 2d Sess. 49-65, 154-159 (1957).

deal primarily with Sections 2 and 3 of the Clayton Act, the net effect of the chapter is to unwrite much of the substance of those sections of the law. . . .

* * *

". . . It was the cumulative weight of its reinterpretations rather than any violent force of specific recommendations, that added up to a proposal of virtual nullification of the Robinson-Patman Act. . . .

* * *

". . . [I]ts interpretation of the 'good faith' issue alone would suffice to reduce the price discrimination law to an empty and useless shell.

"To the committee's interpretation [of the 'good faith' proviso], there are two basic objections. One is that the conclusion rests on unsound economic analysis. The other is that, in effect, the defense is so broadened that it automatically excuses most of the activities included in the substantive offenses."

For these reasons, S. 11 and H.R. 1840 were introduced to overturn the *Standard Oil (Indiana)* decision[105] and to secure "equality of opportunity." These bills would make the "good faith" defense unavailable whenever "the effect of the discrimination may be substantially to lessen competition or tend to create a monopoly in any line of commerce." While vigorously opposed by the Department of Justice,[106] the bill[107] passed the House in 1956 by a vote of 393-3[108] and was favorably reported in the Senate,[109] but could not be brought to a vote before the end of the session.[110] In the 85th Congress, the bill was reintroduced.[111]

---

[105] Standard Oil Co. of Indiana v. Federal Trade Commission, 340 U.S. 231 (1951).

[106] See Bills to Amend Sections 2 and 3 of the Clayton Act, *Hearings Before the Antitrust Subcommittee (Subcommittee No. 5) of the House Committee on the Judiciary*, 84th Cong., 2d Sess., ser. No. 21, 171-173 (1956).

[107] See H.R. REP. No. 2202, 84th Cong., 2d Sess. (1956).

[108] 102 CONG. REC. 9023 (1956).

[109] S. REP. No. 2817, 84th Cong., 2d Sess. (1956).

[110] 102 CONG. REC. 13, 876-77 (1956).

[111] S. 11, 85th Cong., 1st Sess. (1957). See Carlston, *Senate Bill No. 11 and Antitrust Policy*, 11 VAND. L.REV. 129 (1957); Howrey, *Good Faith Meeting of Competition*, in HOW TO COMPLY WITH ROBINSON-PATMAN ACT, 1957 CCH ANTITRUST LAW SYMPOSIUM 46 (1957).

Chapter 6

RESALE PRICE MAINTENANCE AND "FAIR TRADE"

To what extent can a seller lawfully fix the resale price of a commodity and require a purchaser for resale to abide by it? This is the problem of resale price maintenance or vertical price control.[1]

(1) The Legality of Resale Price Maintenance

Resale price maintenance is a restriction on the right freely to sell a commodity. As such it constitutes a restraint on alienation. At common law, a general restraint upon alienation was ordinarily invalid because "obnoxious to public policy, which is best subserved by great freedom of traffic in such things as pass from hand to hand."[2] Resale price maintenance agreements were held unreasonable restraints of trade in *Dr. Miles Medical Co.* v. *John D. Park & Sons Co.*[3]

Since 1890, resale price maintenance agreements have been held to be a violation of section 1 of the Sherman Act.[4] "Fixing minimum prices, like other types of price-fixing, is illegal *per se.*"[5] After the seller has sold his product at prices satisfactory to himself, "the public is entitled to whatever advantage may be derived from competition in the subsequent traffic."[6]

---

[1] "The expression 'vertical price control' refers . . . to pricing through agreements or conspiracies between two or more persons operating at different levels of the same production-distribution-consumption process." KRONSTEIN and MILLER, REGULATION OF TRADE 850 (1953).

[2] John D. Park & Sons v. Hartman, 153 Fed. 24, 42 (6th Cir. 1907); Dr. Miles Medical Co. v. John D. Park & Sons Co., 220 U.S. 373, 404 (1911).

[3] 220 U.S. 373 (1911).

[4] 26 STAT. 209 (1890), 15 U.S.C. § 1 (1952); Dr. Miles Medical Co. v. John D. Park & Sons Co., 220 U.S. 373 (1911).

[5] Schwegmann Bros. v. Calvert Distillers Corp., 341 U.S. 384, at 386 (1951).

[6] *Id.*, at 409.

The courts recognize that a seller has some discretion in choosing his customers and in declining to do business with those who fail to observe his wishes as to resale prices.[7] However, the seller can not enter into agreements, whether express or implied, with all customers which undertake to bind them to observe fixed resale prices because "the parties are combined through agreements designed to take away dealers' control of their own affairs and thereby destroy competition and restrain the free and natural flow of trade amongst the states."[8] Nor can the seller refuse to do business unless "suggested" prices are kept by the retailers where the seller maintains a system of policing such price conditions.[9]

During the depression years of the Thirties, the price cutting and loss leader practices of chain stores led to a clamor by trademark owners and small retailers for government-sanctioned resale price maintenance. Out of these troubled years came the state "fair trade" laws[10] which are the principal matter for discussion in this chapter.

(2) The Nature and Purposes of the "Fair Trade" Laws

In 1931, California enacted the first fair trade statute permitting resale price maintenance on trademarked articles. As amended in 1933, the California statute required all dealers, *including "non-signers" of fair trade contracts*, who knowingly handled a fair traded product to abide by the minimum retail price established in the manufacturer's fair trade contract. Within a few years 44 other states had followed this example.[11]

Fair trade has been characterized in these terms by Senator Humphrey:[12]

> "Fair trade is a form of retail-price maintenance designed to prevent unfair price competition. It is concerned primarily with

---

[7] United States v. Colgate & Co., 250 U.S. 300 (1919).

[8] United States v. A. Schrader's Son, Inc., 252 U.S. 85, 100 (1920).

[9] Federal Trade Commission v. Beechnut Packing Co., 257 U.S. 441 (1922).

[10] The appelation "fair trade" applied to these laws has been called an "attractive misnomer." Circuit Judge Holmes dissenting in Schwegmann Bros. Giant Super Markets v. Eli Lilly & Co., 205 F.2d 788, 796 (5th Cir. 1953). However, it is employed here because it has become the accepted title.

[11] Only Missouri, Texas, Vermont and the District of Columbia have not enacted fair trade laws. For a recent description of the interests and politics at stake in this legislation, see PALAMOUNTAIN, THE POLITICS OF DISTRIBUTION, c. VIII (1955).

[12] *Fair Trade*, Report of the Select Senate Committee on Small Business on a Study on Fair Trade, Based on a Survey of Manufacturers and Retailers, S. REP. No. 2819, 84th Cong., 2d Sess. 1-2 (1956).

predatory price cutting at retail on trademarked products in free and open competition with articles of the same general class produced by others. Its objective is to prevent price cutting on trademarked products which injures the value of the manufacturers' established trademark and the stability of distribution.

"Fair trade is a voluntary program; it is provided for by permissive Federal and State legislation. The manufacturer elects to fair trade and is permitted to do so as long as he does not maintain a monopoly position in the market and his product is freely in competition with that of others. Those wholesalers and retailers electing to sell fair-trade products agree to adhere to the manufacturers' fair-trade price."

By contrast, the Department of Justice and the Federal Trade Commission[13] are opposed to fair trade. The Deputy Attorney General has characterized fair trade as "in fact price fixing and, as such . . . inconsistent with the philosophy of the antitrust laws."[14] The majority of the Attorney General's Committee found that fair trade not only "extends far beyond the essential guarantees of 'loss-leader' control" and thus "strikes not only at promotional price cutting, but at all price reductions which pass to the consumer the economies of competitive distribution."[15]

It should be noted that fair trade merchandise makes up only a relatively small part of the total goods sold in the United States today. The use of fair trade is most prominent in the distribution of drugs and pharmaceuticals, cosmetics and perfumes, household wares, clothing and alcoholic beverages.[16]

(3) "Fair Trade" and the Antitrust Laws

(a) *Prior to* 1952

It is plain that the fair trade laws were inconsistent with the Sherman Act to the extent that they made possible vertical price fixing in interstate commerce. To eliminate such conflict, the

---

[13] See FEDERAL TRADE COMMISSION, REPORT ON RESALE PRICE MAINTENANCE, Summary and Conclusions (1945).

[14] Letter to the Chairman of the Senate District of Columbia Committee, June 3, 1954.

[15] REPORT OF THE ATTORNEY GENERAL'S NATIONAL COMMITTEE TO STUDY THE ANTITRUST LAWS 153 (1955). For this and other reasons, the Committee, in its only major recommendation, proposed repeal of both statutes enabling fair trade to operate in interstate Commerce, the Miller-Tydings Act and the McGuire Act, discussed *infra*.

[16] *Fair Trade*, Report of the Select Senate Committee on Small Business on a Study on Fair Trade, Based on a Survey of Manufacturers and Retailers, S. REP. No. 2819, 84th Cong., 2d Sess. 5 (1956).

Miller-Tydings Act was enacted in 1937.[17] It amended section 1 of the Sherman Act by exempting from its reach resale price maintenance agreements relating to trademarked articles sold in competition with other commodities of the same general class, provided such agreements were lawful under state law as applied to an intrastate transaction.

However, when an attempt was made to apply in interstate commerce the non-signer provision of a state fair trade law to a retailer who had refused to sign a resale price maintenance contract, the Supreme Court held that the Miller-Tydings Act sanctions only "contracts and agreements" but did not extend to the non-signer clause, the effect of which the Court called "price fixing by compulsion."[18] The Court also noted that a statutory provision requiring all non-signers to maintain a fixed price amounts to "horizontal" price fixing (*i.e.*, among competitors), forbidden by the Sherman Act.[19] Congress, impressed among other things by reports of a price war starting after this decision was handed down,[20] thereupon enacted the second fair trade enabling statute, the McGuire Act,[21] which explicitly extended the exemption from the Sherman Act to non-signers.

(b) *Under the McGuire Act*

Passage of the McGuire Act in 1952 has not resolved the fair trade controversies. In its wake we find continued litigation, in both federal and state courts. The Supreme Court has expressed no opinion as to the constitutionality of the McGuire Act and has declined to hear a case in which that issue might have been determined.[22]

Whether the Miller-Tydings and the McGuire Acts provide protection from the antitrust laws depends upon the particular factual situation. In *United States* v. *McKesson & Robbins, Inc.*[23] the Supreme Court held that it is unlawful for an in-

---

[17] 50 STAT. 693 (1937), 15 U.S.C. § 1 (1952).

[18] Schwegmann Bros. v. Calvert Corp., 341 U.S. 384, at 388 (1951).

[19] *Ibid.*

[20] See, *e.g.*, Resale Price Maintenance, *Hearings Before the Antitrust Subcommittee of the House Committee on the Judiciary*, 82d Cong., 2d Sess., ser. No. 12 (1952).

[21] 66 STAT. 631 (1952), 15 U.S.C. § 45 (1952). The McGuire Act amended section 5 of the Federal Trade Commission Act by adding a new subsection (a).

[22] Schwegmann Bros. Giant Super Markets v. Eli Lilly & Co., 346 U.S. 856 (1953). The lower court's decision appears at 205 F.2d 788 (5th Cir. 1953).

[23] 351 U.S. 305 (1956). For an earlier case instituted by the Federal Trade Commission, see Eastman Kodak Co., F.T.C. Dkt. No. 6040 (Jan. 6, 1955). See Note, 64 YALE L.J. 426 (1955).

tegrated manufacturer to enter into fair trade contracts, covering its own products, with independent dealers who compete with the integrated manufacturer's distribution divisions.[24]

UNITED STATES v. McKESSON & ROBBINS, INC.

Supreme Court of the United States 351 U.S. 305 (1956)[25]

"Mr. CHIEF JUSTICE WARREN delivered the opinion of the Court.

* * *

"Appellee, a Maryland corporation with its home office in New York, is the largest drug wholesaler in the United States operating through 74 wholesale divisions located in 35 states, it sells drugstore merchandise of various brands to retailers, principally drugstores, substantially throughout the nation. For the fiscal year ended March 31, 1954, its sales of all drug products amounted to $338,000,000.

"Appellee is also a manufacturer of its own line of drug products, the total sales of which amounted to $11,000,000 for the year ended March 31, 1954. Its manufacturing operation is conducted through a single manufacturing division, McKesson Laboratories, located at Bridgeport, Connecticut. This division, like each of appellee's wholesale divisions, has a separate headquarters and a separate staff of employees, but none of the 75 divisions is separately incorporated. All are component parts of the same corporation and are responsible to the corporation's president and board of directors.

"Appellee distributes its own brand products to retailers through two channels: (1) directly to retailers and (2) through independent wholesalers. The major portion of its brand products is distributed to retailers through its own wholesale division. Appellee also makes direct sales to important retailers through its manufacturing division. Most of the appellee's sales to independent wholesalers are made by its manufacturing division, but its wholesale division sold approximately $200,000 of McKesson brand products to other wholesalers during the fiscal year ended June 30, 1952.

"To the extent possible under state law, appellee requires all retailers of its brand products to sell them at 'fair trade' retail

---

[24] Section 5(a) (5) of the Federal Trade Commission Act expressly states that the Act shall not ". . . make lawful [any] contracts . . . between manufacturers . . . or between wholesalers . . . or between retailers . . . or between persons, firms, or corporations in competition with each other."

[25] Footnotes omitted.

prices fixed by appellee. These prices are set forth in published schedules of wholesale and retail prices.

"Appellee also has 'fair trade' agreements with 21 independent wholesalers who buy from its manufacturing division. Sixteen of these independents compete with appellee's wholesale divisions. The other 5 compete with the manufacturing division for sales to chain drugstores located in their trading areas. On June 6, 1951, in accordance with appellee's 'fair trade' policy, a vice president in charge of merchandising notified appellee's wholesale divisions that—

'None of our wholesale divisions will sell any McKesson products to any wholesaler who has not entered into a fair trade contract with McKesson Laboratories.'

"As a result, 73 of the independent wholesalers who had been dealing with McKesson wholesale divisions entered into 'fair trade' agreements with McKesson by which they bound themselves in reselling its brand products to adhere to the wholesale prices fixed by it. Each of these independent wholesalers is in direct competition with the McKesson wholesale division from which it buys.

". . . The complaint charged that appellee's 'fair trade' agreements with independent wholesalers with whom it was in competition constituted illegal price fixing in violation of Section 1 of the [Sherman] Act. Appellee admitted the contracts, but claimed that they were exempted from the Sherman Act by the Miller-Tydings Act and the McGuire Act.

* * *

"The issue presented is a narrow one of statutory interpretation. The Government does not question the so-called vertical 'fair trade' agreements between McKesson and retailers of McKesson brand products. It challenges only appellee's price-fixing agreements with independent wholesalers with whom it is in competition.

"It has been held too often to require elaboration now that price fixing is contrary to the policy of competition underlying the Sherman Act, and that its illegality does not depend on a showing of its unreasonableness, since it is conclusively presumed to be unreasonable. . . .

* * *

". . . There is no basis for supposing that Congress, in enacting the Miller-Tydings and McGuire Acts, intended any change in the traditional *per se* doctrine. . . .

"In the Miller-Tydings Act, passed as a rider to a District of Columbia Revenue bill, Congress was careful to state that its exemption of certain resale price maintenance contracts from the prohibitions of the antitrust laws 'shall not make lawful any contract or agreement, providing for the establishment or maintenance of minimum resale prices on any commodity herein involved, or between manufacturers, or between producers, or *between wholesalers,* or between brokers, or between factors, or between retailers, or *between persons, firms, or corporations in competition with each other.'* (Emphasis supplied.)

"Fifteen years later Congress attached an almost identical proviso to the McGuire Act. . . .

"Appellee is admittedly a wholesaler with resale price maintenance contracts with 94 other wholesalers who are in competition with it. Thus, even if we read the proviso so that the words 'in competition with each other' modify 'between wholesalers,' the agreements in question would seem clearly to be outside the statutory exemption. . . . These were agreements 'between wholesalers.'

"Any doubts which might otherwise be raised as to the propriety of considering a manufacturer-wholesaler as a 'wholesaler' are dispelled by the last phrase of the proviso in question, which continues the proscription against price-fixing agreements 'between persons, firms, or corporations in competition with each other.' Congress thus made as plain as words can make it that, without regard to categories or labels, the crucial inquiry is whether the contracting parties compete with each other. If they do, the Miller-Tydings and McGuire Acts do not permit them to fix resale prices. . . .

* * *

"Both the Government and appellee press upon us economic arguments which could reasonably have caused Congress to support their respective positions. We need not concern ourselves with such speculation. Congress has marked the limitations beyond which price fixing cannot go. We are not only bound by those limitations, but we are bound to construe them strictly, since resale price maintenance is a privilege restrictive of a free economy.

* * *

"Reversed and remanded.

"Mr. JUSTICE HARLAN, whom Mr. JUSTICE FRANK-FURTER and Mr. JUSTICE BURTON join, dissenting.

* * *

"If we accept the legislative judgment implicit in the Acts that resale price maintenance is necessary and desirable to protect the goodwill attached to a brand name, there is no meaningful distinction between the fair-trade contracts of integrated and non-integrated manufacturers. Certainly the integrated manufacturer has as strong a claim to protection of his goodwill as a non-integrated manufacturer, and the economic effect of the contracts is the same. In both cases price competition in the resale of the branded product is eliminated, and in neither case does the price fixing extend beyond the manufacturer's own product. While the Government concedes the right of a non-integrated manufacturer to eliminate price competition in his products between wholesalers, it finds a vice not contemplated by the Acts when one of the 'wholesalers' is also the manufacturer, for then the contracts eliminate competition between the very parties to the contracts. But in either case, all price competition is eliminated, and I am unable to see what difference it makes between whom the eliminated competition would have existed had it not been eliminated."

It can be expected that the *McKesson* rule will affect other segments of our economy, especially the gasoline industry. In *Esso Standard Oil Co.* v. *Secatore's, Inc.*[26] the plaintiff entered into a three-year contract with the defendant to take effect on May 1, 1954. The defendant, a Massachusetts corporation, operated two large gasoline service stations in East Boston. Plaintiff agreed to sell to the defendant and the defendant agreed to buy from the plaintiff all of its requirements of Esso and Esso Extra gasolines. Defendant was promptly notified when plaintiff entered into fair trade contracts and directed to observe the fair trade prices. Defendant refused to obey these price rules and Esso sued. The suit was dismissed on the authority of the *McKesson* rule, since both parties were in competition with each other in serving filling stations. Such decisions certainly weaken greatly the fair trade protection afforded the gasoline distribution industry by the Miller-Tydings and McGuire Acts.

(c) *Applicability of McGuire Act and "fair trade" laws to imports from a non-"fair trade" state*

Can a state fair trade act protect the domestic trade of the pertinent state from the advertising, offering for sale or sale of goods at prices below the prices stipulated in a fair trade contract where the resale of the products takes place in a non-fair trade jurisdiction? Is the decisive element which determines the applicable law the passing of title of the goods, or the location of the seller, or the place in which "the economic impact of the sales" is felt?

General Electric Co. v. *Masters Mail Order Co. of Washington, D. C.*[27] is in point. This case was tried on stipulated evidence, from which the following facts are apparent: The de-

---

[26] 246 F.2d 17 (1st Cir. 1957), *cert. denied,* 355 U.S. 834 (1957).

[27] 244 F.2d 681 (2d Cir. 1957), *cert. denied,* 355 U.S. 824 (1957). This case was heard by three circuit judges, one of whom, Judge Frank, died before the decision was rendered. Of the two surviving judges, one is in dissent. Judge Waterman was assigned to the case after oral argument and after the death of Judge Frank.

fendant, "Masters D.C.," was wholly owned and supervised by Masters Inc. of New York, "Masters N. Y." Since March 1954 Masters D. C. has run a retail store in Washington, D. C., in which two-thirds of all sales are made to over-the-counter customers. Masters D. C. acquired General Electric products, partly from General Electric dealers in Washington and partly from Masters N. Y. According to a preconceived plan, Masters D. C., knowing of General Electric's fair trade contracts, made sales of General Electric products to consumers in the fair trade states including New York. These sales were all made pursuant to mail orders received at the place of business of Masters D. C. in the District of Columbia directly from the consumers. The orders were all filled by shipments of goods, in original factory cartons, directly to the consumer from the District of Columbia, either by mail or express. Some of such sales were made on a C.O.D. basis. The New York parent firm furnished copies of the mail order blanks of Masters D. C. only to consumers who sought, either in person or by mail, to buy General Electric appliances at the New York store below fair trade prices. In such cases, Masters N. Y. explained that such sales were illegal in New York, but could be effected by mail with Masters D. C. in Washington, D. C.

On the basis of this factual situation, Chief Judge Clark concluded:[28]

> "Our first question is whether the Feld-Crawford Act, so applied, conflicts with the Sherman Antitrust Law's ban on enforcement of resale price maintenance agreements as to goods moving in interstate commerce. *Dr. Miles Medical Co.* v. *John D. Park & Sons Co.*, 220 U.S. 373. Although the McGuire Act carves some exceptions to this long-standing national policy against restraints on trade, we are 'bound to construe them strictly, since resale price maintenance is a privilege restrictive of a free economy.' *United States* v. *McKesson & Robbins, Inc.*, 351 U.S. 305, 316.
>
> "Subsections (a) (2) and (3) of § 2 of the McGuire Act, 15 U.S.C. § 45 (a) (2) and (3), are printed in the margin.[29] The last part of subsection (a) (2) restricts the exception for resale maintenance contracts to contracts governing resales in jurisdictions that have adopted 'fair trade' as a policy. A contract made in a fair trade state, but governing a resale in a non-fair trade state, would be illegal by the terms of the subsection. Subsection

---

[28] 244 F.2d at 683-688. See Note, 71 HARV. L.REV. 374 (1957). See also Sunbeam Corp. v. Masters, Inc., 157 F.Supp. 689 (S.D. N.Y. 1957).

[29] See the appendix of this book under section 5(a) of the Federal Trade Commission Act which was amended by the McGuire Act.

(a) (3) creates an exception for enforcement actions only when the price-cutter is undercutting 'prices prescribed in such contracts'—that is, the contracts described in the previou ssubsection. Therefore no enforcement action lies unless the resales in question occur in a fair trade state.

*   *   *

"Plaintiff protests that our reading of the statute will allow the District of Columbia to impose its policies on economic activities in New York. But the opposite construction will simply allow New York to dominate the economic activities of the District of Columbia (and other like free trade areas). Since Congress has left the regulation of this part of interstate commerce to the option of the individual states, it is inevitable that when a single transaction affects states with conflicting policies one state or the other must see its policies slighted. We have no clearer guide in choosing the dominant state than the language of the statute itself. The trial judge attempted to weigh the defendant's contacts in New York against its contacts in the District, but this approach has no warrant in the congressional language or legislative history.[30] From all that appears Congress was concerned with the place where resales occurred, rather than the place where the retailer's owner resided and exercised supervision over operations.

"Nor do we think that advertisements and offers to sell are to be treated differently from sales themselves. The critical question is still the place of resale, and no enforcement action may be brought for advertising or offering goods for sale below the fair trade prices unless the ad or offer contemplated resales in a fair trade jurisdiction. There is a practical advantage to having all three stages of the seamless process of merchandising governed by the same law, and the wording of the McGuire Act suggests that the three are to be handled together. This was the conclusion of Judge Watkins in *Bissell Carpet Sweeper Co. v. Masters Mail Order Co. of Washington, D.C., supra.,* D.Md., 140 F.Supp. 165, *affirmed* 4 Cir., 240 F.2d 684, noted in 57 Col. L.Rev. 292; and we are in entire agreement with his comprehensive opinion. Hence an enforcement action under the New York statute is valid only if the resales occurred in New York.

"The parties disagree as to whether the defendant's order blanks were offers or only advertisements soliciting offers. Plaintiff views them as offers which were accepted when consumers

---

[30] Its weakness from a realistic point of view is highlighted by the fact that here more than two-thirds of defendant's sales were made over the counter in its extensive three-story store in the District, while the remaining or mail-order sales were by no means limited to New York customers; witness the two federal cases in Maryland that we have cited which also involve this defendant.

in New York signed them and put them in the mail. Defendant contends that the consumers' actions were the real offers which the defendant accepted in the District. We need not resolve the dispute, since Judge Waterman and I are agreed that the place where the contract was made is not controlling. In my view the place where title passed is critical.

"The intent of the parties governs the passage of title between them, although statutes and case law provide guides for ascertaining such intent. Here the predominant interest of both the seller and buyers was to take advantage of the absence of resale price maintenance legislation in the District of Columbia. The defendant's history and operations testify to its concern, and its various pieces of advertising brought home the same desire to New York consumers. For example, one of its order blanks announced 'discounts on all the "fair-traded'" brands of merchandise that are being sold only at list price in 45 states.' Since the parties had the power to determine for themselves where title would pass, they indubitably selected the District of Columbia, where their agreements would be enforceable, rather than New York, where they would not.

* * *

"Quite apart from the McGuire Act, the same result is compelled by New York law.

* * *

"In accordance with these views the order of injunction must be reversed and the action must be dismissed on the merits."

The most important statement in the concurring opinion of Judge Waterman reads as follows:[31]

"To also permit the state of ultimate destination where the consumer resides to apply its fair trade law to such interstate transactions as those now before us would logically require a holding that under the McGuire Act a resale can take place in *two* jurisdictions. It is my belief that the Congress did not intend that New York State can enforce its Feld-Crawford Act both against resident sellers, as has been done in *Raxor Corp.* v. *Goody,* and also against a non-resident seller as by the decision below. For such an anomalous result I find no authority in the language or history of the McGuire Act. In fact, its somewhat equivocal legislative history tends to support the opposite conclusion, that the seller is subject to the applicable law of but one state. See 98 Cong. Rec. 4952-4 (1952). . . .

"In view of my understanding of the McGuire Act I do not find that the New York Feld-Crawford Act has any applicability to the situation before us here. . . . [T]he New York Feld-Crawford Act, in my judgment, cannot be enforced against the

---

[31] 244 F.2d at 689.

defendant, located in the District of Columbia, on the facts in this case; and, as pointed out by Judge Clark, the fact that the defendant is owned by a resident of New York State does not make that Act any more applicable to it than if the defendant were owned by a resident of some other state."

Circuit Judge Lumbard dissented[32] for the reason stated in the district court's opinion.

(4) Recent Developments under State "Fair Trade" Laws

The states enact the actual fair trade laws; the federal statutes (Miller-Tydings and McGuire Acts) only exempt from the prohibition of the federal antitrust laws anyone engaging in fair trade practices sanctioned by a state fair trade statute. Thus it is significant to examine briefly some recent developments affecting the state laws. Such a survey shows that state fair trade statutes have been having hard times.

While the Supreme Court of the United States has not yet ruled on the constitutionality of the McGuire Act, the constitutionality of the state fair trade laws under the respective state constitutions has been considered by two-thirds of the courts of last resort of the 45 states which have adopted fair trade statutes. In the spring of 1958, the high courts of 15 states had upheld the constitutionality of their respective fair trade laws.[33] By the same date, the high courts of 15 states had handed down decisions that their respective fair trade statutes were unconstitutional, either altogether or as applied to non-signers.[34] Thus, there are at present 18 states, and the District of Columbia,[35] where fair trade agreements are either wholly, or with respect to non-signers, unenforceable. To this extent, the Miller-Tydings and McGuire Acts do not apply and fair trade is illegal in interstate commerce under section 1 of the Sherman Act.

In *General Electric Co.* v. *Thrifty Sales, Inc.*[36] the Supreme Court of Utah commented in 1956 on the present trend as to the fair trade laws:

---

[32] 244 F.2d at 691.

[33] These states are: California, Connecticut, Delaware, Illinois, Maryland, Massachusetts, Mississippi, New Jersey, New York, North Carolina, Pennsylvania, South Dakota, Tennessee, Washington, and Wisconsin.

[34] These states are: Arkansas, Colorado, Florida, Georgia, Indiana, Kansas, Louisiana, Michigan, Nebraska, New Mexico, Ohio, Oregon, South Carolina, Utah, and Virginia. For a survey on the pertinent cases, now somewhat incomplete, see Rogers-Kent, Inc. v. General Electric Co., 231 S.C. 636, 99 S.E.2d 665 (1957).

[35] Missouri, Texas, Vermont, and the District of Columbia did not enact fair trade laws.

[36] 5 Utah 2d 326, 301 P.2d 741 (1956).

> "It is significant that after some years of experience under the acts and numerous comprehensive studies covering the economic effects, the administration, and the enforcement of such laws, the majority of the more recent decisions have declared the acts invalid. Since 1952, of the jurisdictions considering the issue for the first time, only four states have upheld them, while eight have found them unconstitutional."

For a recent statement of reasons why such legislation has been held constitutional by 15 high state courts, see *Burche* v. *General Electric Co.*[37] Most of these decisions were strongly influenced by the United States Supreme Court decision in *Old Dearborn Distributing Co.* v. *Seagram Distillers Corp.*[38] where the Court held that the non-signer provision of the fair trade law of California did not work a denial of due process of law, nor of the equal protection of the laws, guaranteed by the Fourteenth Amendment to the Federal Constitution. The decision was based upon the rationale that the manufacturer or distributor has a property right in his trademark, or in the goodwill that the mark symbolizes, as distinguished from the commodity itself. Under this doctrine, ownership of the goodwill remains unchanged, notwithstanding the commodity has been parted with, and entitles the proprietor to fix the resale price even with respect to non-signers. Hence, the price cutting non-signer was held to have unlawfully interfered with a property right and the constitutionality of the Act was upheld.

However, the validity of this rationale has been attacked.[39] "The modern trend is to regard this legislation as a price-fixing statute."[40] In *Bissell Carpet Sweeper Co.* v. *Shane Co., Inc.* the Supreme Court of Indiana stated:[41]

> "The complaint specifically alleges the appellee Shane was not a party to any contract to fix the retail price. It fails to allege from whom Shane purchased the sweepers or when they were purchased. For all that was alleged, Shane could have purchased them in Michigan, where fair trade price fixing is illegal [Cases cited.] Appellant's position is that wilfully and knowingly selling and offering for sale Bissell's sweepers at prices less than fixed by Bissell after notice of the contracts to which Shane was not a party entitled Bissell to relief.

---

[37] 382 Pa. 370, 115 A.2d 361 (1955).

[38] 299 U.S. 183 (1936).

[39] See, *e.g.*, dissenting opinion of Judge Holmes in Schwegmann Bros. Giant Super Markets v. Eli Lilly & Co., 205 F.2d 788, 793 (5th Cir. 1953).

[40] Rogers-Kent, Inc. v. General Electric Co., 231 S.C. 636, 649, 99 S.E. 2d 665, 671 (1957).

[41] ...... Ind. ......, 143 N.E.2d 415, 418, 419, 421 (1957).

"We are not at liberty to substitute our judgment for that of the General Assembly as to whether price fixing is good or bad for the economic life of the state. Conceivably, in a time of depression the benefits might outweigh the disadvantages, while the converse may be true in a time of prosperity or inflation. But the Indiana Constitution on separation of powers and the vesting of the right to enact laws in the General Assembly have the same meaning whatever may be the business or economic condition of the State.

*   *   *

"A *fortiori*, § 66-306, Burns' 1951 Replacement, is broad enough to vest a legislative power to fix prices in private persons. But the Constitution says 'The Legislative authority of the State shall be vested in the General Assembly . . .' Article 4, Section 1. The power to legislate or to exercise a legislative function cannot be delegated to a non-governmental agency or person. *Tucker* v. *State* (1941) 218 Ind. 614, 697, 698, 35 N.E.2d 270 [Footnote omitted.] Nor can the Legislature delegate its law making power to a governmental officer, board, bureau or commission. [Cases cited.] We are not concerned with a statute which places upon an official a duty to execute a law made by the Legislature, or where the law fixes a reasonable and fair rate, price or charge and delegates to a governmental agency the power to find as a fact what is reasonable and fair under proper standards. See *Albert* v. *Milk Control Board of Ind.* (1936), 210 Ind. 283, 300, 200 N.E. 688.

*   *   *

"[I]n the appeal at bar the complaint and the contracts fail to show anything more than attempted legislative price fixing by a contract between the manufacturer and various retailers in the State of Indiana, with no allegation that the appellee Shane ever entered into a contract to sell the sweepers at fair trade prices, or that it induced the breach of contract between Bissell and another party, or that Shane did not acquire the goods in some state, such as Michigan, where such fair trade contracts are held in restraint of trade and void. The complaint rests upon the naked proposition that private parties by contract can make a law binding upon everyone who retails the goods manufactured by Bissell. It is argued that the Fair Trade Act does no more than give an additional property right in a trademark. But if this is to be done, it must be accomplished pursuant to the Indiana Constitution. The General Assembly has no right to abdicate its legislative power to private persons, nor could it even delegate to a governmental agency the power to find what might be a reasonable price without proper safeguards and procedural process. [Footnote omitted.]"

In *General Electric Co.* v. *Wahle*[42] the Supreme Court of Oregon said:

> "Regardless of how its true nature may be camouflaged by high-sounding terms such as 'free and open competition,' 'unfair competition,' 'protection of good will,' etc., it is a matter of common knowledge that it is a price-fixing statute designed principally to destroy competition at the retail level. Protection of the 'good will' of the trademark owner is simply an excuse and not a reason for the law. According to eminent writers in law reviews, pressure for the passage of these Acts came not from the manufacturers or other trademark owners but from distributors—first and foremost the retail druggists associations and then other retail and wholesale distributors."

Hence, state fair trade laws have been held illegal on the ground that they constitute a deprivation of property without due process and thus violate the due process clause of the respective state constitutions. In *Olin Mathieson Chemical Corp.* v. *Francis* the Colorado Supreme Court argued:[43]

> "The Colorado Fair Trade Act grants to private individuals the right to fix prices without providing a standard or fixing the limits within which such prices are to be regulated, and it leaves entirely to certain favored individuals the choice of whether minimum resale prices shall or shall not be fixed, a right which some of such individuals may choose to exercise, while others for reasons of their own may not. . . .

> "The right to contract is a property right, protected by the due process clause of the constitution and cannot be abridged by legislative enactment. . . .

> "To the extent that the Colorado Act is coercive it is lacking in duo process, is confiscatory, and tends to establish a monopoly."

In *General Electric Co.* v. *Thrifty Sales, Inc.*[44] the Supreme Court of Utah held that the state fair trade law was invalid under section 20, article XII of the state constitution, which reads:

> "[A]ny combination . . . having for its object or effect the controlling of the price of any products of the soil, or of any article of manufacture or commerce . . . is prohibited, and hereby declared unlawful, and against public policy."

---

[42] 207 Ore. 302, 317, 296 P.2d 635, 642-643 (1956).

[43] 134 Colo. 160, 176, 177, 301 P.2d 139, 147 (1956). See also Rogers-Kent, Inc. v. General Electric Co., 231 S.C. 636, 99 S.E.2d 665 (1957).

[44] 5 Utah 2d 326, 301 P.2d 741 (1956).

In *General Electric Co.* v. *Wahle*[45] the Supreme Court of Oregon discussed another constitutional ground on which fair trade statutes have been frequently attacked:[46]

> "The enactment of the Fair Trade Act can be justified only upon the theory that it constitutes a reasonable and proper exercise of the inherent police power residing in the state. The police power is broad and far-reaching, and it is difficult, if not impossible, to fix its bounds. Yet an exercise of the police power can never be justified unless it is reasonably necessary in the interests of the public order, health, safety and welfare. The legislature is not the final judge of the limitations of the police power, and, because the legislative action must be reasonably necessary for the public benefit, the validity of the police regulations depends upon whether they can ultimately pass the judicial test of reasonableness. . . . Viewed from a realistic standpoint, it is difficult to find any justification for the Fair Trade Act based upon considerations of the public health, safety, morals, and welfare. We can see no real and substantial connection between the nebulous theory that fixed minimum resale prices are necessary to protect the goodwill of the trademark owner and the welfare of the public."

In several of those states where the non-signer clause has been held invalid, a non-signer is no longer liable in tort for inducing a signer to breach his fair trade contract in order to supply the non-signer with goods below the fair trade price.[47]

(5) The Effectiveness of "Fair Trade"

The machinery of fair trade has continued to be very controversial, especially from an economic point of view. The arguments, pro and con, cannot be repeated here.[48] Apart from that, however, fair trade has run into a number of constantly growing difficulties, which are due only in part to the attitude of numerous unfriendly courts and which seriously endanger its effective-

---

[45] 207 Ore. 302, 296 P.2d 635 (1956).

[46] 207 Ore. at 320, 296 P.2d at 644. See also Skaggs Drug Center v. General Electric Co., ... N. Mex. ......, 315 P.2d 967 (1957).

[47] See, *e.g.*, Sunbeam Corp. v. Gilbert Simmons Associates, Inc., 91 So.2d 335 (Fla. 1956); Sunbeam Corp. v. Hall of Distributors, 142 F.Supp. 609 (E.D. Mich. 1956).

[48] See, *e.g.*, THE "FAIR TRADE" QUESTION (National Industrial Conference Board ed. 1955); Adams, *Resale Price Maintenance: Fact and Fancy*, 64 YALE L.J. 967 (1955); Fulda, *Resale Price Maintenance*, 21 U. CHI. L.REV. 175 (1954). See also YAMEY, THE ECONOMICS OF RESALE PRICE MAINTENANCE (1954).

ness.[49] A recent *Study on Fair Trade, Based on a Survey of Manufacturers and Retailers*, of the Select Senate Committee on Small Business has summarized some of these problems, as seen by fair trading manufacturers and dealers:[50]

"The manufacturers, as proponents of fair trade, naturally have more than a passing interest in having it operate effectively. They wrote unsparingly of its deficiencies. These centered around the rife expansion of discount houses; the difficulties manufacturers are having enforcing their programs; and the considerable expense that many of these enforcement programs and allied litigation entail. The manufacturers overwhelmingly maintained that if fair trade is to be more effective it must be strengthened. The majority thought this could best be done by providing for more stringent enforcement provisions, *e.g.*, by putting teeth into the fair-trade laws such as making violators guilty of a misdemeanor and subject to fines and/or imprisonment. A number of other firms indicated that it is only the non-signer clause that needs revision. Singularly these views were largely those of former fair trade manufacturers who answered the questionnaires.

"Still others felt that revisions of the State laws will not meet the requirements for making fair trade effectively operative. These indicated that Federal legislation, designed to supplement the existing Federal laws or revamp them entirely, is needed. These suggestions included, among other things, providing penalties for fair-trade violations and a national law providing that a manufacturer's price becomes a part of his product, 'in the sense that any unique feature of his product is covered by a patent.' The latter recommendation was predicated on the belief that 'the laws covering patent infringements are less easily violated than are the prices under the fair trade acts.'

"The majority of retailers, in the 45 States which at some time in the past 25 years have enacted fair-trade laws, indicated a desire for fair trade; even those who were not greatly affected by its operation backed the principle and in some instances, firms going out of business maintained that had more stringent fair-trade laws existed they might have continued their operations.

* * *

"Although proponents of the fair trade principle, the majority of the retailers indicated a dissatisfaction with its implementation

---

[49] For an excellent study, see Note, *The Operation of Fair-Trade Programs*, 60 HARV. L.REV. 316 (1955). On September 6, 1956, a key merchandizing official of Westinghouse Electric Corp. announced that sales of small appliances have risen sharply since the company abandoned fair trade a year before. "We feel that after a fair trial our policies have proven successful and we do not intend returning to fair trade." The Washington Post and Times Herald, September 7, 1956, p. 33.

[50] *Fair Trade*, S. REP. No. 2819, 84th Cong., 2d Sess. 21-22 (1956).

under existing laws. Some called for an all-out educational program on the part of manufacturers and wholesalers alike and the
majority called for stricter enforcement at all levels, and some
indicated revisions of the existing laws or the enactment of new
ones are necessary if enforcement of the system is to be practicable.

"In general, the manufacturers and retailers alike favor fair
trade and intend to continue their programs. However, they feel
that fair trade is losing ground and in order to combat this they
indicate the necessity for a stronger fair-trade law if their fair-
trade programs are to be successful."

In March, 1958, fair trade suffered the hardest blow in many
years when the giant General Electric Company abandoned its
policy of maintaining fixed resale prices for small appliances
(except electric bulbs). (As to major appliances and television
sets, General Electric had given up fair trade earlier.) In an-
nouncing its decision, General Electric stated that it had found
its fair trade policy to be "inoperable". In the preceding five
years, the Company had spent almost $5,000,000 to track down
violators and had brought suit against more than 3,000 price
cutters. Other important manufacturers of small appliances, including Sunbeam Corp., McGraw-Edison Co. (toastmaster),
Ronson Corp., and Schick, Inc., followed General Electric's lead.
Within days, vigorous price competition on the distributor's
level made consumer prices drop considerably in many cities
where the manufacturers had hitherto enforced fair trade, including New York City, Chicago and Los Angeles.[51]

Meanwhile, proponents of fair trade introduced a bill in the
House[52] which would legalize resale price maintenance of
branded articles in interstate commerce and, therefore, go far
beyond the fair trade enabling statutes, the Miller-Tydings and
McGuire Acts. The bill, which would amend section 5(a) of the
Federal Trade Commission Act, provides, *inter alia,* that it shall
be lawful for a proprietor, defined as one who identifies merchandise manufactured or distributed by him by the use of his
trademark or trade name, to establish and control stipulated or
minimum resale prices of his merchandise in commerce *by notice*
to his distributors.[53]

---

[51] Time, March 10, 1958, p. 82, col. 3 and p. 83.
[52] H.R. 10527, 85th Cong., 2d Sess. (1958).
[53] *Cf.* also MacLachlan, *A New Approach to Resale Price Maintenance,*
11 VAND. L.REV. 145 (1957), with a formulated draft of a federal fair
trade statute.

Chapter 7

THE FEDERAL TRADE COMMISSION

There are several independent federal commissions which regulate carefully circumscribed areas of our economy.[1] For example, the Federal Power Commission mentioned in chapter 9 regulates the sale and transportation of natural gas in interstate commerce and the interstate transmission of electric power. The Interstate Commerce Commission, oldest of the commissions, regulates the railroads, interstate truck lines and interstate oil pipelines. The Civil Aeronautics Board, the Federal Communications Commission, The Federal Maritime Board, the Federal Reserve Board, and the Atomic Energy Commission regulate various aspects of the industries indicated by their titles.

(1) Purpose and Functions

The Federal Trade Commission was established by Congress in 1914[2] to protect our competitive, free-enterprise economy against unfair practices which would lessen competition or tend to create a monopoly. To carry out this purpose, the Commission is charged with the following main responsibilities:

(1) To prevent unfair methods of competition,[3] including practices which at the same time constitute violations of the Sherman Act,[4] and other unfair and deceptive acts and practices in commerce;[5]

(2) To prevent the dissemination of false or deceptive advertisements of foods, drugs, cosmetics and medical apparatus;[6]

---

[1] For a recent critical analysis, see BERNSTEIN, REGULATING BUSINESS BY INDEPENDENT COMMISSION (1955).

[2] Federal Trade Commission Act, 38 STAT. 717 (1914), as amended, 15 U.S.C. § 41 (1952). The text of the statute, as amended, is set out in the appendix.

[3] F.T.C. Act, § 5, as amended, 15 U.S.C. § 45 (1952).

[4] Federal Trade Commission v. Cement Institute, 333 U.S. 683, 689-695 (1948).

[5] F.T.C. Act, § 5, supra, n.3.

[6] F.T.C. Act, §§ 12-15, 52 STAT. 114-117 (1938), 15 U.S.C. §§ 52-55 (1952).

(3) To prevent certain price and other discriminations,[7] tying and exclusive dealing agreements,[8] mergers and acquisitions,[9] and interlocking directorates;[10]

(4) To prevent unfair methods of competition in export trade and to supervise the registration and operation of associations of American exporters engaged solely in export trade;[11]

(5) To gather and make public factual data concerning economic and business conditions as a basis for remedial legislation, and for the information and protection of the public;[12]

(6 To administer several statutes designed to prevent deceit and insure safety in merchandising certain commodities;[13]

(7) To apply for cancellation of registered trademarks which have been illegally registered or which have been used for purposes contrary to the Lanham Trade Mark Act of 1946.[14]

There is a large area of antitrust law where both the Federal Trade Commission and the Department of Justice have jurisdiction. Section 11 of the Clayton Act[15] provides for dual enforcement of the provisions against price and other discriminations, tying and exclusive dealing agreements, mergers, and interlocking directorates. Furthermore, the Supreme Court has held that "[t]he Commission has jurisdiction to declare that conduct tending to restrain trade is an unfair method of competition even though the selfsame conduct may also violate the Sherman Act."[16] "[T]he [Federal Trade Commission] Act's legislative history shows a strong congressional purpose not only to continue enforcement of the Sherman Act by the Department of

---

[7] Clayton Act, § 2, 38 STAT. 730 (1914), as amended by the Robinson-Patman Act, 52 STAT. 446 (1936), 15 U.S.C. §§ 13(a)-(f) (1952).

[8] Clayton Act, § 3, 38 STAT. 731 (1914), 15 U.S.C. § 14 (1952).

[9] Clayton Act, § 7, 38 STAT. 731 (1914), as amended by the Kefauver-Celler Act, 64 STAT. 1125 (1950), 15 U.S.C. § 18 (1952).

[10] Clayton Act, § 8, 38 STAT. 732 (1914), as amended, 15 U.S.C. § 19 (1952).

[11] Export Trade (Webb-Pomerene) Act, §§ 4-5, 40 STAT. 517 (1918), 15 U.S.C. §§ 64-65 (1952).

[12] F.T.C. Act, § 6, 38 STAT. 721 (1914), 15 U.S.C. § 46 (1952). See, *e.g.,* the Annual Reports of the Commission.

[13] Wool Products Labeling Act, 54 STAT. 1128 (1940), 15 U.S.C. § 68(d) (1952); Fur Labeling Act, 65 STAT. 179 (1951), 15 U.S.C. § 69(f) (1952); Flammable Fabrics Act, 67 STAT. 111 (1953), 15 U.S.C. § 1191 (Supp. IV, 1957).

[14] Lanham Act, § 14, 60 STAT. 433 (1946), 15 U.S.C. § 1064 (1952).

[15] 38 STAT. 734 (1914), as amended, 15 U.S.C. § 21 (1952).

[16] Federal Trade Commission v. Cement Institute, 333 U.S. 683, 693 (1948).

Justice . . . but also to supplement that enforcement through the administrative process of the new Trade Commission."[17]

The problem, then, is how to assure the most efficient cooperation and distribution of work between the Commission and the Antitrust Division of the Department of Justice. In this respect, it has been reported:[18]

> "In June 1948, each agency agreed [footnote omitted] to notify the other by an exchange of cards before initiating any investigation, grand jury proceeding or trade practice conference. Should one agency object to the action proposed, the question of which agency should proceed is submitted to a joint conference. . . .
>
> "Beyond this formal agreement, an enforcement pattern has emerged from case by case action. Thus, apart from cases where Clayton Section 3 forms part of a larger Sherman Act charge, the Department has brought only one case solely under Section 3 of the Clayton Act.[19] Similarly, unless a Clayton Act Section 2 offense comprises an element of Sherman Act violation, the Division apparently recognizes Commission procedures are better suited to primary enforcement of price discrimination bans."

And more recently, the General Counsel of the Federal Trade Commission has confirmed that, in the interest of efficiency, the Department and the Commission have, by common consent, operated under the theory that neither should investigate nor try antitrust suits in areas where the other agency has a particular competency or experience.[20]

(2) Organization and Status

A reorganization of the Federal Trade Commission became effective in 1950 under the Reorganization Act of 1949.[21] Prior to that time the chairman was elected from among the membership of the Commission by the commissioners themselves. Under section 3 of the Reorganization Plan No. 8 of 1950[22] the function of choosing a chairman was transferred to the President. The following testimony of Mr. Howrey, then chairman of the

---

[17] *Id.*, at 692.

[18] REPORT OF THE ATTORNEY GENERAL'S NATIONAL COMMITTEE TO STUDY THE ANTITRUST LAWS 376 (1955).

[19] United States v. United Shoe Machinery Corp., 258 U.S. 451 (1922).

[20] Statement of Mr. Earl Kintner before the Antitrust Subcommittee of the House Committee on the Judiciary, in *Hearings On Professional Sports,* 85th Cong., 1st Sess. (June 19, 1957), Official Verbatim Transcript (mimeo.) 159-160. See also § 1.121 of the Procedures and Rules of Practice For the Federal Trade Commission, as amended to November 12, 1957, 15 U.S.C. § 45 (Supp. V, 1958).

[21] 63 STAT. 203-207 (1949), 5 U.S.C. §§ 133z-133z-15 (1952).

[22] 15 F.R. 3175, 64 STAT. 1264 (1950), 15 U.S.C. § 41 (1952).

Federal Trade Commission, shows this recognition of his changed status:

> "Mr. EVINS: Mr. Howrey, you hold your position as Chairman of the Federal Trade Commission at the pleasure of the President?
>
> Mr. HOWREY: Yes, that is my interpretation of Reorganization Plan No. 8.
>
> Mr. EVINS: Is it also your understanding that you, as Chairman of the Commission, are subject to removal without assignment of any cause whatsoever?
>
> Mr. HOWREY: Yes. It is my understanding, under Reorganization Plan No. 8, which, as you will recall, was issued pursuant to an act of Congress, that the President can fire me at will as Chairman; but not as a member of the Commission.
>
> Mr. EVINS: That, then, is in conflict with this Supreme Court decision that we referred to earlier in which Commissioner Humphrey could not be fired from the Commission?
>
> Mr. HOWREY: It is in conflict in the sense that Congress changed the law."[23]

The case referred to is *Humphrey's Executor* v. *United States*,[24] which involved the attempted removal of a commissioner by President Roosevelt. The Supreme Court there held that the President could not remove a commissioner except for the reasons stated in section 1 of the Federal Trade Commission Act, which are "inefficiency, neglect of duty, or malfeasance in office."

As to the constitutional and statutory concepts underlying the establishment of the Commission, the Court stated in part:[25]

> "The Commission is to be non-partisan; and it must, from the very nature of its duties, act with entire impartiality. It is charged with the enforcement of no policy except the policy of the law. Its duties are neither political nor executive, but predominantly quasi-judicial and quasi-legislative * * * The . . . Commission is an administrative body. . . . Such a body cannot in any proper sense be characterized as an arm or an eye of the executive. . . . To the extent that it exercises any executive function . . . it does so in the discharge and effectuation of its quasi-legislative or quasi-judicial powers, or as an agency of the legislative or judicial department of the government."

---

[23] The Organization and Procedures of the Federal Regulatory Commissions and Agencies and Their Effect on Small Business, *Hearings Before Subcommittee No. 1 of the House Select Committee on Small Business,* 84th Cong., 1st Sess., Part 1, Federal Trade Commission, at 24-25 (1956).

[24] 295 U.S. 602 (1935).

[25] *Id.,* at 624, 628.

The issues summarized in this statement continue to be discussed.[26]

Prior to 1950, the five commissioners appointed by the President operated on the basis of equality and the chairman served as a sort of *primus inter pares*. In 1950, section 1 of Reorganization Plan No. 8 transferred (with certain minor exceptions) from the Commission to the chairman authority over (1) the appointment, promotion, and supervision of personnel employed by the Commission; (2) the distribution of business among such personnel and among the administrative units of the Commission; and (3) the use and expenditure of funds. In addition, the chairman may now delegate authority in administrative and management matters to staff officers. Thus, the reorganization has strengthened the position of the chairman considerably.

In recent years there has been increasing criticism of this new organization of the Commission, by a number of its former and present members among others.[27] On the basis of an investigation, the House Select Committee on Small Business and its Subcommittee No. 1 on Regulatory Agencies and Commissions recommended in 1956 "that the appropriate legislative committees of the Congress consider the following matters in the next Congress:

"1. That the various reorganization plans (sometimes referred to as Hoover Commission plans) applicable to the different independent regulatory agencies such as the Federal Trade Commission . . . be amended to the extent that the Chairman of such agencies be selected by the members thereof, and that the powers placed in the hands of the Chairman by said plans revert to the members of the agencies acting as a body in accordance with usual agency procedure . . . ;

"2. That the independent regulatory agencies be exempted from the Budget Act so that they may submit directly to the Congress, without prior approval by the Bureau of the Budget or any other agency or official of the executive branch, their requests for appropriations; . . .

---

[26] See *Regulatory Agencies and Commissions*, Report of Subcommittee No. 1 of the House Select Committee on Small Business, H.R. REP. No. 2967, 84th Cong., 2d Sess. (1956). For the time prior to 1951, see, *e.g., Antitrust Law Enforcement by the Federal Trade Commission and the Antitrust Division, Department of Justice*, Report of the House Select Committee on Small Business, H.R. REP. No. 3236, 81st Cong., 2d Sess. (1951). See also the papers by Howrey, Clark and Kintner and the panel discussion on the future role of the Commission printed in 10 ABA ANTITRUST SECTION REPORT 40-117 (April 1957).

[27] See *Hearings, supra* n.23.

"3. That the independent regulatory agencies be exempted from the Federal Reports Act in order that they may obtain from private industries and individuals such factual data and information as in their judgment may be necessary to carry out their statutory responsibilities; . . .

"4. That the independent regulatory agencies be exempted from the requirement that they secure prior approval of the Bureau of the Budget or any other agency or official of the executive branch before they submit to the Congress their views concerning legislation affecting their respective agencies and the laws entrusted to them by the Congress; . . .

"5. Whether the independent regulatory agencies should be relieved from the requirement, and the circumstances under which they should be relieved from the requirement, that they secure prior approval of the Solicitor General or any other agency or official of the executive branch to petition the United States Supreme Court to review rulings or decisions made against such independent agencies. . . ."[28]

(3) Procedure

The procedure of the Federal Trade Commission is circumscribed by the procedural provisions contained in the laws administered by the Commission, and the Administrative Procedure Act of 1946.[29] Under the authority of these provisions and in order to assist it in carrying out its functions, the Commission has issued and repeatedly revised its "Procedures and Rules for the Federal Trade Commission".[30] The present rules were adopted by the Commission in May, 1955. They contain a detailed description of the general policy, the functions and procedures of the Commission.

To fulfill its responsibilities, the Commission has authority to make general or industry-wide investigations as well as specific investigations relating to particular firms and practices.[31] The Commission has been characterized as "a guardian of the nation's economy."[32] Most special investigations are initiated on the basis of written complaints by consumers or businessmen.[33]

(a) Informal Procedures

In carrying out its numerous duties, the Commission employs voluntary, or informal, as well as compulsory, or formal, proce-

---

[28] H.R. REP. No. 2967, 84th Cong., 2d Sess. 80-81 (1956).

[29] 60 STAT. 237, as amended, 5 U.S.C. § 1001 (1952).

[30] As amended to November 12, 1957, 15 U.S.C. § 45 (Supp. V, 1958).

[31] F.T.C. Act, § 6, 38 STAT. 721 (1914), 15 U.S.C. § 46 (1952).

[32] Babcock, *Legal Investigation,* in AN ANTITRUST HANDBOOK 385, at 393 (ABA Section of Antitrust Law ed. 1958).

[33] *Id.,* at 387. The amount of such complaints is substantial, *ibid.*

dures. Voluntary procedures for obtaining compliance with the law include (1) stipulations to cease and desist, and (2) staff advice under the anti-merger law.[34]

Neither method leads to an enforceable order. A stipulation consists of a voluntary agreement as to the facts and an agreement to cease and desist from the practices deemed to be violative of the law. If approved by the Commission, the matter is closed without prejudice to the right of the Commission to reopen it.[35] This procedure is extensively used,[36] and results in a considerable saving of time and effort.[37]

The other informal procedure has been adopted by the Commission in order to assist businessmen in foreseeing the legal problems involved in a proposed merger and to give them the benefit of staff views on those problems. On the basis of the facts submitted by the parties and other information available to the Commission, the parties are informed whether or not consummation of the merger would be likely to result in action by the Commission.[38]

(b) *Rulemaking Procedures*

The Wool, Fur and Flammable Fabrics Rules authorized by the respective Acts, the Quantity Limit Rules,[39] which are formal in nature, and the Trade Practice Conference Rules, which are informal, involve rulemaking procedures.

The purpose of trade practice rules is to eliminate and prevent, on a voluntary and industry-wide basis, violations of the laws administered by the Commission. When the Commission, sometimes after a long and expensive trial, has demonstrated that a particular practice of the respondent firm is unlawful, it is faced with the fact that many other firms operating in the same industry are carrying on the same practices. The final decision does not apply to the other firms. This has been a source of great anguish to the firm which is first caught and convicted

---

[34] See Parrish, *Voluntary Procedures*, in AN ANTITRUST HANDBOOK 395 (ABA Section of Antitrust Law ed. 1958).

[35] For details, see §§ 1.51-1.57 of the Procedures and Rules, *supra* n. 30.

[36] See FEDERAL TRADE COMMISSION, ANNUAL REPORT 1957, 61-64 (1957).

[37] The 15 percent increase in funds recommended by the President and granted by the 84th and continued by the 85th Congress made possible a staff increase from 641 to 744. FEDERAL TRADE COMMISSION, ANNUAL REPORT 1957, at 1 (1957).

[38] §§ 1.61-1.63 of the Procedures and Rules, *supra*, n.30. See the discussion in chapter 3.

[39] Authorized by section 2(a) of the Clayton Act, as amended by the Robinson-Patman Act. See the discussion in chapter 5.

because it fears that it will lose business to its competitors, so long as they continue the forbidden trade practices.[40] But the Commission cannot enjoin the practices of the other firms until proceedings have been brought against each of them.

This defect has been mitigated to some extent by the adoption of the trade practice conference as a supplemental means of preventing unlawful trade practices. It depends for its success on the voluntary support of the industry members. The purpose of the conference is the establishment by the Commission of trade practice rules. This procedure[41] affords an opportunity for voluntary participation by the industry members in the drafting of rules to provide for elimination or prevention of unfair methods of competition, unfair or deceptive acts or practices and other illegal trade practices.

Under this procedure, rules have been prepared and published by the Commission for approximately 160 industries, ranging from the photoengraving industry of the southeastern states to the subscription and mail order book publishing industry.

Trade practice conference rules have no force of law in themselves. They are advisory only.[42] They are interpretations of the law, neither requiring more, nor tolerating less, than what the statutory provisions on which they are based require. The Commission can proceed only on the basis that the activity in question violates one of the laws which the Commission has the duty to enforce. However, the rules do help the industry members to understand what the statutes and court decisions prohibit, as far as their industry is concerned.

(c) *Formal Procedure*

Where the parties refuse to cooperate during an investigation, compulsory measures become necessary. The Federal Trade Commission Act provides the Commission with (1) the power of access to documentary evidence,[43] (2) the power to require annual and special reports from the firm,[44] and (3) the power of subpoena.[45] Section 10 provides for serious penalties for fail-

---

[40] See Moog Industries, Inc. v. Federal Trade Commission, 78 S.Ct. 377 (1958), discussed *infra*.

[41] §§ 2.21-2.32 of the Procedures and Rules, *supra*, n.30. See Parrish, *supra*, n.34, at 398-402.

[42] Standard Distributors, Inc. v. Federal Trade Commission, 211 F.2d 7, 13 (2d Cir. 1954).

[43] § 9, 38 STAT. 722 (1914), 15 U.S.C. § 49 (1952).

[44] § 6(b), 38 STAT. 721 (1914), 15 U.S.C. § 46 (1952). *Cf.* United States v. Morton Salt Co., 338 U.S. 632, 647-651 (1950).

[45] § 9, *supra* n.43.

ure to comply with the lawful requirements of the Commission.[46] "This combination of fact-finding power represents the broadest power available to any agency of the government."[47]

Recently, however, the power of the Commission to issue subpoenas in proceedings brought under the Clayton Act became controversial, as the following decision illustrates.

MENZIES v. FEDERAL TRADE COMMISSION
United States Court of Appeals for the Fourth Circuit
242 F.2d 81 (1957)[48]

"PARKER, Chief Judge.

"These are appeals from an order enforcing subpoenas *duces tecum* issued by the Federal Trade Commission pursuant to Section 9 of the Federal Trade Commission Act, 15 U.S.C.A. § 49. The subpoenas were issued in proceedings before the Commission in which three corporations were charged with violation of Section 2(d) of the Clayton Act as amended by the Robinson-Patman Act, 15 U.S.C.A. § 13(d). The contentions on appeal are that the subpoenas are invalid on the ground that the Commission does not have power to issue subpoenas under Section 9 of the Federal Trade Commission Act in proceedings had before it for enforcement of the Clayton Act and that, even if this power exists, the subpoenas are violative of the provisions of the Fourth Amendment to the Constitution of the United States.

* * *

"It is not without significance that for more than forty years the Federal Trade Commission, in proceedings had before it under the Clayton Act, has issued subpoenas such as it issued here and has issued many thousands of such subpoenas. While we agree that this is not conclusive as to its power to issue them, it is not reasonable to suppose that the power would have gone unchallenged for so long a period in such a sensitive field of the law, if there were any real doubt as to its existence.

"The Federal Trade Commission Act, 15 U.S.C.A. § 41 *et seq.*, and the Clayton Act, 15 U.S.C.A. § 12 *et seq.*, were before

---

[46] 38 STAT. 722 (1914), 15 U.S.C. § 50 (1952).

[47] Babcock, *supra* n.32, at 386. For a discussion of the proceedings, see Kern, *Hearings on Complaints*, in AN ANTITRUST HANDBOOK 405 (ABA Section of Antitrust Law ed. 1958); Kintner, *Post-Hearing Procedures and Compliance, id.*, at 425. *Cf.* also Gwynne, *Current Enforcement of Federal Trade Commission Acts*, in 1957 CCH ANTITRUST LAW SYMPOSIUM 20 (1957).

[48] *Cert. denied*, 353 U.S. 457 (1957). *Accord*, Federal Trade Commission v. Reed, 243 F.2d 308, 309 (7th Cir. 1957), *cert. denied*, 355 U.S. 823 (1957); Federal Trade Commission v. Tuttle, 244 F.2d 605, 610 (2d Cir. 1957), *cert. denied*, 354 U.S. 925 (1957); Federal Trade Commission v. Rubin, 245 F.2d 60 (2d Cir. 1957). See Note, 70 HARV. L.REV. 1476 (1957), and Note, 57 COLUM. L.REV. 890 (1957).

Congress at the same time and were in *pari materia*, dealing with the same general subject matter, restraints of trade and unfair competition. The Clayton Act (38 Stat. 730) laid down substantive rules of law and provided for their enforcement by courts and administrative agencies. The Federal Trade Commission Act created the Commission as an administrative agency and conferred certain powers upon it, among others the power to enter cease and desist orders upon a finding of unfair competition and to conduct investigations as to 'the organization, business, conduct, practices and management of any corporation engaged in commerce, excepting banks and common carriers * * * and its relation to other corporations and to individuals, associations and partnerships.' 38 Stat. 717-724, 15 U.S.C.A. § 46. Authority to enforce compliance with the provisions of the Clayton Act, except as to banks and common carriers, was conferred by Section 11 of that Act on the Federal Trade Commission; and this could mean nothing else than that, in carrying out this provision, the Commission should exercise the powers with respect to investigations and hearing vested in it by the Act of its creation. Among such powers, was the power to examine documents and witnesses and issue subpoenas. This was provided in Section 9 of the Act.

* * *

"Contention is made that the language 'for the purposes of this Act' limits the power of examining witnesses and issuing subpoenas to proceedings and investigations authorized by the Act creating the Commission and that the power may not be exercised in an enforcement provision which the Commission is authorized by the Clayton Act to conduct. This, we think, is an unreasonable and forced construction of the language used, the manifest purpose of which was to give the Commission the power of subpoena and examination in connection with any investigation or proceeding which it was authorized by law to conduct. The language in question is 'for the purposes of this Act;' and one of the purposes of the Act was to vest the Commission with adequate powers to conduct investigations and proceedings with respect to restraints of trade and unfair competition. When duties of investigation or enforcement are imposed upon the Commission by another act or acts, the reasonable intendment is that it shall exercise the power conferred upon it by law in the discharge of such duties.

* * *

"It is conceded that if the Commission were conducting an investigation under Section 5 or Section 6 of the Trade Commission Act into the discriminatory practices of the corporations here being investigated, it would have power to issue subpoenas under Section 9 of the Act and to use the information thus obtained in a subsequent proceeding to enforce the provisions of the Clayton Act. Certainly the power of the Commission to issue subpoenas and conduct the investigation is not less because of the fact that it gives notice in advance that the information obtained is to be so used; and the filing of the complaint under the Clayton Act amounts to no more than this. To deny such power to the Commission would in large measure defeat the purpose which Congress manifestly had in mind in the enactment of these statutes; and we find nothing in the language or history of either statute which at this late day requires such a result.

 * * *

"Affirmed."

In *Federal Trade Commission* v. *Tuttle*,[49] the Second Circuit had to deal with the question of the power of the Commission under Section 9 of the Act to subpoena documents and records of third parties.

". . . The argument of respondent on that point is that the subpoena power is limited to documents and records of the corporation being investigated or proceeded against, which in this case would be the Spaulding corporation and possibly the Rawlings corporation. Respondents stress the use of the word 'such' in the first sentence of Section 9. . . .

". . . The respondent argues that its antecedent in the first sentence of Section 9 is 'documentary evidence of any corporation being investigated or proceeded against.' That contention might appear to be reasonable if we read only the language of the first sentence of Section 9 disregarding the other provisions of Section 9; the purpose and policy of the Federal Trade Commission Act; its legislative history; the Congressional intent; and the effect of respondent-appellee's construction of Section 9, if adopted, upon the Commission's functioning under the Act. . . .

 * * *

"Respondent's narrow construction of the first sentence of the first paragraph of Section 9 is in direct conflict with the broad provisions of the fifth paragraph of that section, relating to the taking of testimony by deposition 'in any proceeding or investigation pending under this Act.'

 * * *

"The limited construction of the word 'such,' as contended for by the respondents, would also result in this anomalous situation —that oral testimony could be elicited by the Commission in examining a witness under subpoena, concerning transactions re-

---

[49] 244 F.2d 605, 611, 613, 615 (2d Cir. 1957), *cert. denied,* 354 U.S. 925 (1957). See also Federal Trade Commission v. Bowman, 149 F.Supp. 624 (N.D. Ill. 1957), *affirmed,* 248 F.2d 456 (7th Cir. 1957).

ported in the books and records of the individual or partnership, but the books and records themselves could not be subpoenaed.

*   *   *

"A correct interpretation of the long first sentence of Section 9 of the Federal Trade Commission Act should recognize the fact that it grants two separate powers to the Commission, and that the language granting those distinct powers is separated by a semi-colon. The first grants the right of access to and the right to copy any documentary evidence of the corporation being investigated or proceeded against. The second grants a subpoena power for the production of documentary evidence relating to any matter under investigation.

"In the second half of the first sentence of Section 9 the words 'the production of all such documentary evidence relating to any matter under investigation' should be construed to mean 'the production of all documentary evidence relating to any matter under investigation,' thus eliminating the word 'such.' That will comply with the policy and purposes of the Act itself."

(4) Evidence

The purpose of all of the proceedings of the Commission, after a complaint has been issued, is to enable the Commission to make findings of fact, supported by the evidence of record, upon which conclusions can be based as to whether the matter complained of violates the antitrust laws. The evidentiary principles followed by this Commission are the same as are applicable in hearings before other administrative agencies. The Commission is not obliged to apply in its hearings the rules of evidence developed for court proceedings.[50] Thus, while the basic safeguards respecting the use of evidence in trials also apply to its hearings, the Commission's rules do not go into detail beyond such fundamental precepts, and their effect is largely determined from case to case. The very general character of those rules was recently summarized as follows by Chief Judge Stephens:[51]

"In the early history of the development of federal administrative agencies it was thought by some of the federal courts that the silence of the Congress, in statutes creating agencies, on the subject of the rules of evidence and procedure freed the agencies from the so-called 'technical rules' or 'strict rules' of evidence, pleading, and procedure; and some state statutes expressly assumed to free local administrative agencies from such rules.

---

[50] Federal Trade Commission v. Cement Institute, 333 U.S. 683, 705 (1948).

[51] Dissenting, in Dolcin Corp. v. Federal Trade Commission, 219 F.2d 751, at 753-759 (D.C. Cir. 1954), *cert. denied,* 348 U.S. 981 (1955).

But it was ultimately decided in the United States courts that administrative agencies are not relieved from the essentials of the adjective law for the reason that those essentials embrace the essentials to fair hearing contemplated by the due process clause of the Constitution. The rulings of the Supreme Court on this subject are epitomized in *Ohio Bell Tel. Co.* v. *Comm'n.* (1937), 301 U.S. 292, 304, 305.

* * *

"The Federal Trade Commission has in its own rules recognized the force of the quoted rulings. The Commission's Rule 18 (a) provides that the trial examiner 'shall admit relevant, material and competent evidence, but shall exclude irrelevant, immaterial and unduly repetitious evidence.' The Commission's Rule 14 (e) provides that the trial examiner 'is charged with the duty of conducting a fair and impartial hearing . . .' The Commission's Rule 15 (a) provides:

'Every party respondent shall have the right of due notice, cross-examination, presentation of evidence, objection, exception, motion, argument, appeal and all other fundamental rights * * * ,[The Federal Trade Commission Rules appear in their amended form in 15 U.S.C. § 45 (Supp. V, 1958).]

"One of the fundamentals of fair hearing in the Anglo-American legal system is that *both* sides shall be fully heard before a case is decided and a judgment entered. This means that all of the competent, relevant, material, non-cumulative evidence available to each party shall be heard and considered before the tribunal, whether court or administrative agency, decides. Moreover, the requirement that each party's competent, relevant, material, non-cumulative evidence shall be admitted and considered before a final decision is reached is applicable, subject to one limitation discussed below, as well to newly discovered evidence not available to a party by the exercise of due diligence during a trial as to evidence available and offered while a trial is in process. A party discovering, after the close of an adjudicatory proceeding, new evidence not discoverable by the exercise of due diligence during the proceeding would as much be denied full hearing by refusal of the tribunal to reopen the case and consider such evidence as if he had during the trial met with refusal by the tribunal to hear evidence then offered. Motions for new trial on the ground of newly discovered evidence are provided for by the Federal Rules of Civil Procedure. See Rule 60(b). . . . Moreover, the Federal Trade Commission Act itself provides, in Section 5(b), 38 STAT. 720 (1914), as amended, 15 U.S.C. § 45(b) (1952), for the reopening of a case by the Commission itself at any time before the filing of the record under a petition for review, and provides also, in Section 5(c), 38 STAT. 720 (1914), as amended, 15 U.S.C. § 45(c) (1952), for the adducing of additional evidence before the Commission, after the filing of the record and pending review, upon order of the court of appeals. . . .

"The most recent rulings of the Supreme Court pertinent to the question presently under discussion are *Universal Camera Corp.* v. *Labor Bd.*, 340 U.S. 474 (1951) and *Labor Board* v. *Pittsburgh S.S. Co.*, 340 U.S. 498 (1951).

* * *

"There is but one limitation upon the duty of a court or commission to reopen for newly discovered competent, relevant, material, non-cumulative evidence, to wit, that evidence must be of such character as will probably bring about a result different from that reached by the tribunal without such evidence. . . ."

(5) Enforcement and Judicial Review of F.T.C. Orders

We must distinguish between cease and desist orders based on Section 5 of the Federal Trade Commission Act, and those issued under Section 11 of the Clayton Act. The statutory procedure which governs in the former case makes the order unattackable if the respondent does not appeal the matter to a federal court of appeals within 60 days after the order issues. Violation of such an order is punished by penalty collected through a civil suit brought in the federal district courts by, and at the discretion of the Department of Justice.[52]

Cease and desist orders issued under the Clayton Act do not automatically become final upon the expiration of a fixed period of time. If the respondent fails or neglects to obey the order, the Commission must proceed for enforcement in a United States court of appeals. In applying for enforcement, the Commission has to show that a violation of the order has occurred.[53] While there is a civil penalty provision in the Federal Trade Commission Act, the only remedy available to the Government under the Clayton Act is a proceeding for contempt.

Recently, the Supreme Court passed upon the following important enforcement aspect of the Clayton Act, on which two courts of appeals had disagreed:

---

[52] F.T.C. Act, § 5(1), 52 STAT. 111 (1938), 15 U.S.C. § 45(1) (1952).

[53] Clayton Act, § 11, 38 STAT. 734 (1914), 15 U.S.C. § 21 (1952). Federal Trade Commission v. Ruberoid Co., 343 U.S. 470, 479 (1952).

MOOG INDUSTRIES, INC. v. FEDERAL TRADE COMMISSION

FEDERAL TRADE COMMISSION v. C. E. NIEHOFF & CO.

Supreme Court of the United States 78 S.Ct. 377 (1958)[54]

"PER CURIAM.

"The general question presented by these two cases is whether it is within the scope of the reviewing authority of a Court of Appeals to postpone the operation of a valid cease and desist order of the Federal Trade Commission against a single firm until similar orders have been entered against that firm's competitors. In proceedings arising out of alleged violations of the price discrimination provisions of the Clayton Act, § 2, 38 Stat. 730, as amended by the Robinson-Patman Act, 49 Stat. 1526, 15 U.S.C. § 13, two Courts of Appeals reached opposed results on this underlying issue. In order to resolve the conflict we granted certiorari, 353 U.S. 908, 982.

"In No. 77, Petitioner (Moog Industries, Inc.) was found by the Commission to have violated the Act and was ordered to cease and desist from further violation. 51 F.T.C. 931. Petitioner sought review in the United States Court of Appeals for the Eighth Circuit. Upon affirmance of the order, 238 F.2d 43, petitioner moved the court to hold the entry of judgment in abeyance on the ground that petitioner would suffer serious financial loss if prohibited from engaging in pricing practices open to its competitors. The court denied the requested relief.

"In No. 110, respondent (C. E. Niehoff & Co.) requested the Commission to hold in abeyance the cease and desist order that had been recommended by the hearing examiner, on the ground that respondent would have to go out of business if compelled to sell at a uniform price while its competitors were not under similar restraint. The Commission found that respondent had violated the Act and, in issuing its order, denied respondent's request. 51 F.T.C. 1114, 1153. On review in the United States Court of Appeals for the Seventh Circuit, the Commission's determination of statutory violation was affirmed; however, the court (one judge dissenting) directed that the cease and desist order should take effect 'at such time in the future as the United States Court of Appeals for the Seventh Circuit may direct, *sua sponte* or upon motion of the Federal Trade Commission.' 241 F.2d 37, 43.

"In view of the scope of administrative discretion that Congress has given the Federal Trade Commission, it is ordinarily

---

[54] *Cf.* P. & D. Mfg. Co., Inc. v. Federal Trade Commission, 245 F.2d 281, 282 (7th Cir. 1957), *cert. denied*, 355 U.S. 884 (1957); E. Edelmann & Co. v. Federal Trade Commission, 239 F.2d 152 (7th Cir. 1956), *cert. denied*, 78 S.Ct. 426 (1958).

not for courts to modify ancillary features of a valid Commission order. This is but recognition of the fact that in the shaping of its remedies within the framework of regulatory legislation, an agency is called upon to exercise its specialized, experienced judgment. Thus, the decision as to whether or not an order against one firm to cease and desist from engaging in illegal price discrimination should go into effect before others are similarly prohibited depends on a variety of factors peculiarly within the expert understanding of the Commission. Only the Commission, for example, is competent to make an initial determination as to whether and to what extent there is a relevant 'industry' within which the particular respondent competes and whether or not the nature of that competition is such as to indicate identical treatment of the entire industry by an enforcement agency. Moreover, although an allegedly illegal practice may appear to be operative throughout an industry, whether such appearances reflect fact and whether all firms in the industry should be dealt with in a single proceeding or should receive individualized treatment are questions that call for discretionary determination by the administrative agency. It is clearly within the special competence of the Commission to appraise the adverse effect on competition that might result from postponing a particular order prohibiting continued violations of the law. Furthermore, the Commission alone is empowered to develop that enforcement policy best calculated to achieve the ends contemplated by Congress and to allocate its available funds and personnel in such a way as to execute its policy efficiently and economically.

"The question, then, of whether orders such as those before us should be held in abeyance until the respondents' competitors are proceeded against is for the Commission to decide. If the question has not been raised before the Commission, as was the situation in No. 77, a reviewing court should not in any event entertain it. If the Commission has decided the question, its discretionary determination should not be overturned in the absence of a patent abuse of discretion. Accordingly, the judgment in No. 77 is affirmed, and the judgment in No. 110 is vacated and the cause remanded to the Court of Appeals with directions to affirm the order of the Commission in its entirety.

"*It is so ordered.*

"Mr. JUSTICE WHITTAKER took no part in the consideration or decision of these cases."

Chapter 8

EQUITY, CRIMINAL AND DAMAGE SUITS

Congress has harnessed together several procedural devices to achieve the ends of the antitrust laws: administrative agency actions by the Federal Trade Commission, equity suits brought either by the Department of Justice, Antitrust Division, or by private persons, damage suits and criminal actions. The prior chapter was devoted to the role of the Federal Trade Commission. We here briefly discuss some recent developments as to the remaining modes of enforcement.

(1) Equitable Relief

The antitrust laws empower federal district courts to prevent and to restrain violations of the antitrust laws.

Injunctions may be sought either by the attorney general[1] or by private persons.[2] Justice Rutledge referred to the nature of injunctions under the antitrust laws in the following terms:[3]

"The antitrust injunction suit is in form 'a proceeding in equity.' In substance, it is a public prosecution, with civil rather than criminal sanctions, for vindication of public right and for redress and prevention of public injury. To regard the fashioning of appropriate relief in such a suit as identical with the same function in private litigation is to disregard at once the former's statutory origin, its public character, and the public interest it protects. The equitable garb of the proceeding therefore does not determine or conceal its true character. Nor does it limit the

---

[1] Section 4 of the Sherman Act, 26 STAT. 209 (1890), 15 U.S.C. § 4, (1952) and Section 15 of the Clayton Act, 38 STAT. 736 (1914), 15 U.S.C. § 25 (1952), reprinted in the appendix. For a discussion of the general principles and procedures applied by the Antitrust Division of the Department of Justice in investigating and trying antitrust cases, see the various papers reprinted in AN ANTITRUST HANDBOOK at 235-329 and 435-517 (ABA Section of Antitrust Law ed. 1958).

[2] Section 16 of the Clayton Act, 38 STAT. 737 (1914), 15 U.S.C. § 26 (1952), reprinted in the appendix.

[3] Hartford-Empire Co. v. United States, 323 U.S. 386, at 441-442 (1945), Justice Rutledge dissenting in part.

required relief merely to what will prevent repetition of the illegal conduct by which the combination has been formed, its property acquired, and its dominating position secured."

The purpose and extent of the antitrust injunction were discussed in *Local* 167 v. *United States*:[4] "The United States is entitled to effective relief [in antitrust cases]. To that end the decree should enjoin acts of the sort that are shown by the evidence to have been done or threatened in furtherance of the conspiracy. It should be broad enough to prevent evasion. In framing its provisions doubts should be resolved in favor of the Government and against the conspirators."

(a) *Neutralizing unlawful power*

In the field of equitable relief, Judge Wyzanski's careful considerations in *United States* v. *United Shoe Machinery Corp.*[5] deserve special attention. It is interesting to note that there was no separate evidentiary hearing on relief in this case. Instead, Judge Wyzanski not only heard testimony relating to United's practices but he also explored alternative courses of conduct. He questioned witnesses at considerable length concerning the feasibility of various measures for relief. Subsequent to trial, the parties were given full opportunity to submit briefs and oral argument on that question.

The combined procedure lends itself to immediate enforcement of appropriate remedies in the event the suit terminates in a decision adverse to the defendant. This permits an earlier restoration of competitive conditions while eliminating further protracted and expensive pleadings and hearings.

The carefully formulated legal and economic considerations underlying the moderate provisions for relief in this opinion make it a worthwhile study on equitable remedy. The court applied a combination of remedies which shows the nature and flexibility of equitable relief in rectifying situations violating the antitrust laws. For these reasons, we here present the pertinent part of the opinion:[6]

---

[4] 291 U.S. 293, at 299 (1934).

[5] 110 F.Supp. 295 (D. Mass. 1953), *aff'd per curiam*, 347 U.S. 521 (1954). For a discussion of the principles governing enforcement, see, *e.g.*, Kilgore, *Antitrust Judgments and Their Enforcement*, in AN ANTITRUST HANDBOOK 331 (ABA Section of Antitrust Law ed. 1958); and Brown, *Injunctions and Divestiture*, *id.*, at 535. Considerations shaping enforcement policies are discussed by Hansen, *Current Antitrust Policy*, in 1957 CCH ANTITRUST LAW SYMPOSIUM 25 (1957).

[6] 110 F.Supp. at 346-351.

"Opinion on Remedy.

"Where a defendant has monopolized commerce in violation of § 2, the principal objects of the decree are to extirpate practices that have caused or may hereafter cause monopolization, and to restore workable competition in the market.

"A trial judge, until he is otherwise directed by the Supreme Court or Congress, (see 110 F.Supp. 345, footnote 2, *supra*), must frame a decree upon the basis of the presuppositions underlying *Aluminum* and *Griffith*. He must accept these as the premises of the current interpretation of § 2 of the Sherman Act. Concentrations of power, no matter how beneficently they appear to have acted, nor what advantages they seem to possess, are inherently dangerous. Their good behavior in the past may not be continued; and if their strength were hereafter grasped by presumptuous hands, there would be no automatic check and balance from equal forces in the industrial market. In the absence of this protective mechanism, the demand for public regulation, public ownership, or other drastic measures would become irresistible in the time of crisis. Dispersal of private economic power is thus one of the ways to preserve the system of private enterprise. Moreover, well as a monopoly may have behaved in the moral sense, its economic performance is inevitably suspect. The very absence of strong competitors implies that there cannot be an objective measuring rod of the monopolist's excellence, and the test of its performance must, therefore, be largely theoretical. What appears to the outsider to be a sensible, prudent, nay even a progressive policy of the monopolist, may in fact reflect a lower scale of adventurousness and less intelligent risk-taking than would be the case if the enterprise were forced to respond to a stronger industrial challenge. Some truth lurks in the cynical remark that not high profits but a quiet life is the chief reward of monopoly power. And even if a particular enterprise seeks growth and not repose, an increased rate in the growth of ideas does not follow from an increased concentration of power. Industrial advance may indeed be in inverse proportion to economic power; for creativity in business as in other areas, is best nourished by multiple centers of activity, each following its unique pattern and developing its own esprit de corps to respond to the challenge of competition. The dominance of any one enterprise inevitably unduly accentuates that enterprise's experience and views as to what is possible, practical, and desirable with respect to technological development, research, relations with producers, employees, and customers. And the preservation of any unregulated monopoly is hostile to the industrial and political ideals of an open society founded on the faith that tomorrow will produce better than the best.

"Yet a trial judge's decree attempting to recreate a competitive market should be drafted in the spirit which has been attributed to Lord Acton—the most philosophical mind that has ever been directed to the evils of concentration of power. 'No one can be sure what view Acton would have adopted on contemporary economic issues. What is certain is the principles and tests he would have employed. Of every proposal he would have asked, Is it just? Is it in accordance with the permanent will of the community? Is it practicable? Will it be efficient? Will it increase or diminish real freedom?' Fasnacht, Acton's Political Philosophy (1952), p. 124.

"Judges, in prescribing remedies have known their own limitations. They do not *ex officio* have economic or political training. Their prophecies as to the economic future are not guided by unusually subtle judgment. They are not so representative as other branches of the government. The recommendations they receive from government prosecutors do not always reflect the overall approach of even the executive branch of the government, sometimes not indeed the seasoned and fairly informed judgment of the head of the Department of Justice. Hearings in the court do not usually give the remote judge as sound a feeling for the realities of a situation as other procedures do. Judicial decrees must be fitted into the framework of what a busy, and none too expert, court can supervise. Above all, no matter with what authority he is invested, with what facts and opinions he is supplied, a trial judge is only one man, and should move with caution and humility.

"That considerations of this type have always affected antitrust courts is plain from the history of the *Standard Oil, American Tobacco* and *Alcoa* cases. To many champions of the antitrust laws these cases indicate judicial timidity, economic innocence, lack of conviction, or paralysis of resolution. Yet there is another way of interpreting this judicial history. In the antitrust field the courts have been accorded, by common consent, an authority they have in no other branch of enacted law. Indeed, the only comparable examples of the power of judges is the economic rule they formerly exercised under the Fourteenth Amendment, and the role they now exercise in the area of civil liberties. They would not have been given, or allowed to keep, such authority in the antitrust field, and they would not so freely have altered from time to time the interpretation of its substantive provisions, if courts were in the habit of proceeding with the surgical ruthlessness that might commend itself to those seeking absolute assurance that there will be workable competition, and to those aiming at immediate realization of the social, political, and economic advantages of dispersal of power.

"Such self-restraining considerations have peculiar force in this case. Until Alcoa lost its case in 1945, there was no significant reason to suppose that United's conduct violated § 2 of the Sherman Act. The Supreme Court has three times, in *United States* v. *Winslow*, 227 U.S. 202, *United States* v. *United Shoe Machinery Company of N.J.*, 247 U.S. 32, and *United Shoe*

Machinery Corp. v. *United States,* 258 U.S. 451, reviewed aspects of this company's, or its predecessor's, activities. What United is now doing is similar to what it was then doing, but the activities which were similar stood uncondemned,—indeed, one ought to go further and say they were in part endorsed. On the face of these decisions, it would be anomalous to charge the officers of United with any moral deficiency.

"In the light of these general considerations, it is now meet to consider four of the principal problems respecting a proposed decree: first, dissolution, second, treatment of the leases, third, divestiture of supply activities, and fourth, patents.

"The Government's proposal that the Court dissolve United into three separate manufacturing companies is unrealistic. United conducts all machine manufacture at one plant in Beverly, with one set of jigs and tools, one foundry, one laboratory for machinery problems, one managerial staff, and one labor force. It takes no Solomon to see that this organism cannot be cut into three equal and viable parts.

"Nor can the division of United's business be fairly accomplished by dividing the manufacture of machinery into three broad categories, and then issuing an injunction restraining the Beverly plant from manufacturing two broad categories of machine types, and vesting in each of two new companies the right to manufacture one of those categories. Such an order would create for the new companies the most serious type of problems respecting the acquisition of physical equipment, the raising of new capital, the allotment of managerial and labor forces, and so forth. The prospect of creating three factories where one grew before has not been thought through by its proponents.

"A petition for dissolution should reflect greater attention to practical problems and should involve supporting economic data and prophesies such as are presented in corporate reorganization and public utility dissolution cases. Moreover, the petition should involve a more formal commitment by the Attorney General, than is involved in the divergent proposals that his assistants have made in briefs and in oral arguments addressed to the Court.

"On the whole, therefore, the suggested remedy of dissolution is rejected.

"From the opinion on defendant's violations it follows that some form of relief regarding defendant's leases and leasing practices is proper and necessary.

"The Government does not propose that United should cease leasing machines. It does suggest that this Court order defendant to eliminate from the leases those provisions found to be restrictive, to offer for sale every type of machine which it offers for lease, and to make the sales terms somewhat more advantageous to customers, than the lease terms.

"The Court agrees that it would be undesirable, at least until milder remedies have been tried, to direct United to abolish leasing forthwith. United is free to abolish leasing if it chooses to do so, but this Court hesitates to lay down any absolute ban for two reasons. First, if a ban were immediately applied, a substantial number of shoe factories would probably be put out of business, for they have not the assets, nor the capacity to borrow, requisite to purchase machines, even on conditional sales agreements. Second, if this Court forbade United to lease machines, it could not apply a similar ban to its competitors. This would constitute for United a major not a minor competitive handicap if one accepts the testimony of the large number of shoe manufacturers who have already expressed their preference for leasing rather than buying machines. How deeply rooted is this preference might be disputed; but it cannot be denied that virtually all the shoe manufacturers who took the stand, and the 45 shoe manufacturers who were selected as a sample by the Court, expressed a preference for the leasing system. It is, of course, possible that through inertia, fear of reprisal, or other motives, those who opposed the leasing system did not speak up. Moreover, Compo, which is United's chief rival, and which the Government claims was a chief victim of United policies, favors the leasing system, and might encourage shoe factories to continue leasing.

"Although leasing should not now be abolished by judicial decree, the Court agrees with the Government that the leases should be purged of their restrictive features. In the decree filed herewith, the term of the lease is shortened, the full capacity clause is eliminated, the discriminatory commutative charges are removed, and United is required to segregate its charges for machines from its charges for repair service. For the most part, the decree speaks plainly enough upon these points. Yet, on two matters, a further word is in order.

"The decree does not prohibit United from rendering service, because, in the Court's view, the rendition of service, if separately charged for, has no exclusionary effects. Moreover, the rendition of service by United will keep its research and manufacturing divisions abreast of technological problems in the shoe manufacturing industry; and this will be an economic advantage of the type fostered by the Sherman Act.

"Nor does the decree attempt to deal with that feature of United's pricing policy which discriminates between machine types. To try to extirpate such discrimination would require either an order directing a uniform rate of markup, or an order subjecting each price term and each price change to judicial supervision. Neither course would be sound. Some price discrimination, if not too rigid, is inevitable. Some may be justified as resting on patent monopolies. Some price discrimination is economically desirable, if it promotes competition in a market where several multiproduct firms compete. And while price discrimination has been an evidence of United's monopoly power, a buttress to it, and a cause of its perpetuation, its eradication cannot be accomplished without turning United into a public utility, and the Court into a public utility commission, or requiring United to observe a general injunction of non-discrimination between different products—an injunction which would be contrary to sound theory, which would require the use of practices not followed in any business known to the Court, and which could not be enforced.

"The Court also agrees with the Government that if United chooses to continue to lease any machine type, it must offer that type of machine also for sale. The principal merit of this proposal does not lie in its primary impact, that is, in its effect in widening the choices open to owners of shoe factories. For present purposes it may be assumed that the antitrust laws are not designed, chiefly, if at all, to give a customer choice as to the selling methods by which the supplier offers that supplier's own product. The merit of the Government's proposal is in its secondary impact. Insofar as United's machines are sold rather than leased, they will ultimately, in many cases, reach a second-hand market. From that market, United will face a type of substitute competition which will gradually weaken the prohibited market power which it now exercises. Moreover, from that market, or from United itself, a competitor of United can acquire a United machine in order to study it, to copy its unpatented features, and to experiment with improvements in, or alterations of, the machine. Thus, in another and more direct way, United's market power will be diminished.

"Furthermore, the creation of a sales market together with the purging of the restrictive features of the leases will, in combination, gradually diminish the magnetic hold now exercised by what United properly describes as the partnership features of the leasing system. As United's relationships with its customers grow feebler, competitors will have an enhanced opportunity to market their wares.

"Two objections to this proposal should now be answered.

"First, United emphasizes the point that if a decree requires United to offer for sale all machine types which it leases, the decree will discriminate against United because its competitors will be subject to no parallel injunction. United says that this discrimination violates United's legal rights. In support of this contention, United relies upon the language in *Hartford-Empire Company* v. *United States*, 323 U.S. 386, 409-410, in which a judicial decree was modified, because it placed a defendant 'for the future, "in a different class than other people"'. But that ruling of the Supreme Court of the United States does not apply to the case at bar, because, through its own action, United has already put itself in a class different from any of its competitors.

It has used its leases to monopolize the shoe machinery market. And if leasing continues without an alternative sales system, United will still be able to monopolize that market. To root out monopolization and to bring United, in the future, in the same class as its competitors, it is necessary not merely to place limitations upon United's leases, but also to require United to offer for sale any machine type which it leases. While, on its face, the decree seems to discriminate against United, in the context of the market situation created by United itself, the effect of the decree is to break down barriers erected by a monopolizer, so that, hereafter, there may be no wall between the class in which it is and the class in which its competitors are.

"A second possible objection to the decree is that it confers upon United's competitors the unearned opportunity to copy the unpatented features of United's machines. These competitors get a free ride.

"In reply, it might be enough to say that there does not appear to be any federal or local, statutory or common law, principle protecting United's interest in these unpatented features. See *Cheney Bros.* v. *Doris Silk Corp.*, 2 Cir., 35 F.2d 279. That is, the decree takes from United nothing which the policy of our law protects. A further answer is that if the creation of a sales alternative to leasing is, as this Court believes, necessary to dissipate United's monopoly power, the Court should not withhold its decree because its effect is to allow competitors to copy United's design. *Cf. Fashion Originators' Guild of America, Inc.* v. *Federal Trade Commission*, 312 U.S. 457, 468.

"The Government goes one step further and asks the Court to require defendant to make its sales terms more attractive to customers than any lease terms it offers. One difficulty with this proposal is that, instead of redressing the balance between United and its competitors, it would give a marked advantage to such of United competitors as chose to continue leasing machines. But there are even more serious practical objections. If this Court were to direct United to make its sales terms more favorable than lease terms, and to keep that discrimination effective every time that new terms were set, every time that new machine types were introduced, and every time that money rates changed in the financial world, this Court would be creating administrative problems which would require its continuous judicial supervision. To avoid the difficulties just stated, it seems to the Court sufficient to direct defendant, if it offers any machine type for lease, to set such terms for leasing that machine as do not make it substantially more advantageous for a shoe factory to lease rather than to buy a machine. Admittedly, there is in this direction some flexibility. But defendant is forewarned by the decree itself that if it abuses this flexibility, the Court after the entry of this decree may modify it. Thus the decree invokes the precedent not of Drace, but of Damocles and Dionysius.

Compare *Appalachian Coals, Inc.* v. *United States*, 288 U.S. 344, 378.

"One other phase of the decree to which this opinion should expressly avert is the method of handling those subsidiaries and branches which produce supplies in fields which United has monopolized. The clearest example are nails and tacks, and eyelets for the shoe machinery market. These are large scale monopolizations attributable to the machinery monopoly. And United should be divested of its business of manufacturing and distributing these particular supplies, because this is the kind of dissolution which can be carried out practically, and which will also reduce monopoly power in each of the affected supply fields. Logically, the same principle might be applied to those other parts of United's enterprise which manufactures other supplies that United monopolizes. But in each of the other cases where this might at first blush seem reasonable, the supply is technically so intimately related to a machine as to be naturally manufactured by the maker of the machine, or the supply is sold in such small annual volume, or the difficulties of enforcing divestiture of part of the plant are so obvious, as to make the extension of the decree to those instances undesirable.

"No similar practical difficulties exist in ordering United to divest itself of its business of distributing supplies manufactured by companies which are not part of United's organization. The annual dollar volume of some of these supplies, if looked at individually, is often not large; but the annual volume of all of them together is roughly $4½ million. The specifications for some of these supplies did originate with United, but their continued manufacture does not require United's assistance. Their distribution could be economically undertaken, if not by the several manufacturers, by a new supply distributor. And United ought not to be allowed to continue these distributorships because they flowed to United partly, at any rate, as an indirect consequence of United's prohibited monopolization of shoe machinery. To be sure, other advantages flowed to United from its monopolization; but the particular advantages inherent in the large scale distribution of supplies are, as already noted, easily severable, and would probably lead to the organization of a new supply company, or the expansion of an existing supply company, which could become in time a manufacturer of certain machine types, or a source of repair service. Thus the total effect would be to develop avenues for the dissipation of United's monopoly power in the machinery field.

"Similar reasoning dictates the decree's treatment of patents. Defendant is not being punished for abusive practices respecting patents, for it engaged in none, except possibly two decades ago in connection with the wood heel business. It is being required to reduce the monopoly power it has, not as a result of patents, but as a result of business practices. And compulsory licensing,

on a reasonable royalty basis, is in effect a partial solution, on a
non-confiscatory basis. In regard to patents, as in regard to the
termination of supply distributorships, the decree does no more
than what defendant's own expert recognized would be appropriate if the Court found defendant had monopolized the shoe
machinery market."

(b) *Consent decrees*

There are times when a person charged with violating a federal antitrust law chooses to forego his right to a trial of the
facts and agrees to be bound by a court order based on stipulated facts. Such an order is a judicial act binding on both the
Government and the defendant just as if it had been entered
after litigation.[7]

Of 171 civil antitrust actions terminated between 1935 and
1950, 134, or 78 per cent, were settled by consent judgment and
37 were tried.[8] Between May 1, 1953, and March 1, 1956, of the
106 civil cases terminated, 80, or 75 per cent, resulted in consent
decrees.[9]

The Government is interested in consent judgments because
it believes it can thereby obtain effective enforcement of the
antitrust laws without the cost in men and resources of a protracted trial. Based on a recent study, the Department of Justice found that the average litigated case required 5½ years from
filing of the complaint to entry of final judgment. By contrast,
consent decrees required an average of 2½ years.[10]

Defendants are interested in the consent judgment route because they avoid the bad publicity a public trial might bring,
and the court order entered by consent cannot be used as a
basis for a treble damage suit.[11] As 75 per cent of private treble

---

[7] United States v. Swift & Co., 286 U.S. 106, 114-115 (1932). For a
recent review of the history, nature, and use of consent decrees, see Comment, *A Re-Analysis of Consent Decrees,* 55 MICH. L.REV. 92 (1956),
and materials and authorities cited therein. See also Barnes, *Settlement by
Consent Judgment,* in 4 ABA ANTITRUST SECTION REPORT 8 (April
1954).

[8] Quoted by the Assistant Attorney General in charge of the Antitrust
Division, in Distribution Problems, *Hearing Before Subcommittee No. 5 of
the Select House Committee on Small Business,* Part V, Antitrust Consent
Decrees, A Case Study—The A. T. & T. Consent Decree, 84th Cong., 2d
Sess., at 6 (1956).

[9] *Ibid.*

[10] *Id.,* 4. For the fiscal year ending June 30, 1958, Congress appropriated $3,785,000 to the Department of Justice for the enforcement of anti-
trust laws. 71 STAT. 55 (1957).

[11] See Section 5 of the Clayton Act in the appendix and the discussion
under "Damage Suits" later in this chapter.

damage suits follow successful Government prosecution, a consent judgment sharply cuts the possibilities of success in a subsequent private treble damage suit.[12]

The possible contents, scope, and importance of consent decrees can best be shown by presenting an example. One of the most interesting and far-reaching consent decrees ever entered has been entered recently in *United States* v. *United Fruit Co.*[12a] United and its subsidiaries are a fully integrated business engaged in Latin America and in the United States in the production, purchase, transportation, processing, handling, distribution, and sale of bananas. In 1954, suit was brought by the Attorney General under the Wilson Tariff Act and sections 1 and 2 of the Sherman Act, on the grounds that United had restricted and monopolized the banana business on various levels, being in a position, for example, to dictate banana prices in the United States and to exclude competitors. United had built up its great banana monopoly through its ownership of most of the land suitable for growing bananas in Latin America, through its control over International Railways of Central America, through its control over a fleet of ships transporting bananas to the United States, and through control over the distribution of bananas in the United States.

Rather than spend further years fighting an antitrust suit which it might lose in the end, United agreed (1) to dispose of its interest in a banana selling corporation and thus to be confined to importing; (2) to omit numerous restrictive trade practices or agreements involving the production, transportation and importation of bananas; (3) to divest itself of its interest in a railway in Central America; and, most importantly, (4) to create, out of its own assets, a new independent competitor capable of importing into the United States nine million stems of bananas per year. This is roughly a third of United Fruit's present imports. The detailed consent decree sets forth the method of accomplishing these ends. The following are its most important provisions:

---

[12] Distribution Problems, *Hearing Before the Subcommittee No. 5 of the Select House Committee on Small Business*, Part V, Antitrust Consent Decrees, A Case Study—The A. T. & T. Consent Decree, 84th Cong., 2d Sess. 7 (1956).

[12a] 1958 CCH TRADE CASES Para. 68,941 (E.D.La. 1958).

"Final Judgment

"SEYBOURNE, H. LYNNE, District Judge.

"Plaintiff United States of America, having filed its complaint herein on July 2, 1954, and its amended complaint herein on January 12, 1956, and defendant, United Fruit Company having appeared and having filed its answer to the amended complaint on February 10, 1956, denying the substantive allegations thereof, and plaintiff and said defendant having severally consented to the making and entry of this Final Judgment without trial or adjudication of any issue of fact or law herein and without admission in respect to any issue;

"Now, Therefore, before any testimony has been taken and without trial or adjudication of any issue of fact or law herein, and upon consent of the parties hereto, it is hereby

"Ordered, Adjudged, and Decreed as follows:

    * * *

IV

"United is enjoined and restrained from engaging anywhere in the United States, directly or indirectly, in the business of ripening, processing and selling bananas, provided, however, that United may continue the present business of Banana Selling Corporation until its liquidation, which shall be completed within nine months from the effective date of this Final Judgment, and provided, further, that nothing in this Final Judgment shall restrain or prohibit United from salvaging, processing and selling to anyone bananas which arrive at a United States port in a ripened or damaged condition or which are damaged at the terminal.

    * * *

VII

"(A) Not later than June 30, 1966, United shall divest itself of all of the capital stock (whether common or preferred) or other proprietary interest in International Railways of Central America that United then owns, either (1) by a private sale of the said capital stock to purchasers who have no relationship or affiliation directly or indirectly with United, or (2) by sale of the said capital stock on the open market on the New York Stock Exchange, the London Stock Exchange or on any other stock exchange on which the said stock may be listed, or (3) by a private sale of part of the said capital stock to purchasers who have no relationship or affiliation directly or indirectly with United and by sale of the other part on the open market or on a stock exchange as aforesaid.

"(B) At any time and from time to time prior to June 30, 1966 United may dispose of all or any part of any stock or proprietary interest which it now owns in International Railways of Central America, either by private sale to purchasers who have no relationship or affiliation directly or indirectly with

United, or by sale on the open market on any stock exchange in which the stock may be listed.

"(C) On and after the date on which United shall have divested itself of all of its capital stock and proprietary interest in International Railways of Central America, as provided for in subsections (A) and (B) above, United and its officers and directors are enjoined and restrained from acquiring or holding, directly or indirectly, any legal or beneficial interest in any capital stock of International Railways of Central America.

VIII

"(A) United shall distribute to the shareholders of United all the capital stock of a company (hereinafter referred to as the 'New Company') organized by United and having from United assets (or all of the capital stock of a company or companies owning directly or indirectly such assets), including liquid assets, producing banana lands and banana purchase arrangements, ships, terminal arrangements, and other essential accessory assets, reasonably calculated to be capable of importing into the East Coast, Gulf Coast and/or West Coast ports of the United States approximately 9,000,000 stems of bananas per year and staffed with managerial and other personnel in a manner reasonably calculated to enable the New Company to conduct the operations of the banana business available to it by virtue of its properties and assets. . . . Prior to or contemporaneously with such distribution of stock, United shall take such actions or enter into such arrangements as are reasonably calculated to enable the New Company to distribute and sell bananas imported by it in such of the three major geographical marketing areas of the United States as the management of the New Company shall determine to be in its best interests in the light of all relevant factors. . . . If a distribution of the capital stock of a company organized by United is not made pursuant to the provisions of this paragraph (A), then

"(B) United shall sell to an Eligible Person (as hereinafter defined) production and transportation assets (or the capital stock of a company or companies owning directly or indirectly such assets), including producing banana lands or banana purchase arrangements, ships, and other essential accessory assets, reasonably calculated to be capable of importing annually into the East Coast, Gulf Coast and/or West Coast ports of the United States approximately 9,000,000 stems of bananas per year. . . .

* * *

"(D) The term 'Eligible Person' as used in this Final Judgment shall mean any individual, group or business organization, other than Standard Fruit and Steamship Company, that is not owned or controlled by United and in which United has no stock interest directly or indirectly and that makes a showing that it intends to engage in the importation of bananas into the United States.

"(E) Not later than June 30, 1966 United shall submit to this Court for approval a plan for compliance with the obligation imposed upon United by the provisions of Paragraphs (A), (B) or (C) above and shall serve upon the plaintiff a copy of the plan a reasonable time in advance of the submission. The plan shall provide for compliance with reasonable promptness but in any event not more than four (4) years after final approval of the plan.

"If, after hearing, the Court considers that performance of the plan will constitute compliance with the obligations provided by that Paragraph of this Article VIII under which the plan is submitted, the Court shall approve the plan. If the Court considers that performance of the plan will not constitute compliance with one or more of such obligations and specifies the obligation or obligations provided by such Paragraph as to which it considers the plan deficient, the Court shall require United promptly to prepare and propose for approval amendments calculated to achieve such compliance and if the Court considers that performance of the plan as so amended will constitute compliance with the obligations of such Paragraph, the Court shall approve the plan as so amended.

"Performance of such a plan approved as originally submitted or as amended shall be deemed to be full compliance with the obligations imposed upon United by this Article VIII.

    ❋ ❋ ❋

X

"(A) United is ordered and directed within two months after the entry of this Final Judgment to submit to its stockholders any portions of this Final Judgment as to which the consent of the stockholders is required by the corporate charter of United, and the board of directors of United shall recommend to said stockholders that said consent be given. If the required consent is given, on the day following United shall file with this Court a statement of that fact and the date of filing shall be the effective date of this Final Judgment.

"(B) This Final Judgment shall be of no further force and effect and this cause shall be restored to the docket for prompt trial without prejudice to either party if within three months from the date of entry of this Final Judgment the required majority in interest of the stockholders of United have not consented to all portions of this Final Judgment as to which such consent is required by the corporate charter of United.

    ❋ ❋ ❋

XVI

"Jurisdiction is retained for the purpose of enabling any of the parties to this Final Judgment to apply to this Court at any

time for such further orders and directions as may be necessary
or appropriate for the construction or carrying out of this Final
Judgment or for the modification or termination of any of the
provisions thereof, and for the enforcement of compliance therewith and punishment of violations thereof."

(c) *Applicability of antitrust decrees to third parties*

An antitrust decree is not binding upon, and therefore does
not determine the contractual rights of, a third party who was
not before the court. *General Aniline and Film Corp.* v. *Bayer
Co.*[13] However, the Attorney General of the United States was
able subsequently to nullify this state court decision so far as
General Aniline was concerned by making that company a party
to the antitrust proceeding. This was accomplished by serving
a supplemental complaint on General Aniline and persuading
the federal court to enlarge the decree against Bayer in order to
enjoin General Aniline from carrying out, or enforcing, any of
the contracts which were the basis of the original proceeding
against Bayer and which had been held to be illegal because in
violation of the antitrust laws.[14]

(d) *Derivative shareholder suits*

In *Fanchon & Marco, Inc.* v. *Paramount Pictures*[15] the court
recognized as proper the use of a derivative shareholder suit
under Section 16 of the Clayton Act[16] against a person not connected with the corporation: "[T]he antitrust derivative action
is quite thoroughly recognized as a proper suit in equity in those
cases which have questioned its availability at law, since the
shareholder's right to sue in the corporate stead must be first
established."

In *Schechtman* v. *Wolfson*,[17] an intracorporate derivative action by shareholders against directors of their own corporation
based on a violation of Section 8 of the Clayton Act (interlocking directorates), the plaintiff asked for an award of counsel's
fee. The district court denied the petition on the ground that
the primary remedy was with the Federal Trade Commission
from which plaintiff could have obtained "gratuitously" everything for which he now sued the corporation.

---

[13] 188 Misc. 929, 64 N.Y.S. 2d 492 (1946), *aff'd* 281 App. Div. 668, 117
N.Y.S. 2d 497 (1952); 305 N.Y. 479,113 N.E. 2d 844 (1953). See Note,
Consent Decrees and Absent Cartel Participants, 56 YALE L.J. 396 (1947).

[14] United States v. Bayer Co., Inc., 135 F.Supp. 65 (S.D. N.Y. 1955).

[15] 202 F.2d 731, at 734 (2d Cir. 1953).

[16] 38 STAT. 737 (1914), 15 U.S.C. § 26 (1952).

[17] 141 F.Supp. 453 (S.D. N.Y. 1956), *aff'd on other grounds,* 244 F.2d
537 (2d Cir. 1957). See Note, 66 YALE L.J. 413 (1957).

The court of appeals opposed this view:[18]

"There is nothing in the statute which restricts remedy against interlocking directorates to action by the Commission. It seems well known that the Commission has found little occasion, and perhaps little incentive, to take action in the premises. [Citation omitted.] Apparently competitors, who could sue under 15 U.S.C. § 15 or § 26, have little motivation to pursue this obviously preventive remedy against antitrust violations until there is more direct prospect of harm and of treble damages than mere interlocking suggests. . . . Vicarious prosecution has been quite usual and presumably effective in various areas of public interest, and there seems little doubt but that the spur of counsel fees adds greatly to the likelihood of private law enforcement. As urged in several critical notes on this case, 70 Harv. L.Rev. 369; 66 Yale L.J. 413; 105 U. of Pa. L.Rev. 261; 9 Stan. L.Rev. 387, it seems not in the public interest to require shareholders to await delaying or non-existent agency action. Enforcement of antitrust policy will be better advanced by complementary action within the group of both public and private interests. . . ."

(2) Criminal Suits

(a) *Scope and procedure*

What types of antitrust offenses are prosecuted criminally? The Assistant Attorney General in Charge of the Antitrust Division of the Department of Justice recently stated:[19]

"In general, the following types of offenses are prosecuted criminally: (1) price fixing; (2) other violations of the Sherman Act where there is proof of a specific intent to restrain trade or to monopolize; (3) a less easily defined category of cases which might generally be described as involving proof of use of predatory practices (boycotts, for example) to accomplish the objective of the combination or conspiracy; (4) the fact that a defendant has previously been convicted of or adjudged to have been, violating the antitrust laws may warrant indictment for a second offense. There are other factors taken into account in determining whether to seek an indictment in cases that may not fall precisely in any of these categories. The Division feels free to seek an indictment in any case where a prospective defendant has knowledge that practices similar to those in which he is engaged have been held to be in violation of the Sherman Act in a prior civil suit against the other persons.

    * * *

---

[18] 244 F.2d at 539. Footnote omitted. *Cf.* also Kogan v. Schenley Industries, Inc., 1956 CCH TRADE CASES Para. 68,554 (D. Del. 1956).

[19] Quoted in REPORT OF THE ATTORNEY GENERAL'S NATIONAL COMMITTEE TO STUDY THE ANTITRUST LAWS 350 (1955).

"It should also be added that in determining to bring a case on the criminal side, the Department does not foreclose itself from filing a companion civil case against the same defendants. This is done in situations where it is believed that in addition to the criminal penalties, effective injunctive relief can be obtained. On the other hand, we avoid filing civil actions where nothing more is involved than ordinary price fixing, because an injunction against price fixing adds nothing to the injunctions already contained in the Sherman Act itself."

Before a criminal action is brought, the following procedures are followed by the Antitrust Division:[20]

"In the first instance, a recommendation is made by the attorney in charge of the particular investigation. If he is in the field, his recommendation is then reviewed by his field office chief. It is then reviewed by the appropriate litigation section chief in Washington. The section chief's decision is reviewed by the first or second assistant to the Assistant Attorney General and by the Assistant Attorney General. Review at the various levels is effected not only by oral conferences, but also by written memomanda of facts detailing the evidence against each proposed defendant."

(b) *Criminal penalties under the Sherman Act*

Prior to 1955, the maximum fine for a criminal violation of the Sherman Act was $5,000. According to an analysis of the Antitrust Division, the average of fines assessed during the period from January 1, 1946, to February, 1954 was approximately $2,600. Numerous fines ranging from $100 to $500 were imposed.[21]

By Act of July 7, 1955,[22] Congress amended Sections 1, 2 and 3 of the Sherman Act by increasing the maximum fine to $50,000.

Heavy fines have been imposed under this provision. On June 18, 1957, a district judge imposed fines totalling $187,500 and suspended sentences against Safeway Stores, Inc., a corporation, and two individuals. The defendants pleaded *nolo contendere* to three charges: Count I, conspiracy to monopolize the retail grocery business in various cities in Texas and New Mexico, in violation of the Sherman Act; Count II, an attempt to monopolize such business in violation of the same Act; Count III, sales of goods in Texas at prices lower than those exacted in other parts of the United States, in violation of Section 3 of the Robin-

---

[20] *Ibid.* See Dobey, *Criminal Antitrust Trials,* in AN ANTITRUST HANDBOOK 277 (ABA Section of Antitrust Law ed. 1958).

[21] *Id.,* at 352.

[22] 69 STAT. 282 (1955), 15 U.S.C. §§ 1-3 (Supp. IV, 1957).

son-Patman Act. The fines and sentences were as follows: Safeway Stores, Inc.—$50,000 (Count I), $50,000 (Count II), and $5,000 (Count III); (2) Lingan A. Warren—$35,000 and a sentence of one year's imprisonment to be probated (Count I), $35,000 and one year's imprisonment to be probated and to run concurrently with the prison sentence of the first Count (Count II), and $5,000 (Count III); (3) Earl Cliff—$4,000 and one year's sentence to be probated (Count I), and $3,500 (Count II). Mr. Cliff was not named in Count III.[23]

(c) *Nolo contendere*

United States v. *Norris*[24] established that if a plea of *nolo contendere* is accepted by the court it is an implied confession of guilt and, for the purposes of the case only, equivalent to a plea of guilty. *Hudson* v. *United States*[25] established that a sentence of either fine and/or imprisonment may be imposed after a plea of *nolo contendere* was accepted.

In *United States* v. *Safeway Stores, Inc.*,[26] the district court, in view of the charges above stated and a civil suit pending before it, permitted the defendants to change their pleas from not guilty to *nolo contendere*. The decision presents an interesting discussion of two serious objections of the Government to the change in plea which the court rejected.

> "One of the principal grounds for objection is that Safeway is a multiple offender, and has been convicted or has plead *nolo contendere* in at least five other cases. . . .
>
> ＊　＊　＊
>
> "This record, says the Government, shows a disrespect by Safeway of the law. If this be accepted as a fact, it still does not follow that the defendants' plea of *nolo contendere* should be rejected in the case at the bar. The fact that the courts accepted pleas of *nolo contendere* in four of five cases cited by the Government indicates that the courts regarded this as the most practical, logical and just disposition of the cases. It has not been contended that justice was not done in those cases by acceptance of pleas of *nolo contendere*.
>
> ＊　＊　＊

---

[23] Criminal No. 9584 (N.D. Texas), CCH TRADE REGULATION REPORTS, Para. 45,003 (Case 1263). A total of $697,000 in fines were meted out in antitrust criminal suits during the first half of 1957. Dept. of Justice Press Release of August 19, 1957.

[24] 281 U.S. 619 (1930).

[25] 272 U.S. 451 (1925).

[26] 1957 CCH TRADE CASES Para. 68,770, at p. 73,133-136 (N.D. Texas 1957). See also United States v. B. F. Goodrich Co., 1957 CCH TRADE CASES Para. 68,713 (D. Colo. 1957).

"These prior convictions should have more bearing upon the sentence of punishment to be assessed than upon the issue pertaining to the acceptance or rejection of Safeway's plea of *nolo contendere*. In spite of a bad past record, there is nothing to prevent the court from permitting Safeway to enter its 'plea of guilt in Latin' and assessing the appropriate punishment forthwith.

"Another reason urged by the Government for rejecting Safeway's offered plea of *nolo contendere* is that acceptance would deprive private litigants of the benefits to be derived from a verdict of guilty under Section 5 of the Clayton Act. Under this section a contested judgment or decree rendered in a suit brought by the Government under the antitrust laws shall be *prima facie* evidence against the defendants as to all matters respecting which judgment or decree would be an estoppel as between the parties thereto.

". . . [T]he Court's view in the instant case has been accurately expressed as follows:[27]

'. . . the Government's responsibility in bringing cases of this nature is to vindicate the public interest in preserving a competitive economy rather than to redress private wrongs and recover damages for injuries sustained by individuals.'

"It is fundamental that the primary responsibility of the Government in a criminal case involves the consideration of public interests, not private interests.

"As stated by Judge Tolin in *United States* v. *Jones,* 119 F.Supp. 288 at 290 (S.D. Cal. 1954):

'. . . it is always important for Courts to avoid permitting criminal prosecutions to be used as a means of redressing civil wrongs and, by means of a criminal judgment, procuring either directly or indirectly some advantage in a civil case.'

"The Government cites the case of *United States* v. *Standard Ultramarine and Color Co.,* 137 F.Supp. 167 (S.D. N.Y. 1955) in support of its position. In that case six corporations were charged with conspiring to fix and maintain prices in the sale of dry colors throughout a nine year period. The volume of business involved amounted to some 37½ per cent of the total national sales. The Court rejected the defendants' plea of *nolo contendere*. The aggravated nature of the offense is indicated by the Court's reference to the offense as 'one of the more serious infractions of the law' (page 172). The Court in *Ultramarine* was concerned about securing the benefits of the criminal judgment for private litigants. However, the reasoning of *Ultramarine* strongly indicates that the Court took this position because no companion civil suit had been filed by the Govern-

---

[27] Part V (pp. 1-2) of Bill of Particulars Filed by the United States Pursuant to Order of the Court, dated December 6, 1956. . . .

ment. *Ultramarine* distinguished the holding therein from that in *U.S.* v. *Cigarette Merchandising Assn.*, 136 F.Supp. 212 (S.D. N.Y. 1955) where a plea of *nolo contendere* had been granted upon the point that in the *Cigarette* case a companion civil suit had been filed, whereas in the *Ultramarine* case there was no civil suit which might aid private litigants.

"In the case at bar there is a civil suit pending on this Court's docket which may be brought to trial by the Government.

    * * *

"This Court does not believe that Congress intended that pleas of *nolo contendere* be refused in criminal antitrust cases for the purpose of aiding private litigants under Section 5 of the Clayton Act. That section, as amended (69 STAT. 283; 15 U.S.C. § 16) in the concluding paragraph provides:

'That this section shall not apply to consent judgments *or to decrees entered before any testimony has been taken* or to judgments or decrees entered in actions under Section 4a'.

"If such had been the intent of Congress it would have been a simple matter to delete the phrase '*or decrees entered before any testimony has been taken*' from this provision of Section 5a of the Clayton Act, and by so doing private litigants would have secured the benefit of criminal convictions as *prima facie* evidence upon acceptance of a plea of *nolo contendere*. It must be assumed that Congress was aware of the fact that a plea of *nolo contendere* results in a judgment *before any testimony has been taken*.

    * * *

"By the Act of June 29, 1940 (54 STAT. 688) Congress conferred upon the Supreme Court the authority to prescribe the Federal Rules of Criminal Procedure. The rules became effective March 21, 1946, after having been reported to Congress by the Attorney General in January 1945; and Rule 11 has expressly provided that 'a defendant may plead not guilty, guilty, or with the consent of the Court, *nolo contendere*.' In the years since the promulgation of these rules no legislation has been enacted that could be construed as withdrawing from the court its discretion under Rule 11 concerning *nolo contendere* pleas. It must be assumed that Congress is satisfied with the rule and its application.

    * * *

"While the condition of the Court's docket would not be reason for the acceptance of the pleas of *nolo contendere,* the fact is that all other litigation in the Fort Worth, Abilene and San Angelo Divisions of the Northern District of Texas would necessarily be delayed and all other litigants would be denied the right to speedy trial during the trial of this case, estimated at a minimum of three months, if such pleas be not accepted. The benefits to be derived from a long, expensive trial are not sufficient in the instant case to justify the rejection of defendants' offered pleas of *nolo contendere.* The savings of time and expense has been recognized as a factor in the acceptance of pleas of *nolo contendere.*"

(d) *Statute of limitations*

This has been the subject of recent legislation. A criminal prosecution must now be commenced within a period of five years from the date the offense was committed. The applicable statute provides that "no person shall be prosecuted, tried, or punished for any offense, not capital, unless the indictment is found or the information is instituted within five years next after such offense shall have been committed."[28]

(3) **Damage Suits**

Section 4 of the Clayton Act[29] allows a person injured as a result of a violation by the defendant of the antitrust laws to bring a private suit for treble damages.[30] In other words, the plaintiff must establish that he sustained pecuniary damages[31] as a result of the defendant's wrongdoing.[32]

The award for treble damages is statutory and leaves no discretion to judge or jury. "The amount of [the] verdict was required by statute to be trebled by the judgment. In this respect neither the jury nor either court had any discretion. The verdict [of the jury] should represent actual damages sustained and

---

[28] 68 STAT. 1145 (1954), 18 U.S.C. § 3282 (Supp. V, 1958).

[29] 38 STAT. 731 (1914), 15 U.S.C. § 15 (1952); for the wording, see appendix. This section also provides for recovery of cost of suit, including a reasonable attorney's fee. However, the latter right accrues to the party injured and not to his attorney. First Iowa Hydro Elec. Coop. v. Iowa-Illinois Gas & Elec. Co., 245 F.2d 630, 632 (8th Cir. 1957), *cert denied,* 355 U.S. 871 (1957).

[30] For recent writings, see, *e.g.,* Clark, *The Treble Damage Bonanza,* 52 MICH. L.REV. 363 (1954); and Comment, *Antitrust Enforcement by Private Parties: Analysis of Developments in the Treble Damage Suit,* 61 YALE L.J. 1010 (1952).

[31] Turner Glass Corp. v. Hartford-Empire Co., 173 F.2d 49, at 51 (7th Cir. 1949), *cert denied,* 338 U.S. 830, *rehearing denied,* 338 U.S. 881 (1949).

[32] With respect to the proper evidence and measure of damages, see the recent decisions in Flintkote Co. v. Lysfjord, 246 F.2d 368 (9th Cir. 1957), and Enterprise Industries, Inc. v. Texas Co., 240 F.2d 457 (2d Cir. 1957), *cert. denied,* 353 U.S. 965 (1957).

two-thirds of the judgment is a penalty which Congress has seen
fit to impose in such case upon a guilty defendant."[33]

A controversy has developed concerning who is to be regarded as "any person . . . injured in his business or property"
within the meaning of Section 4. Recovery has been denied to
a landlord of a competitor injured by the defendant although
the landlord had a percentage rental.[34] Likewise, recovery was
denied to a patent licensor who would have received royalties
from one of the defendant's competitors injured by the defendant's violations of the antitrust laws.[35] Judge Wyzanski recently
stated:[36]

> "[D]espite its broad language Section 4 of the Clayton Act
> does not give a private cause of action to a person whose losses
> result only from an interruption or diminution of profitable re-
> lationships with the party directly affected by alleged violations
> of the antitrust laws. . . . [Otherwise, B]usinessmen would be
> subjected to liabilities of indefinable scope for conduct already
> subject to drastic private remedies. Courts aware of these con-
> siderations have been reluctant to allow those who were not in
> direct competition with the defendant to have a private action
> even though as a matter of logic their losses were foreseeable.
> Congress has failed to amend the antitrust laws on this point in
> the face of repeated decisions. It seems to have been content
> for the judiciary to take a position narrower than that often
> applied in non-statutory tort cases and in cases where plaintiffs
> are not allowed a multiple recovery."

Section 5 of the Clayton Act[37] gives a wronged private person
the right in a treble damage suit to meet his burden of proof to

---

[33] Bigelow v. R.K.O. Radio Pictures, 150 F.2d 877, at 873 (7th Cir.
1945), *reversed on other grounds,* 327 U.S. 251 (1946). Although, thus
characterized as a "penalty," it has been held that unlike other penalties,
the right to sue under Section 4 survives the death of either party. See
Barns Coal Corp. v. Retail Coal Merchants Ass'n, 128 F.2d 645, at 649
(4th Cir. 1942).

[34] Melrose Realty Co. v. Loew's, Inc., 234 F.2d 518, 519 (3d Cir. 1956),
cert. denied, 352 U.S. 890 (1956); Harrison v. Paramount Pictures, Inc.,
211 F.2d 405 (3d Cir. 1954), *cert. denied,* 348 U.S. 828 (1954); *cf.* Walder
v. Paramount Publix, 132 F.Supp. 912, 916 (S.D. N.Y. 1955). *Contra,*
Congress Building Co. v. Loew's, Inc., 246 F.2d 587 (7th Cir. 1957);
Tower Building Corp. v. Loew's, Inc., 1956 CCH TRADE CASES Para.
68,537 (N.D. Ill. 1956).

[35] Production Inventions, Inc. v. Trico Products Co., 224 F.2d 678 (2d
Cir. 1955), *cert. denied,* 350 U.S. 936 (1955).

[36] Snow Crest Beverages, Inc. v. Recipe Foods, Inc., 147 F.Supp. 907,
at 909 (D. Mass. 1956).

[37] 38 STAT. 731 (1914), as amended, 69 STAT. 283 (1955), 15 U.S.C.
§ 16 (Supp. V, 1958). Under the concluding paragraph of this provision,
consent judgments may not be used as evidence in subsequent private

the extent of proving a *prima facie* case of violation of the anti-trust laws by simply introducing evidence of the conviction or enjoining of the defendant in a prior antitrust suit brought by the federal Government.[38] This provision is part of a legislative policy of minimizing the burden of litigation for injured private suitors and of enlisting private persons to aid in enforcement of the antitrust laws.[39]

The use of damage suits has recently been assessed in these terms:

> "During the Sherman Act's first 50 years, private antitrust plaintiffs succeeded in only 13 of 175 actions brought.[40] Since World War II, however, this picture has altered sharply. From June 1947 to June 1951, private antitrust suits pending in District Courts jumped from 118 to 367. Recoveries, moreover, increased almost correspondingly. Since 1951, growth has been even more rapid."[41]

(a) *United States can now sue for damages*

In *Georgia* v. *Evans*[42] the Supreme Court held that a state may sue for treble damages where injured by a violation of the antitrust laws.[43] Three years later the Court held that a state may also sue for treble damages as *parens patria*.[44]

The same Court held in 1941 that Congress did not intend to give the United States the right to sue for treble damages, especially as Congress had given the federal government three potent weapons for enforcing the Sherman Act: criminal prosecution under Sections 1, 2 and 3; injunction under Section 4; and seizure of property under Section 6.[45] This case law has been superseded by recent statute.[46] Section 4A of the Clayton Act

---

treble damage suits. This exception serves to encourage quick settlement of antitrust cases and, consequently, speedy elimination of restrictive trade abuses. See discussion on consent decrees, *supra*.

[38] Emich Motors Corp. v. General Motors Corp., 340 U.S. 558 (1951).

[39] 51 CONG. REC. 16319 (1914). See Emich Motors Corp. v. General Motors Corp., 340 U.S. 558 (1951).

[40] ANNUAL REPORT OF THE ATTORNEY GENERAL 233 (1938).

[41] REPORT OF THE ATTORNEY GENERAL'S NATIONAL COMMITTEE TO STUDY THE ANTITRUST LAWS 378 (1955).

[42] 316 U.S. 159 (1942).

[43] Section 7 of the Sherman Act, which allowed treble damage suits and which is mentioned in this and some other cases of the same period, was superseded by Section 4 of the Clayton Act.

[44] Georgia v. Pennsylvania Railroad Co., 324 U.S. 439, at 450 (1945).

[45] United States v. Cooper Co., 312 U.S. 600 (1941).

[46] 69 STAT. 282 (1955), 15 U.S.C. § 15a (Supp. V, 1958), amended the Clayton Act by adding a new Section 4A and repealed Section 7 of the Sherman Act. See Forkosch, *Suggested Limitation Upon the 1955 Amendment Permitting the United States to Sue for Treble Damages—An Analysis*, 1 ANTITRUST BULL. 289 (1955).

now reads:

> "Whenever the United States is hereafter injured in its business or property by reason of anything forbidden in the antitrust laws it may sue therefor in the United States district court for the district in which the defendant resides or is found or has an agent, without respect to the amount in controversy, and shall recover actual damages by it sustained and the cost of suit."

(b) *Statute of limitations*

Prior to 1955, the antitrust laws did not provide a federal statute of limitations for private actions. Consequently, there was always the problem of what state law should determine the maximum time allowed between the antitrust injury and the private suit for relief.[47] Considerable confusion and conflict followed.

Congress has provided a solution by amending the Clayton Act.[48] A new Section 4B provides for a uniform four-year statute of limitations in all private antitrust suits.

> "Any action to enforce any cause of action under Sections 4 or 4A shall be forever barred unless commenced within four years after the cause of action accrued. No cause of action barred under existing law on the effective date of this Act shall be revived by this Act."

Section 5 of the Clayton Act was also amended by the same statute. Under old Section 5 the running of the applicable state statute of limitations was suspended only during the pendency of an antitrust action brought by the federal Government. Under new Section 5(b) the running of the statute of limitations is suspended during the pendency of the Government suit and for one year thereafter. The private party enjoying such a suspension is required to commence his action either within the suspension period or within four years after the cause of action accrued.[49]

---

[47] See REPORT OF THE ATTORNEY GENERAL'S NATIONAL COMMITTEE TO STUDY THE ANTITRUST LAWS 380-385 (1955).

[48] 69 STAT. 283 (1955), 15 U.S.C. § 15b (Supp. V, 1958).

[49] "(b) Whenever any civil or criminal proceeding is instituted by the United States to prevent, restrain, or punish violations of any of the antitrust laws, but not including any action under Section 4A, the running of the statute of limitations in respect of every private right of action arising under said laws and based in whole or in part on any matter complained of in said proceedings shall be suspended during the pendency thereof and for one year thereafter: *Provided, however,* That whenever the running of the statute of limitations in respect of a cause of action arising under Section 4 is suspended hereunder, any action to enforce such cause of action shall be forever barred unless commenced either within the period of suspension or within four years after the cause of action accrued." 69 STAT. 283 (1955), 15 U.S.C. § 16 (Supp. V, 1958).

Chapter 9

REGULATED INDUSTRIES AND THE ANTITRUST LAWS

Certain industries in the United States are closely regulated in their activities because of the character of their functions and service. The regulatory statutes are usually justified on such grounds as public health, welfare and interest, and national defense. As the antitrust laws are also intended to serve the public interest, there should be no conflict, in the last analysis, between the ultimate purpose of the regulation of a public utility, for example, and the antitrust provisions forbidding monopoly and price fixing.

Interestingly, Congress has often provided that the antitrust provisions shall apply, if only to a limited degree, to certain industries heavily regulated by federal or state agencies. To illustrate this proposition we here present three illustrations: commercial banking; certain aspects of the petroleum industry, particularly pipelines; and atomic energy.

(A) COMMERCIAL BANKING

Since the economic nature of this "industry" is unique, and has necessitated the application of both state and federal regulation to the most comprehensive extent, the competitive activities of commercial banks deserve separate treatment. In recent years, these activities have been most characteristically evident in a vast growth of branch banking and a sharp acceleration in the rate of mergers.

(1) The Nature of Competition in Commercial Banking

As in other important industries, oligopoly generally prevails in commercial banking. In any given banking market relatively few banks compete with each other, since the entry of newcomers is seriously restricted by statutory provisions and by the practice of regulatory agencies. As in other industries characterized by relatively few sellers, we find competition in services rather than in prices charged for credit or for checking account

services. Commercial banks must meet competition from enterprises which provide more or less related services, such as savings banks, savings and loan institutions and personal finance
corporations. However, since only commercial banks offer checking account services and still make most short-term business
loans, they may be regarded essentially as a distinct "industry."

While these facts and the recent bank merger movement point
to similarities with the competitive pattern in other important
industries, the decisive difference between banking and industry
generally is that banking is much more regulated. Competition
among commercial banks is restricted in the following ways:[1]

> "The size and type of loans banks can make is limited; the
> type of investments they can undertake is regulated; the reserve
> they must hold against deposits is governed by regulating author-
> ity; limits are placed on dividends; examinations by public
> authority are made on a regular basis—merely to name a few of
> the regulations under which banks operate. Moreover, it is sig-
> nificant that throughout all these laws, regulations and super-
> visory controls, there runs one objective that appears paramount
> to all others—that banks be safe, sound and capable of meeting
> the needs of the community for essential banking services.

> ❋ ❋ ❋

> "Moreover, it is relevant to note that in supporting their objec-
> tive to foster the soundness and capability of banks, the super-
> visory authorities place certain definite limits on the competitive
> process. For example, banking is not a business which anyone
> can enter who has the necessary capital and who desires to go
> into it. Indeed, existing banks are not even free to expand as
> they may desire. The supervisory authorities—the Comptroller
> of the Currency, the Federal Reserve Board, the F.D.I.C. [Fed-
> eral Deposit Insurance Corporation], or the various State bank-
> ing agencies—exercise control over entry into banking; they con-
> trol the ability of existing banks to establish new branches; and
> their approval is usually required for any increase in capital
> stock. . . . Hence one of the primary requisites for free com-
> petition—freedom of entry—is generally absent in banking. Like-
> wise, the general level of interest rates which banks charge are
> subject at least to indirect control, and thus limits are set on the
> general level of bank earnings. This is the result of various
> activities of the Federal Reserve Board—open market operations,
> changes in the rediscount rate, and regulation of reserve require-

---

[1] Statement of John J. McCloy, Chairman of the Board of Directors of
the Chase-Manhattan Bank of New York, in: Bank Mergers, *Hearings Before Antitrust Subcommittee* (*Subcommittee No. 5*) *of the House Committee on the Judiciary,* 84th Cong., 1st Sess., ser. No. 7, at 20-21 (1955).

ments, for example—which are designed to control the supply of money in our economy."

This statement indicates that bank supervision and regulation have a number of purposes different from the policy underlying the antitrust laws. Three purposes conflicting with a policy of preservation of complete freedom of competition may be stated:

(a) Since the public entrusts money to the banks it is in the public interest that banks be honestly operated, keep accurate books, and make sound investments. As contrasted with other industries, the elimination of weak and less efficient bank competitors by bankruptcy is regarded as a price too high for the community to pay. Consequently, the establishment of any new banking office has to be justified by proving the "need" of the community for its services. In other words, the applicant practically has to prove that existing bank facilities will not become unprofitable.

(b) In the public interest, bank assets have to be sufficiently liquid so that banks can immediately meet possible withdrawals of their demand deposits. The liquidity position of banks is enhanced by borrowing and rediscounting privileges at Federal Reserve banks.

(c) Federal Reserve monetary policy limits or permits expansion of the total volume of bank credit and bank deposits. The aims of this facet of monetary regulation are to foster orderly economic growth and a stable dollar. Federal Reserve monetary policy exerts important controls over the total flow of bank credit and money, but the distribution of bank credit and deposits among individual banks depends on the choice of the owners of the deposits. To that extent, commercial banks like sellers in other industries have to face competition among each other, mainly in the field of services.

(2) Government Supervision of Banking

The Federal Reserve Act of December 23, 1913,[2] created a Federal Reserve Board to supervise the operations of the 12 Federal Reserve banks and their branches newly established in Federal Reserve districts throughout the country. The objectives of the Federal Reserve System may be summarized as follows: (1) the establishment of an elastic currency and credit system; (2) the inauguration of a nation-wide collection system; (3) better bank supervision; (4) aid in government financing; and (5) national credit management.

---

[2] 38 STAT. 251 (1913), 12 U.S.C. § 221 (1952).

Congress bolstered the banking system by enacting the Banking Acts of June 16, 1933,[3] and of August 23, 1935.[4] These Acts aimed at strengthening individual banks by providing restrictions on group banking and underwriting. For the same reason and in order to protect deposits, the Federal Deposit Insurance Corporation (FDIC) was established.[5] "In the main, the rescue work of the FDIC has for its objective the merging of weak banks with their sounder neighbors. To make mergers attractive to the sounder institutions, the FDIC has been quite generous in providing direct financial aid."[6]

The table reprinted overleaf from Kent, Money and Banking 185 (3d ed. 1956) shows the main regulatory and supervisory powers of the banking authorities and the distribution of these powers.[7]

(3) Mergers

(a) *Present concentration tendencies in banking*

"The special nature of the functions performed by banks, the fact they are closely supervised, the limits on entry and expansion of facilities, and to a certain extent on earnings, dictate in large measure the unique structure of banking in the United States—a structure in which there are large banks, medium-sized

---

[3] 48 STAT. 162, 12 U.S.C. § 21 (1952).

[4] 49 STAT. 684, 12 U.S.C. § 21 (1952).

[5] 48 STAT. 168 (1913), as amended, 12 U.S.C. § 264 (1952).

[6] KENT, MONEY AND BANKING 207 (3d ed. 1956). See also Alhadeff & Aldaheff, *Recent Bank Mergers,* 69 Q.J.ECON. 503, 521 (1955), quoting FDIC ANNUAL REPORT 1949, 3-5; and *Bank Mergers and Concentration of Banking Facilities,* Staff Report to Subcommittee No. 5 of the House Committee on the Judiciary, 82d Cong., 2d Sess. 57 (1952).

[7] The authors have added the last item (authority to approve acquisitions and mergers).

DISTRIBUTION OF SUPERVISORY POWERS AMONG BANKING AUTHORITIES[8]

		Exercised with respect to		
Powers	*National banks*	*State member banks*	*State non-member insured banks*	*State non-member non-insured banks*
Issuance of charters	CC	State	State	State
Approval of changes in name, changes in capitalization, issue and retirement of capital notes and debentures, etc.	CC	State FR	State FDIC	State
Authority to establish, change location of, & discontinue branches	CC	State FR	State FDIC	State
Admission to the Federal Reserve System	CC	FR		
Admission to deposit insurance	CC	FR	FDIC	
Authority to exercise trust powers	FR	State	State	State
Examinations	CC (FR) (FDIC)	State FR (FDIC)	State FDIC	State
Reports of condition	CC FR FDIC	State FR FDIC	State FDIC	State
Determination of reserve requirements	FR	State FR	State	State
Limitation of interest payments on deposits	FR	State FR	State FDIC	State
Receiver in case of insolvency	FDIC	State or FDIC	State or FDIC	State
Approval of acquisitions and mergers	CC	State FR[9]	State FDIC[9]	State

---

[8] Explanation for abbreviations used: "CC" for Comptroller of the Currency; "FR" for the Board of Governors and other officials of the Federal Reserve System; "FDIC" for Federal Deposit Insurance Corporation; and "State" for state supervisory authorities. Parentheses indicate that powers are not commonly exercised.

[9] The approval of the federal agency is required only if the combined capital and surplus of the merging banks are diminished by the transaction.

banks, and small banks, all of which are necessary for a healthy economy and the well-being of the country."[10]

However, with a sharp acceleration in the bank merger rate of the last few years, concentration in banking with its impact on competition has become one of the major antitrust problems.

In April 1955, there were 14,314 banks in the United States, including both commercial and mutual savings banks.[11] In 1952, the bank merger rate was 100. In 1953, there were some 115 bank mergers. In 1954, 206 mergers occurred.[12] "In 1955, 232 previously independent banks had ceased operations in the United States as a result of consolidations and mergers. In the 3 years 1953-1955, there were 556 bank absorptions, more than twice the number of such transactions in the preceding years."[13]

"The size of the banks involved in these transactions has varied widely. In some cases small banks have been purchased by other small banks; in other cases, local banks have been acquired by large city banks; in still other cases giant financial institutions have merged with each other. The effect of bank mergers has been to increase the concentration of banking resources in almost every important financial center in the United States. New York City alone, in the year 1955, witnessed several of the largest bank mergers in American financial history. Among these were the merger of the Chase National Bank, having total assets of about $5.7 billion, with the Bank of Manhattan Co. which had assets of $1.6 billion and the Bronx County Trust Co. which had assets of $76 million; the merger of the National City Bank of New York, having total assets of about $5.8 billion, with the First National Bank of New York, which had assets of over $700 million; and the merger of the Bankers Trust Company of New York, which had assets of $2.2 billion, with the Public National Bank & Trust Company of New York, which had assets of almost $600 million.

"Data submitted to the subcommittee showed the percentage of total commercial bank assets owned by the single largest, the

---

[10] Statement of John J. McCloy in Bank Mergers, *Hearings Before Antitrust Subcommittee (Subcommittee No. 5) of the House Committee on the Judiciary,* 84th Cong., 1st Sess., ser. No. 7, at 21 (1955).

[11] *Ibid.*

[12] *Id.,* at 23.

[13] *Corporate Mergers and Acquisitions,* Staff Report of the Subcommittee on Antitrust and Monopoly of the Senate Committee on the Judiciary, S. REP. No. 132, 85th Cong., 1st Sess., at 65 (1957). For the time prior to 1953, see *Bank Mergers and Concentration of Banking Facilities,* Staff Report to Subcommittee No. 5 of the House Committee on the Judiciary, 82d Cong., 2d Sess. 12-25 (1952); *Concentration of Banking in the United States,* Staff Report of the Board of Governors of the Federal Reserve System to the Subcommittee on Monopoly of the Select Senate Committee on Small Business, 82d Cong., 2d Sess. (1952).

2 largest and the 4 largest banks in 16 important cities in the United States. In each case the 4 leading banks own more than 60 per cent of total commercial banking assets in that city."[14]

Several causes of these mergers have been cited: uneven rates of growth of different banks, lending restrictions (the maximum unsecured loan to one borrower is limited to ten per cent of a bank's capital and surplus), higher operating costs and lower profits of smaller banks, management problems, and the desire for branch bank expansion.[15] An interesting analysis of this last cause has been published:[16]

> "The growing importance of branch banking during the last twenty years is producing a striking change in the formal structure of the commercial banking system in the United States. On December 31, 1934, branch offices comprised only 16 per cent of total commercial banking offices; by December 31, 1954, branch offices were 31 per cent of the total.[17] In two decades, the number of branch offices more than doubled, and branch offices virtually doubled as a percentage of total commercial banking offices.[18] . . .
>
> "The acceleration of the trend towards branch banking during the past two or three years is due to several factors. First, many branch banks have exhibited a spectacular rate of growth. Indeed, the largest bank in the country, the Bank of America, with resources exceeding nine billion dollars, has outgrown the traditional giants of the banking system, the Wall Street Banks. . . .
>
> "Second, branch banking helps to ease the earnings problems posed by the population shift from metropolitan centers to suburban and outlying areas.
>
>   * * *
>
> "Non-economic factors have also stimulated the trend toward branch banking. Considerations of prestige, or the desire for sheer size of banks are no doubt important in stimulating individual bank expansion—and an excellent way to become a banking giant is to expand the number of branches. . . .
>
> "The drive to establish and expand branch banking systems has proceeded along two main lines: establishing *de novo*

---

[14] *Report on Corporate Mergers and Acquisitions, id.,* at 65-66.

[15] For a critical examination of these merger motives, see Alhadeff & Alhadeff, *Recent Bank Mergers,* 69 Q.J. ECON. 503, 504 *et seq.* (1955). The authors conclude that two basic factors seem to have motivated the sharp acceleration of the bank merger rate: (1) pressures resulting from uneven rates of growth by different banks, and (2) the desire to establish or expand branch bank systems. *Id.,* at 531.

[16] *Id.,* at 515-19. See also the basic study on branch banking by D. A. ALHADEFF, MONOPOLY AND COMPETITION IN BANKING (1954).

[17] Computed by Federal Reserve Bulletin, Feb. 1955, p. 208.

[18] *Ibid.* There were 3,007 branches of commercial banks on December 31, 1934, and 6,306 on December 31, 1954.

branches, and acquiring existing banks and converting them into branches of the acquiring bank. . . . In 1942 and 1943, slightly less than one-third of the banks acquired in all commercial bank mergers became branches of the acquiring banks. By 1948, this figure had risen to 75 per cent, and, *by 1954, 85 per cent of all acquired banks were converted into branches of the acquiring bank.*[19]

"Acquisitions rather than *de novo* branches are often motivated by both business and legal reasons. When a bank is acquired, and converted into a branch, the staffing problem is usually solved automatically. . . . Far more important, the branch does not have to build its deposits from zero, and it benefits from existing banker-customer loan relationships. . . . A *de novo* branch must satisfy the regulatory authorities of the 'need' for its existence, and that is not always easy when other banks already exist in the area. Moreover, it would be difficult to obtain authorization for as many *de novo* branches as could be obtained in a large, multi-bank merger. Indeed, some state laws make it easier to acquire a bank and convert it into a branch than to open a *de novo* branch."

(b) *The present state of the law*

The extent to which national and local branch banking as a form of concentration may develop depends on state law. Some states permit interstate branch banking. Others prohibit it altogether. The remainder have some limited type of branch banking. Under these laws and regulations, antitrust considerations do not play any important role. Hence, the "most powerful restriction on bank mergers—the prohibition against interstate branch banking is not part of federal antitrust legislation."[20]

Bank holding companies were established in an attempt to circumvent branch banking restrictions in state laws. Some state legislatures struck back by prohibiting bank holding companies. On the federal level, the Bank Holding Company Act of May 6, 1956,[21] was enacted to prevent, in effect, the future expansion of about 28 existing holding companies across state lines, to control new holding company formations and additional holding company bank acquisitions through the Board of Governors, and to require bank holding companies to divest themselves of their non-banking interests.[22]

---

[19] For 1948, Patman Report, *op.cit.*, Part I, p. 556; for 1954, Federal Reserve Bulletin, Feb. 1955, p. 208. Emphasis supplied.

[20] Alhadeff & Alhadeff, *Recent Bank Mergers*, 69 Q.J. ECON. 503, 523 (1955).

[21] 70 STAT. 133, 12 U.S.C. § 1841 *et seq.* (Supp. III, 1956).

[22] *Cf.*, Belgrano, *Bank Holding Company Legislation and Competition*, 73 BANKING L.J. 34, 36, 134-135 (1956).

Under Section 3 of this Act, every bank holding company that proposes to acquire additional banks must first obtain the consent of the Board of Governors of the Federal Reserve System. In determining whether to give such approval the Board is required to consider whether the proposed acquisition would be consistent with adequate and sound banking, the public interest, *and the preservation of competition* in the field of banking. But the Act also requires the Board to consider the financial history and condition of the holding company and the banks involved, their prospects and the character of their management, and the needs of the community concerned.

In New York State, which has at present only one state-wide bank holding company, the problem of branch banking has recently arisen in the form of two questions: Should the large New York City banks, restricted by state law to the five boroughs, be permitted to establish branches in the suburbs? And should they be permitted to gain branches indirectly through new holding companies? The test was raised by the First National City Bank of New York in an application to the Federal Reserve Board to obtain approval under the Bank Holding Company Act of 1956 to set up and become part of a bank holding company which would acquire the largest bank in Westchester County. In this connection, the Bank Holding Company Act does not affect the right of the New York State legislature to block the First National by enacting legislation prohibiting bank holding companies (Section 7). If the First National should succeed in circumventing the New York State laws limiting branch banking via the Board of Governors of the Federal Reserve System, it is possible that the state legislature will be forced to enact legislation permitting state banks the same freedom in order to avoid possible large scale conversion of state banks to national banks.

Apart from the specific problem of branch banking, it should be noted that much of the specific bank merger legislation on both state and federal levels has made it easy for banks to merge. In a recent Staff Study of the Senate Subcommittee on Antitrust and Monopoly, the present legal situation as to bank mergers has been summarized as follows:[23]

> "Under present State and Federal banking statutes various bank supervisory agencies have responsibility for approving or disapproving bank mergers, depending upon the nature of the

---

[23] *Corporate Mergers and Acquisitions,* Staff Report of the Subcommittee on Antitrust of the Senate Committee on the Judiciary, S. REP. No. 132, 85th Cong., 1st Sess. 66-67 (1957); see also the Table on the distribution of supervisory powers among banking authorities, reprinted *supra.*

transaction. This responsibility is incomplete and somewhat over-lapping. The Comptroller of the Currency is required to pass upon all mergers where the surviving institution is a national bank. Where the surviving bank is a State-chartered institution, the merger must be approved by the appropriate State banking authority. However, if the continuing or acquiring State-chartered bank is a member of the Federal Reserve System, the approval of the Board of Governors of that System is also required, but only if the combined capital and surplus of the merging banks are diminished by the transaction. Where the surviving State-chartered bank is not a member of the Federal Reserve System but is insured by the Federal Deposit Insurance Corporation, the approval of the transaction by that body is also required, but again, only if the combined capital and surplus are to be impaired. Where the surviving institution is a non-member non-insured bank, or where the bank which survives is a State-chartered bank and the combined capital and surplus of the merging banks are not reduced, no approval is required by any Federal agency. The largest bank merger in the history of this country, that of the Chase National Bank into the Bank of Manhattan Co., a State-chartered institution, was in the latter category, and thus, regardless of its effect, not legally subject to any requirement for approval by any Federal banking agency.[24]

"In those cases in which Federal approval of a bank merger is required at present, the statutory criteria for approval do not include any reference to the effect of the proposed transaction upon banking competition."

In spite of these events, there is little doubt that an important objective of Government policy has been, and today seems to be more than ever before, the preservation of banking as an essentially competitive industry. This follows not only from specific banking statutes such as the Bank Holding Company Act of 1956, but also from the general antitrust laws and the present legislative activity in Congress.

There is no doubt that Section 1 (restraint of trade) and 2 (monopoly) of the Sherman Act as well as Section 7 of the Clayton Act (acquisitions and mergers) apply to banks. Judge Barnes, then assistant attorney general in charge of the Antitrust Division of the Department of Justice, stated:[25]

---

[24] Note by the authors: Under New York law, the Superintendent of Banks can refuse agreement to a merger if competition is unduly affected. The superintendent, apparently lacking facilities to make a proper determination, approached the Department of Justice to determine whether it saw anything wrong with the merger. The Department noted that Section 7 of the Clayton Act did not apply and concluded that neither Section 1 nor 2 of the Sherman Act were violated.

[25] Testimony in Legislation Affecting Corporate Mergers, *Hearings Before the Subcommittee on Antitrust and Monopoly of the Senate Commit-*

"In the more than 60 years since the Sherman Act's passage no one has suggested its provisions did not apply to banks as to all other sectors of American business.

"Similarly, in the Transamerica case,[26] never was it urged that unamended Section 7 did not apply with equal force to both banks and non-banking corporations. And finally, in its 1950 amendment to Section 7, Congress reiterated prohibitions on stock acquisitions to fit banks the same as all other corporations."

Section 11 of the Clayton Act vests authority to enforce compliance with Section 7 "in the Federal Reserve Board where applicable to banks, banking associations, and trust companies." However, when Congress in 1950 amended Section 7 of the Clayton Act in order to broaden the section's reach by including not only the acquisition of the stock but also of the *assets* of another corporation, it allowed banks to escape the enlarged scope of the provision. The pertinent language in paragraph 1 of Section 7 reads "and no corporation *subject to the jurisdiction of the Federal Trade Commission* shall acquire the whole or any part of the assets of another corporation." (Emphasis supplied.) As Section 11 vests jurisdiction over banks in the Federal Reserve Board, the new Section 7 clause does not apply to banks.

Significantly, the Federal Reserve Board has only once attempted to enforce unamended Section 7 of the Clayton Act (which only covered mergers consummated by stock acquisition), and then unsuccessfully. As the case involves one of the most spectacular segments of the banking industry, we present an extensive extract from the decision.

TRANSAMERICA CORP. v. BOARD OF GOVERNORS OF THE FEDERAL RESERVE SYSTEM

United States Court of Appeals for the Third Circuit
206 F.2d 163 (1953)[27]

"MARIS, Circuit Judge.

"Transamerica Corporation, a corporation of Delaware, has petitioned this court to review an order of the Board of Governors of the Federal Reserve System entered against it under Section 11 of the Clayton Act, 15 U.S.C.A. § 21, to enforce

tee on the Judiciary, 84th Cong., 2d Sess., at 159 (1956). See also A. A. Berle, Jr., *Banking Under the Anti-Trust Laws*, 49 COL. L.REV. 589 (1949); Gruis, *Antitrust Laws and Their Application on Banking*, 73 BANKING L.J. 793 (1956).

[26] Transamerica Corporation v. Board of Governors of the Federal Reserve System, 206 F.2d 163 (3d Cir. 1953), *cert. denied,* 346 U.S. 901 (1953), reprinted *infra.*

[27] *Cert. denied,* 346 U.S. 901 (1953).

compliance with Section 7 of the Act, 15 U.S.C.A. § 18. The Board's complaint was issued June 24, 1948 charging Transamerica with having violated Section 7 in that for many years it and its predecessors have continuously and systematically been acquiring the stocks of independent commercial banks located in the five States of California, Oregon, Nevada, Washington and Arizona, and that the effect of such acquisitions may be to substantially lessen competition, restrain commerce or tend to create a monopoly.

"Hearings were held on the Board's complaint before a member of the Board as hearing officer. The hearing officer submitted recommended findings to the Board to which exceptions were filed. After hearing the exceptions the Board, two members dissenting, on March 27, 1952 entered the order here challenged, finding that Transamerica's acquisitions and ownership of the stocks of the various banks named in the complaint constitute a violation of Section 7 of the Clayton Act and requiring Transamerica to divest itself of all such stocks, except that of Bank of America National Trust and Savings Association, within an over-all period of two years and ninety days.

* * *

"It may readily be admitted that Congress in the past customarily dealt with the banking business by special legislation directed solely to that end. This it did under its fiscal and currency powers. [Footnote omitted.] Indeed, more than 100 years ago the Supreme Court had held that banking was not commerce.[28] It is, therefore, doubtless true that the members of Congress in enacting Section 7 of the Clayton Act in 1914 did not specifically contemplate that 'corporations engaged in commerce' would include banks. We find nothing in the legislative history, however, to indicate that Congress did not intend by Section 7 to exercise its power under the commerce clause of the Constitution to the fullest extent. The avowed purpose of the Clayton Act was to supplement the Sherman Act, 15 U.S.C.A. §§ 1-7, 15 note, by arresting in their incipiency those acts and practices which might ripen into a violation of the latter act. Since the general language of the Sherman Act was designed by Congress 'to go to the utmost extent of its Constitutional power in restraining trust and monopoly agreements,'[29] the supplementary general language of the Clayton Act was undoubtedly intended to have the same all inclusive scope.

"We turn then to the merits of the case. The Transamerica group had its origin in 1904 when A. P. Giannini organized the Bank of Italy (now Bank of America National Trust and Sav-

---

[28] Nathan v. Louisiana [1850], 8 How. 73, 49 U.S. 73.
[29] United States v. South-Eastern Underwriters' Association, 1944, 322 U.S. 533, 558.

ings Association) with headquarters in San Francisco. This bank is said to be the largest bank in the world, due principally to the fact that more than 550 independent banks and branches in the State of California have been acquired and either converted into branches of Bank of America or merged or consolidated with it. Until 1917 these acquisitions were made by individual officers of the bank, who pledged their personal credit when stock of an independent bank was being purchased. In that year Stockholders Auxiliary Corporation, a Transamerica predecessor, was organized and this company thereupon acted as purchaser of independent banks in California destined for inclusion within the Bank of America system.

"In 1918 another corporation, Bancitaly Corporation, was organized by A. P. Giannini, the largest stockholder of which was Stockholders Auxiliary Corporation. This company acquired the stocks of various banks located in New York City and certain foreign countries. Later on it also acquired stock interests in California banks. In 1924 still another corporation was formed called Americommercial Corporation and it, too, acquired controlling stock interests in California banks. In 1928 Transamerica Corporation, the petitioner here, was organized to take over stock control of Bank of America and its affiliated companies. Since that time Transamerica has acted as purchaser of independent banks in California for Bank of America.

"In 1930 Transamerica acquired The First National Bank of Portland, Oregon, which has since become the principal Transamerica branch banking system in that state. In 1934 it acquired the First National Bank in Reno, Nevada, the name of which has subsequently been changed to First National Bank of Nevada. In 1936 it acquired the National Bank of Tacoma, Washington, the name of which was later changed to National Bank of Washington. In 1937 it acquired the First National Bank of Arizona at Phoenix, the Phoenix National Bank and the Phoenix Savings Bank & Trust Company (the latter being an affiliate of the Phoenix National Bank). The Phoenix National Bank and the First National Bank of Arizona at Phoenix were later consolidated as the First National Bank of Arizona. Numerous subsequent acquisitions of independent banks were made by Transamerica in these four states, most of which have been converted into branches of the banks just mentioned.

"Commencing in 1937 Transamerica, which then held substantially all the stock of Bank of America, began a program of voluntary disposal of these holdings. In that year it distributed 58% of this stock to its own shareholders. By 1948 Transamerica's holding of Bank of America stock had been reduced to 22.88% and by 1951 to 7.66%. On October 20, 1952 the last of the stock was disposed of so that today Transamerica has no stock interest whatever in Bank of America. Also upon the death of L. M. Giannini on August 19, 1952 the two corporations

ceased to have any director in common. [Footnote omitted.]
The Board, nonetheless, in its findings of fact included Bank of
America in the Transamerica banking group, along with 47
majority owned banks which Transamerica had acquired in the
five states, since it regarded Transamerica as still exercising effective control over Bank of America in spite of its then com-
paratively small stock interest. The Board did not include Citi-
zens National Trust and Savings Bank of Los Angeles, in which
Transamerica also has a minority stock interest, however, since
it did not find that Transamerica exercises control over that bank.

"The Board's findings of fact set forth the growth, by years,
in banking offices, deposits and loans of the Transamerica banking group. This growth has been steady. The Transamerica
group controls approximately 645 or 41% of all commercial
banking offices in the five-state area. In addition the Transamerica group holds approximately 39% of all commercial bank
deposits and approximately 50% of all commercial bank loans in
the five-state area. [Footnote omitted.] On the basis of such
overall figures as these and without any findings as to the competitive effect of Transamerica's bank acquisitions in the communities in which the banks operate the Board reached its conclusion that the acquisitions violate Section 7 of the Clayton Act
and accordingly called for the order of divestment here under
review.

"It will be recalled that Section 7 makes unlawful the acquisition of the stock of two or more corporations engaged in interstate commerce where its effect 'may be to substantially lessen
competition between such corporations, or any of them, whose
stock or other share capital is so acquired, * * * or tend to
create a monopoly of any line of commerce.' The contention of
Transamerica is that the Board's findings wholly fail to furnish
support to the conclusion that the effect of Transamerica's acquisitions of bank stocks may be to substantially lessen competition between the acquired banks or that those acquisitions may
tend to create a monopoly in the banking business.

"We think that Transamerica's contention with respect to substantial lessening of competition must be sustained. The ban
imposed by Section 7 in this regard is solely against stock acquisitions which may have the effect of substantially lessening competition between the companies acquired. The application of
this clause obviously requires a preliminary determination of the
area of effective competition between the companies involved
before the question of competition between them may be considered. The Board has made such a determination in this case,
finding that the business of commercial banks is largely local and
confined to the communities in which they operate and in which
customers may conveniently visit them.

* * *

"Likewise it must appear that substantial competition exists between the acquired companies which may be subject to substantial lessening as the result of their acquisition by a common owner. [Footnote omitted.] In the present case the Board has made no findings with respect to either present or possible future competition between the individual acquired banks in the communities in which they operate. Indeed it rejected evidence on this subject offered by Transamerica. Moreover as to 38 of the acquired banks there could hardly be a finding of such competition since none of them is located in the same community as any other acquired bank. While the remaining 10 banks are not eliminated by this geographic test the mere showing of common ownership will not support an inferential finding that competition between them exists and may be lessened. [Footnote omitted.]

"The Board's ultimate finding on this score was 'that the effect of its [Transamerica] holding and use of such stocks may be to substantially lessen competition and restrain commerce in commercial banking in the States of California, Oregon, Nevada, Arizona and Washington.' This finding is deficient in two respects. It is not directed to competition between the acquired banks, the only competition with which Section 7 is concerned. And it sets up a five-state area of competition for which there is no support in the evidence and which is inconsistent with its own specific finding on this point to which we have already referred. So far as concerns the portion of this finding that the effect of these stock acquisitions may be to restrain commerce in commercial banking in the five-state area it is sufficient to say that the Board did not refer to it in this court either in its brief or in oral argument and evidently does not rely upon it.

* * *

"By cumulating the acquisition of banks by Transamerica throughout the five-state area and including Bank of America (in which Transamerica no longer has any stock interest) the Board shows the growth of a banking group which, it asserts, is moving toward a monopoly in banking in the five states. We agree that this quantitative analysis discloses a tremendous concentration of banking capital, and thereby of economic power, in the hands of the Transamerica group which may be unwise and against sound public policy. It may well be in the public interest to curb the growth of this banking colossus by appropriate legislative or administrative action. This, however, is not for us to decide. Our only question is whether the theory upon which the Board based its decision meets the legal tests which are required under Section 7 of the Clayton Act to determine whether Transamerica's bank stock acquisitions tend to create a monopoly of commercial banking. We are compelled to agree with Transamerica that it does not do so.

* * *

"[U]nder Section 7, contrary to the rule under Section 3, the the lessening of competition and the tendency to monopoly must appear from the circumstances of the particular case and be found as facts before the sanctions of the statute may be invoked. Evidence of mere size and participation in a substantial share of the line of business involved, the 'quantitative substantiality' theory relied on by the Board, is not enough.

* * *

"We conclude that since the Board failed to find the facts as to lessening competition and tendency to monopoly in the areas of effective competition actually involved, its order is unsupported by the necessary findings and cannot stand."

Although decided under the old Section 7, this case is not only important with respect to the determination of the relevant market but also points to the evidence deemed necessary to prove an acquisition illegal. However, it seems doubtful whether the decision can be fully reconciled with the doctrine laid down recently in *United States* v. *E. I. du Pont de Nemours & Co.,*[30] discussed in chapter 3.

(c) *Federal legislative efforts to control mergers*

There is felt generally a need for strengthening the law with respect to bank mergers. In recent years, the problem has received considerable attention in both the House of Representatives and the Senate. The bills which have been introduced take two different approaches.

The first type of bill would amend *Section 7 of the Clayton Act* so as to bring acquisitions of bank *assets* under its coverage. The bills would also require *prior notice* of most proposed bank mergers to be given to the Attorney General and the Board of Governors of the Federal Reserve System. Under these bills the legality of any bank merger would be determined primarily on the basis of its effect on competition. Enforcement of Section 7 with respect to banks would be vested concurrently in the Board of Governors of the Federal Reserve System and in the Attorney General in line with the concurrent jurisdiction principle applicable to other types of mergers under Section 7.[31]

---

[30] 353 U.S. 586 (1957).

[31] This has been the view taken by the antitrust subcommittees of the Congress, the Federal Trade Commission and the Attorney General; *Corporate Mergers and Acquisitions,* Staff Report of the Subcommittee on Antitrust and Monopoly of the Senate Committee on the Judiciary, 85th Cong., 1st Sess. 66 (1957); *Corporate and Bank Mergers,* Interim Report of the Antitrust Subcommittee (Subcommittee No. 5) of the House Committee on the Judiciary, 84th Cong., 1st Sess. 26-37, 40-41, 172 *et seq.*

As contrasted therewith, "[t]he three federal bank supervisory agencies proposed that the present authority for *advance approval* of bank mergers by those agencies under the *banking statutes* be broadened to include all bank mergers, regardless of the effect upon capital structure, wherever the surviving institution is a national bank, a member of the Federal Reserve System, or is insured by the Federal Deposit Insurance Corporation; that the criteria for approval be amended to include the effect on banking competition among the various factors to be considered; and that these three agencies be vested with final authority over all bank-merger transactions. Under this proposal the appropriate banking agency might, if it wished, require the opinion of the Attorney General but would not be obliged either to make such a request or to follow the recommendation received."[32] These bills would leave Section 7 of the Clayton Act unchanged.

(B) ASPECTS OF THE OIL AND GAS INDUSTRY

(1) General Comment

The domestic petroleum industry is exceeded in size only by agriculture, the railroads and the combined worth of gas and electric utilities.[33] Several of the largest and most dynamic companies in the United States are based on oil and natural gas.[34]

(1955); H.R. REP. No. 1417, 84th Cong., 1st Sess. (1955); Hon. Herbert Brownell, Jr., *Statement Before the Senate Banking and Currency Committee 'To Amend and Revise the Statutes Governing Financial Institutions and Credit,'* 2 ANTITRUST BULL. 519 (1957).

[32] *Report on Corporate Mergers and Acquisitions, id.,* at 67; see also Regulation of Bank Mergers, *Hearings Before a Subcommittee of the Senate Committee on Banking and Currency,* 84th Cong., 2d Sess. (1956); *Regulation of Bank Mergers,* Report of the Committee on Banking and Currency, S. REP. No. 2583, 84th Cong., 2d Sess. (1956); Hon. Martin, Chairman of the Board of Governors of the Federal Reserve System, *Statement Before the Antitrust Subcommittee of the House Committee on the Judiciary,* March 8, 1957, 43 FED. RESERVE BULL. 271 (March 1957).

[33] Gross investment in the petroleum industry was estimated at $40.4 billion as of December 31, 1955. REPORT OF THE ATTORNEY GENERAL PURSUANT TO SECTION 2 OF THE JOINT RESOLUTION OF JULY 28, 1955, CONSENTING TO AN INTERSTATE COMPACT TO CONSERVE OIL AND GAS, hereinafter cited as REPORT, at 23 (September 1, 1956).

[34] Ranked either on the basis of total assets or net profits, 5 of the 10 largest concerns in the United States are oil companies. Ranked on an asset basis, the list of the 25 largest United States companies would include 10 of the major oil companies. Fortune Magazine, *Directory of the 500 Largest United States Industrial Corporations* (July 1956).

The Oil industry itself also displays a high degree of integration. 54 of the companies operating refineries owned, as of 1950, 34.8 per cent of pro-

These facts together with the wasting nature of the commodities account for the interest of federal and state Governments in the exploration, development, transportation, processing and marketing aspects of oil and gas, an interest which has taken the form of regulations, assistance,[35] and, where necessary, antitrust action.[36]

Increasing domestic requirements for petroleum and its products have resulted in the investment of great sums of money in foreign countries by American corporations acting alone or in concert with other firms. Their quest has affected our foreign policy. Defense considerations have raised commercial transactions relating to foreign oil fields to the level of international relations. At the same time, Congress has been constantly concerned lest the actions of these American oil companies abroad violate the American antitrust laws.[37]

The oil and gas industry in its largest sense presents a kaleidoscopic picture of competition on the one hand and Government imposed restrictions on the other. No part of the industry is completely free of the whiplash of the antitrust laws and yet the

---

ducing oil wells, 89.1 per cent of refinery crude oil capacity, 80.8 per cent of the crude oil transmission trunk lines, 46.1 per cent of tanker dead weight tonnage, 17.4 per cent of the tank cars and 51.4 per cent of the service stations. See REPORT 24-27. For further information, see Dirlam, *The Petroleum Industry*, in THE STRUCTURE OF AMERICAN INDUSTRY 236, and readings suggested, *id.*, at 272-273 (Adams ed., 2d rev. ed. 1954).

[35] *E.g.*, to encourage exploration for oil, Congress has granted substantial tax benefits to producers of oil and gas: 68A STAT. 77, 207, 208 (1954), 26 U.S.C. §§ 263(c), 611, 613(b) (Supp. 1956).

[36] For example, in United States v. Standard Oil Co. of New Jersey, Civil No. 86-27 (S.D. N.Y.), the Government in 1953 charged 5 defendant American oil companies with a conspiracy in conjunction with 2 major foreign companies and others, to restrain and monopolize the interstate and foreign commerce of the United States in petroleum and its products. There has been no final decision in this case.

In 1957, some 25 per cent of the professional staff of the Antitrust Division of the Department of Justice was engaged upon oil matters. SECOND REPORT OF THE ATTORNEY GENERAL PURSUANT TO SECTION 2 OF THE JOINT RESOLUTION OF JULY 28, 1955, CONSENTING TO AN INTERSTATE COMPACT TO CONSERVE OIL AND GAS, hereinafter cited as SECOND REPORT, at 62 (September 1, 1957).

[37] See *The International Petroleum Cartel*, Federal Trade Commission Report to the Subcommittee on Monopoly of the Select Senate Committee on Small Business, 82d Cong., 2d Sess. (1952); *Petroleum, The Antitrust Laws and Government Policies*, Report of the Subcommittee on Antitrust and Monopoly of the Senate Committee on the Judiciary, S. REP. No. ...., 85th Cong., 1st Sess. 6 (1957). This latter investigation was commenced after the closing of the Suez Canal.

area where such discipline might be applied is restricted by Government action and regulation.

The early days of the oil industry were marked with severe competition. Control was exercised by monopolists or would-be monopolists through ownership of refineries and the oil pipelines.[38] This led to dissolution of the Standard Oil trust for violation of the Sherman Act.[39] Similarly, oligopolistic control of natural gas pipelines later led to enactment of the Natural Gas Act.[40]

Discovery of enormous new oil fields during the first decades of the twentieth century caused erratic flooding of the market with volumes of fuel which could only be absorbed, if at all, by plunges in the selling price. Subsequent increases in market demand would then drive the price up as the fuel supply grew relatively more scarce. Such wild fluctuation resulted in wasteful production methods, a boom-or-bust oil economy and demands for some form of disciplined production and development of oil in the field.

After years of discussion and the failure of the depression-spawned National Industrial Recovery Act,[41] the states in which producing oil and gas fields are located entered into an agreement in 1935 which is called the Interstate Oil Compact. Designed to encourage conservation through proper production and development of oil and gas reserves, the compact has continued in effect since that date, renewed from time to time with the approval of Congress.[42] Membership of the Interstate Oil Compact has expanded from the original six signatories to a total of 26 states. Three other states and the Territory of Alaska are associate members.[43]

---

[38] See 1 TARBELL, THE HISTORY OF THE STANDARD OIL COMPANY, c. 2 (1925).

[39] Standard Oil Co. v. United States, 221 U.S. 1 (1911). This dissolution brought about divorcement of 12 pipeline systems from Standard Oil. Only one of these pipelines exists today as a common carrier. The remainder have either disappeared or function solely as intrastate transporters. *Petroleum, The Antitrust Laws and Government Policies,* Report of the Subcommittee on Antitrust and Monopoly of the Senate Committee on the Judiciary, S. REP. No. ......, 85th Cong., 1st Sess. 27 (1957).

[40] 52 STAT. 821-833 (1938), as amended, 15 U.S.C. §§ 717-717w (1952).

[41] Declared unconstitutional in Schechter Corp. v. United States, 295 U.S. 495 (1935).

[42] The power of a state to enter into compacts is governed by the Constitution of the United States, Art. I, sec. 10. The most recent congressional approval of the Interstate Oil Compact is to be found in 69 STAT. 419 (1955).

[43] REPORT 53-54.

Article V of the Compact presently reads:

> "It is not the purpose of this compact to authorize the states joining herein to limit the production of oil or gas for the purpose of stabilizing or fixing the price thereof, or create or perpetuate a monopoly, or to promote regimentation, but is limited to the purpose of conserving oil and gas and preventing the avoidable waste thereof within reasonable limitations."

Congress does not intend that this compact serve to permit price fixing forbidden by the antitrust acts. Therefore, the Attorney General has been directed to make an annual report to Congress as to whether the actions of the states have been consistent with Article V of the compact.

Preliminary studies of the Attorney General indicate that the effect of the Compact Commission[44] on conservation is "mainly the result of voluntary adherence by the states to the views of the Commission, and not of any formal compulsion emanating from that agency."[45] As we shall see below, the oil and gas conservation practices by the producing states serve to restrict the domestic supply to a close balance with estimated demand. However, the Attorney General's studies apparently have not yet justified a report to Congress that the Compact Commission's activities amount to unlawful price fixing.[46]

It is the state agencies which actually regulate oil and gas production. The principal producing states have set up regulatory machinery which ensures (1) that the oil and gas producers in the state produce no more than enough to meet market requirements for those commodities from sources within the state, and (2) that the predetermined overall production within the state is assigned on a *pro rata* basis to the producers located in the state.[47] This latter step is called proration.

"In determining what the probable market demand will be, the States ordinarily use the forecast of market demand which is published regularly by the Bureau of Mines. That is supplemented in each State by local information which the State agency may have available. This may include 'nominations' by purchasers, that is, estimates by major crude producers of the amount which they expect to purchase within the period, both

---

[44] Article VI of the Compact provides for the establishment of a Commission.

[45] REPORT 57.

[46] See SECOND REPORT 30.

[47] The basic Texas regulations are set out in VERNON'S REVISED CIVIL STATUTES OF THE STATE OF TEXAS, Art. 6049d.

statewide and from particular fields."[48] The amount of oil in storage is also considered. "Out of the consideration of these factors by the State agency, a determination is made of the probable demand which is used as the basis for the statewide allowable over the forthcoming period. That is the amount of crude oil which the agency will permit all the wells in the State to produce during the proration period."[49]

To assist the producing states in enforcing their proration laws during the depression years, Congress enacted in 1935 the Conolly "Hot Oil" Act.[50] This statute forbids the movement in interstate commerce of oil produced, transported or withdrawn from storage in violation of applicable state proration statutes. Intended as an emergency measure, the Act has proved such a helpful adjunct to state regulation that it is still an effective federal law.[51]

Despite frequent assurances that the elaborate state and federal machinery controlling production of oil and gas is not a price-fixing mechanism, there are some who assert the contrary.[52] However, neither the Attorney General nor Congress has as yet concluded that the price effect of the state regulations constitutes price fixing forbidden by the antitrust laws.[53]

To demonstrate more clearly this interesting combination of Government control, competition and antitrust regulation, let us examine two industries which exist solely to transport oil and natural gas to market by pipelines which cross state lines. In other words, we will limit this discussion to interstate pipelines.[54]

(2) Interstate Oil Pipelines

The Interstate Commerce Commission has had jurisdiction over pipelines transporting oil and petroleum products in inter-

---

[48] REPORT 59.

[49] Id., at 60.

[50] 49 STAT. 30 (1935), 15 U.S.C. §§ 715-715m (1952).

[51] 56 STAT. 381 (1942), 15 U.S.C. § 715l (1952).

[52] See, e.g., Carmical, No Plot is Needed: Law Rigs Oil Price, New York Times, February 24, 1957, Sec. 3; Emergency Oil Lift Program and Related Oil Problems, Joint Hearings Before Subcommittees of the Senate Committees on the Judiciary and on Interior and Insular Affairs, 85th Cong., 1st Sess., Part I, 456 (1957).

[53] SECOND REPORT 49. Cf. also id., at 118-119.

[54] Intrastate pipeline rates are sometimes regulated by state commissions.

state commerce since 1906.[55] Pipelines so regulated are held to be common carriers like the railroads.[56]

As of December 31, 1955, approximately 85 pipeline companies reported to the Commission as common carriers.[57] It is significant to an understanding of this segment of the oil industry that only one of these 85 pipelines is not owned by an oil company.[58]

A person desiring to construct an interstate oil pipeline need not obtain any prior authorization from the Interstate Commerce Commission. Thus private industry determines how, when and where an oil pipeline is to be constructed. Economic factors are, therefore, decisive in such construction.[59]

At the time operation of an oil pipeline is commenced, there must be on file with the Commission tariffs setting out the rates to be charged for the transportation service. Thereafter, the pipeline companies must file periodic reports and keep their accounts in a form prescribed by regulation.[60]

The Commission has the power to review and change the rates established by the oil pipeline companies under its jurisdiction.[61] The Commission has given little public evidence of the exercise of its rate powers.[62] The most significant action in this field took place on December 23, 1941 when the Attorney General filed a

------

[55] 34 STAT. 584 (1906), as amended, 41 STAT. 474 (1920), 49 U.S.C. § 1(b) (1952). There are about 100,000 miles of crude oil and petroleum products lines in the United States, not all of which are in interstate commerce. See UREN, PETROLEUM PRODUCTION ENGINEERING 35-36 (1950).

[56] The Pipe Line Cases, 234 U.S. 548 (1914). *Cf.* United States v. Champlin Refinery Co., 341 U.S. 290 (1951).

[57] *Petroleum, The Antitrust Laws and Government Policies,* Report of the Subcommittee on Antitrust and Monopoly of the Senate Committee on the Judiciary, S. REP. No. ...., 85th Cong., 1st Sess. 27 (1957).

[58] *Ibid.*

[59] For example, it is alleged that the availability of low cost oil from Latin America and the Middle East for delivery to east coast ports has resulted in a lack of incentive to construct oil pipelines from domestic sources to those same markets. Emergency Oil Lift Program and Related Oil Problems, *Joint Hearings Before Subcommittees of the Senate Committees on the Judiciary and on Interior and Insular Affairs,* 85th Cong., 1st Sess., Part 1, 345, 368 (1957).

[60] See Uniform System of Accounts prescribed for pipe line companies by the Interstate Commerce Commission, revised to July 1, 1953.

[61] See KOOKENBOO, CRUDE OIL PIPELINES AND COMPETITION IN THE OIL INDUSTRY (1955); WOLBERT, AMERICAN PIPELINES (1952).

[62] SHARFMAN, THE INTERSTATE COMMERCE COMMISSION, Part II, 98 (1931).

complaint[63] against 53 common carrier pipeline companies and their 36 oil company shipper-owners charging them with engaging in unlawful rebates from the tariff charged by the pipelines in violation of Sections 2 and 6 of the Interstate Commerce Act and Section 1 of the Elkins Act.[64] On the same date, all defendants entered into a consent judgment enjoining them from continuing the forbidden rebate practice. The decree also enjoined any payments to shipper-owners in excess of 7 per cent of the I.C.C. valuation of the pipeline company's property.[65]

On October 11, 1957 the Attorney General filed four motions in the Federal Court against certain of the pipelines and one shipper-owner for violation of the consent decree.[66]

Small oil producers who do not share in the ownership of these interstate pipelines[67] are constantly fearful that they are being denied pipeline connections with the refineries and, ultimately, with the market, by the major integrated companies who own over 90 per cent of oil pipeline capacity.[68] The Subcommittee on Antitrust and Monopoly of the Senate Committee on the Judiciary recently recommended, in view of charges of discrimination made by independent non-integrated producers before that subcommittee, that the Department of Justice initiate an immediate investigation along the following lines:

"(a) Monopolization of common-carrier pipeline transportation, including extent of interest in trucking.

(b) Use of controlled pipelines to deny independent producers a competitive market for crude oil.

(c) Use of controlled pipelines to restrict sources of oil to independent refineries.

(d) Crude oil price discrimination against producers.

(e) Pipeline proration."[69]

---

[63] United States v. The Atlantic Refining Co., Civil No. 14060 (D.C., 1941).

[64] 24 STAT. 379, 380 (1887), 41 STAT. 479, 483 (1920), 49 U.S.C. §§ 2, 6 (1952); 32 STAT. 847 (1903), 34 STAT. 587 (1906), 49 U.S.C. § 41 (1952).

[65] Consent judgment in Civil No. 14060 (Dec. 23, 1941). Hearings scheduled by the Subcommittee on Antitrust and Monopoly of the Senate Committee on the Judiciary in October, 1957, were intended to concentrate on this consent judgment.

[66] Department of Justice Press Release of October 11, 1957.

[67] The non-integrated or independent producers account for less than 40 per cent of domestic crude oil output. REPORT 26.

[68] *Petroleum, The Antitrust Laws and Government Policies,* Report of the Subcommittee on Antitrust and Monopoly of the Senate Committee on the Judiciary, S. REP. No. ......, 85th Cong., 1st Sess. 31 (1957).

[69] *Id.,* at 7.

Under the present state of the law, producers cannot compel interstate oil pipelines to connect with their wells except in case of pipelines constructed on Government lands. In the latter case, the pipeline company is allowed to construct only on condition that it serve as a common carrier for all producers in the vicinity of the pipeline.[70]

(3) Interstate Natural Gas Pipelines

There are over 400,000 miles of natural gas lines in the United States. Ten per cent are in the form of field and gathering lines, thirty per cent represent transmission lines, and the remainder distribution lines.[71] We are here concerned only with those transmission lines carrying natural gas in interstate commerce.

Jurisdiction over sales for resale in interstate commerce and transportation in interstate commerce is vested by the Natural Gas Act[72] in the Federal Power Commission.[73] This statute was designed to protect the producers of natural gas, as well as the ultimate household consumer, from the powerful interstate pipeline companies.[74] Federal legislation was necessary because the Supreme Court had held that the states lacked the power to regulate this industry.[75]

The Federal Power Commission exercises minute control over the construction and operation of the facilities of regulated pipeline companies and the rates that they charge. No interstate pipeline can be constructed or enlarged and no service undertaken or abandoned by such a pipeline company without prior authorization of the Commission. This authorization is given, after appropriate public hearing, in the form of a certificate of public convenience and necessity.[76]

---

[70] 41 STAT. 449 (1920), 49 STAT. 678 (1935), 67 STAT. 557 (1953), 30 U.S.C. § 185 (Supp. 1956).

[71] 1955 GAS FACTS 57 (American Gas Association ed. 1955). The large oil companies do not own the natural gas pipeline companies although they do supply them with natural gas.

[72] 52 STAT. 821-833 (1938), as amended, 15 U.S.C. §§ 717-717w (1952). The Commission also regulates the producers of natural gas selling to the interstate pipelines. For the problems in this field, see the symposia presented in 44 GEO. L.J. 551-723 (1956), and in 19 LAW & CONTEMP. PROB. 323-473 (1954).

[73] More than 100 natural gas pipeline companies report to the Federal Power Commission. See FEDERAL POWER COMMISSION, STATISTICS OF NATURAL GAS COMPANIES (1956).

[74] See 52 STAT. 871 (1938), 15 U.S.C. § 717 (1952).

[75] Missouri v. Kansas Gas Co., 265 U.S. 298 (1924).

[76] See Kansas Pipe Line & Gas Co., 2 F.P.C. 29 (1939).

The Commission cannot compel a pipeline company to enlarge its facilities.[77] Thus the initiative as to how, when and where an interstate natural gas pipeline will be constructed or expanded lies with private industry.

To obtain a certificate for the construction of new pipeline facilities, the company is ordinarily required to demonstrate

(1) that it has adequate natural gas reserves under contract in oil and gas reservoirs in identified fields to meet its daily gas requirements for the life of the contracts between itself and its customers (usually 20 years);

(2) that the proposed construction is technically feasible, and will perform the proposed service at reasonable costs;

(3) that there is a market for the proposed natural gas service at rates which will make the project economic; and

(4) that the project can be financed.

The rates of natural gas pipeline companies, like those of many public utilities, are rigorously regulated. The success of rate regulation depends in no small part on the fact that the pipeline companies must keep their books and accounts in a prescribed way.[78]

Protection of the consumer against exploitation by the pipeline company is the primary duty of the Federal Power Commission.[79] But in setting rates the Commission must also consider the investor interest. In *Federal Power Commission* v. *Hope Natural Gas Co.*[80] Justice Douglas noted that the Commission "was not bound to the use of any single formula or combination of formulae in determining rates. . . . Under the statutory standard of 'just and reasonable' it is the result reached, not the method employed, which is controlling."[81] He further stated, "the investor interest has a legitimate concern with the financial integrity of the company."[82]

Section 7(g) of the Natural Gas Act[83] allows the Commission to authorize construction of a competing natural gas pipeline into an area already being served by a pipeline company. Sev-

---

[77] Panhandle Eastern Pipe Line Co. v. Federal Power Commission, 204 F.2d 675 (3d Cir. 1953).

[78] Uniform System of Accounts prescribed for natural gas companies subject to the provisions of the Natural Gas Act.

[79] Federal Power Commission v. Hope Natural Gas Co., 320 U.S. 591, 610 (1944).

[80] 320 U.S. 591 (1944).

[81] 320 U.S. at 602.

[82] 320 U.S. at 603.

[83] 52 STAT. 824 (1938), 56 STAT. 83 (1942), 61 STAT. 459 (1946), 15 U.S.C. §717f(g) (1952).

eral attempts to obtain authorization to construct such new lines have been successful. Thus, New England is now served by two pipeline companies,[84] the New York City area by two pipeline companies,[85] and the New Jersey area by three.[86] All of these pipelines extend over a thousand miles to gas supply sources in Texas and Louisiana.

A battle is presently being waged before the Commission to determine whether a second pipeline company should be allowed to serve the Chicago area.[87] This second pipeline would run from a connection with an existing pipeline system in the State of Tennessee, past Chicago, to interconnect with Trans-Canada Pipe Line Ltd. at the Canada-Minnesota border. En route this proposed pipeline traverses the areas now being served or proposed to be served by four other interstate natural gas pipeline companies.

As a result of this fight, the Governor of Wisconsin has charged that several gas companies have conspired to keep the second pipeline from being constructed. A grand jury investigation has been authorized into this alleged violation of the antitrust laws.[88]

There has not been any important court decision involving application of the antitrust laws to these regulated interstate natural gas pipelines. Perhaps this results from their close supervision. Certainly the Commission recognizes that the antitrust laws are applicable.[89] "[T]he grant of monopolistic privileges, subject to regulation by governmental bodies, does not carry an exemption, unless one be expressly granted, from the antitrust laws, or deprive the courts of jurisdiction to enforce them."[90] Indeed, Section 20(a) of the Natural Gas Act provides that the

---

[84] The second pipeline was authorized by F.P.C. Opinion No. 259, issued August 6, 1953.

[85] The second pipeline was authorized by F.P.C. Opinion No. 279, issued December 28, 1954.

[86] The second and third pipelines were authorized by 7 F.P.C. 24, issued May 29, 1948, and Opinion No. 279, issued December 28, 1954, respectively.

[87] F.P.C. Dkt. No. G-9454 et al.

[88] The Wall Street Journal, November 26, 1957, p. 28.

[89] See F.P.C. Opinion No. 303 issued June 21, 1957, mimeo., p. 22. "The Commission, while it 'has no power to enforce the Sherman Act as such . . . [and] cannot decide definitely whether the transaction contemplated constitutes . . . an attempt to monopolize which is forbidden by that Act . . . ,' nevertheless, [it] cannot without more ignore the [Act]." City of Pittsburgh v. Federal Power Commission, 237 F.2d 741, at 754, (D.C. Cir. 1956).

[90] Pennsylvania Water & Power Co. v. Consolidated Gas, 184 F.2d 552, 560 (4th Cir. 1950), cert. denied, 340 U.S. 906 (1950).

Commission "may transmit such evidence as may be available
. . . concerning apparent violations of the Federal antitrust laws
to the Attorney General, who, in his discretion, may institute the
necessary criminal proceedings."[91]

On July 22, 1957, the Acting Attorney General announced the
filing of a complaint charging that the recent acquisition by El
Paso Natural Gas Company of the common stock of Pacific
Northwest Pipeline Corporation may substantially lessen competition or tend to create a monopoly in violation of Section 7
of the Clayton Act. El Paso is the sole outside supplier of natural gas to California. Pacific Northwest supplies the northwestern states and is the sole importer of natural gas from Canada
west of the Rocky Mountains.[92]

El Paso has since filed with the Federal Power Commission
an application seeking authorization to merge Pacific Northwest
into El Paso.[93] This move may be prompted by the hope that
Commission sanction of the merger will nullify the prosecution
since Congress gave the Commission special jurisdiction over
natural gas companies, which jurisdiction includes mergers.[94]

(C) ASPECTS OF THE ATOMIC ENERGY INDUSTRY

In the first two sections of this chapter, we presented examples
of industries which commenced their operations in a laissez-
faire atmosphere and were gradually confined by governmental
regulation. Their development exemplifies what has occurred
in other industries which today are highly regulated, such as
the railroads, ocean shipping, the air lines and gas and electric
utilities.

In this section we present a rare example of the opposite
trend. The atomic energy industry came into existence under
complete wartime Government monopoly. Since the inception of
this industry, federal control has been gradually diminished by
statute and regulation in an attempt to encourage an increasing

---

[91] 52 STAT. 832 (1938), 15 U.S.C. § 717s(a) (1952).

[92] United States v. El Paso Natural Gas Co., Civil No. 143-57 (D. Utah
1957), Department of Justice Press Release of July 22, 1957.

[93] F.P.C. Dkt. No. G-13019.

[94] See Colorado Interstate Gas Co., 10 F.P.C. 105 (1951); Interstate
Natural Gas Co. v. Southern Colorado Gas Co., 209 F.2d 380, 384 (9th
Cir. 1953); Michigan Consolidated Gas Co. v. Panhandle Eastern Pipe Line
Co., 173 F.2d 784, 789 (6th Cir. 1949). Section 7 of the Clayton Act provides in part: "Nothing contained in this section shall apply to transactions
duly consummated pursuant to authority given by the . . . Federal Power
Commission. . . ." But see United States v. El Paso Natural Gas Co.,
1957 CCH TRADE CASES Para. 68,872 (D.C. Utah 1957), *cert. denied,*
78 S.C. 553 (1958).

participation by private enterprise. In order to encourage the development of free competition in this process of liberation, a number of antitrust and other competitive safeguards have been introduced. Meanwhile, many aspects of atomic energy industry remain closely regulated.

It is too early to judge the outcome of this experiment. At the present time economic considerations in such areas as the utilization of atomic energy for the generation of electricity appear to be a greater deterrent to the increasing role of private enterprise than the statutory ambiance. Nonetheless, a brief survey of recent legislative and administrative actions designed to encourage competition in this industry may be of general interest in a consideration of the function of antitrust legislation in regulated fields of our economy.

(1) The Pattern of Government Regulation

Atomic energy in the United States developed under three types of Government control. The first lasted from 1942 to 1946 and was the most complete. It "was imposed by the military and continued the control by secrecy which had been initiated by scientists after their recognition of fission in early 1939."[95]

The second type of Government control dates from January 1, 1947, when the Atomic Energy Commission, a civilian agency, assumed responsibility of atomic matters under the Atomic Energy Act of 1946.[96] This second period which lasted until 1954, was still characterized by a far-reaching Government monopoly over development of atomic energy. Private firms could not own fissionable material or the facilities to produce it.[97] They were excluded from using such material[98] and could participate in the development of atomic energy only under licenses issued by the Atomic Energy Commission.[99] Any patents developed were accessible to the Government and to all licensed firms.[100]

A third type of Government regulation began with the enactment of the most recent Atomic Energy Act on August 30,

---

[95] Dunlavey, *Government Regulation of Atomic Industry*, 105 U. PA. L.REV. 295 (1957).

[96] 60 STAT. 755 (1946), 42 U.S.C. §§ 1801-1819 (1952).

[97] 60 STAT. 760 (1946), 42 U.S.C. §§ 1804, 1805 (1952).

[98] *Ibid.*

[99] 60 STAT. 764 (1946), 42 U.S.C. § 1807 (1952).

[100] 60 STAT. 768 (1946), 42 U.S.C. § 1811 (1952).

1954.[101] Many factors resulted in a new policy of the Government.[102] As the Attorney General stated in a recent speech:[103]

"Still necessary was development of atomic weapons within the existing framework of controls and secrecy. Feasible now, however, was international cooperation with our Allies in atomic matters.[104] Finally, it was necessary to open the field to widespread industry participation to achieve rapid development or commercial atomic application.

"Consequently, this legislation sought to end total governmental monopoly. It relaxed the prohibitions over private participation in atomic developments, allowed freer access to hitherto restricted technological data and permitted private ownership and use of production and utilization facilities. In effect, a full measure of competition was now permitted within the framework of an industry still closely regulated.

"Passage of this legislation occasioned lengthy hearings[105] and sharp differences of opinion. The legislative history of the Act —bills, hearings, reports and Congressional debates—fills three enormous volumes."[106]

In summary, the new statute provides a compromise between the need for control in the interest of public health, safety, common defense and security on the one hand, and, on the other, the desire to establish free enterprise and free competition in a new and important sector of our economy. However, one writer concludes:[107]

"[T]he security and safety controls exerted by the Commission in its regulatory capacity are not in themselves inconsistent with the competitive assumptions of the antitrust laws, at least as they apply to the manufacturers of equipment and material.

---

[101] 68 STAT. 919 (1954), as amended, 42 U.S.C. §§ 2011-2281 (Supp. III, 1956).

[102] For a discussion of these factors, see Palfrey, *Atomic Energy: A New Experiment in Government-Industry Relations,* 56 COLUM. L.REV. 367, 369-372 (1956).

[103] Brownell, Address on "Atomic Energy and Free Enterprise" before the Section on Antitrust Law, New York State Bar Association, January 24, 1957.

[104] See, *e.g., Conference on the Statute of the International Atomic Energy Agency by Congressional Advisers,* Report of the Joint Committee on Atomic Energy, 85th Cong., 1st Sess. (1957).

[105] *Hearings Before the Joint Committee on Atomic Energy on S. 3323 and H.R. 8862, To Amend the Atomic Energy Act of 1946,* 83d Cong., 2d Sess. (1954).

[106] U.S. ATOMIC ENERGY COMMISSION, LEGISLATIVE HISTORY OF THE ATOMIC ENERGY ACT OF 1954 (Public Law 703), 83d Cong., 3 Vol. (1955).

[107] Palfrey, *Atomic Energy: A New Experiment in Government-Industry Relations,* 56 COLUM. L.REV. 367, 386 (1956).

These controls are not designed to regulate entry, prices, or the obligation to serve except as security and safety factors require."

(2) The Antitrust Safeguards in the Atomic Energy Act of 1954

Congress has recognized the importance of free competition in the atomic energy industry by stating in the declaration of policy, which is contained in Section 1 of the Act:[108]

". . . the development, use, and control of atomic energy shall be directed so as to promote world peace, improve the general welfare, increase the standard of living, *and strengthen free competition in private enterprise.*" [Emphasis added.]

"The strengthening of free competition in private enterprise is, therefore, one of the fundamental criteria to be applied by the Atomic Energy Commission in all its activities in the performance of its statutory responsibilities."[109]

To prevent any developments which might come into conflict with this policy, Congress included express antitrust provisions in the 1954 Act. The most basic safeguard of competition is embodied in Section 105, which provides for normal application of the antitrust laws to the civilian atomic energy industry. Section 105(a) reads in part:[110]

"Nothing contained in this Act, including the provisions which vest title to all special nuclear material in the United States, shall relieve any person from the operation of the . . . [Sherman Act, Wilson Tariff Act,[111] Clayton Act,[112] and Federal Trade Commission Act[113]]."

To insure the cooperation of the Atomic Energy Commission in enforcement of the antitrust laws, Section 105(b) of the Atomic Energy Act[114] provides:

"The Commission shall report promptly to the Attorney General any information it may have with respect to any utilization of special nuclear material or atomic energy which appears to violate or to tend toward the violation of any of the foregoing Acts, or to restrict free competition in private enterprise."

In addition to this general affirmation of the applicability of the antitrust laws, the last sentence of Section 105(a) provides:

---

[108] 68 STAT. 921 (1954), 42 U.S.C. § 2011(b) (Supp. III, 1956).

[109] Jacobs and Melchior, *Antitrust Aspects of the Atomic Energy Industry,* 25 GEO. WASH. L.REV. 508 (1957).

[110] 68 STAT. 938, 42 U.S.C. § 2135 (Supp. III, 1956).

[111] 28 STAT. 570 (1894), 15 U.S.C. §§ 8-11 (1952).

[112] 38 STAT. 730 (1914), 15 U.S.C. §§ 12-27 (1952).

[113] 38 STAT. 717 (1914), 15 U.S.C. §§ 41-58 (1952).

[114] 68 STAT. 938, 42 U.S.C. § 2135 (Supp. III, 1956).

"In the event a licensee is found by a court of competent jurisdiction, either in an original action in that court or in a proceeding to enforce or review the findings or orders of any Government agency having jurisdiction under the laws cited above, to
have violated any of the provisions of such laws in the conduct
of the licensed activity, the [Atomic Energy] Commission may
suspend, revoke, or take such other action as it may deem necessary with respect to any license issued by the Commission under
the provisions of this Act."

Before any commercial license is granted, the Atomic Energy
Commission is required to notify the Attorney General of the
proposed license and conditions thereof. The Attorney General
then has to advise the Commission whether

"the proposed license would tend to create or maintain a situation inconsistent with the antitrust laws, and such advice shall
be published in the Federal Register."[115]

The Attorney General has recently commented upon this and
other provisions as follows:[116]

"This provision, patterned after earlier surplus property disposal laws[117] makes available to the Commission analysis of any
special anticompetitive considerations presented. Antitrust advice, however, need not be controlling. For the Commission
must also weigh the necessities of defense and security and public health and safety. . . .

"As the Act now stands, then, the Commission must issue
commercial licenses on a nonexclusive basis to all applicants who
meet the conditions the Act sets forth.[118] This provision promises the widest possible participation of all interested in entering
the atomic field. It reduces the possibility that the limited number of Government contractors already in the field will retain
their exclusive position.

"That possibility is further decreased by the action of the Commission in permitting vital dissemination of restricted data.[119]
Dissemination opens up to newcomers great areas of technologi-

---

[115] Section 105(c) of the Atomic Energy Act, *ibid.*

[116] Brownell, Address on "Atomic Energy and Free Enterprise" before
the Section on Antitrust Law, New York State Bar Association, January 24,
1957. For a more detailed study by two members of the Antitrust Division,
see Jacobs and Melchior, *Antitrust Aspects of the Atomic Energy Industry,*
25 GEO. WASH. L. REV. 508, 513-518 (1957). The speech has been
published in 1957 CCH ANTITRUST LAW SYMPOSIUM 11-19 (1957).

[117] Sec. 207 of the Federal Property and Administrative Services Act of
1949, 63 STAT. 391, 40 U.S.C. § 485 (1952).

[118] Sec. 103(b), 68 STAT. 936 (1954), 42 U.S.C. § 2133(b) (Supp. III.,
1956).

[119] AEC Regulation "Access to Restricted Data," 21 FED. REG. 810
(February 4, 1956), amended 21 FED. REG. 5633 (August 1, 1956).

cal information hitherto available only to the contractors under the earlier Government program.[120]

"Concern with anticompetitive considerations, let me emphasize, does not end with issuance of any commercial license. Licenses, once issued, are still subject to the antitrust laws. And licenses may be revoked by the Commission if subsequent information would warrant refusal of a license on an original application.[121] We interpret this language to include instances where a later investigation reveals anti-competitive factors unknown to this Department at the time the license was issued."

In contrast with these views, one writer has called the safeguards written into the licensing provisions "elusive and deceptive."[122]

The second group of provisions designed to promote competition in atomic energy industry relates to patents in this field. Again, we quote the Attorney General of the United States for the views and policy of the present administration:[123]

"Considerable discussion arose over the present law's patent provisions.[124] The patent system is a fundamental factor contributing to the outstanding technological development of American industry. Many believed, therefore, that any curtailment of traditional patent rights would obstruct full and speedy development.[125]

"However, technology's importance in this highly scientific field inspired the belief that curtailment of certain patent rights was necessary for competition to flourish. Particularly, the technical advantages gained by Atomic Energy Commission con-

---

[120] However, see the discussion of the problems remaining in this area, involving AEC's use of its discretion, in Green, *Information Control and Atomic Power Development*, 21 LAW & CONTEMP. PROB. 91 (1956).

[121] Sec. 186(a), 68 STAT. 955 (1954), 42 U.S.C. §2236(a) (Supp. III, 1956).

[122] Adams, *Atomic Energy: The Congressional Abandonment of Competition*, 55 COLUM. L.REV. 158, 169 (1955).

[123] Brownell, Address on "Atomic Energy and Free Enterprise" before the Section on Antitrust Law, New York State Bar Association, January 24, 1957.

[124] The patent provisions of the Act are extensively analyzed in Boskey, *Patents Under the New Atomic Energy Act*, 36 J. PAT. OFF. SOC'Y 867 (1954); Spear, *Compulsory Licensing of Patents under the Atomic Energy Act of 1954*, 43 GEO. L.J. 211 (1955); Becket and Merriman, *Will the Patent Provisions of the Atomic Energy Act of 1954 Promote Progress or Stifle Invention?* 37 J. PAT. OFF. SOC'Y 38 (1955); Ooms, *Some Suggestions Relating to Patent Provisions in Atomic Energy Legislation to Protect the Public Interest*, 38 J. PAT. OFF. SOC'Y 38 (1956); Boskey, *Progress and Patents in Atomic Energy: The Military and the Civilian Uses*, 34 TEXAS L.REV. 867 (1956).

[125] See, for example, the views of Rep. Cole, Chairman of the Joint Committee, H. REP. No. 2181, 83d Cong., 2d Sess. 96 *et seq.* (1954).

tractors before the passage of the Act suggested that important areas might be closed off to newcomers. The President called for temporary provisions to meet this need; as he put it:[126]

'Until industrial participation in the utilization of atomic energy requires a broader base, considerations of fairness require some mechanism to assure that the limited number of companies, which as Government contractors now have access to the program, cannot build a patent monopoly which would exclude others desiring to enter the field. I hope that participation in the development of atomic power will have broadened sufficiently in the next five years to remove the need for such provisions.'

"The Act, as passed, provides that any patent issued before September 1, 1959, may be declared by the Commission, under certain conditions, to be affected with a public interest. The Commission itself may then use or license the invention or discovery covered by the patent.[127]

"This provision has been criticized on the grounds that the conditions governing compulsory licensing are too strict and the period during which it may be invoked too short.[128] Significantly, however, no special problems seem to have arisen under this provision. Moreover, other sections of the Act relating to patents reinforce this section's effort to insure equality of opportunity.

"Section 159, for instance, carefully preserves the Government's paramount rights to invention made by the individual concerns in the course of their work under contract.[129] Similar provisions were included in larger contracts during the period of Government monopoly.

"An even more significant protection for the general public is found in Section 152.[130] It provides a statutory affirmation of the Government's rights in inventions resulting from work under Atomic Energy Commission contracts and extends those rights to other areas. Unless the Commission should, in its discretion, waive its claim, any invention made *or conceived* under any contract, arrangement 'or other relationship' with the Commission, regardless of whether the relationship involved the expenditure of funds by the Atomic Energy Commission, 'shall be deemed to have been made or conceived by the Commission.' This means that no person or firm can gain private patent advantages from ideas originating through past or future Government connection.

---

[126] H.R. DOC. No. 328, 83d Cong., 2d Sess. 7 (1954).

[127] Sec. 153, 68 STAT. 945 (1954), 42 U.S.C. § 2183 (Supp. III, 1956).

[128] *E.g.,* Adams, *Atomic Energy: The Congressional Abandonment of Competition,* 55 COLUM. L.REV. 158 (1955).

[129] 68 STAT. 948 (1954), 42 U.S.C. § 2189 (Supp. III, 1956).

[130] 68 STAT. 944 (1954), 42 U.S.C. § 2182 (Supp. III 1956). See, Palfrey, *Atomic Energy: A New Experiment in Government-Industry Relations,* 56 COLUM. L.REV. 367, 383 (1956).

"A final patent safeguard is the provision respecting antitrust violations in the use of atomic energy patents.[131] The statute specifically authorizes the courts to require reasonable royalty licensing of patents involved in antitrust violations. While courts already have this power included within their general equity remedies, Congress has here clearly directed appropriate use of that remedy in this field."

Again, opinions differ as to the effectiveness of the patent provisions in promoting competition.[132] However, as no case has yet been decided in this field, the workability of the antitrust provisions remains to be seen.

(3) Government Efforts to Promote Competition

As we have already remarked, one of the principal tasks assigned to the Atomic Energy Commission by statute is the strengthening of free competition in the private atomic energy industry. "This statutory purpose can be effectuated by the Commission in its licensing policy, in its procurement and other contracting policies, and in its policies relating to the classification and availability of information."[133]

Certain of the conditions now present in the atomic energy industry may contribute to future antitrust violations. It has been noted:[134]

"There is already in evidence a marked tendency in the field of atomic energy for companies in activities in this field to do so on a joint basis. This tendency may be motivated by such factors as the lack of adequate fuels and facilities, large initial financial investments required and possibility of large public liability. The areas in which joint activities are found include research and development programs, mining and processing arrangements, construction and operation of various types of reactors, joint insurance programs and industrial study groups.

"The companies involved in many of these joint ventures are among the largest utilities and industrial concerns in their respective fields of activity. The concern from an antitrust standpoint stems principally from the fact that these joint ventures

---

[131] Sec. 158, 68 STAT. 947 (1954), 42 U.S.C. § 2188 (Supp. III, 1956).

[132] Adams, *Atomic Energy: The Congressional Abandonment of Competition*, 55 COLUM. L.REV. 158, 167, 171 (1955); Palfrey, *Atomic Energy: A New Experiment in Government-Industry Relations*, 56 COLUM. L. REV. 367, 387 (1956); Jacobs and Melchior, *Antitrust Aspects of the Atomic Energy Industry*, 25 GEO. WASH. L.REV. 508, 533-534 (1957).

[133] Jacobs and Melchior, *Antitrust Aspects of the Atomic Energy Industry*, 25 GEO. WASH. L.REV. 508, 519 (1957).

[134] *Id.*, at 522; see also Dunlavey, *Government Regulation of Atomic Industry*, 105 U. PA. L.REV. 295, 372 (1957).

will bring into close association a number of firms which are actual or potential competitors."

The Attorney General has shown an awareness of this problem:[135]

"It is in the area of licensing and patents that the extent of competition in civilian development of atomic energy will largely be determined.

"There were special problems in this area. During the period of Government monopoly, much of the Atomic Energy Commission operation and research had been performed by private firms under contract. Private firms had thus gained access to a great deal of restricted data, acquired the necessary scientific staffs, and had accumulated a mass of technological know-how. Without effective controls to offset these advantages, it was feared that potential newcomers to the industry would be deterred by the dominant position these firms would quickly achieve.[136]

"Provisions of the Act designed to ensure competition received careful consideration in the light of these special problems.[137] Many conflicting proposals were made.[138] Not surprisingly, therefore, the terms of the resulting statute are, in large part, the product of compromise."[139]

The Atomic Energy Commission is attempting to broaden the competitive base in this new industry.[140] The Attorney General has briefly reported on these activities and the efforts of the Department of Justice:[141]

"Since the passage of the 1954 Act, the Department of Justice has worked closely with the Atomic Energy Commission.

---

[135] Brownell, Address on "Atomic Energy and Free Enterprise" before the Section on Antitrust Law, New York State Bar Association, January 24, 1957.

[136] See Adams, *Atomic Energy: The Congressional Abandonment of Competition*, 55 COLUM. L.REV. 158 (1955), reprinted as Chapter VII in ADAMS & GRAY, MONOPOLY IN AMERICA, (1955).

[137] Similar problems with respect to Government research and development work generally are discussed in REPORT OF THE ATTORNEY GENERAL PURSUANT TO SECTION 708(e) OF THE DEFENSE PRODUCTION ACT OF 1950, AS AMENDED (November 9, 1956).

[138] See for example: Sec. 106 of H.R. 8862 and its companion bill, S. 3323, 83d Cong., 2d Sess. (1954); Sec. 105 of H.R. 9759 as introduced, 83d Cong., 2d Sess. (1954).

[139] H.R. REP. No. 2666, 83d Cong., 2d Sess. 30 (1954).

[140] Jacobs and Melchior, *Antitrust Aspects of the Atomic Energy Industry*, 25 GEO. WASH. L.REV. 508, 519-521 (1957).

[141] Brownell, Address on "Atomic Energy and Free Enterprise" before the Section on Antitrust Law, New York State Bar Association, January 24, 1957.

We have assisted the Commission in formulating regulations[142] governing civilian participation in atomic energy developments to ensure the implementation of the competitive safeguards in the Act.[143] We have also consulted on general competitive problems involved in development of this new industry.

"An example of the problems so far raised concerns the issuance of research and development licenses to private firms under Section 104 of the Act.[144] Because of the heavy expenses involved in construction and operation of experimental power reactors and other types of laboratory equipment, there has been a tendency to organize joint participation among a number of firms. Although the companies seeking such licenses jointly may not presently be engaged in the same industries, such activities still require considerable careful study, from a comparative point of view, both as to present actions in the experimental stages and in future activities when the commercial stage is reached. In the case of public utilities, I might add, such licenses for joint activities also raise the possibility of questions under the Public Utilities Holding Company Act.[145]

"The volume of competitive problems in this field has not yet been large. Despite the glowing promise of the atom's commercial development, such promise is still but a hope. Aside from the use of radioisotopes, activities in the field are still completely experimental.[146]

"Yet, this experimental work shows that the industry will not be limited to a mere handful of previous participants. Virtually all segments of industry are alert to the possibilities of this new and dynamic field.[147] More than 1,000 persons and firms have already been granted access permits by the Commission to obtain technological information.[148]

---

[142] 10 CFR p. 3 *et seq.* (Supp. 1955). AEC regulations are also collected in 2 CCH ATOMIC ENERGY LAW REP. 15,001 *et seq.*

[143] See, for example, Secs. 50.70 and 50.71, concerning inspections, records, and reports, 21 F.R. 360, 2 CCH ATOMIC ENERGY LAW REP. 15,064.

[144] 68 STAT. 937 (1954), 42 U.S.C. § 2134 (Supp. III, 1956).

[145] 49 STAT. 838 (1935), 15 U.S.C. § 79 (1952). See the general discussion on this subject in Murray, *Atomic Electric Energy and the Holding Company Act,* 24 J.B. ASS'N D.C. 20 (1957).

[146] A compilation of pertinent data on all current developments in construction of nuclear reactors for research and for experimental power plants in the United States, both Federal and private, is contained in *Nuclear Reactors, Built, Building or Planned in the United States as of October 1, 1956,* 1 CCH ATOMIC ENERGY LAW REP. 2721.

[147] See Ooms, *Some Suggestions Relating to Patent Provisions in Atomic Energy Legislation to Protect the Public Interest,* 38 J. PAT. OFF. SOC'Y 38, 46 (1956).

[148] AEC Press Release No. 948, December 31, 1956, p. 8.

"Nevertheless, we will keep a close eye on the developing situation in atomic energy. We will continue close consultations with the Commission and will advise them immediately of any situation which, in our judgment, may appear to present a serious tendency toward anticompetitive concentration. We are also prepared to inform Congress, without delay, of any need which may develop for changes in the basic statutes to provide additional competitive safeguards.

"The techniques of preventive action, though not entirely new to antitrust enforcement, here find their greatest opportunity for useful application. . . . We are confident that the development of a great new industry in the spirit of full and free competition can be accomplished."

Chapter 10

RESTRAINTS IN INTERNATIONAL TRADE

(A) PROTECTION OF THE AMERICAN ECONOMIC ORDER

The preceding chapters have indicated some of the current limits within which business activities must be conducted in the United States to prevent harm to the American economic order. The same limits exist in that portion of the American economy in which foreign corporations operate, inasmuch as the premise of antitrust regulation is one of general economic policy.[1]

In the furtherance of this public policy, antitrust has logically been extended to American business transactions involving foreign parties from the earliest time that such cases came before the courts.[1a] The Supreme Court itself took the first step in establishing a long tradition when it ordered both British and American defendants in the *American Tobacco* case[2] to abrogate their agreement confining themselves to their respective domestic markets. Its opinion dealt at length with the illegality of market divisions under the Sherman Act and concluded that the agreement was prohibited, assuming without discussion that the matter was one for adjudication under American law.

Similar cases followed during the succeeding forty years, in which American business organizations were adjudged in viola-

---

[1] A recent restatement of this policy is found in the REPORT OF THE ATTORNEY GENERAL'S NATIONAL COMMITTEE TO STUDY THE ANTITRUST LAWS 1 and 2 (1955):

"* * * Antitrust is a distinctive American means for assuring the competitive economy on which our political and social freedom under representative government in part depends . . . [T]he essentials of antitrust are today proclaimed by both political parties as necessary to assure economic opportunity and some limitation on economic power incompatible with the maintenance of competitive conditions."

[1a] The problems of antitrust in international commerce are treated in two new books, BREWSTER, ANTITRUST AND AMERICAN BUSINESS ABROAD (1958), and FUGATE, FOREIGN COMMERCE AND THE ANTITRUST LAWS (1958).

[2] United States v. American Tobacco Co., 221 U.S. 106 (1911).

tion of the antitrust laws for agreeing with foreign competitors to restrict or withhold their participation in foreign markets and, in most of the arrangements, to monopolize or restrain as well the domestic trade in their products. An American carrier was found guilty, in 1911, of granting discriminatory rates to users who avoided its competitors' facilities.[3] It appeared that the concern had undertaken this discrimination as its part of a cartel agreement with Canadian carriers, who were joined in the case. The Supreme Court voided the contract insofar as it required an illegal act to be done by an American in the United States, and did not heed the foreigners' complaint that their cartel had thus been rendered inoperative.

In 1927, the Mexican sisal monopoly was broken on a finding that American participators had taken steps to monopolize the American distribution of the fibre.[4]

The remaining cases in this series presented factual situations analogous to the tobacco agreement, though with added complexities in the form of patent and trademark manipulations. These new means were employed to effectuate market divisions in the chemical,[5] titanium,[6] electrical,[7] and roller-bearing[8] industries, which resulted in the entrenching of the American participants in positions of competitive superiority or monopoly with relation to the domestic market. All of these cartels were emasculated by the courts under similar applications of the antitrust law, whether the foreign conspirators were parties to the case or not. The rationales of these decisions were identical in their simplicity:

> "It is suggested that this Court is without jurisdiction to consider conduct abroad, on part of foreign corporations, relating to the commerce of foreign nations. Unquestionably, if the gravamen of the complaint were to impeach the Aussig agreement as such, or the BTP-Laporte quota arrangement as such, the point would be well taken. But that is not the gist of the complaint.

---

[3] United States v. Pacific & Arctic Railway & Navigation Co., 228 U.S. 87 (1913).

[4] United States v. Sisal Sales Corp., 274 U.S. 268 (1927).

[5] United States v. General Dyestuffs Corp., 57 F.Supp. 642 (S.D. N.Y. 1944); United States v. Bayer, Civil No. 15-364 (S.D. N.Y. 1941); United States v. Imperial Chemical Industries, Ltd., 100 F.Supp. 504 (S.D. N.Y. 1951).

[6] United States v. National Lead Co., 63 F.Supp. 513 (S.D. N.Y. 1945), aff'd, 332 U.S. 319 (1947).

[7] United States v. General Electric Co., 80 F.Supp. 989 (S.D. N.Y. 1948); United States v. General Electric Co., 82 F.Supp. 753 (D.N.J. 1949), 115 F.Supp. 835 (S.D. N.Y. 1953).

[8] United States v. Timken Roller Bearing Co., 341 U.S. 593 (1951).

On the contrary, it has been alleged and proved that a conspiracy was entered into, in the United States, to restrain and control the commerce of the world, including the foreign commerce of the United States. The several agreements relating to manufacture and trade within the European markets are but some of the links in the chain which was designed to enthral the entire commerce in titanium. The object of the government's attack is a conspiracy in the United States affecting American commerce, by acts done in the United States as well as abroad. . . .

"The argument has been advanced that this court cannot invalidate contracts with parties who are not within the court's jurisdiction and amenable to its order.[9]

"The absence of NL's foreign associates will, of course, place a practical limitation upon the scope of the court's decree; it does not prevent the court from finding a violation as the facts warrant, and from restraining those within the reach of its mandate from continuing a conspiracy in defiance of the Sherman Act.

* * *

"The second line of evidence is that American producers cannot do business successfully in a cartelized world except on cartel terms; and that, to abstain from such business, would amount to a greater restraint on trade than is involved in joining the cartel; . . . For the courts it is conclusive that Congress has not yet validated such a solution to the problem. Until it does, private agreement and combination and private regulation may not substitute for legislation. Only Congress, not the courts, may grant the required immunity."[10]

No different rationalization for applying antitrust, despite foreign participation in the restraints, can be found in any line of cases. Thus, no court has explicitly used a distinction between public and private law in considering this extension of economic policy. As a concept, indeed, such a distinction is unknown in

---

[9] * * * Whatever may be the scope of this rule, it has not interfered with the action of the courts in striking down systems deemed violative of the antitrust laws even though such systems included leases, licenses, and other forms of agreements, and the lessees, licensees, and other parties to the agreements were not before the court. . . .
Were the rule advocated by NL allowed to operate in the field of restraints upon the foreign commerce of the United States, it would paralyze the enforcement of the law in all cases where one or more of the parties to the conspiracy was an alien corporation over whom the court could acquire no personal jurisdiction. The courts do not so readily permit a frustration of valid national policy. The flexibility of the decree which the court can frame allows for a great degree of accommodation. An example of that is J. I. Case Co. v. N.L.R.B., 1944, 321 U.S. 332.

[10] United States v. National Lead Co., 63 F.Supp. 513, 524, 525, 526 (S.D. N.Y. 1945).

American law. As a practical consideration, it is perhaps implied, in the economic field, within the public policy approach through which the courts have effectuated the antitrust laws' superiority to all private agreements limiting competition. But this superiority demanded recognition by sheer force of statute, since it was expressed by the Sherman Act precisely in derogation of the formerly prevalent "freedom of contract,"[11] with the result that the national interest in the economic order was placed as a standard in what might otherwise be called a field of "private law."

Outside of the basic series of cases outlined above, there exists a decision, not involving an American party, which constitutes an apparent departure from the automatic application of domestic law on the basis of national interest. Judge Learned Hand approached the problem as follows, in the *Alcoa* case:

> "[W]e are concerned only with whether Congress chose to attach liability to the conduct outside the United States of persons not in allegiance to it. . . . Nevertheless, it is quite true that we are not to read general words, such as those in this Act, without regard to the . . . limitations which generally correspond to those fixed by the 'Conflict of Laws'."[12]

His use of the term, "conflict of laws," is deceiving unless it is noted that Judge Hand belongs to the so-called "local law" or "realistic" school. Whether in commercial or tort cases, he proclaims as his law, "the law of the place where I sit."[13] According to Judge Hand, "[N]o court can enforce any law but that of its own sovereign, and, when a suitor comes to a jurisdiction foreign to the place of the tort, he can only invoke an obligation recognized by that sovereign. A foreign sovereign under civilized law imposes an obligation of its own as nearly homologous as possible to that arising in the place where the tort occurs. . . ."[14]

Based on this premise, the use of conflicts law preserves the superiority of the economic order as surely as the direct application of domestic law.[15] This is clear from the fact that Judge Hand in the *Alcoa* case considered Congressional intent first, and only contemplated consulting conflicts of law in the absence of

---

[11] Addyston Pipe and Steel Co. v. United States, 175 U.S. 211 (1899).

[12] United States v. Aluminum Co. of America, 148 F.2d 416, 443 (2d Cir. 1945).

[13] Direktion der Disconto-Gesellschaft v. United States Steel Corp., 300 Fed. 741, 744 (S.D. N.Y. 1924).

[14] Guinness v. Miller, 291 Fed. 769, 770 (S.D. N.Y. 1923), *modified*, 269 U.S. 71 (1925).

[15] See the discussion of Alcoa in Section E, *infra*.

a specific enough expression of the will of Congress. The Judge found that such an intent existed and went no further.

Another line of cases, involving unfair competition rather than cartels, appears likewise inconsistent with the approach of the cartel decisions. This line began in 1909 with the *American Banana* case, the very first to consider the application of the Sherman Act to a transaction with foreign elements. While that decision established an entirely different solution from the one followed today in cartel cases, its rationale was early restricted to the facts of the case and has never been discussed at length by any cartel decision since *Sisal*, in 1927. Recently, however, considerable attention has been given in antitrust literature and appellants' briefs to attempts at broadening the *American Banana* rule to encompass what to this day the courts have considered *dictum*. For this reason, it may be profitable to examine that rule briefly.

Justice Holmes, writing the *American Banana* opinion, used a rule of conflict of laws known as the "territorial" theory to deny the American Banana Company damages under the Sherman Act against an alleged conspiracy between the United Fruit Company and the government of Costa Rica to seize American's plantations, as well as against certain acts of unfair competition by United alone. The Justice concluded:[16]

> "A conspiracy in this country to do acts in another jurisdiction does not draw to itself those acts and make them unlawful, if they are permitted by the local law. . . ."

It is noteworthy that Justice Holmes gave no weight to the national interest represented in the statute, but considered the rights granted under it comparable to mere tort rights. Of course, the suit was a private one, and it had not yet become established that such enforcement of antitrust is as much in the national interest as in the plaintiff's own.[17] Further, not only was the time of this decision one still largely unconcerned with public interests in the economic order, but the Justice himself belonged to the laissez-faire school of economics which he considered to represent the prevailing sense of society in his era.

The case itself was soon distinguished and not allowed to impede application of the antitrust laws in the main line of cartel decisions following it. Thus, in the *Sisal* case, the Court pointed

---

[16] American Banana Co. v. United Fruit Co., 213 U.S. 347, 359 (1909).

[17] See chapter 8, *supra*. United Fruit itself can testify that since American Banana the law has come full circle, United States v. United Fruit Co., 1958 CCH TRADE CASES Para. 68,941 (E.D. La. 1958), reprinted in chapter 8, *supra*.

to acts done on American soil as bringing the antitrust laws into play:

> "The United States complain of a violation of their laws within their own territory by parties subject to their jurisdiction, not merely of something done by another government at the instigation of private parties."[18]

A number of antitrust laws were passed by Congress after the *Banana* case. The *Alkali* opinion used this fact to suggest the implied annihilation of those *Banana* principles, if any there were, contrary to the applicability of antitrust against foreign transactions. Deciding the leading case on the Webb-Pomerene Act,[19] Judge Kaufmann wrote:[20]

> "Far from restricting the application of the antitrust laws abroad, the Webb Act made what, at the time of its passage, were wide extensions in the extraterritorial effect of those laws designed to preserve competition. *The oft distinguished Banana case had at that time left in doubt the extent to which the Sherman Act applied to extraterritorial restraints of trade.*"[21]

As a minority comment in the Attorney General's Committee Report[22] points out, these distinguishing and abrogating decisions have not rejected the territorial limitation placed by the *Banana* case on the illegality of acts of unfair competition done abroad. Nonetheless, it has become clear that the *Banana* case has a more limited application even in that sphere than at first appeared. Its principles were not allowed to prevent an injunction against an unlicensed "school" in the United States which thrived on the awarding of worthless medical and other diplomas to South American correspondence "students." Calling this unfair competition against reputable schools, the court wrote:[23]

> "Congress has the power to prevent unfair trade practices in foreign commerce by citizens of the United States, although some of the acts are done outside the territorial limits of the United States. * * * The exercise by the United States of its sovereign control over its commerce and the acts of its resident citizens therein is no invasion of the sovereignty of any other

---

[18] United States v. Sisal Sales Corp., 274 U.S. 268, 276 (1927); see also United States v. National Lead Co., *supra* n.6.

[19] 40 STAT. 516 (1918), 15 U.S.C. §§ 61-65 (1952). See, *infra*, Section C.

[20] United States v. United States Alkali Export Association, 86 F. Supp. 59, 67 (S.D. N.Y. 1949).

[21] Italicized part represents the footnote at this point in the text.

[22] REPORT OF THE ATTORNEY GENERAL'S NATIONAL COMMITTEE TO STUDY THE ANTITRUST LAWS 67, footnote 5 (1955).

[23] Branch v. Federal Trade Commission, 141 F.2d 31, 35 (7th Cir. 1944),

country or any attempt to act beyond the territorial jurisdiction of the United States."

Trademarks have also received protection beyond that apparently allowed by *American Banana*. Using a competitor's trade name in Mexico, well known there though registered only in the United States, constituted unfair competition by the American individual so using it, against the Bulova Company in *Steele* v. *Bulova Watch Co.*[24]

That these developments are not of the same nature as those in cartel cases is now apparent from the recently decided *Vanity Fair* case.[25] Vanity alleged that the defendants, acting in conspiracy, had committed acts of unfair competition in Canada. Plaintiff, a Pennsylvania corporation, and defendant, a Canadian corporation, concurrently held the "Vanity Fair" trade mark in their respective countries of incorporation. Each used its trademark in the general field of lingerie.

> "During the years 1945-1953 the defendant ceased to use its own 'Vanity Fair' trademark, purchased branded merchandise from the plaintiff, and sold this merchandise under advertisements indicating that it was of United States origin and of plaintiff's manufacture. . . . In 1953, defendant resumed the use of its own trademark 'Vanity Fair' and, simultaneously, under the same trademark, sold plaintiff's branded merchandise and cheaper merchandise of Canadian manufacture." [25a]

No danger to the American economic order existed in the practice complained of by Vanity. It was rather a case concerned with the protection of an American property right which the court considered unenforceable against a foreigner abroad. On these facts, the decision is not only consistent with the current application of antitrust to international agreements[26] but it clarifies by contrast the basis for that application. It now becomes apparent that the obligation imposed on Mr. Steele in the *Bulova* case stemmed not from antitrust considerations, but from the provisions of the Lanham Trade-Mark Act,[27] which bound him as an American.

The courts have continued to apply antitrust regulation to the type of case which began with *American Tobacco*, and have done so without any further elaboration of rationale. The re-

---

[24] 344 U.S. 280 (1952).

[25] Vanity Fair Mills v. T. Eaton Co., Ltd., 234 F.2d 633 (2d Cir. 1956), *cert. denied*, 352 U.S. 871 (1956), *rehearing denied*, 352 U.S. 913 (1956).
[25a] *Id.*, at 638.

[26] The two lines have been considered irreconcilable. Oliver, *Extraterritorial Application of United States Legislation Against Restrictive or Unfair Trade Practices*, 51 AM.J.INT.L. 380, 384 (1957).

[27] 60 STAT. 427 (1946), 15 U.S.C. §§ 1051-1127 (1952).

newed attacks on this tradition following the aftermath of the *ICI* case[28] focused attention on the *Holophane* case[29] as a new opportunity to test the law on international agreements. On the applicability of antitrust to contracts entered into with foreign companies the lower court offered no comment, but assumed its propriety with the statement that the cartel agreements were in violation of the Sherman Act. The court went on to decree that all those provisions were void and were not to be honored by the parties thereto, and enjoined Holophane from refusing to fill orders from abroad as required by the agreement.[30]

The Supreme Court, in a *per curiam* opinion, affirmed the judgment and this much of the decree unanimously, despite the fact that the briefs before it had contained extensive arguments on the law of conflicts, public international law, and considerations of international relations.[31] Thus the case has become added authority for the reasoning established since *American Tobacco* in cartel cases, and an implicit rejection of international law, public or private, as applicable to them.

Footnoting, as it were, this rejection, and supplying another case to the growing line of cartel decisions, the *Oldham* opinion disposed of the newest challenge to domestic antitrust law, the "antitrust" provisions which have been included in recent commercial treaties of the United States:[32]

"In 1953 the United States and Japan entered into a Treaty of Friendship, Commerce and Navigation. The effect of the Treaty is to accord 'national treatment' and 'most favored nation treatment' by one party to nationals of the other party. . . .

"Article XVIII of the Treaty states:

'1. The two Parties agree that business practices which restrain competition, limit access to markets or foster monopolistic control, and which are engaged in or made effective by one or more private or public commercial enterprises . . . may have harmful effects upon commerce between their respective territories. Accordingly, each Party agrees upon the request of the other Party to consult with respect to any such prac-

---

[28] See below, Section F.

[29] United States v. Holophane Co., Inc., 119 F.Supp. 114 (S.D. Ohio 1954), *affirmed*, 352 U.S. 903 (1956). See *infra* p. 251.

[30] United States v. Holophane Co., Inc., 1954 CCH TRADE CASES Para. 67,679 (S.D. Ohio 1954). See *infra* p. 283.

[31] For the oral argument on these points before the Court, see Oliver, *Extraterritorial Application of United States Legislation Against Restrictive or Unfair Trade Practices*, 51 AM.J.INT.L. 380, 382 (1957).

[32] United States v. R. P. Oldham Co., 152 F.Supp. 818, 822-823 (N.D. Cal. 1957).

tices and to take such measures as it deems appropriate with a view to eliminating such harmful effects.'

* * *

It is contended by the defendants that Article XVIII provides the exclusive remedy available to the government in reaching the conspiracy charged in the indictment.

"I cannot agree that Article XVIII was intended to provide any such exclusive remedy. The language of this Article is permissive rather than mandatory. If it had been intended that the Article should operate as a *pro tanto* revocation of the antitrust laws, the Article could easily have been so worded. The tenor of the entire Treaty is *equal* treatment to nationals of the other party, not *better* treatment. In view of these considerations, I conclude that Article XVIII was intended to supplement the antitrust laws, not replace them.

"Even if Article XVIII were held to provide an exclusive remedy for antitrust violations, the defendant importers would have no standing to invoke this Article. All are American corporations. Certainly the Treaty was not intended to exempt nationals from the sanctions of their own country's laws. *Cf. Skiriotes* v. *State of Florida*, 313 U.S. 69 (1941).

"Nor do I think Kinoshita & Co., Ltd., U.S.A., would have any standing to invoke Article XVIII. Though wholly owned by a Japanese corporation, the defendant Kinoshita is an American corporation organized under the law of California. Article XXII of the Treaty is the only article devoted to definition of terms used in the Treaty. After defining 'national treatment' and 'most favored nation treatment' in paragraphs 1 and 2, respectively, Article XXII goes on in paragraph 3 to define 'companies,' and then states:

'* * * Companies constituted under the applicable laws and regulations within the territories of either Party *shall be deemed companies thereof* and shall have their judicial status recognized within the territories of the other party.' (Emphasis added.)

* * *

Thus by the terms of the Treaty itself, as well as by established principles of the law, a corporation, organized under the laws of a given jurisdiction, is a creature of that jurisdiction, with no greater rights, privileges or immunities than any other corporation of that jurisdiction.[33]"

Whatever the lengths to which an antitrust decree may go, to this day the principle remains clear that the antitrust laws as

---

[33] But of course, the rights of an alien owned corporation may be *less* than those of domestically owned corporations. See Clark v. Uebersee Finanzkorporation, A.G., 332 U.S. 480 (1947); Daimler Co. v. Continental Tyre and Rubber Co., (1916) A.C. 307 (H.L.).

such apply to cartel agreements and international monopolies involving American parties, regardless of the place of the contracts involved. The law applied is domestic law, and it is applied to further the policy of antitrust to protect the American economic order.[34]

Most of the following sections will, therefore, deal with the limitations imposed upon domestic law by the peculiarities of cases involving foreign parties and acts done abroad. The basic law applicable is that already discussed in the preceding chapters.

Extensions to cases not involving American parties will be analyzed separately. After considering the question of illegality as such, the problem of what sanctions and remedies may be applied to acts found to be illegal is dealt with under decrees.

One section will also consider the criticisms and suggestions that have been offered from the point of view of foreign courts and international private and public law scholars.

(B) RESTRAINTS ON DOMESTIC TRADE UNDER AGREEMENTS WITH FOREIGNERS

(1) Private Agreements Between American and Foreign Firms

Originally, and to this day, the typical case bringing foreign acts and parties under the antitrust laws has involved agreements between an American and a foreign business organization to restrain each other's operation and, sometimes, those of competitors in their respective countries or in the world market. For brevity, this class of cases will henceforth be referred to as the cartel[35] cases. They are considered below according to the methods they employ to stabilize competition.

(a) *Direct restraints*

Price fixing and division of markets are the usual goals of international cartels. The domestic law, which generally outlaws all explicit agreements to fix prices and divide markets, has been applied without elaboration to such cartels.

The clearest case of illegal price fixing in international transactions is illustrated by an agreement between Norwegian sardine dealers and American distributors fixing resale prices for the sardines in the United States.[36]

---

[34] *Accord,* Timberg, *Extraterritorial Jurisdiction Under the Sherman Act,* 11 RECORD 101, 109 (1956).

[35] The term "Cartel" is used in its American sense, signifying a combination in restraint of international trade.

[36] United States v. A.B.C. Canning A/S, CCH TRADE CASES, Supp. Vol. IV, para. 4213 (S.D. N.Y. 1931).

No less unlawful is an understanding to set prices between American and foreign competitors with regard to goods in both markets. An agreement of this sort was involved in the *Timken* case,[37] where the parties agreed on prices of products sold by each in the other's territory.

Both such price schemes have been brought under the domestic standard expressed in the *Socony Vacuum* case:

> "The reasonableness of prices has no constancy due to the dynamic quality of business facts underlying price structures. . . . Any combination which tampers with price structures is engaged in an unlawful activity. . . . The Act places all such schemes beyond the pale and protects that vital part of our economy against any degree of interference."[38]

Outright market allocations between competitors are equally illegal on their face. This principle was established in the *Tobacco* case[39] for international markets, and refined in *National Lead*. The latter case explicitly held the division of foreign markets between American and foreign competitors to be such a violation of the Sherman Act.[40]

It is as true in international as in domestic cases, however, that a reasonable market division may be excused if it is ancillary to a contract of sale. This exception is illustrated by a contract between Kodak and Dresden dividing their markets after Kodak's purchase of Dresden's photographic paper business in certain areas. Since that business was based on a secret process, the court found that Kodak had "bought the business of the Dresden Company to which the territorial rights were merely incidental and protective," rather than buying the territorial rights "to which the business of the Dresden Company was a mere incident."[41]

But the realities of the circumstances, not the mere presence of a sale, are always considered where the excuse of ancillary agreement is pleaded.[42]

A final point of comparison between domestic and foreign application of the Sherman Act prohibitions is on the allowability of reasonableness as an excuse. Price fixing and market division admit no evidence for the purpose of demonstrating their rea-

---

37 United States v. Timken Roller Bearing Co., 341 U.S. 593 (1951).
38 United States v. Socony-Vacuum Oil Co., 310 U.S. 150, 221 (1940).
39 United States v. American Tobacco Co., 221 U.S. 106 (1911).
40 United States v. National Lead Co., 63 F.Supp. 513, 525 (S.D. N.Y. 1945).
41 Eastman Kodak Co. v. Sutherland, 52 F.2d 592, 595 (3d Cir. 1931).
42 United States v. Holophane Co., Inc., 119 F.Supp. 114, Finding of Fact No. 19 (S.D. Ohio 1954).

sonableness. This is the significance of their designation by the courts as *per se* unreasonable. Despite some criticism, the doctrine limiting the justification and excusability of such restraints seems firmly established, especially after the *Northern Pacific* decision.[43]

This rule seems particularly applicable to international restraints. Its rationale in domestic cases has been that the question whether a certain price scheme or market division has a substantially bad effect on competition is too difficult, if not impossible, to answer in a judicial proceeding. To make such a determination in an international case might require considering conditions outside the United States, perhaps even extending the inquiry to the entire world market.[44] The rule is applicable, on this premise, to indirect restrictions as well. In the industrial property cases, the illegality of the agreements is established upon proof that their principal result could only be price fixing or market division.

The *Holophane* opinion illustrates a typical small cartel as well as the approach of the courts in determining the illegality of such an arrangement.

UNITED STATES v. HOLOPHANE CO., INC.

United States District Court for the Southern District of Ohio
119 F.Supp. 114 (1954)

"UNDERWOOD, Chief Judge.

"This is an action by the United States of America to prevent and restrain the defendant, Holophane Company, Inc., from engaging in an allegedly unlawful combination and conspiracy, and from being a party to contracts allegedly in restraint of interstate and foreign trade and commerce in violation of Section 1 of the Sherman Anti-Trust Act, 26 STAT. 209 (1890), 15 U.S.C.A. § 1.

* * *

"Findings of Fact.

"1. The defendant is a corporation, organized and existing under the laws of the State of Delaware, and maintaining offices in New York, New York, and a factory in Newark, Ohio. It is

---

[43] Northern Pacific Railway Co. v. United States, 78 S.Ct. 514 (1958), reprinted and discussed in chapter 4, *supra*. The trend toward *per se* rules was criticized specifically as to international cases in Oppenheim, *Federal Antitrust Legislation: Guideposts to a Revised National Antitrust Policy,* 50 MICH. L.REV. 1139, at 1175 (1952).

[44] United States v. Timken Roller Bearing Co., 341 U.S. 593, 599 (1951). *Cf.* REPORT OF THE ATTORNEY GENERAL'S NATIONAL COMMITTEE TO STUDY THE ANTITRUST LAWS 83 (1955); Carlston, *Antitrust Policy Abroad,* 49 Nw.U. L.REV. 713 (1954).

engaged in the manufacture and sale of prismatic glassware and illuminating appliances containing prismatic glassware.

* * *

"3. Holophane Limited, hereinafter referred to as 'Limited,' a joint stock company organized and existing under the laws of the United Kingdom with offices and principal place of business in London, England, is named as a co-conspirator. . . .

"4. La Societe Anonyme Francaise Holophane, hereinafter referred to as 'Francaise,' a corporation organized and existing under the laws of France, with offices and principal place of business in Paris, France, is named as co-conspirator. . . .

* * *

"9. Otis A. Mygatt held the controlling stock interest in both 'Limited' and 'Francaise' in 1925. 'Limited' held all of the stock of the Holophane Glass Co., Inc. Each company was separately managed. . . .

"10. In 1925, a group of executives, engineers and employees of the afore-mentioned Holophane Glass Company, Inc., organized the predecessor company of the defendant, for the purpose of purchasing the Holophane Glass Company, Inc., from 'Limited.' . . .

* * *

"12. On September 15, 1925, the defendant's predecessor and 'Limited' entered into a trading agreement which was characterized by Joel B. Liberman as a reciprocal trade and patent agreement of great value. It was signed on behalf of 'Limited' by H. Hepworth Thompson as Managing Director, and Charles Franck as Vice President. It contained no termination date, and was in effect at the time of the trial.

"The essential features of the agreement are as follows:

(a) The territory of the defendant's predecessor is defined as that part of the Continent of America north of the Panama Canal and adjacent islands (not including West Indies), the Philippine Islands, the Republic of Cuba, and the Empire of Japan. The territory of 'Limited' is defined as the whole of the world except the territory of the defendant's predecessor and the Republic of France and its Colonies.

(b) Each party agrees to use every means in its power to prevent the exportation from its territory into the territory of the other, of products sold or manufactured by it, except with the consent in writing of that party.

(c) Each party agrees that it will not carry on trade in the territory of the other, except at the request and for the benefit of that party.

(d) Each party agrees that it will neither apply for nor obtain patent or trademark protection in the territory of the other, except at the request and for the benefit of that party.

(e) Each party agrees to communicate and assign every invention, design, discovery or improvement and trademark to the other, and render any aid necessary to enable the other to secure proper protection in its territory.

(f) Each party agrees to supply to the other, when requested, Holophane products at a price equal to factory cost, plus 30%, delivered at place of manufacture.

(g) The agreement defines 'Holophane products' as any product sold under the trademark or trade name 'Holophane' and-or manufactured or sold by either company.

"13. On June 29, 1926, defendant's predecessor and 'Francaise' entered into a patent and manufacturing agreement which . . . in all of its essential terms is identical to the trading agreement between defendant's predecessor and 'Limited.' The agreement defines the territory of 'Francaise' as the Republic of France and its Colonies. . . .

* * *

"15. * * * Although the agreements cover the entire world, the defendant admits that in 1925 there were many countries in the world in which neither the defendant, 'Limited' nor 'Francaise' carried on business; other countries in which they made only occasional or isolated sales; and that even to date there are a number of countries in which none of the three companies had made any substantial effort to develop a market.

* * *

"16. * * *

(c) On June 11, 1945, defendant and 'Limited' entered into an intercompany buying agreement, which elaborated upon that provision in the 1925 trading agreement which required the parties to supply each other with Holophane products. The new arrangements permitted a party to ship to and invoice directly, a customer located in the territory of the other but only at the request and for the benefit of the party owning the territory. It further permitted the selling company to render engineering service directly to the customer to assure the securing of the order. Accordingly, new formulae were devised for determining the profit due the party into whose territory the shipment was made in order to compensate the selling company for the clerical and engineering service rendered.

It was also agreed that, with regard to any direct inquiries or purchase orders received by either company from the territory of the other, such orders or inquiries would be referred to that company for instructions.

* * *

"18. In fulfillment of its obligations under the agreements with 'Limited' and 'Francaise,' the defendant has imposed upon its customers and dealers contractual obligations not to export products purchased from it into the territory of 'Limited' and 'Francaise.' The defendant rejects orders and requests for quotations from its customers whenever it suspects that the order is to be shipped into the territory of either 'Francaise' or 'Limited,' and refers such customers either to 'Francaise' or 'Limited'. This practice of the defendant has substantially affected the foreign commerce of its customers.

"19. Although the defendant's answer alleges that the restrictive agreements were 'reasonable and necessary for the protection of the business and good will sold,' the defendant failed to establish . . . that the agreements were subordinate to the alleged lawful purpose. The evidence establishes that the restrictive agreements were designed to eliminate competition between the parties and with outsiders in all markets of the world, and were neither measurable by, limited to, nor subordinate to the reasonable necessities of the sale.

"20. The restrictive arrangements between the defendant and the co-conspirators, 'Limited' and 'Francaise,' are in unreasonable restraint of the interstate and foreign commerce of the United States in prismatic glassware. . . .

"21. The intended effects of the agreements between the defendant and the co-conspirators will continue unless prevented by this Court.

"Conclusions of Law.

"1. The court has jurisdiction of the subject matter hereof and of the defendant, and the complaint states a cause of action against the defendant under the provisions of the Act of July 2, 1890, entitled 'An act to protect trade and commerce against unlawful restraints and monopolies,' as amended, commonly known as the Sherman Act, 15 U.S.C.A. § 1 *et seq.*

"2. Beginning in or about 1925 and continuing at all times thereafter to the date of these findings, the defendant and the co-conspirators have been continuously engaged in a combination and conspiracy in restraint of trade and commerce in prismatic glassware and illuminating appliances containing prismatic glassware among the several states of the United States and with foreign nations and have been and are now parties to contracts, agreements and understandings in restraint of such trade and commerce; all in violation of Section 1 of the Sherman Act.

"3. Plaintiff is entitled to a decree."

(b) *Restraints through industrial property*

Much discussion has centered on the use of patents and trademarks and on the limits within which they are lawful subjects of agreement.

". . . American manufacturers are particularly worried with respect to the following questions in connection with agreements with foreign companies, whether controlled or independent concerns:

(A) Is it proper for them to enter into an agreement applicable to a group of countries as well as to a single country?

"Assuming that an agreement between an American company and a foreign company for exclusive manufacturing and exclusive distribution, involving patent licensing, trademark licensing or communication of know-how is legal if applicable only to the country where the foreign company is located, does such an agreement become unlawful if it grants such rights to the foreign company for a group of countries?

"One would have thought that the question should be answered in the affirmative. What difference does it make ultimately whether the American manufacturer enters into 20 such agreements with companies in 20 separate countries or into a single license agreement with one company covering these 20 countries?

* * *

(B) Is it proper for the American manufacturer to restrict himself from importing and selling his own products in the territory of the licensee and to restrict the licensee from importing and selling the licensee's products in the United States?

* * *

(C) Is it unlawful agreement for the American company to require the foreign licensee to use the trademark of the American company and no other trademark?"[45]

The answers to these questions can be determined by examining the domestic patent arrangements which have been found to violate the antitrust laws. Such an inquiry reveals that the courts have applied consistent tests and have in fact expressed principles not at all unlike those proposed in the literature.[46] The *Crown Zellerbach* opinion presented the following classic formulation:

"Antitrust considerations are not to override the limited monopoly conferred by a patent, nor may a patent be employed beyond its scope for purposes condemned by the Sherman Act.

". . . The limited monopoly granted to an inventor cannot be made to serve as the instrumentality of unlawful combination, or 'as a peg upon which to attach contracts with former or prospective competitors, touching business relations other than the making and vending of patented devices.' *United States* v. *Line Material Co.*, 333 U.S. 287, 304 (1948). The value of the

---

[45] A Study of the Antitrust Laws, *Hearings Before the Subcommittee on Antitrust and Monopoly of the Senate Committee on the Judiciary,* 84th Cong., 1st Sess., Part IV (Foreign Trade), at 1730-1731 (1956).

[46] For a critical evaluation of the cases in this field, see *The Patent System and the Modern Economy,* Study of the Subcommittee on Patents, Trademarks, and Copyrights of the Senate Committee on the Judiciary, 84th Cong., 2d Sess. (1957).

patent monopoly lies largely in its transferability, through licensing arrangements. But patent licenses cannot be used simply as a means for dividing a market among competitors, and of eliminating competition beyond the scope of the patent claims. *United States* v. *United States Gypsum Co.,* 333 U.S. 364 (1948); *Hartford-Empire Co.* v. *United States,* 323 U.S. 386 (1945). The complaint sets up a situation where patent licenses have been utilized to support a system of pervasive control in the paper towel cabinet and paper towel industry. Regardless of the possible legality of each of the agreements and practices standing alone, their total effect, qualified by the alleged unlawful purpose to restrain trade, will suffice to support the complaint against a motion to dismiss."[47]

A division of markets is a logical and allowable result of an exclusive license to a product patent. Where the market division is sought by collecting all patents in the field, the courts have found a case of using the patent for restraint of trade rather than the protection of inventions. In the international cases, this has been the basis for finding the various patent arrangements illegal.

Some of these cases have also involved grant-back and cross-licensing arrangements as well as patent pools, all of which were found to be used primarily for a division of foreign markets. They confirm the general observation that

". . . contractual arrangements relating to patents and patent rights are generally outside the patent law and are tested by general law, including the antitrust laws, which prohibit combinations in restraint of trade. The restraint inherent in a valid patent is not the result of combination and is not forbidden."[48]

As a rule, these remarks should apply to the use of trademarks in the division of markets. The *Timken* case[49] is authority that they do, although there the parties also had agreed explicitly to divide their markets.

Generally, an examination of the facts found by the courts in industrial property cases provides a clear basis for deciding the legality of any arrangement.[50] A more explanatory rule than that which declares illegal any restraint beyond one natural to

---

[47] United States v. Crown Zellerbach Corp., 141 F.Supp. 118, 126 (N.D. Ill. 1956).

[48] *Antitrust Problems in the Exploitation of Patents,* a Staff Report to Subcommittee No. 5 of the House Committee on the Judiciary, 84th Cong., 2d Sess. 6 (1957).

[49] United States v. Timken Roller Bearing Co., 341 U.S. 593 (1951).

[50] An excellent analysis of the domestic cases is found in *Review of the American Patent System,* Report of the Subcommittee on Patents, Trademarks, and Copyrights of the Senate Committee on the Judiciary, 84th Cong., 2d Sess. (1956).

the industrial property itself, would be too particular to describe the breadth of the actual decisions.[51]

(2) Agreements Involving American Firms and Foreign Governments

(a) *Participation by foreign government corporations*

In a case involving an alleged international petroleum cartel, a party to the agreement was a foreign government corporation. The only consideration of law raised by this situation concerned the immunity of such an agency to service of process in an investigation of details of the cartel. Other parties were accorded no special privilege derived from the participation of a sovereign in the agreement. Practically, however, the effect of the decision might be to hamper the preparation of evidence against the rest of the cartel, and possibly prevent prosecution.

On the liability of government corporations, the *Petroleum* case established the rule that a private corporation enjoys sovereign immunity when it is used in pursuance of a governmental function, such as national defense.

> "A special grand jury has been convened in the District of Columbia to investigate possible violations of Title 15 U.S.C.A. §§ 1-23, Federal Antitrust Laws. Voluminous subpoenas *duces tecum* have been served on various oil companies. . . .
>
>   ❋ ❋ ❋
>
> "Anglo-Iranian Oil Company, Ltd., is a British Company, whose headquarters are located in London. It has offices in other parts of the world, including an office at 610 Fifth Avenue, New York City, New York, where the present subpoena *duces tecum* was served. A general appearance was entered by counsel for that company.
>
> "Although the British Government has a capital investment of approximately 35% of the total capital, it dominates the ownership of the 'ordinary shares' which carry with them the greater portion of voting rights and thus controls the company.
>
>   ❋ ❋ ❋
>
> "The first issue is whether the corporate entity involved in the Anglo-Iranian Oil Company is of such a character as to be recognized as a unit of the British Government. Under the circumstances at hand this would also require an observation to be made as to the relationship existing between the corporate-agent and the Foreign Sovereign's governmental functions and duties.

---

[51] See Derenberg, *Impact of the Antitrust Laws on Trade-Marks in Foreign Commerce,* 27 N.Y.U. L.REV. 414 (1952).

". . . Anglo-Iranian came into being as the result of an agreement between Anglo-Persian Oil Company, Ltd., and the British Government in the year 1914. The latter acquired its interest in this company to insure a proper supply of petroleum, crude oil and other products for the British Fleet. In the agreement drawn up with Anglo-Persian Oil Company there appears the following clause:

'Paragraph 13. A large consumer like the Admiralty, with the national interest of naval defense in its keeping, cannot, however, place itself in a position of dependence for vital supplies upon a few large companies whose interests are necessarily cosmopolitan and financial, * * *. It is important and essential in naval interest to secure that at least one large British Oil Company shall be maintained, having independent control of considerable supplies of natural petroleum, and bound to the Government by financial and contractual obligations * * *'.

* * *

"This court notes that one of Great Britain's contentions before the International Court of Justice in 1951, with regard to the Iranian Oil disputes, was that the agreement of 1933 between Iran and the Anglo-Iranian Oil Company was in effect a treaty or convention between *two sovereign states* and therefore the International Court of Justice did have jurisdiction over the controversy. (Emphasis supplied.)

"This court is of the impression that the corporation, Anglo-Iranian Oil Company, is indistinguishable from the Government of Great Britain. . . .

* * *

"The consequences of a successful prosecution of Anglo-Iranian here would in reality be to charge and find the British Government guilty of violating a law of the United States which imposes criminal penalties.

"This court has compared *United States* v. *Deutsche Kalisyndikat Gesellschaft*, D.C., 31 F. 2d 199, where it was held a suit by the United States Government to enjoin violations of antitrust laws was maintainable against a corporation organized under the general corporation law of France and in which France owned eleven-fifteenths of the capital stock. However, the French Government was involved in a commercial venture, entirely divorced from any governmental function. There is a vast distinction between a seafaring island-nation maintaining a constant supply of maritime fuel and a government seeking additional revenue in the American markets and causing a direct injury in the United States to our domestic commercial structure."[52]

---

[52] In re Investigation of World Arrangements with Relation to the Production, Transportation, Refining and Distribution of Petroleum, 13 F.R.D. 280, 288, 290-291 (D. D.C. 1952).

It still appears that an American business organization may not enter a more restrictive agreement with a government corporation than with any private foreign business, where a world cartel is its goal.[53] The court in the above case recognized this principle by allowing the subpoena power to reach the American participants. It should be noted also that immunity under international law did not legalize the acts of the British company, but only protected it from judicial and administrative process.[54]

The *Kalisyndikat* case, distinguished by the court in the *Petroleum* case, above, continues to be authority for the proposition that a foreign corporation may not engage in restraints in the domestic American market, even if its own government controls or regulates it.

> "A foreign sovereign cannot authorize his agents to violate the law in a foreign jurisdiction, or to perform any sovereign or governmental functions within the domain of another sovereign, without his consent. He, therefore, cannot claim as a matter of comity or otherwise that the act of the alleged agent in such case is the act of the sovereign, and that a suit against the agent is in fact a suit against the sovereign. This is especially so when such alleged agent is a foreign corporation, or an officer, agent, or employee of a foreign corporation, which is doing business here only by consent, which cannot be assumed to be given, except on condition that they shall be subject to our laws."[55]

(b) *Participation by government-regulated foreign corporations*

No issue of immunity is raised where an organization based on a government-granted monopoly or franchise enters a restraint agreement with American firms.

Recently, however, much emphasis has been placed on the national interest of foreign governments in the preservation of monopolies and cartels, and it has been suggested that the antitrust laws of the United States should not be applied to such business entities.[56] The present status of the law in America must be considered under its proper aspects if it is to be clearly presented. A distinction therefore is made here between the law on agreements entered into by such foreign organizations with

---

[53] For cases involving only the foreign commerce of the United States, see Section C, *infra*.

[54] The immunity problem is analyzed by Wedderburn, *Sovereign Immunity of Foreign Public Corporations*, 6 INT'L. & COMP. L.Q. 290 (1957). See Section F, *infra*.

[55] United States v. Deutsche Kalisyndikat Gesellschaft, 31 F.2d 199, 203 (S.D. N.Y. 1929).

[56] See Section G, *infra*.

American firms to restrict an American market, and the law applied to the doing of business in the United States by such an organization acting alone, or outside America in cooperation with American firms. The latter situations are dealt with in Sections E and C, respectively, of this chapter.

The law applied to specially franchised foreign corporations which enter into combinations in the American market continues to be represented by the *Sisal* case.[57] There, the Mexican Government granted a monopoly to a producer of sisal fibre. The producer thus became the sole supplier of sisal to the United States, whereupon he entered into arrangements with certain American firms to monopolize the importation and distribution of the fibre in this country. Pointing to numerous restraints exercised by the American agents under the agreements, the Supreme Court held the Sherman Act applicable to these activities and upheld the injunction against the Mexican monopoly and its American partners ordering them to desist from such restraining practices in the domestic market.

The Department of Justice is applying this rule of law in its suit against the *Swiss Watch* cartel.[58] It has urged a requirement that the cartel cease to exercise any restrictive control over its watches once they are sold to the American importers. The cartel was alleged to have required buyers to sell at specified prices and blacklisted any importer refusing to comply.

(C) RESTRAINTS ON FOREIGN TRADE

(1) Restraints Imposed by Agreements

It is apparent that the cases discussed in previous sections involved restraints on the foreign trade of the United States, but their essential characteristic consisted of the restraint on the domestic market. It was this element which brought domestic law to bear upon the agreements as a matter of course. A number of cases, however, have dealt with foreign trade directly. Therefore, they require consideration from this point of view, to determine how far American domestic law is applied to foreigners in that market.

Under the Webb-Pomerene Act,[59] American firms may cooperate in conducting their export business, without violating the antitrust laws. But it is clear from the Act itself that no restraint

---

[57] United States v. Sisal Sales Corp., 274 U.S. 268 (1927).

[58] See Section E, *infra*, for other aspects of the case. United States v. Watchmakers of Switzerland Information Center, Inc., Civ. No. 96-170 (S.D. N.Y., filed Oct. 19, 1954).

[59] 40 STAT. 516 (1918), 15 U.S.C. §§ 61-65 (1952).

will be allowed against American competitors who are not connected with the export association, nor will any anti-competitive effect on the domestic market be tolerated.

From the *Alkali* case,[60] it further appears clear that an export association may not be allowed to enter international cartel agreements. Such a restraint is an interference with American exports and imports and is covered by the antitrust laws. In other words, an export association has no privilege in this regard over an individual trader. Its exemption extends only to agreements among its members as to their exports.

> "Viewing the Webb Act, in the light of contemporaneous interpretation of the antitrust laws, considering the impact of the Act when read as a whole, and giving careful attention to the entire legislative history of its passage, the conclusion is irresistible that the Webb-Pomerene Act affords no right to export associations to engage on a world-wide scale in practices so antithetical to the American philosophy of free competition. The international agreements between defendants allocating exclusive markets, assigning quotas in sundry markets, fixing prices on an international scale, and selling through joint agents are not those 'agreements in the course of export trade'. . . ."[61]

Cooperation between Webb-Pomerene associations and their foreign competitors may exist without formal agreement. The British Monopolies and Restrictive Practices Commission reported an example of such an arrangement in the rubber tire market.

> "397. Dunlop have stated that, in view of the competition which had to be faced in the 1920s, both Dunlop and the American manufacturers found the export market unprofitable, largely because of false reports of competitive prices. Both parties, therefore, have considered it advisable to adopt the practice of consulting, quite informally, through the Rubber Export Association of America, before changes in export prices are made, although neither side is bound by any agreement. This Association is a corporation formed in 1918 under the Webb-Pomerene Act, which, subject to certain provisos, permits American manufacturers to cooperate in export trade in order to compete effectively with foreign manufacturers and companies. The export companies of all the larger American tyre manufacturers are members of this Association, which is stated to provide means for exchanging information on all rubber export matters, and the result of these exchanges is a common price policy.

---

[60] United States v. United States Alkali Export Association, 86 F.Supp. 59 (S.D. N.Y. 1949).

[61] *Id.*, at 70.

"398. It appears that consultation between the R.E.A. and Dunlop, which relates solely to price movements and results in no allocation of markets, has taken place since 1925, and that this has resulted substantially in a common world price level in all markets where the prices of tyres are not determined by local manufacture. . . .

"399. . . . Generally speaking, the ceiling for export prices (f.o.b.) has been the wholesale domestic price level in the U.S.A. or the United Kingdom, whichever is the lower at the time, but we are told that this arises not from any agreement between Dunlop and the R.E.A. but because both wish to discourage exports by 'domestic' traders who, having no expert knowledge of conditions overseas, might prejudice the market by sending out unsuitable types of tyres if export prices were higher than domestic prices. . . .

"400. Dunlop consider that if it were not for these consultations with the R.E.A., there would probably be a price war with the American groups in world markets. These groups, with their large domestic turnover allied to a low ratio of export, could afford to export at a loss. The result, in Dunlop's view, might be the elimination of the smaller British manufacturers and a serious fall in prices, leading to a reduction in the total value of United Kingdom exports and a general deterioration in the terms of trade."[62]

The legality of this alleged price leadership in the tire market is open to question. It may be that the use of a Webb-Pomerene association to promote price equality would bring the case under the prohibition of the Webb Act itself. In any event, there is no question that the situation involves the domestic market of the United States, for it affects both American exports and imports and involves parties competing in the American market. Should it come before the courts, the operation might therefore be regarded from the point of view of cartel regulation, discussed in the previous section, rather than as a case of foreign commerce alone.

A further limitation on Webb-Pomerene activities deals with the relation between the parties themselves, but is of interest because it may restrict the advantages of an association as against its foreign competitors. *Minnesota Mining* struck down the use of joint subsidiaries by Webb-Pomerene associates:

"Exculpation is also sought under the terms of the Webb-Pomerene Act. . . . This is no cover for defendants' conduct.

---

[62] THE MONOPOLIES AND RESTRICTIVE PRACTICES COMMISSION, REPORT ON THE SUPPLY AND EXPORT OF PNEUMATIC TYRES 84 (December 8, 1955).

The statute is by its first section limited to that sort of 'export trade' which consists of 'commerce in goods ° ° ° exported ° ° ° from the United States ° ° ° to any foreign nation.' As the House Committee on the Judiciary stated, 'The object of this bill is to aid and encourage our manufacturers and producers to extend our foreign trade.' To use American capital, no matter how profitably, to extend the exclusively internal trade of a foreign country may contract but is unlikely to extend our foreign trade. Nothing in the statute, nor in its legislative history, nor in the penumbra of its policy justifies or has any bearing upon the right of defendants to join in establishing and financing factories in foreign lands. Export of capital is not export trade."[63]

Outside the Webb-Pomerene provisions, when an individual American firm enters agreements with foreign businesses to restrict its trade abroad, without undertaking any restraints on its domestic operations, the reasoning of the cartel cases no longer applies. True, such an agreement might be said to have an effect on American business, insofar as it affects the business of the particular American party. No case has even been litigated on these facts, but a *dictum* in the *ICI* case casts doubt on the validity of such an arrangement:

"[T]he proof here shows an American concern, already established in a foreign local market, and a British concern, which has a foothold in the same local market, combining to form a jointly owned company to the end that the same foreign market may be developed for their mutual benefit and profits divided on an agreed basis. To this, and as an incident to the formation of the foreign company, we find added by agreement not only joint contribution of capital investment but a pooling of patents and processes owned by the parent companies. That a foreign company created under such conditions by concerted action of actual or potential competitors meets the tests of *per se* legality is open to serious question. But, with a dubious nod, we assume that it does; . . ."[64]

The court thus formulated specifically the issue which exists in one of the few areas which the cases have left open for speculation. Discussion as to the propriety of antitrust application abroad has been most impassioned, particularly in this area. It may be said, generally, that proponents of greater freedom in foreign arrangements have appealed essentially to the customs

---

[63] United States v. Minnesota Mining & Mfg. Co., 92 F.Supp. 947, 963 (D. Mass. 1950).

[64] United States v. Imperial Chemical Industries, Ltd., 100 F.Supp. 504, 557 (S.D. N.Y. 1951).

prevalent abroad,[65] while their opposite numbers have pointed out that an American firm, as a practical matter, is always part of the domestic market. One ground for agreement suggests itself from such a statement of the controversy. Where the "customs" abroad amount to a legal requirement, the American firm will more likely be free to participate in restrictive arrangements.[66] This proposition will be explored below. Otherwise, the American organization might, perhaps, be allowed to con-

---

[65] "When foreign businessmen, including Americans, go into England, they must conduct their business as it is conducted there. It is not always easy for the foreigner to get into the local 'club' but it would be equally difficult for him to survive if he did not play according to the local rules. The Government does not tell businessmen what to do or what not to do. Each industry in trade makes its own rules, some very loose, some very tight, and in many cases no rules at all. The problem of finding out the rules and observing them is one of the essentials a foreign businessman has to learn.

✿ ✿ ✿

"In the view of the London Chamber, it is incomprehensible to American businessmen abroad that their Government should pursue them in their legitimate business projects, and endeavor to encompass them with laws which were obviously intended to apply to Americans operating at home. No one in America is harmed by any arrangement which an American company might make in a foreign country with a national of that foreign country, which arrangement is to be wholly operated outside of the state.

✿ ✿ ✿

"In answering the contention that arrangements and agreements made abroad may have consequences within the United States, the London chamber expressed the view that unfavorable consequences to our country now obtain under the present interpretation of our antitrust laws. They cited these consequences as follows:

(1) The discouragement of our overseas investments.
(2) The loss of income to our country, with its consequent harmful effect on our economy.
(3) We will lose our associations with overseas industries, with all the benefits this provides.
(4) We shall drive our overseas associations to seek arrangements with other companies in other countries, where freedom of trade exists.
(5) We shall miss a great opportunity to promote international good will, and shall prejudice our position of friendliness and stifle international good will toward us.
(6) We risk being isolated.

✿ ✿ ✿

"At the conferences in Paris and Rome, with the American chambers of commerce, the same viewpoint expressed by the London chamber was reiterated." *Foreign Trade Conferences*, Staff Memorandum of the Subcommittee on Antitrust and Monopoly of the Senate Committee on the Judiciary, 84th Cong., 1st Sess. 5-15 (1955).

[66] This is usually the case in fields where the national interest predominates, *e.g.*, natural resource exploitation, transportation, and national defense. The governmental requirements of nations in this regard are dis-

form with the customs by establishing an independent subsidiary. The possibilities available under that method are discussed in the section on subsidiaries.

(2) Restraints Imposed by Foreign Law and Policy

In discussing legal restraints, it is essential to establish a distinction between permissive and mandatory foreign law, as well as between policies of public and private economic protection. Never has it been doubted that American firms must conduct their foreign operations in compliance with all mandatory laws and rules of public policy. The *Minnesota Mining* decision recognized this principle in considering the legality of agreements limiting exports:

> "But they say, and their exhibits are offered to show, that the reason that they no longer make substantial exports from the United States to those areas is that they cannot do so profitably because of the economic and political barriers that others have erected. The diminution of their American exports to those areas, they allege, is not the consequence of their design or desire or conduct. The fault lies not in themselves but in their destiny determined by the machinations of foreign rulers and by the desires of foreign peoples.

> "With part of the defendants' argument there can be no legitimate quarrel. It is axiomatic that if over a sufficiently long period American enterprises, as a result of political or economic barriers, cannot export directly or indirectly from the United States to a particular foreign country at a profit, then any private action taken to secure or interfere solely with business in that area, whatever else it may do, does not restrain foreign commerce in that area in violation of the Sherman Act. For, the very hypothesis is that there is not and could not be any American foreign commerce in that area which could be restrained or monopolized."[67]

A case more in point on the facts is that recently filed against certain large American oil companies.[68] The defendants collaborated in the development of Saudi Arabian Government concessions under requirements established by the Arabian government to safeguard that country's interests. The effects of this participation were not only the exclusion of American competitors, but also a division of the world market in Middle East oil among

cussed in MILLER, LES GOUVERNEMENTS ET LES PLACEMENTS PRIVES A L'ETRANGER (France, 1950).

[67] United States v. Minnesota Mining & Mfg. Co., 92 F.Supp. 947, at 958 (D. Mass. 1950).

[68] United States v. Standard Oil Co. of New Jersey, Civil No. 86-27 (S.D. N.Y. filed June 8, 1953).

the participants and the complete cartelization of a substantial source of American crude oil imports. Significantly, the complaint recognizes the validity of all the restraints, not only on the foreign but even on the domestic commerce of the United States, required by the express policy of Saudi Arabia. Those acts of defendants which the allegations attack are conduct which the Government believes to have gone beyond such requirements.

American participation in the reorganized former Anglo-Iranian Oil Company affords an even stronger indication of the legality of restraints flowing from mandatory foreign requirements. The Iranian Government set up a world cartel to operate the petroleum industry in accordance with the interests of the country. The United States endorsed and aided the negotiations leading to the establishment of the new organization.[69]

The rule is embodied in the following provision of a consent judgment issued by Judge Ryan:

> "Defendant ASR is enjoined and restrained from directly or indirectly entering into, adhering to, maintaining or furthering any contract, agreement, understanding, plan or program, whether in the nature of a cartel or other non-competitive arrangement, with any other person (*except a foreign government*) engaged in the mining, smelting, refining or sale of primary lead (a) to restrict the import into, or export from, the United States of lead ore, lead concentrates, lead bullion, or primary lead or (b) to fix, establish or maintain any price or prices for the sale of lead ore, lead concentrates, lead bullion, or primary lead in the domestic or foreign commerce of the United States; provided, that this Section VI shall not apply to any act in a foreign country which defendant ASR can show was *officially* required of defendant ASR by the government thereof." [Emphasis supplied.][70]

Somewhat different is the problem of foreign grants of monopoly power to American firms which seek to obtain such a franchise by bargaining rather than under any governmental policy. During the second world war, an American corporation negotiated an agreement with the Mexican Government under which the American firm was to establish a chemical plant in return for a monopoly in certain lines and a transfer of seized German patents. The arrangement was abandoned after a protest by the

---

[69] See Current Antitrust Problems, *Hearings Before Antitrust Subcommittee (Subcommittee No. 5) of the House Committee on the Judiciary,* 84th Cong., 1st Sess., Part II, Ser. No. 3, 709 (1955).

[70] United States v. American Smelting and Refining Co., Civil No. 88-249, 1957 CCH TRADE CASES Para. 68,836 (S.D. N.Y. 1957).

United States Government and the threat of competitors to enter similar agreements with other governments.

There was no indication given as to whether a suit against the perfected arrangement could have been brought with any expectation of success. However, as the Government of Mexico was offering a mere incentive, which it could have avoided if the American firm were prevented by the antitrust laws from accepting, the monopoly was not a matter of foreign law, policy or even convenience. It would have been a private arrangement, and the American party should have been kept from taking advantage of its monopoly.

With respect to governmental policies not concretely evidenced by franchise or express regulation, there is no case holding whether they excuse agreements restraining the foreign market. But in view of the scrutiny given explicit regulations in the above cases, greater effectiveness would seem to be imparted to the policies which a government might deem important in fields affected by American antitrust laws if they were enacted into some formal expression of the sovereign will. This is suggested by the *Minnesota Mining* case:

> "Defendants' contention is that after 1929 it was impractical to continue to export a large volume of coated abrasives from America to Britain because of Empire preference measures including official tariff restrictions and the more subtle aspects of a 'Buy British' campaign. And these restraints became more effective when in the fall of 1931 the pound went off the gold standard.
>
> "It is not claimed that the United Kingdom imposed a legal ban upon imports of abrasives. Nor is it asserted that economically *no* American coated abrasives could be profitably exported to the British market. The precise contention is that it was economically *impracticable* to continue to export to Britain a *large* volume of such abrasives. Stated another way this means, as we shall see, only that it was more profitable to make abrasives in Britain than to export them to Britain.
>
> * * *
>
> "In short, this Court finds as an ultimate fact that defendants' decline in exports to the United Kingdom is attributable less to import and currency restrictions of that nation and to the preferential treatment afforded to British goods by British customers than to defendants' desire to sell their British-made goods at a large profit rather than their American-made goods at a smaller profit and in a somewhat (but not drastically) reduced volume."[71]

---

[71] 92 F.Supp. at 959, 960.

(D) SUBSIDIARIES

It was seen above that the foreign commerce of the United States is directly affected by restraints upon exports. But is it affected at all by restraints upon the local trade of foreign subsidiaries?

The general rule discernible in the cases below is that whenever a subsidiary is used by its parent as a device to achieve a result, forbidden by the antitrust laws if the parent were to act alone, the corporate entity will be disregarded. Conversely, however, the parent may be able to enter restrictive agreements with its subsidiary which would be illegal when entered with an independent corporation.[72]

The cases which have been decided on this point in international commerce have always involved a rather clear competitive benefit derived by the parent rather than by the subsidiary as such. The question of whether, under the antitrust laws, the foreign subsidiary alone may profit from a local restraint agreement with its local competitors, which in no way limits participation by American competitors in the foreign market or by its foreign partners in the American market, has never been litigated.

Illegal benefit may come to the parent directly, when the subsidiary is an organ of an express cartel agreement between its shareholders. Such was the role of the Duperial and other joint companies declared illegal in the *ICI* case.

> "The history of each of these companies demonstrates the unlawful purpose with which they were organized, and demonstrates that they were used as instruments by which territories and countries were divided and assigned for trade and commerce. It also reveals that these companies were intended to and did effect a restraint of American foreign trade and regulation and suppression of competition between ICI, du Pont and other American concerns in the non-exclusive territories."[73]

Investment in a foreign company is not in itself suspect. If an American competitor uses stock in a foreign corporation to influence the policies of that firm to the end that competition with the parent is restrained, only then is the "investment" considered a restraint on interstate or foreign commerce. Such an organi-

---

[72] For a valuable summary of law and opinion on subsidiaries, see Graham, *Antitrust Problems of Corporate Parents, Subsidiaries, Affiliates and Joint Venturers in Foreign Commerce*, 9 ABA ANTITRUST SECTION REPORT 32 (August 1956), and materials cited therein; see also Hale, *Joint Ventures: Collaborative Subsidiaries and the Antitrust Laws*, 42 VA. L.REV. 927 (1956).

[73] United States v. Imperial Chemical Industries, Ltd., 100 F.Supp. 504, 559 (S.D. N.Y. 1951).

zation then becomes a meeting place for competing interests. But even then, the remedy against the abuse is different from that decreed against the mere arm of a cartel. This is evident from the decree in the *General Electric* case:

> "The recent case of *United States* v. *Imperial Chemical Industries*, D.C. S.D. N.Y. 1952, 105 F.Supp. 215, does not dictate that divestiture should be ordered here. There divestiture of foreign companies owned jointly by United States and British corporations which had conspired to divide the world market in explosives and chemicals was ordered, but in that case the jointly owned foreign firms were organized for the specific purpose of doing the unlawful acts, which was not the basis of General Electric's and IGE's foreign investments."[74]

Only partially controlled subsidiaries were included in this prohibition. Companies owned by more than 50% of their stock were treated under the same considerations as the defendants.

Partial ownership of a foreign company, it may be implied, prevents the American "investor" from making intramural arrangements without regard for their effect as restraints of trade. Were it to divide the world market between itself and its wholly-owned subsidiary, no objection could be made that its right to export was impaired. But where the American investor does not own a controlling interest, as in *Timken*,[75] the "subsidiary" is in effect a foreign corporation, and agreements with it have the effect of limiting its competition in America which the controlling majority might otherwise have decided to exercise.

But it would also seem that even where the American company controls its subsidiary, substantial foreign stockholders may seek concessions for their benefit. This was the Government's contention as regarded such subsidiaries in the *General Electric* case above.

> "The Government opposed any change in the Section as originally drawn asserting that by association of General Electric or IGE in relation with other owners, such as another defendant in this case, where they would own a bare 51% of the stock they would escape from the safeguards set up in this Section. In such case, however, the entity would come within the definition of subsidiary as contemplated in Section II of this Judgment, and would be subject to all the restraints imposed by the general injunctions contained therein. In the provision as originally writ-

---

[74] United States v. General Electric Co., 115 F.Supp. 835, at 876 (D. N.J. 1953).

[75] United States v. Timken Roller Bearing Co., 83 F.Supp. 284, at 312 (N.D. Ohio 1949), *modified and affirmed,* 341 U.S. 593 (1951).

ten General Electric's objection would appear to have justification and relationships with foreign subsidiaries could not be maintained in practice. Hence the Section was reformed to meet this objection."[76]

It is fair to imply from this answer that the courts will also look to the substance of any arrangements with partially-owned but controlled subsidiaries, to prevent any arrangements restricting the parent's position in relation to its foreign competitors.

In all of the above situations it was clear that American imports and exports were affected by some specific arrangement to that end. This, then, rather than the existence of the foreign subsidiary organization may be taken as the test of legality.

The amount of business done by an American concern through its foreign subsidiary also affects American trade, but not in the same direct manner. For this reason, it is not clear whether an agreement by such a subsidiary, established for that purpose, with its local foreign competitors limiting production, setting prices or dividing foreign markets, would be prohibited under the antitrust laws. There is no question that the law could be interpreted as forbidding such practices, but it is not certain that it would be, without more of an involvement by the American parent. In this connection, it is interesting to note certain arrangements reported by the British Restrictive Practices Commission. Subsidiaries of American radio tube manufacturers have allegedly entered the local arrangements governing the entire British industry in its internal relationship as well as its relations with continental competitors.[77]

Another aspect of the subsidiary problem is presented by the American subsidiaries of foreign companies. It is clear that the subsidiary, whether regarded as a foreign or an American company, cannot enter restrictive agreements with American firms. Agreements by subsidiaries, partly owned by Americans with the foreign parent company should be judged under the same standards as applied above.

The American subsidiary of a foreign company has usually played a role in controversies over the presence of its parent in the United States.

But the question may also arise whether a subsidiary can be regarded as an independent American company if thereby it re-

---

[76] United States v. General Electric Co., 115 F.Supp. 835, at 876 (D. N.J. 1953).

[77] THE MONOPOLIES AND RESTRICTIVE PRACTICES COMMISSION, REPORT ON THE SUPPLY OF ELECTRONIC VALVES AND CATHODE RAY TUBES (December 20, 1956).

ceives a favored position in the American market. This essentially was the question in the *Guerlain* case.[78] The court decided to pierce the corporate veil and consider the subsidiary as an arm of an integrated international company.

But would the corporate veil be pierced if the foreign parents of two American subsidiaries, established as competitors in the American market, should enter an agreement limiting the competition between their subsidiaries, or if they should merge, abroad, and thus automatically cause the unified operation of the American firms? The question is open. Whatever answers might be indicated today are more likely to be found in the cases covered in the following section.

(E) FOREIGN COMBINATIONS AND MONOPOLIES

(1) Private Combinations

Only one case has ever involved application of the antitrust laws to a restraint of trade not involving American parties. Part of the *Alcoa* decision[79] was based on the determination that a world aluminum cartel allocating quotas for its members' exports to the United States did not include American conspirators.[80] As a result, the case is cited as authority for the tests to be used in determining the point at which purely foreign arrangements come under American law.

Judge Hand stated his premises thus:

"[I]t is settled law . . . that any state may impose liabilities, even upon persons not within its allegiance, for conduct outside its borders that has consequences within its borders which the state reprehends; *and* these liabilities other states will ordinarily recognize. . . . [F] or argument we shall assume that the [Sherman] Act does not cover agreements [among foreigners], even though intended to affect imports or exports, unless its performance is shown actually to have had some effect upon them. Where both conditions are satisfied, the situation certainly falls within *United States* v. *Pacific* & *Arctic R.* & *Navigation Co.,* 228 U.S. 87; *Thompson* v. *Cayser,* 243 U.S. 66, and *United States* v. *Sisal Sales Corp.,* 274 U.S. 268. . . ."[81]

Factually, however, the case is not precedent for a general rule that foreign cartels intended to affect domestic American trade may not operate legally in the United States. Although

---

[78] United States v. Guerlain, Inc., 155 F.Supp. 77 (S.D. N.Y. 1957), reprinted in Section F, *infra.*

[79] United States v. Aluminum Co. of America, 148 F.2d 416, 439-445 (2d Cir. 1945).

[80] 148 F.2d at 441.

[81] 148 F.2d at 443, 444.

Judge Hand expressly found that the American parent of the Canadian company involved in the cartel could not be held responsible for its subsidiary's participation therein, the interests of Alcoa were so fully represented in the arrangement that the case cannot safely be interpreted without according weight to this fact. It was clear that Alcoa was improving its domestic position as a result of the cartel's export restrictions. The manner in which those restrictions were administered by the cartel, to keep down exports to Alcoa's markets, betrayed a hidden control by the American company.

To allow for the limitations imposed by the facts, the rule might be stated that an international cartel, of which no American is a member, operates illegally in American commerce, if an American competitor's interests are safeguarded or promoted by the cartel as though he were a member, albeit no formal agreement, nor permission, to that end can be found.[82]

Doubtless it is true that the antitrust policy could be extended to all firms dealing with the United States, resulting in the extreme possibility of excluding from doing business with, as well as in, America any companies practicing, singly or with other foreigners, restraints which denied a competitive market to American buyers or sellers.

The Government is currently attempting to apply such a rule in the *Swiss Watch* case.[83] The Swiss watch industry is governed by a comprehensive cartel convention, which regulates the conduct of both internal and foreign commerce. The United States government has instituted suit against the cartel, alleging that it exercised monopolistic control over Swiss exports to America, had entered into agreements with American importers restricting the prices and disposition of its exports, and had practiced blacklisting against non-complying American importers.

A petition in the complaint by the Government provides for the termination of blacklisting and of all agreements with American importers regulating the disposition of articles after sale to such importers. It goes further, however, and requires the Swiss cartel convention to cancel its rule that all exports to the United

---

[82] For a similar view, see Brewster, *Extraterritorial Effects of the U.S. Antitrust Laws: "An Appraisal,"* 11 ABA ANTITRUST SECTION REPORT 70 (July 1957).

[83] United States v. Watchmakers of Switzerland Information Center, Inc., Civil No. 96-170 (S.D. N. Y. 1954). Of course, even the broadest extension of Alcoa recognizes the legality of combinations required by foreign law, and the present case so indicates, as shown in the following subsection. The presumption in this attempt must therefore be that no foreign legal requirement applies.

States be approved by the members. The latter provision of the complaint appears to follow the broad rule of the *Alcoa* case as stated by Judge Hand, and may thus afford a test of its validity, should it appear that no American interests are protected by this cartel.

To date, however, it is not the nature of the foreign business but that of its transactions with Americans which is judged by the standards of American law. Thus the resale conditions and blacklisting practices employed by the Swiss watch cartel must be measured by domestic law,[84] as they involve obligations imposed on Americans and on goods already in the American market.

One exception to this approach suggests itself. If a foreign export association were to operate in the American market, its legality might be challenged on the grounds that its avowed purpose, more efficient competition against foreign combinations, would be inapposite in this market where the antitrust laws are available to combat such competitors. This argument might be used against associations formed under the new German antitrust law which exempts associations for such purposes specifically.[85]

There may be situations in which the nature of the transaction itself is colored by the foreign corporation's very character as a foreigner. Such a corporation, even though acting singly and without monopolistic power abroad, may be able to exercise a restraint upon the American market because of its foreign position through what otherwise appears to be a lawful transaction with an American company. In this connection the following district court decision recently illustrated the possibilities of price maintenance through a trademark transaction. The legal tests which the court employed in condemning the scheme are somewhat doubtful, especially those for determining the relevant market. But the case indicates the policy behind the limitations placed on the use of industrial property and the vigor with which the courts seek enforcement of that policy. It may even be that the case succeeds in validly applying the general rule limiting trademark use, for in effect it reaches a result which

---

[84] See chapter 4 on Exclusive Dealing, *supra*.

[85] Law Against Restraints of Competition of July 27, 1957, (1957) Bundesgesetzblatt I, 1081 (Germany), section 6. For an English translation of the statute, see 8 WIRTSCHAFT UND WETTBEWERB 33-55 (Germany 1958). For a discussion of section 6, see Kronstein, *"Cartels" Under the New German Cartel Statute*, 11 VAND. L.REV. 271, 281-283 (1958), and Schwartz, *Antitrust Legislation and Policy in Germany—A Comparative Study*, 105 U. PA. L.REV. 617, 656-662 (1957).

protects competing distributors from the exercise by a manufacturer of a restraint-power granted by statute only to an independent trademark purchaser.[86]

". . . The defendants are American corporations marketing
trademarked toilet goods of better quality and relatively high
price. Each of the American companies is closely associated with
a French company that originated the trade name, first marketed
products under the trademarks and supplies the products, manufactured under secret formulae, sold by the American company,
or the essential ingredients of those products. . . .

"In each case the French company has given to its associated
American company an exclusive right to distribute its products
in the United States and has transferred to the American company trademark rights intended to be sufficient to justify registration in the United States Patent Office on the basis of a claim
of ownership by the American company. And each of the defendants has filed with the Bureau of Customs, United States
Treasury, certificates of registration of certain trademarks for the
purpose of preventing the competitive importation of products
bearing those trademarks without the written consent of the
American registrant, under the terms of § 526 of the Tariff Act
of 1930.

* * *

"I have found as a fact in each case, beyond a gnawing doubt,
that the defendant and its French counterpart constitute a single
international enterprise. . . .

"The Government urges a construction of § 526 of the Tariff
Act of 1930 that is not to be derived from a literal reading of the
words of the statute. Subsection (a) of § 526 reads as follows:

'It shall be unlawful to import into the United States any
merchandise of foreign manufacture, if such merchandise, or
the label, sign, print, package, wrapper, or receptacle, bears a
trademark owned by a citizen of, or by a corporation or association created or organized within, the United States, and
registered in the Patent Office by a person domiciled in the
United States, under the provisions of Sections 81 to 109 of
Title 15, and if a copy of the certificate of registration of such
trademark is filed with the Secretary of the Treasury, in the
manner provided in Section 106 of said Title 15, unless written consent of the owner of such trademark is produced at the
time of making entry.'

"The Government contends that this provision may apply only
to the advantage of an independent American trademark owner

---

[86] United States v. Guerlain, Inc., 155 F.Supp. 77, at 79, 80, 83, 87
(S.D. N.Y. 1957), *probable jurisdiction noted,* 78 S.Ct. 429 (1958). The
action is based on s. 2 of the Sherman Act; see Note, 71 HARV. L.REV.
564 (1958). Footnotes omitted.

which may, by registering a trademark of a foreign producer in its own name, prevent the importation of authentic products by anyone else. But it is argued that the provision does not apply to the American part of a single international enterprise to enable it to prevent the importation into the United States of authentic products sold abroad by the foreign part of the enterprise. Despite the absence of specific language to that effect in the legislation, I am constrained to agree, in view of the litigated history of the issue involved and of the legislative history of the section.

* * *

". . . In the definition of the relevant market, the defendants maintain that the recent decision in the cellophane case, *United States* v. *E. I. du Pont de Nemours & Co., supra,* is dispositive.

* * *

"The defendants stress heavily the sentence in the *Cellophane* case that the '. . . power that, let us say, automobile or soft-drink manufacturers have over their trademarked products is not the power that makes an illegal monopoly.' But such power of the defendants over their trademarked products is not here under attack. What is under attack is, in effect, an attempt (successfully executed) by each defendant, as a part of a single international business enterprise, to limit the resale price of its products for the express purpose of excluding competition and controlling prices. Purchasers from the French part of the enterprise are prevented, by means of the utilization of § 526 [of the Tariff Act of 1930] from competing in the United States with the American part of the same enterprise. Such exclusion, if it were accomplished by agreement, would violate § 1 of the Sherman Act. For, '[a] distributor of a trademarked article may not lawfully limit by agreement, express or implied, the price at which or the person to whom its purchaser may resell, except as the seller moves along the route which is marked by the Miller-Tydings Act.' *United States* v. *Bausch & Lomb Co.,* 321 U.S. 707, 721, quoted in *United States* v. *McKesson & Robbins,* 351 U.S. 304, 310. These defendants have achieved the same result unilaterally, without agreement, with the effect of expanding their trademarked monopolies beyond their proper scope. In the *Cellophane* case [351 U.S. 377 (1956)] there was no evidence that du Pont had attempted to control the use or resale of cellophane, and there is nothing in the case to indicate that the power of a manufacturer of a trademarked product may not be expanded into an illegal monopoly. It is in the context of the extension of a statutory monopoly into illegal proportions by deliberately exclusionary conduct that the relevant market must be defined."

Certain restrictions, at first blush not applicable to Americans, would be added to those of the domestic law in foreign cases under the rationale in *Guerlain* that the law may not be used by a foreign-dominated company to foster cartel conditions in the American market. With reference again to the transactions of foreign combinations, the question would arise whether a foreign monopoly or cartel can take advantage of the fair trade laws.

It has been established that the Miller-Tydings Act applies its exemption impliedly to the Wilson Tariff Act.[87] The McGuire Act, however, requires that a fair traded product be in free and open competition with commodities of the same general class in the American market.[88] This raises the question whether the Swiss watch exporters, for instance, operating under cartel conditions in their export transactions, may avail themselves of resale price maintenance contracts.

The answer would appear to be fairly simple upon a direct application of the principles governing domestic trade. If Swiss watches were found to be an integral part of the American watch market, they would be in competition therein. But if Swiss watches and parts constituted a relevant market in themselves, they clearly would not be. The considerations given weight by the court in the *Guerlain* case, however, complicate the issue. There, the court considered the use of American law to establish restraints, not contemplated by such law, as vitiating the legality of advantages claimed under it. With respect to fair trade, this would seem to imply that the exception granted to resale price maintenance contracts under federal law would not apply when such a contract was used by a foreign combination or monopoly to strengthen its position in the American market, just as the trademark exemption in *Guerlain* could not be used to eliminate competing distributors.[89] While no case has considered this point generally, much less with respect to fair trade, it is one which may play a part in future decisions in the field of foreign commerce.

---

[87] 28 STAT. 570 (1894), as amended, 15 U.S.C. § 8 (1952). See Adams-Mitchell Co. v. Cambridge Distributing Co., Ltd., 189 F.2d 913 (2d Cir. 1950).

[88] See chapter 6, *supra*, on resale price maintenance and "fair trade" laws.

[89] The apparently discriminatory treatment of the foreign firm in Guerlain stemmed from the advantage it might otherwise achieve in having its subsidiary treated as a separate concern. The principle would seem to apply to a foreign combination or monopoly, though fair trade itself promotes some restraint in trade, since no American competitor could initially achieve a similar status under American law.

(2) Foreign Government Franchises

The *Swiss Watch* case presents a further point for consideration in the fact that certain provisions of the Swiss cartel arrangement are required by Swiss law. The cartel itself may even be considered as a government regulated industry, especially with respect to exports.

> "In view of representations by the Swiss Government that certain Swiss laws and regulations may be directly involved in a second matter regarding watchmaking machinery, this matter remains under study in order to permit further consultation between the two Governments. The United States Government is hopeful that resolution of this matter can be facilitated through mutual cooperation between the two Governments.
>
>   * * *
>
> 'By this action filed today the Department seeks to enjoin restrictive practices imposed upon the watch industry. *No attempt is made by this suit to regulate or control the operations of the Swiss watch industry in Switzerland.* The complaint deals only with practices effectuated in the United States which relate to the domestic and foreign commerce of this country."[90] [Emphasis supplied.]

On the other hand, the governmental character of the Swiss domestic arrangements plays no part in determining the legality of the cartel's control over American distributors and sales. As soon as something other than a mere sale is consummated with an American, the transaction itself is subject to the antitrust laws, regardless of governmental requirements controlling the foreign seller.[91]

To this date, the remedy considered proper to reach foreign franchises which do not engage in any objectionable practices in the American market continues to be diplomatic consultation, as evidenced by the above press release.

(F) PROCEDURAL ASPECTS

(1) Service of Process and Subpoena

In our discussion of the amenability of foreign corporations to antitrust regulation, it is apparent that the substantive law implicitly delineates the activities which bring foreign business under the jurisdiction of American law. This jurisdiction is asserted by service of process in order to bring the party to court. However, the corporation itself need not be in the United States.

The manner of lawfully reaching such foreign corporations is circumscribed by the requirements of due process, the Federal

---

[90] Press Release, Department of Justice, October 19, 1954.

[91] This corresponds to the Kalisyndikat rule, discussed, *supra*, Section B.

Rules of Civil Procedure, and specific statutory provisions for antitrust cases.[92]

In general, service must be such as to give reasonably certain notice to the defendant of the suit brought. The *Scophony* case[93] established the rule that service on a person integrally connected with the foreign corporation is sufficient to bring that company to court.

Wholly-owned American subsidiaries may be served to reach their foreign parent corporation only if the subsidiaries are acting solely as agents of their parents. Thus distributors and jointly owned trade associations were found to be connected sufficiently for service of process purposes with the business of the foreign manufacturers in *United States* v. *Watchmakers of Switzerland Information Center, Inc.*[94]

The connection with the foreign corporation must be such that the foreigner may be said to be doing business through the American agent. This "doing business" is to be determined on the basis of practical business conceptions instead of hair-splitting legal technicalities encrusted upon the "found"—"present"— "carrying-on-business" sequence.[95]

A distinction, however, is made between "doing" and "transacting" business. The *De Beers* decision[96] relied upon this difference in denying the liability of foreign diamond manufacturers to service of process through bank accounts which they had established merely to facilitate transactions with American buyers. The case further held that an office established to purchase equipment and conduct an advertising campaign was not sufficiently connected with the business of the foreign corporation. This seems to be contrary to the later holding in the *Swiss Watch* case.[97] It also appears to be narrower than an earlier decision of the same court,[98] which stated that such activities subjected the foreign company to service of a subpoena *duces tecum.*

---

[92] See section 12 of the Clayton Act, 15 U.S.C. § 22 (1952); International Shoe Co. v. State of Washington, 326 U.S. 310 (1945).

[93] United States v. Scophony Corp. of America, 333 U.S. 795 (1948).

[94] 133 F.Supp. 40 (S.D. N.Y. 1955).

[95] United States v. Scophony Corp. of America, 333 U.S. 795, 808 (1948).

[96] United States v. De Beers Consolidated Mines, Ltd., 1948-1949 CCH TRADE CASES Para. 62,248 (S.D. N.Y. 1948).

[97] United States v. Watchmakers of Switzerland Information Center, Inc., 133 F.Supp. 40 (S.D. N.Y. 1955).

[98] In re Grand Jury Subpoenas Duces Tecum Addressed to Canadian International Paper Co., et al., 72 F.Supp. 1013 (S.D. N.Y. 1947).

It seems to be easier to conclude that a subsidiary in the United States is acting for its foreign parent, when subpoenas are involved. Two cases have recently held that service of a subpoena on a subsidiary was valid. The business relation was considered thus in the *Siemens* case:

> "In 1954 the two German Siemens corporations established a jointly owned subsidiary, a Delaware corporation, upon which the subpoena in question was served. Siemens (N.Y.) acts as representative of the German organizations in this country. It assists in the negotiation of contracts, servicing contracts and advising potential customers. It also advises and assists Siemens with respect to patents and patent licenses and it furnishes general technical, economic and financial information from this country. To a minor extent it sells products of the Siemens enterprise and purchases a small amount of American products for Siemens in Germany. It devotes itself exclusively to the business of Siemens. For these services it receives a flat allowance of $17,500 per month, plus a 5% price differential with respect to sales made for Siemens or purchases made on Siemens' account.
>
> * * *
>
> "In addition, however, the intercorporate history shows that the New York organization is no more than an *alter ego* for the German parents. . . .
>
> "[I]t is my opinion that at least for the purpose of sustaining process in aid of an investigation into crime, particularly a violation of the antitrust laws, it is the duty of this Court to pierce the corporate veil with respect to a wholly owned subsidiary, such as here presented. . . ."[99]

A party over whom jurisdiction has been asserted may be required by subpoena to produce records and documents belonging to affiliates or found outside of the United States.

The parent is required to produce records of a subsidiary in which it could elect a majority of the directors either through its own voting rights in the subsidiary or through its power over other corporations. If the affiliate is a jointly owned company, the same rules apply, provided a majority of the stock is reachable through the corporations which are under subpoena.[100]

Presence in a foreign country of subpoenaed documents is in itself no excuse for quashing the subpoena. The burden is on the served corporation to show that foreign law prevents re-

---

[99] In the Matter of the Grand Jury Subpoena Duces Tecum Addressed to Siemens & Halske A.G., 1957 CCH TRADE CASES, Para. 68,763 (S.D. N.Y. 1957).

[100] In re Investigation of World Arrangements, 13 F.R.D. 280, 285 (D.D.C. 1952).

moval, and that all steps that might be taken under such law to secure permission for removal have been attempted.[101]

(2) Decrees

Considerations of conflict with foreign law become truly pertinent in the formulation of decrees. Throughout the presentation of the substantive law, the emphasis has been on the jurisdiction of antitrust laws over the matter of the action. Jurisdiction over the person was of concern in the law on compulsory process. The question of jurisdiction in connection with decrees for the first time involves the issue of what effects may be produced in a foreign country as a result of the declaration by the court that an unlawful restraint on the domestic or foreign commerce of the United States has been perpetrated.

Equity, acting *in personam*, may order the persons under its jurisdiction to do any act.[102] This rule is limited by the practical considerations of enforceability and certain excuses of impossibility which are recognized as available to the defendant.

Enjoining the defendants from pursuing the terms of an illegal agreement, or from doing illegal acts, automatically affects established rights in foreign countries to the extent that such countries continue to recognize them and can enforce compliance. Nonetheless, certain elements are basic to the drafting of every antitrust decree. Any acts contributing essentially to the illegal restraint may be enjoined, and any acts essentially necessary to restore the competitive market may be commanded by the court. The presumption is that all foreign countries affected will recognize the validity of such a decree as one issued to protect the American economic order and to undo the effects of an illegal act of an American or foreign defendant.

Such is the reasoning of the court in the *ICI* case:

> "Our power so to regulate is limited and depends upon jurisdiction *in personam*. The effectiveness of the exercise of that power depends upon the recognition which will be given to our judgment as a matter of comity by the courts of the foreign sovereign which has granted the patents in question."[103]

On this basis, the court proceeded to order all the acts it deemed necessary, always aware of the fact that any one or more of them might be impossible of performance. As to acts allegedly governed by mandatory foreign law, the court exer-

---

[101] *Id.*, at 286.

[102] Penn v. Lord Baltimore, (1750) 1 Ves. 444.

[103] United States v. Imperial Chemical Industries, Ltd., 105 F.Supp. 215, 229 (S.D. N.Y. 1952).

cised due caution, but stated, in connection with allegedly applicable patent regulations:

> "This should not deter us from making directions we feel are required, even though the application of them be limited in operation by the possible action of an official of a foreign sovereign."[104]

Acts governed by the ordinary rules of contracts and property were ordered under this reasoning:

> "What credit may be given to such an injunctive provision by the courts of Great Britain in a suit brought by BNS to restrain such importations we do not venture to predict. We feel that the possibility that the English courts in an equity suit will not give effect to such a provision in our decree should not deter us from including it."[105]

A clause to exempt defendants where compliance would be against foreign law was included in the *General Electric* case.[106] Similar attitudes were taken toward foreign law in other cases.[107]

What is meant by such "saving" clauses is clearly not that everything which would be permitted in a foreign country is left unchanged by the decree. The decree intends total compliance with its provisions, except where they conflict with mandatory foreign laws or regulations or unless a foreign court prevents such compliance. Thus, in the *Holophane* case,[108] the command to export to the United Kingdom is limited by the import laws of that country and proof of such laws would excuse failure to comply to the extent forbidden.

---

[104] *Id.*, at 230.

[105] *Id.*, at 231.

[106] United States v. General Electric Co., 115 F.Supp. 835, 878 (D. N.J. 1953):

> "A. Philips shall not be in contempt of this Judgment for doing anything outside of the United States which is required or for not doing anything outside of the United States which is unlawful under the laws of the government, province, country or state in which Philips or any other subsidiaries may be incorporated, chartered or organized or in the territory of which Philips or any such subsidiaries may be doing business. . . ."

[107] Consent decree in the Potash (Equity No. 41-124 (S.D. N.Y. 1929)) and Quinine (Adm. No. 98-242 (S.D. N.Y. 1928)), cartel cases. Most recently, such a clause was included in the far-reaching decree in United States v. United Fruit Co., 1958 CCH TRADE CASES Para. 68,941 (E.D. La. 1958), reprinted in chapter 8, *supra.*

[108] United States v. Holophane Co., Inc., 119 F.Supp. 114 (S.D. Ohio 1954).

The comity which the *ICI* case mentioned[109] appeared to be lacking in Great Britain, where a court refused to allow return of certain patents as required by the American decree.[110] ICI had licensed the patents in question to British Nylon Spinners, a British corporation, outside American jurisdiction and not a party to the case. That company successfully sought to enjoin ICI from complying with the American decree to return the patents to their originators.

> "[T]here is no doubt that it is competent for the court of a particular country, in a suit between persons who are either nationals or subjects of that country or are otherwise subject to its jurisdiction, to make orders in personam against one such party—directing it, for example, to do something or to refrain from doing something in another country affecting the other party to the action. As a general proposition, that would not be open to doubt. But the plaintiffs in this case (unlike Imperial Chemical Industries) are neither subjects nor nationals of the United States, nor were they parties to the proceedings before his Honour, nor are they otherwise subject to his jurisdiction."[111]

Looking back at the intimations of this holding found in the *ICI* case, it is apparent that Judge Ryan merely predicted wrongly the decision of a court which he himself admitted had the competence to decide the rights of British Nylon Spinners.[112] Convinced that British Nylon Spinners had guilty knowledge, the Judge proceeded to postulate the outcome of the suit. It is clear that, far from usurping the prerogative of British justice, Judge Ryan recognized it and provided for it in his decree.[113]

The experience of this aftermath, however, may have had some cautionary effect on later cases. The Supreme Court of the United States[114] divided equally on that section of the *Holophane* decree of the District Court which ordered positive acts, and unanimously affirmed the rest of the judgment and decree.

---

[109] United States v. Imperial Chemical Industries, Ltd., 105 F.Supp. 215, 229 (S.D. N.Y. 1952).

[110] British Nylon Spinners, Ltd. v. Imperial Chemical Industries, Ltd., (1953) Ch. 19 (1952). The case is fully presented by Kahn-Freund, Note, 18 MODERN L.REV. 65 (1955).

[111] (1953) Ch. at 25.

[112] 105 F.Supp. at 230. *Accord,* Hansen, *Enforcement of the United States Antitrust Laws by the Department of Justice to Protect Freedom of United States Trade,* 11 ABA ANTITRUST SECTION REPORT 75, 85 (July 1957).

[113] For a realistic appraisal of the ICI aftermath, see Timberg, *Antitrust and Foreign Trade,* 48 Nw.U.L.REV. 411, 413 (1953).

[114] Holophane Co., Inc. v. United States, 352 U.S. 903 (1956).

As a result, that decree was not disturbed. Here are the provisions ordering positive acts:

"Defendant is ordered and directed:

"A. To use reasonable efforts, including but not limited to the use of present or subsequent distributors or wholly-owned subsidiaries, to promote the sale and distribution of said products in foreign markets, including the territories of 'Limited' and 'Francaise.' Nothing contained in this paragraph shall be construed as requiring the exportation by the defendant of any such products in violation of the valid patent or trademark or trade-name rights of any person in any foreign country. If . . . such exportation can be made into certain countries only by means of unmarked glass or the adoption of another trademark or trade-name for such exportation, then the defendant shall, within one year from the date hereof, have available sufficient quantities of unmarked glass or glass marked with a new trademark to be distributed under a new trade-name, if necessary, to meet reasonable anticipated foreign demand.

"B. To offer said products for sale and export to the territories of 'Limited' and 'Francaise' at prices and upon terms and conditions of sale not discriminatory as compared to those offered to purchasers for use or re-sale in the United States.

"C. To take the following specific steps to promote and develop export sales of said products:

"(1) To circularize within one year from the date of this Judgment known potential distributors of said products in the territory of 'Limited' and 'Francaise,' seeking to employ their services in selling and distributing said products.

"(2) Beginning six months from the date of this Judgment and for a period of five years thereafter, to insert advertisements at reasonable intervals in trade journals of appropriate circulation in all countries in which said products manufactured by 'Limited' or 'Francaise' are sold in substantial quantities, of the manufacture and availability for sale of said products.

"(3) To circularize within one year from the date of this Judgment all persons who from January 1, 1948 to date of this Judgment have made written inquiry to the defendant respecting the purchase or distribution of said products, exported to any country in the territory of 'Limited' or 'Francaise' informing them of the manufacture and availability for sale of said products.

"(4) To respond in writing to all persons who from the date of Judgment make written inquiry to the defendant respecting the purchase or distribution of said products for export to the territory of 'Limited' or 'Francaise,' advising them of the manufacture and availability for sale of said products. * * *"[115]

---

[115] 1954 CCH TRADE CASES Para. 67,679 (S.D. Ohio 1954).

(G) ANTITRUST POLICY IN RELATION TO INTERNA-TIONAL AND FOREIGN LAW

Much has been written on the antitrust decisions involving foreign corporations from the point of view of international private and international public law, as well as the law of other countries.[116]

With respect to alleged conflicts between such decisions and international private law, objections have been raised principally on the basis that normal contract law has been abandoned for the missionary aims of American antitrust.[117] Contracts, it is said, which are governed by the law of foreign parties, either by agreement or under the principles of conflicts law, should not be abrogated on the grounds that they do not comply with another country's policies.[118]

American courts, however, have never considered antitrust enforcement as a matter governed by the rules of conflicts, and those advocating their application are in wide disagreement as to the principles which may be pertinent.[119] Nonetheless, it is interesting to note that even within the law of conflicts, provisions exist which can be used to preserve national economic interests.

It is at least debatable whether British conflicts law forecloses the excuse of illegality of a contract under the law of one party.[120] In any case, conflicts law today clearly admits the

---

[116] The alleged clash of these with American antitrust is delineated in Friedmann and Verloren van Themaat, *International Cartels and Combines,* in ANTITRUST LAWS: A COMPARATIVE SYMPOSIUM 469 (Friedmann ed., 1956). JESSUP, TRANSNATIONAL LAW 39 *et seq.* (1956).

[117] An excellent foreign presentation of American antitrust law, together with a mild criticism on this ground, is found in PETITPIERRE, L'APPLICATION DU DROIT ANTITRUST DES ETATS UNIS D'AMERIQUE A LEUR COMMERCE EXTERIEUR (Switzerland 1956).

[118] Much quoted in this connection are Haight, *International Law and Extraterritorial Application of the Antitrust Laws,* and Whitney, *Sources of Conflict Between International Law and the Antitrust Laws,* 63 YALE L.J. 639 and 655, resp. (1954).

[119] The confused state of this law is discernible from Hansard, *U.S. Antitrust Process Beyond Our Borders: Jurisdiction and Comity,* address before the Fifth Annual Meeting, Section on Antitrust Law, New York State Bar Association, published in 1953 CCH ANTITRUST LAW SYMPOSIUM 44 (1953). For the authors' views, see Kronstein, *Crisis of "Conflict of Laws",* 37 GEO. L.J. 483 (1949). See also Brewster, *Extraterritorial Effects of the U.S. Antitrust Laws: "An Appraisal,"* 11 ABA ANTITRUST SECTION REPORT 65, 69 (July 1957).

[120] WOLFF, PRIVATE INTERNATIONAL LAW 450(1945).

precedence of the *"ordre public."*[121] All contracts are governed by the law of the parties as to acts required to be done by such parties, when the national interest of the countries involved is at stake. Thus no one denies that currency controls, license requirements and other general measures for the protection of economies prevail over any agreement entered by a party subject to them. Similarly, the antitrust laws if applied only to the regulation of American trade, cannot be avoided by any act other than that of the United States Congress itself.[122]

Wengler has analyzed the antitrust cases in this light, and holds the American law applicable under the theory of *"ordre public."* He extends the law to the regulation of American exporters, but doubts its validity as applied to effects felt only by foreign competitors of those exporters.[123] In cases of conflict, the rule applicable, he says, is that of the most rigorous law governing the transaction.[124] Where no conflict exists, he expects that American law might even be enforced as such by foreign courts, provided they do not find that the pertinent antitrust provision is a "political" law promoting the American economy at others' expense.[125]

Most interesting to note, the severity of the conflicts themselves is on the wane, as antitrust policies advance in other countries. Britain[126] and Germany[127] not only find themselves now in the antitrust camp,[128] rendering the previous clash of ideolo-

---

[121] CHESHIRE, PRIVATE INTERNATIONAL LAW 234 (5th ed. 1957), limits the rule to *"ordre public international,"* which would nonetheless seem to include economic protection.

[122] *Contra,* Haight, *Antitrust Laws and the Territorial Principle,* 11 VAND. L.REV. 27, 55 (1957).

[123] Wengler, *Laws Concerning Unfair Competition and the Conflict of Laws,* 4 AM. J. COMP. L. 167, 180 (1955).

[124] *Id.* at 181.

[125] *Id.* at 184.

[126] Monopolies and Restrictive Practices (Inquiries and Control)Act, 11 and 12 Geo. 6, c.66 (1948), as amended; Monopolies and Restrictive Practices Commission Act, 1 and 2 Eliz. 2, c.51 (1953); Restrictive Trade Practices Act, 4 and 5 Eliz. 2, c. 68 (1956). See Grunfeld, *Antitrust Law in Britain Since the Act of* 1956, 6 AM.J.COMP.L. 439 (1957), and authorities cited therein.

[127] See *supra,* n. 85.

[128] For a summary of foreign tendencies, see *Foreign Legislation Concerning Monopoly and Cartel Practices,* Report of the Department of State to the Subcommittee on Monopoly of the Senate Select Committee on Small Business, 82 Cong., 2d Sess. (1952). For a synoptic treatment of European cartel controls as well as the international implications of American antitrust, see WEEBERS, CONTROLE OP INTERNATIONALE KARTELS (Netherlands 1957). See also the authorities cited in footnote 8 of the preface.

gies a difference of degree, but are quite naturally also in the position of exercising an influence on international transactions beyond their borders as regards restrictive trade practices.[129] Suspicion that American antitrust is destructive of other economies should now be allayed, at least in those countries.

Particularly in view of this growth of understanding, the remaining differences with American law can, without threatening much strife, be left to the corrective devices of each country. This seems fairer, given a common policy, than expecting the American judge dealing with an international transaction to resolve differences automatically in favor of foreign defendants, especially where the judge lacks a specific realization of the peculiar needs of the foreign country's economy, which undoubtedly accounts for those differences.[130]

International public law does not command any different attitude. It should be noted first, that no general international law exists, either by multilateral treaty or out of custom, that might impose upon a state obligations superior to its own regulations applicable to its own economic order. Such public international law binding the United States as does exist is found in the provisions of bilateral treaties, which in no way alter the domestic practice of the United States in cases involving foreign corporations. The most comprehensive of these treaties with respect to antitrust policy contain provisions similar to the clauses

---

[129] The foreign applicability of British antitrust law has been said to stop short of the *Alcoa* extension. See Shawcross, *English Restrictive Practice Legislation; Extraterritorial Effect of U.S. Antitrust Laws,* 11 ABA ANTITRUST SECTION REPORT 111, 115, (July 1957). But the British rule as recorded in the legislative history by the then President of the Board of Trade, appears practically very close to the American. See Mr. Thorneycroft's testimony, House of Commons Debates, 13 July 1955.

For the foreign effect of the German law, see Schwartz, *Antitrust Legislation and Policy in Germany—A Comparative Study,* 105 U. PA. L.REV. 617, at 658 (1957). For a European comment, adopting foreign effects as natural, see Meinhardt, *Conflict Avoidance in the Law of Patents and Trade-Marks,* 21 LAW & CONTEMP. PROB. 533, 543 (1956). He concludes, at 548: "If the parties choose a law other than that of the country of protection [of industrial property], the rules of public policy of the country of protection, such as exchange control regulations, provisions against the abuse of monopoly, prohibition of assignment of trade-marks without the goodwill, or restrictions in granting licenses under trade-marks, must be observed."

[130] *Cf.* Friedmann, *A Comparative Analysis,* in ANTITRUST LAWS: A COMPARATIVE SYMPOSIUM 519 (Friedmann ed., 1956).

of the United States-Japanese Treaty which were considered in the *Oldham* case.[131]

Attempts at world-wide understanding in antitrust matters have continued to fail. The collapse of ITO[132] has been followed by the postponement of the United Nations program for publicizing cartel activities.[133] Nevertheless, the spirit underlying these attempts is followed by the United States. In the Swiss watch case, consultations were held to resolve difficulties stemming from the clash between Swiss protective laws and American free trade market policy.

> "Prior to the filing of this suit, consultations were held between representatives of the Department of Justice, in conjunction with Department of State officials, and representatives of the Swiss Government. The discussions, which were conducted in a cordial atmosphere, were undertaken to clarify the complex issues involved."[134]

The Attorney General's Committee also examined this field and recommended continuation of the present consultation practice.[135]

Contrary to some allegations of rigidity, a decided flexibility flows from the nature of American antitrust enforcement. Under American concepts, enforcement of antitrust laws is never mandatory. The Department of Justice, as well as the Federal Trade Commission, has discretion to sue or prosecute. Usually, each chooses to act against violations which it deems most dangerous to the economy or in situations where the applicable law requires clarification. This discretion also has been utilized consistently to adapt antitrust concepts to special national security or policy requirements. A very definite part of antitrust law is

---

131 United States v. R. P. Oldham Co., 152 F.Supp. 818 (N.D. Cal. 1957). See Section A, *supra*.

132 See *Final Act of the United Nations Conference on Trade and Employment*, United States Department of State Publication 3117, Commercial Policy Series 113 (1948).

133 See Kopper, *International Regulation of Cartels—Current Proposals*, 40 VA.L.REV. 1005 (1954); Timberg, *Restrictive Business Practices, Comparative Legislation and the Problems That Lie Ahead*, 2 AM.J. COMP.L. 445 (1953); Timberg, *Restrictive Business Practices as an Appropriate Subject for United Nations Action*, 1 ANTITRUST BULL. 409 (1955); Montague, *Limitations on What UN Can Do Successfully: The Proposed UN Program on Restrictive Business Practices, id.*, at 441 (1955).

134 Department of Justice, Press Release, October 19, 1954. It should be noted that concurrently with this case, American tariffs on Swiss watches and parts were raised under the escape clause in the tariff agreement with Switzerland.

135 REPORT OF THE ATTORNEY GENERAL'S NATIONAL COMMITTEE TO STUDY THE ANTITRUST LAWS 97 (1955).

contained in these administrative decisions. Recently, the Suez crisis demonstrated the flexibility which this discretionary power imparts to antitrust enforcement. The Government heeded the demands of the world economy and permitted a combination of American oil companies to make the arrangements necessary to alleviate the situation.[136]

As in the case of regulated domestic industries, antitrust sometimes cedes to larger considerations in foreign cases. Its respect for explicit foreign law and policy may be considered from this point of view. The integrated international oil companies are the result of this respect, and of the subordination of competition to the requirements of conservation, national defense and the regulations of foreign countries. Interestingly enough, with regard to the integrated oil industry foreign comment has been most critical of insufficient antitrust enforcement by the United States government. A report of the United Nations Economic Council for Europe blames high gasoline prices in Europe on American abuses of conservation policy and cartel agreements between American and Middle East interests.[137]

Whatever opinion might be advocated on the effect of American antitrust on world commerce, certain facts are never superfluous in the discussion. American antitrust laws in fact set certain limits on American-foreign business arrangements and on the use of capital abroad. These limits are no more definite nor obscure than the rest of the American law.[138] Some foreign, and domestic, businessmen may be surprised to find an arrange-

---

[136] See Emergency Oil Lift Program and Related Oil Problems, *Joint Hearings Before Subcommittees of the Senate Committees on the Judiciary and on Interior and Insular Affairs*, 85th Cong., 1st Sess., Parts 1-4 (1957); *Petroleum, The Antitrust Laws and Government Policies*, Report of the Subcommittee on Antitrust and Monopoly of the Senate Committee on the Judiciary, 85th Cong., 1st Sess. (1957). A more critical view of current possibilities for adaptation is taken by SPECIAL COMMITTEE ON ANTITRUST LAWS AND FOREIGN TRADE OF THE ASSOCIATION OF THE BAR OF THE CITY OF NEW YORK, PRELIMINARY REPORT ON NATIONAL SECURITY AND FOREIGN POLICY IN THE APPLICATION OF AMERICAN ANTITRUST LAWS TO COMMERCE WITH FOREIGN NATIONS (1957).

[137] UNITED NATIONS ECONOMIC COMMISSION FOR EUROPE, THE PRICE OF OIL IN WESTERN EUROPE (1955). The only judicial material available to date is the decision in United States v. Standard Oil Co. of California, 155 F.Supp. 121 (S.D. N.Y. 1957), which should be read in conjunction with this report.

[138] *Contra*, and with a comprehensive annotation of materials, Hale and Hale, *Monopoly Abroad: The Antitrust Laws and Commerce in Foreign Areas*, 31 TEX.L.REV. 493 (1953).

ment illegal, and their disappointment cannot be denied.[139] But from the point of view of any given nation today, disappointments are to be expected in its economic dealings with a competing and still somewhat different economy. Such disappointments cannot be avoided as long as the economies involved must protect themselves from different threats. They can only be minimized by alert responsiveness to progress in the respective nations' communities of interest through *ad hoc* negotiations and commercial treaties. With this attitude, perhaps, the discussion on America's flexibility to its neighbors' needs may be more fruitful, at least more multilateral, than under those premises which would resolve everything in a wholesale surrender of American antitrust interests to every real or imaginary consideration of foreign commerce.

---

[139] For a foremost practitioner's viewpoint, see Dean, *Extraterritorial Effects of the U.S. Antitrust Laws: "Advising the Client,"* 11 ABA ANTI-TRUST SECTION REPORT 88 (July 1957).

APPENDIX

TEXT OF THE
FEDERAL ANTITRUST LAWS

Sherman Act
Clayton Act
Robinson-Patman Act
Federal Trade Commission Act

SHERMAN ACT[1]

Sec. 1. Every contract, combination in the form of trust or otherwise, or conspiracy, in restraint of trade or commerce among the several States, or with foreign nations, is hereby declared to be illegal: *Provided,* That nothing herein contained shall render illegal, contracts or agreements prescribing minimum prices for the resale of a commodity which bears, or the label or container of which bears, the trade mark, brand, or name of the producer or distributor of such commodity and which is in free and open competition with commodities of the same general class produced or distributed by others, when contracts or agreements of that description are lawful as applied to intrastate transactions, under any statute, law, or public policy now or hereafter in effect in any State, Territory, or the District of Columbia in which such resale is to be made, or to which the commodity is to be transported for such resale, and the making of such contracts or agreements shall not be an unfair method of competition under section 5, as amended and supplemented, of the Act entitled "An Act to create a Federal Trade Commission, to define its powers and duties, and for other purposes," approved September 26, 1914: *Provided further,* That the preceding proviso shall not make lawful any contract or agreement, providing for the establishment or maintenance of minimum resale prices on any commodity herein involved, between manufacturers, or between producers, or between wholesalers, or between brokers, or between factors, or between retailers, or between persons, firms, or corporations in competition with each other. Every person who shall make any contract or engage in any combination or conspiracy hereby declared to be illegal shall be deemed guilty of a misdemeanor, and, on conviction thereof, shall be punished by fine not exceeding fifty thousand dollars, or by imprisonment not exceeding one year, or by both said punishments, in the discretion of the court.[2]

Sec. 2. Every person who shall monopolize, or attempt to monopolize, or combine or conspire with any other person or persons, to monopolize any part of the trade or commerce among the several States, or with foreign nations, shall be deemed guilty of a misdemeanor, and, on conviction thereof, shall be punished by fine not exceeding fifty thousand dollars, or by imprisonment not exceeding one year, or by both said punishments, in the discretion of the court.[3]

Sec. 3. Every contract, combination in form of trust or otherwise, or conspiracy, in restraint of trade or commerce in any Territory of the United States or of the District of Columbia, or in restraint of trade or commerce between any such Territory and another, or between any such Territory or Territories and any State or States or the District of Columbia, or with foreign nations, or between the District of Columbia and

---

[1] 26 STAT. 209 (1890), as amended, 15 U.S.C. §§ 1-7 (1952), as amended, 15 U.S.C. §§ 1-3 and 15 (Supp. IV, 1957).
[2] 26 STAT. 209 (1890), as amended by the Miller-Tydings Act, 50 STAT. 693 (1937), 15 U.S.C. § 1 (1952), as amended, 15 U.S.C. § 1 (Supp. IV, 1957).
[3] 26 STAT. 209 (1890), as amended, 15 U.S.C. § 2 (Supp. IV, 1957).
[4] 26 STAT. 209 (1890), as amended, 15 U.S.C. § 3 (Supp. IV, 1957).

any State or States or foreign nations, is hereby declared illegal. Every person who shall make any such contract or engage in any such combination or conspiracy shall be deemed guilty of a misdemeanor, and, on conviction thereof, shall be punished by fine not exceeding fifty thousand dollars, or by imprisonment not exceeding one year, or by both said punishments, in the discretion of the court.[4]

Sec. 4. The several circuit courts[5] of the United States are hereby invested with jurisdiction to prevent and restrain violations of this act; and it shall be the duty of the several district attorneys of the United States, in their respective districts, under the direction of the Attorney General, to institute proceedings in equity to prevent and restrain such violations. Such proceedings may be by way of petition setting forth the case and praying that such violation shall be enjoined or otherwise prohibited. When the parties complained of shall have been duly notified of such petition the court shall proceed, as soon as may be, to the hearing and determination of the case; and pending such petition and before final decree, the court may at any time make such temporary restraining order or prohibition as shall be deemed just in the premises.[6]

Sec. 5. Whenever it shall appear to the court before which any proceeding under section four of this act may be pending, that the ends of justice require that other parties should be brought before the court, the court may cause them to be summoned, whether they reside in the district in which the court is held or not; and subpoenas to that end may be served in any district by the marshal thereof.[7]

Sec. 6. Any property owned under any contract or by any combination, or pursuant to any conspiracy (and being the subject thereof) mentioned in section one of this act, and being in the course of transportation from one State to another, or to a foreign country, shall be forfeited to the United States, and may be seized and condemned by like proceedings as those provided by law for the forfeiture, seizure, and condemnation of property imported into the United States contrary to law.[8]

Sec. 7. [This section, which was superseded by section 4 of the Clayton Act, *infra*, was repealed, 69 STAT. 283 (1955), 15 U.S.C. § 15 (Supp. IV, 1957), effective January 7, 1956.]

Sec. 8. The word "person", or "persons", wherever used in this act shall be deemed to include corporations and associations existing under or authorized by the laws of either the United States, the laws of any of the Territories, the laws of any State, or the laws of any foreign country.[9]

CLAYTON ACT[10]

Sec. 1. "Antitrust laws," as used herein, includes the Act entitled "An Act to protect trade and commerce against unlawful restraints and monopolies," approved July second, eighteen hundred and ninety; sections seventy-three to seventy-seven, inclusive, of an Act entitled "An Act to reduce taxation, to provide revenue for the Government, and for other purposes," of August twenty-seventh, eighteen hundred and ninety-four; an Act entitled "An Act to amend sections seventy-three and seventy-six of the Act of August twenty-seventh, eighteen hundred and ninety-four, entitled 'An Act to reduce taxation, to provide revenue for the Government, and for other purposes,' " approved February twelfth, nineteen hundred and thirteen; and also this Act.

"Commerce," as used herein, means trade or commerce among the several States and with foreign nations, or between the District of Columbia or any Territory of the United States and any State, Territory, or foreign nation, or between any insular possessions or other places under the jurisdiction of the United States, or between any such possession or place and any State or Territory of the United States or the District of Columbia or any foreign nation, or within the District of Columbia or any Territory or any insular possession or other place under the jurisdiction of the United States: *Provided,* That nothing in this Act contained shall apply to the Philippine Islands.

The word "person" or "persons" wherever used in this Act shall be deemed to include corporations and associations existing under or authorized by the laws of either the United States, the laws of any of the Territories, the laws of any State, or the laws of any foreign country.[11]

---

[5] The circuit courts were abolished and their powers and duties imposed upon the district courts of the United States, 36 STAT. 1167 (1911).
[6] 26 STAT. 209 (1890), as amended, 15 U.S.C. § 4 (1952).
[7] 26 STAT. 210 (1890), 15 U.S.C. § 5 (1952).
[8] 26 STAT. 210 (1890), 15 U.S.C. § 6 (1952).
[9] 26 STAT. 210 (1890), 15 U.S.C. § 7 (1952).
[10] 38 STAT. 730 (1914), as amended, 15 U.S.C. §§ 12-27 (1952), as amended, 15 U.S.C. §§ 15, 15a, 15b, 16 (Supp. IV, 1957).
[11] 38 STAT. 730 (1914), 15 U.S.C. § 12 (1952).

Sec. 2. (a) It shall be unlawful for any person engaged in commerce, in the course of such commerce, either directly or indirectly, to discriminate in price between different purchasers of commodities of like grade and quality, where either or any of the purchases involved in such discrimination are in commerce, where such commodities are sold for use, consumption, or resale within the United States or any Territory thereof or the District of Columbia or any insular possession or other place under the jurisdiction of the United States, and where the effect of such discrimination may be substantially to lessen competition or tend to create a monopoly in any line of commerce, or to injure, destroy, or prevent competition with any person who either grants or knowingly receives the benefit of such discrimination, or with customers of either of them: *Provided,* That nothing herein contained shall prevent differentials which make only due allowance for differences in the cost of manufacture, sale, or delivery resulting from the differing methods or quantities in which such commodities are to such purchasers sold or delivered: *Provided, however,* That the Federal Trade Commission may, after due investigation and hearing to all interested parties, fix and establish quantity limits, and revise the same as it finds necessary, as to particular commodities or classes of commodities, where it finds that available purchasers in greater quantities are so few as to render differentials on account thereof unjustly discriminatory or promotive of monopoly in any line of commerce; and the foregoing shall then not be construed to permit differentials based on differences in quantities greater than those so fixed and established: *And provided further,* That nothing herein contained shall prevent persons engaged in selling goods, wares, or merchandise in commerce from selecting their own customers in bona fide transactions and not in restraint of trade: *And provided further,* That nothing herein contained shall prevent price changes from time to time where in response to changing conditions affecting the market for or the marketability of the goods concerned, such as but not limited to actual or imminent deterioration of perishable goods, obsolescence of seasonal goods, distress sales under court process, or sales in good faith in discontinuance of business in the goods concerned.

(b) Upon proof being made, at any hearing on a complaint under this section, that there has been discrimination in price or services or facilities furnished, the burden of rebutting the prima facie case thus made by showing justification shall be upon the person charged with a violation of this section, and unless justification shall be affirmatively shown, the Commission is authorized to issue an order terminating the discrimination: *Provided, however,* That nothing herein contained shall prevent a seller rebutting the prima facie case thus made by showing that his lower price or the furnishing of services or facilities to any purchaser or purchasers was made in good faith to meet an equally low price of a competitor, or the services or facilities furnished by a competitor.

(c) It shall be unlawful for any person engaged in commerce, in the course of such commerce, to pay or grant, or to receive or accept, anything of value as a commission, brokerage, or other compensation, or any allowance or discount in lieu thereof, except for services rendered in connection with the sale or purchase of goods, wares, or merchandise, either to the other party to such transaction or to an agent, representative, or other intermediary therein where such intermediary is acting in fact for or in behalf, or is subject to the direct or indirect control, of any party to such transaction other than the person by whom such compensation is so granted or paid.

(d) It shall be unlawful for any person engaged in commerce to pay or contract for the payment of anything of value to or for the benefit of a customer of such person in the course of such commerce as compensation or in consideration for any services or facilities furnished by or through such customer in connection with the processing, handling, sale, or offering for sale of any products or commodities manufactured, sold, or offered for sale by such person, unless such payment or consideration is available on proportionally equal terms to all other customers competing in the distribution of such products or commodities.

(e) It shall be unlawful for any person to discriminate in favor of one purchaser against another purchaser or purchasers of a commodity bought for resale, with or without processing, by contracting to furnish or furnishing, or by contributing to the furnishing of, any services or facilities connected with the processing, handling, sale, or offering for sale of such commodity so purchased upon terms not accorded to all purchasers on proportionately equal terms.

(f) It shall be unlawful for any person engaged in commerce, in the course of such commerce, knowingly to induce or receive a discrimination in price which is prohibited by this section.[12]

Sec. 3. It shall be unlawful for any person engaged in commerce, in the course of such commerce, to lease or make a sale or contract for sale of goods, wares, merchandise, machinery, supplies or other commodities, whether patented or unpatented, for use, consumption or resale within the United States or any Territory thereof or the District of Columbia or any insular possession or other place under the jurisdiction of

---

[12] 38 STAT. 730 (1914), as amended by section 1 of the Robinson-Patman Act, 49 STAT. 1526 (1936), 15 U.S.C. § 13 (a)-(f) (1952).

the United States, or fix a price charged therefor, or discount from, or rebate upon, such price, on the condition, agreement or understanding that the lessee or purchaser thereof shall not use or deal in the goods, wares, merchandise, machinery, supplies, or other commodities of a competitor or competitors of the lessor or seller, where the effect of such lease, sale, or contract for sale or such condition, agreement or understanding may be to substantially lessen competition or tend to create a monopoly in any line of commerce.[13]

Sec. 4. Any person who shall be injured in his business or property by reason of anything forbidden in the antitrust laws may sue therefor in any district court of the United States in the district in which the defendant resides or is found, or has an agent, without respect to the amount in controversy, and shall recover threefold the damages by him sustained, and the cost of suit, including a reasonable attorney's fee.[14]

Sec. 4A. Whenever the United States is hereafter injured in its business or property by reason of anything forbidden in the antitrust laws it may sue therefor in the United States district court for the district in which the defendant resides or is found or has an agent, without respect to the amount in controversy, and shall recover actual damages by it sustained and the cost of suit.[15]

Sec. 4B. Any action to enforce any cause of action under sections 4 or 4A shall be forever barred unless commenced within four years after the cause of action accrued. No cause of action barred under existing law on the effective date of this Act shall be revived by this Act.[16]

Sec. 5. (a) A final judgment or decree heretofore or hereafter rendered in any civil or criminal proceeding brought by or on behalf of the United States under the antitrust laws to the effect that a defendant has violated said laws shall be prima facie evidence against such defendant in any action or proceeding brought by any other party against such defendant under said laws or by the United States under esction 4A, as to all matters respecting which said judgment or decree would be an estoppel as between the parties thereto: *Provided,* That this section shall not apply to consent judgments or decrees entered before any testimony has been taken or to judgments or decrees entered in actions under section 4A.

(b) Whenever any civil or criminal proceeding is instituted by the United States to prevent, restrain, or punish violations of any of the antitrust laws, but not including an action under section 4A, the running of the statute of limitations in respect of every private right of action arising under said laws and based in whole or in part on any matter complained of in said proceeding shall be suspended during the pendency thereof and for one year thereafter: *Provided, however,* That whenever the running of the statute of limitations in respect of a cause of action arising under section 4 is suspended hereunder, any action to enforce such cause of action shall be forever barred unless commenced either within the period of suspension or within four years after the cause of action accrued.[17]

Sec. 6. The labor of a human being is not a commodity or article of commerce. Nothing contained in the antitrust laws shall be construed to forbid the existence and operation of labor, agricultural, or horticultural organizations, instituted for the purposes of mutual help, and not having capital stock or conducted for profit, or to forbid or restrain individual members of such organizations from lawfully carrying out the legitimate objects thereof; nor shall such organizations, or the members thereof, be held or construed to be illegal combinations or conspiracies in restraint of trade, under the antitrust laws.[18]

Sec. 7. No corporation engaged in commerce shall acquire directly or indirectly, the whole or any part of the stock or other share capital and no corporation subject to the jurisdiction of the Federal Trade Commission shall acquire the whole or any part of the assets of another corporation engaged also in commerce, where in any line of commerce in any section of the country, the effect of such acquisition may be substantially to lessen competition, or to tend to create a monopoly.

No corporation shall acquire, directly or indirectly, the whole or any part of the stock or other share capital and no corporation subject to the jurisdiction of the Federal Trade Commission shall acquire the whole or any part of the assets of one or more corporations engaged in commerce, where in any line of commerce in any section of the country, the effect of such acquisition, of such stocks or assets, or of the use of such stock by the voting or granting of proxies or otherwise, may be substantially to lessen competition, or to tend to create a monopoly.

This section shall not apply to corporations purchasing such stock solely for investment and not using the same by voting or otherwise to bring about, or in attempting to

---

[13] 38 STAT. 731 (1914), 15 U.S.C. § 14 (1952).
[14] 38 STAT. 731 (1914), 15 U.S.C. § 15 (1952).
[15] 69 STAT. 282 (1955), 15 U.S.C. § 15a (Supp. IV, 1957).
[16] 69 STAT. 283 (1955), 15 U.S.C. § 15b (Supp. IV, 1957).
[17] 38 STAT. 731 (1914), as amended, 15 U.S.C. § 16 (Supp. IV. 1957).
[18] 38 STAT. 731 (1914), 15 U.S.C. § 17 (1952).

bring about, the substantial lessening of competition. Nor shall anything contained in this section prevent a corporation engaged in commerce from causing the formation of subsidiary corporations for the actual carrying on of their immediate lawful business, or the natural and legitimate branches or extensions thereof, or from owning and holding all or a part of the stock of such subsidiary corporations, when the effect of such formation is not to substantially lessen competition.

Nor shall anything herein contained be construed to prohibit any common carrier subject to the laws to regulate commerce from aiding in the construction of branches or short lines so located as to become feeders to the main line of the company so aiding in such construction or from acquiring or owning all or any part of the stock of such branch lines, nor to prevent any such common carrier from acquiring and owning all or any part of the stock of a branch or short line constructed by an independent company where there is no substantial competition between the company owning the branch line so constructed and the company owning the main line acquiring the property or an interest therein, nor to prevent such common carrier from extending any of its lines through the medium of the acquisition of stock or otherwise of any other common carrier where there is no substantial competition between the company extending its lines and the company whose stock, property, or an interest therein is so acquired.

Nothing contained in this section shall be held to affect or impair any right heretofore legally acquired: *Provided,* That nothing in this section shall be held or construed to authorize or make lawful anything heretofore prohibited or made illegal by the antitrust laws, nor to exempt any person from the penal provisions thereof or the civil remedies therein provided.

Nothing contained in this section shall apply to transactions duly consummated pursuant to authority given by the Civil Aeronautics Board, Federal Communications Commission, Federal Power Commission, Interstate Commerce Commission, the Securities and Exchange Commission in the exercise of its jurisdiction under section 10 of the Public Utility Holding Company Act of 1935, the United States Maritime Commission,[19] or the Secretary of Agriculture under any statutory provision vesting such power in such Commission, Secretary, or Board.[20]

Sec. 8. No private banker or director, officer, or employee of any member bank of the Federal Reserve System or any branch thereof shall be at the same time a director, officer, or employee of any other bank, banking association, savings bank, or trust company organized under the National Bank Act or organized under the laws of any State or of the District of Columbia, or any branch thereof, except that the Board of Governors of the Federal Reserve System may by regulation permit such service as a director, officer, or employee of not more than one other such institution or branch thereof; but the foregoing prohibition shall not apply in the case of any one or more of the following or any branch thereof:

(1) A bank, banking association, savings bank, or trust company, more than 90 per centum of the stock of which is owned directly or indirectly by the United States or by any corporation of which the United States directly or indirectly owns more than 90 per centum of the stock.

(2) A bank, banking association, savings bank, or trust company which has been placed formally in liquidation or which is in the hands of a receiver, conservator, or other official exercising similar functions.

(3) A corporation, principally engaged in international or foreign banking or banking in a dependency or insular possession of the United States which has entered into an agreement with the Board of Governors of the Federal Reserve System pursuant to section 25 of the Federal Reserve Act.

(4) A bank, banking association, savings bank, or trust company, more than 50 per centum of the common stock of which is owned directly or indirectly by persons who own directly or indirectly more than 50 per centum of the common stock of such member bank.

(5) A bank, banking association, savings bank, or trust company not located and having no branch in the same city, town, or village as that in which such member bank or any branch thereof is located, or in any city, town, or village contiguous or adjacent thereto.

(6) A bank, banking association, savings bank, or trust company not engaged in a class or classes of business in which such member bank is engaged.

(7) A mutual savings bank having no capital stock.

Until February 1, 1939, nothing in this section shall prohibit any director, officer, or employee of any member bank of the Federal Reserve System, or any branch thereof, who is lawfully serving at the same time as a private banker or as a director, officer, or employee of any other bank, banking association, savings bank, or trust company, or any branch thereof, on the date of enactment of the Banking Act of 1935, from continuing such service.

---

[19] Now the Federal Maritime Board.
[20] 38 STAT. 731 (1914), as amended by the Kefauver-Celler Act, 64 STAT. 1125 (1950), 15 U.S.C. § 18 (1952).

The Board of Governors of the Federal Reserve System is authorized and directed to enforce compliance with this section, and to prescribe such rules and regulations as it deems necessary for that purpose.

No person at the same time shall be a director in any two or more corporations, any one of which has capital, surplus, and undivided profits aggregating more than $1,000,000, engaged in whole or in part in commerce, other than banks, banking associations, trust companies, and common carriers subject to the Act to regulate commerce, approved February fourth, eighteen hundred and eighty seven, if such corporations are or shall have been theretofore, by virtue of their business and location of operation, competitors, so that the elimination of competition by agreement between them would constitute a violation of any of the provisions of any of the antitrust laws. The eligibility of a director under the foregoing provision shall be determined by the aggregate amount of the capital, surplus, and undivided profits, exclusive of dividends declared but not paid to stockholders, at the end of the fiscal year of said corporation next preceding the election of directors, and when a director has been elected in accordance with the provisions of this Act it shall be lawful for him to continue as such for one year thereafter.

When any person elected or chosen as a director or officer or selected as an employee of any bank or other corporation subject to the provisions of this Act is eligible at the time of his election or selection to act for such bank or other corporation in such capacity his eligibility to act in such capacity shall not be affected and he shall not become or be deemed amenable to any of the provisions hereof by reason of any change in the affairs of such bank or other corporation from whatsoever cause, whether specifically excepted by any of the provisions hereof or not, until the expiration of one year from the date of his election or employment.[21]

[Sec. 8A, as added in 1933, 48 STAT. 194, was repealed in 1935, 49 STAT. 717, 15. U.S.C. § 19 a (1952).]

[Sec. 9 was repealed by the Criminal Code in 1948, 62 STAT. 864, section 21 of which enacted similar provisions[22].]

Sec. 10. No common carrier engaged in commerce shall have any dealings in securities, supplies, or other articles of commerce, or shall make or have any contracts for construction or maintenance of any kind, to the amount of more than $50,000, in the aggregate, in any one year, with another corporation, firm, partnership, or association when the said common carrier shall have upon its board of directors or as its president, manager, or as its purchasing or selling officer, or agent in the particular transaction, any person who is at the same time a director, manager, or purchasing or selling officer of, or who has any substantial interest in, such other corporation, firm, partnership, or association, unless and except such purchases shall be made from, or such dealings shall be with, the bidder whose bid is the most favorable to such common carrier, to be ascertained by competitive bidding under regulations to be prescribed by rule or otherwise by the Interstate Commerce Commission. No bid shall be received unless the name and address of the bidder or the names and addresses of the officers, directors, and general managers thereof, if the bidder be a corporation, or of the members, if it be a partnership or firm, be given with the bid.

Any person who shall, directly or indirectly, do or attempt to do anything to prevent anyone from bidding or shall do any act to prevent free and fair competition among the bidders or those desiring to bid shall be punished as prescribed in this section in the case of an officer or director.

Every such common carrier having any such transactions or making any such purchases shall, within thirty days after making the same, file with the Interstate Commerce Commission a full and detailed statement of the transaction showing the manner of the competitive bidding, who were the bidders, and the names and addresses of the directors and officers of the corporations and the members of the firm or partnership bidding; and whenever the said commission shall, after investigation or hearing, have reason to believe that the law has been violated in and about the said purchases or transactions, it shall transmit all papers and documents and its own views or findings regarding the transaction to the Attorney General.

If any common carrier shall violate this section it shall be fined not exceeding $25,000; and every such director, agent, manager or officer thereof who shall have knowingly voted for or directed the act constituting such violation or who shall have aided or abetted in such violation shall be deemed guilty of a misdemeanor and shall be fined not exceeding $5,000, or confined in jail not exceeding one year, or both, in the discretion of the court.[23]

Sec. 11. Authority to enforce compliance with sections 2, 3, 7, and 8 of this Act by the persons respectively subject thereto is hereby vested in the Interstate Commerce Commission where applicable to common carriers subject to the Interstate Com-

---

[21] 38 STAT. 732 (1914), as amended, 15 U.S.C. § 19 (1952).
[22] 62 STAT. 730 (1948), 18 U.S.C. § 660 (1952).
[23] 38 STAT. 734 (1914), 15 U.S.C. § 20 (1952).

merce Act, as amended; in the Federal Communications Commission where applicable to common carriers engaged in wire or radio communication or radio transmission of energy; in the Civil Aeronautics Board where applicable to air carriers and foreign air carriers subject to the Civil Aeronautics Act of 1938; in the Federal Reserve Board where applicable to banks, banking associations, and trust companies; and in the Federal Trade Commission where applicable to all other character of commerce to be exercised as follows:

Whenever the Commission or Board vested with jurisdiction thereof shall have reason to believe that any person is violating or has violated any of the provisions of sections 2, 3, 7, and 8 of this Act, it shall issue and serve upon such person and the Attorney General a complaint stating its charges in that respect, and containing a notice of a hearing upon a day and at a place therein fixed at least thirty days after the service of said complaint. The person so complained of shall have the right to appear at the place and time so fixed and show cause why an order should not be entered by the Commission or Board requiring such person to cease and desist from the violation of the law so charged in said complaint. The Attorney General shall have the right to intervene and appear in said proceeding and any person may make application, and upon good cause shown may be allowed by the Commission or Board, to intervene and appear in said proceeding by counsel or in person. The testimony in any such proceeding shall be reduced to writing and filed in the office of the Commission or Board. If upon such hearing the Commission or Board, as the case may be, shall be of the opinion that any of the provisions of said sections have been or are being violated, it shall make a report in writing, in which it shall state its findings as to the facts, and shall issue and cause to be served on such person an order requiring such person to cease and desist from such violations, and divest itself of the stock, or other share capital, or assets, held or rid itself of the directors chosen contrary to the provisions of sections 7 and 8 of this Act, if any there be, in the manner and within the time fixed by said order. Until a transcript of the record in such hearing shall have been filed in a United States court of appeals, as hereinafter provided, the Commission or Board may at any time, upon such notice, and in such manner as it shall deem proper, modify or set aside, in whole or in part, any report or any order made or issued by it under this section.

If such person fails or neglects to obey such order of the Commission or Board while the same is in effect, the Commission or Board may apply to the United States court of appeals, within any circuit where the violation complained of was or is being committed or where such person resides or carries on business, for the enforcement of its order, and shall certify and file with its application a transcript of the entire record in the proceeding, including all the testimony taken and the report and order of the Commission or Board. Upon such filing of the application and transcript the court shall cause notice thereof to be served upon such person, and thereupon shall have jurisdiction of the proceeding and of the question determined therein, and shall have power to make and enter upon the pleadings, testimony, and proceedings set forth in such transcript a decree affirming, modifying, or setting aside the order of the Commission or Board. The findings of the Commission or Board as to the facts, if supported by substantial evidence, shall be conclusive. If either party shall apply to the court for leave to adduce additional evidence, and shall show to the satisfaction of the court that such additional evidence is material and that there were reasonable grounds for the failure to adduce such evidence in the proceeding before the Commission or Board, the court may order such additional evidence to be taken before the Commission or Board and to be adduced upon the hearing in such manner and upon such terms and conditions as to the court may seem proper. The Commission or Board may modify its findings as to the facts, or make new findings, by reason of the additional evidence so taken, and it shall file such modified or new findings, which, if supported by substantial evidence, shall be conclusive, and its recommendations, if any, for the modification or setting aside of its original order, with the return of such additional evidence. The judgment and decree of the court shall be final, except that the same shall be subject to review by the Supreme Court upon certiorari as provided in section 1254 of title 28, United States Code.

Any party required by such order of the Commission or Board to cease and desist from a violation charged may obtain a review of such order in said United States court of appeals by filing in the court a written petition praying that the order of the Commission or Board be set aside. A copy of such petition shall be forthwith served upon the Commission or Board, and thereupon the Commission or Board forthwith shall certify and file in the court a transcript of the record as hereinbefore provided. Upon the filing of the transcript the court shall have the same jurisdiction to affirm, set aside, or modify the order of the Commission or Board as in the case of an application by the Commission or Board for the enforcement of its order, and the findings of the Commission or Board as to the facts, if supported by substantial evidence, shall in like manner be conclusive.

The jurisdiction of the United States court of appeals to enforce, set aside, or modify orders of the Commission or Board shall be exclusive.

Such proceedings in the United States court of appeals shall be given precedence over cases pending therein, and shall be in every way expedited. No order of the Commission or Board or the judgment of the court to enforce the same shall in anywise relieve or absolve any person from any liability under the antitrust Acts.

Complaints, orders, and other processes of the Commission or Board under this section may be served by anyone duly authorized by the Commission or Board, either (a) by delivering a copy thereof to the person to be served, or to a member of the partnership to be served, or to the president, secretary, or other executive officer or a director of the corporation to be served; or (b) by leaving a copy thereof at the principal office or place of business of such person; or (c) by registering and mailing a copy thereof addressed to such person at his principal office or place of business. The verified return by the person so serving said complaint, order, or other process setting forth the manner of said service shall be proof of the same, and the return post-office receipt for said complaint, order, or other process registered and mailed as aforesaid shall be proof of the service of the same.[24]

Sec. 12. Any suit, action, or proceeding under the antitrust laws against a corporation may be brought not only in the judicial district whereof it is an inhabitant, but also in any district wherein it may be found or transacts business; and all process in such case may be served in the district of which it is an inhabitant, or wherever it may be found.[25]

Sec. 13. In any suit, action, or proceeding brought by or on behalf of the United States subpoenas for witnesses who are required to attend a court of the United States in any judicial district in any case, civil or criminal, arising under the antitrust laws may run into any other district: *Provided,* That in civil cases no writ of subpoena shall issue for witnesses living out of the district in which the court is held at a greater distance than one hundred miles from the place of holding the same without the permission of the trial court being first had upon proper application and cause shown.[26]

Sec. 14. Whenever a corporation shall violate any of the penal provisions of the antitrust laws, such violation shall be deemed to be also that of the individual directors, officers, or agents of such corporation who shall have authorized, ordered, or done any of the acts constituting in whole or in part such violation, and such violation shall be deemed a misdemeanor, and upon conviction therefor of any such director, officer, or agent he shall be punished by a fine of not exceeding $5,000 or by imprisonment for not exceeding one year, or by both, in the discretion of the court.[27]

Sec. 15. The several district courts of the United States are hereby invested with jurisdiction to prevent and restrain violations of this Act, and it shall be the duty of the several district attorneys of the United States, in their respective districts, under the direction of the Attorney General, to institute proceedings in equity to prevent and restrain such violations. Such proceedings may be by way of petition setting forth the case and praying that such violation shall be enjoined or otherwise prohibited. When the parties complained of shall have been duly notified of such petition, the court shall proceed, as soon as may be, to the hearing and determination of the case; and pending such petition, and before final decree, the court may at any time make such temporary restraining order or prohibition as shall be deemed just in the premises. Whenever it shall appear to the court before which any such proceeding may be pending that the ends of justice require that other parties should be brought before the court, the court may cause them to be summoned whether they reside in the district in which the court is held or not, and subpoenas to that end may be served in any district by the marshal thereof.[28]

Sec. 16. Any person, firm, corporation, or association shall be entitled to sue for and have injunctive relief, in any court of the United States having jurisdiction over the parties, against threatened loss or damage by a violation of the antitrust laws, including sections two, three, seven, and eight of this Act, when and under the same conditions and principles as injunctive relief against threatened conduct that will cause loss or damage is granted by courts of equity, under the rules governing such proceedings, and upon the execution of proper bond against damages for an injunction improvidently granted and a showing that the danger of irreparable loss or damage is immediate, a preliminary injunction may issue: *Provided,* That nothing herein contained shall be construed to entitle any person, firm, corporation, or association, except the United States, to bring suit in equity for injunctive relief against any common carrier subject to the provisions of the Act to regulate commerce, approved February fourth, eighteen hundred and eighty seven, in respect of any matter subject to the regulation, supervision, or other jurisdiction of the Interstate Commerce Commission.[29]

---

[24] 38 STAT. 734 (1914), as amended, 15 U.S.C. § 21 (1952).
[25] 38 STAT. 736 (1914), 15 U.S.C. § 22 (1952).
[26] 38 STAT. 736 (1914), 15 U.S.C. § 23 (1952).
[27] 38 STAT. 736 (1914), 15 U.S.C. § 24 (1952).
[28] 38 STAT. 736 (1914), 15 U.S.C. § 25 (1952).
[29] 38 STAT. 737 (1914), 15 U.S.C. § 26 (1952).

Sec. 17. Section two hundred and sixty three of an Act entitled "An Act to codify, revise, and amend the laws relating to the judiciary," approved March third, nineteen hundred and eleven, is hereby repealed.[30]

[Sections 18 and 19 were repealed by the Criminal Code in 1948, 62 STAT.997.]

Sec. 20. No restraining order or injunction shall be granted by any court of the United States, or a judge or the judges thereof, in any case between an employer and employees, or between employers and empployees, or between employees, or between persons employed and persons seeking employment, involving, or growing out of, a dispute concerning terms or conditions of employment, unless necessary to prevent irreparable injury to property, or to a property right, of the party making the application, for which injury there is no adequate remedy at law, and such property or property right must be described with particularity in the application, which must be in writing and sworn to by the applicant or by his agent or attorney.

And no such restraining order or injunction shall prohibit any person or persons, whether singly or in concert, from terminating any relation of employment, or from ceasing to perform any work or labor, or from recommending, advising, or persuading others by peaceful means so to do; or from attending at any place where any such person or persons may lawfully be, for the purpose of peacefully obtaining or communicating information, or from peacefully persuading any person to work or to abstain from working; or from ceasing to patronize or to employ any party to such dispute, or from recommending, advising, or persuading others by peaceful and lawful means so to do; or from paying or giving to, or withholding from, any persons engaged in such dispute, any strike benefits or other moneys or things of value; or from peaceably assembling in a lawful manner, and for lawful purposes; or from doing any act or thing which might lawfully be done in the absence of such dispute by any party thereto; nor shall any of the acts specified in this paragraph be considered or held to be violations of any law of the United States.[31]

[Sections 21-25 were repealed by the Criminal Code in 1948, 62 STAT. 864, section 1 of which enacted similar provisions[32].]

Sec. 26. If any clause, sentence, paragraph, or part of this Act shall, for any reason, be adjudged by any court of competent jurisdiction to be invalid, such judgment shall not affect, impair, or invalidate the remainder thereof, but shall be confined in its operation to the clause, sentence, paragraph, or part thereof directly involved in the controversy in which such judgment shall have been rendered.[33]

ROBINSON-PATMAN ACT[34]

[Section 1 of this Act amends section 2 of the Clayton Act and can be found under that heading. Section 2 referred to matters arising prior to the effective date of the Robinson-Patman Act which were based on the old section 2 of the Clayton Act.].

Sec. 3. It shall be unlawful for any person engaged in commerce, in the course of such commerce, to be a party to, or assist in, any transaction of sale, or contract to sell, which discriminates to his knowledge against competitors of the purchaser, in that, any discount, rebate, allowance, or advertising service charge is granted to the purchaser over and above any discount, rebate, allowance, or advertising service charge available at the time of such transaction to said competitors in respect of a sale of goods of like grade, quality, and quantity; to sell, or contract to sell, goods in any part of the United States at prices lower than those exacted by said person elsewhere in the United States for the purpose of destroying competition, or eliminating a competitor in such part of the United States; or, to sell, or contract to sell, goods at unreasonably low prices for the purpose of destroying competition or eliminating a competitor.

Any person violating any of the provisions of this section shall, upon conviction thereof, be fined not more than $5,000 or imprisoned not more than one year, or both.[35]

Sec. 4. Nothing in this Act shall prevent a cooperative association from returning to its members, producers, or consumers the whole, or any part of, the net earnings or surplus resulting from its trading operations, in proportion to their purchases or sales from, to, or through the association.[36]

---

[30] 38 STAT. 737 (1914). The first, second, and fourth paragraphs of this section have been repealed by the Criminal Code in 1948, 62 STAT. 997.
[31] 38 STAT. 738 (1914), 29 U.S.C. § 52 (1952).
[32] 62 STAT. 701, 844, and 828 (1948), as amended, 18 U.S.C. §§ 402, 3691, and 3285 (1952).
[33] 38 STAT. 740 (1914), 15 U.S.C. § 27 (1952).
[34] 49 STAT. 1526 (1936), 15 U.S.C. §§ 13 (a)-(f), 13a, 13b, 21a (1952).
[35] 49 STAT. 1528 (1936), 15 U.S.C. § 13a (1952).
[36] 49 STAT. 1528 (1936), 15 U.S.C. § 13b (1952).

FEDERAL TRADE COMMISSION ACT[37]

Sec. 1. A commission is hereby created and established, to be known as the Federal Trade Commission (hereinafter referred to as the commission), which shall be composed of five commissioners, who shall be appointed by the President, by and with the advice and consent of the Senate. Not more than three of the commissioners shall be members of the same political party. The first commissioners appointed shall continue in office for terms of three, four, five, six, and seven years, respectively, from the date of the taking effect of this Act, the term of each to be designated by the President, but their successors shall be appointed for terms of seven years, except that any person chosen to fill a vacancy shall be appointed only for the unexpired term of the commissioner whom he shall succeed: *Provided, however,* That upon the expiration of his term of office a Commissioner shall continue to serve until his successor shall have been appointed and shall have qualified. The commission shall choose a chairman from its own membership.[38] No commissioner shall engage in any other business, vocation, or employment. Any commissioner may be removed by the President for inefficiency, neglect of duty, or malfeasance in office. A vacancy in the commission shall not impair the right of the remaining commissioners to exercise all the powers of the commission.[39]

Sec. 2. The commission shall appoint a secretary, who shall receive a salary, payable in the same manner as the salaries of the judges of the courts of the United States, and it shall have authority to employ and fix the compensation of such attorneys, special experts, examiners, clerks, and other employees as it may from time to time find necessary for the proper performance of its duties and as may be from time to time appropriated for by Congress.

With the exception of the secretary, a clerk to each commissioner, the attorneys, and such special experts and examiners as the commission may from time to time find necessary for the conduct of its work, all employees of the commission shall be a part of the classified civil service, and shall enter the service under such rules and regulations as may be prescribed by the commission and by the Civil Service Commission.

All of the expenses of the commission, including all necessary expenses for transportation incurred by the commissioners or by their employees under their orders, in making any investigation, or upon official business in any other places than in the city of Washington, shall be allowed and paid on the presentation of itemized vouchers therefor approved by the commission.

Until otherwise provided by law, the commission may rent suitable offices for its use.

The General Accounting Office shall receive and examine all accounts of expenditures of the commission.[40]

Sec. 3. [The first two paragraphs of this section contain temporary provisos.]

The principal office of the commission shall be in the city of Washington, but it may meet and exercise all its powers at any other place. The Commission may, by one or more of its members, or by such examiners as it may designate, prosecute any inquiry necessary to its duties in any part of the United States.[41]

Sec. 4. The words defined in this section shall have the following meaning when found in this Act, to wit:

"Commerce" means commerce among the several States or with foreign nations, or in any Territory of the United States or in the District of Columbia, or between any such Territory and another, or between any such Territory and any State or foreign nation, or between the District of Columbia and any State or Territory or foreign nation.

"Corporation" shall be deemed to include any company, trust, so-called Massachusetts trust, or association, incorporated or unincorporated, which is organized to carry on business for its own profit or that of its members, and has shares of capital or capital stock or certificates of interest, and any company, trust, so-called Massachusetts trust, or association, incorporated or unincorporated, without shares of capital or capital stock or certificates of interest, except partnerships, which is organized to carry on business for its own profit or that of its members.

"Documentary evidence" includes all documents, papers, correspondence, books of account, and financial and corporate records.

---

[37] 38 STAT. 717 (1914), as amended, 15 U.S.C. §§ 41-58 (1952), as amended, 15 U.S.C. §§ 41-46 (Supp. IV, 1957).
[38] See now Reorganization Plan No. 8, effective May 24, 1950, 64 STAT. 1265, 15 F.R. 3175, discussed in chapter 7.
[39] 38 STAT. 717 (1914), as amended, 15 U.S.C. § 41 (1952).
[40] 38 STAT. 718 (1914), as amended, 15 U.S.C. § 42 (Supp. IV, 1957).
[41] 38 STAT. 719 (1914), 15 U.S.C. § 43 (1952).

"Acts to regulate commerce" means the Act entitled "An Act to regulate commerce," approved February 14, 1887, and all Acts amendatory thereof and supplementary thereto and the Communications Act of 1934 and all Acts amendatory thereof and supplementary thereto.

"Antitrust Acts," means the Act entitled "An Act to protect trade and commerce against unlawful restraints and monopolies," approved July 2, 1890; also sections 73 to 77, inclusive, of an Act entitled "An Act to reduce taxation, to provide revenue for the Government, and for other purposes," approved August 27, 1894; also the Act entitled "An Act to amend sections 73 and 76 of the Act of August 27, 1894, entitled 'An Act to reduce taxation, to provide revenue for the Government, and for other purposes,' " approved February 12, 1913; and also the Act entitled "An Act to supplement existing laws against unlawful restraints and monopolies, and for other purposes," approved October 15, 1914.[42]

Sec. 5. (a) (1) Unfair methods of competition in commerce, and unfair or deceptive acts or practices in commerce, are hereby declared unlawful.

(2) Nothing contained in this Act or in any of the Antitrust Acts shall render unlawful any contracts or agreements prescribing minimum or stipulated prices, or requiring a vendee to enter into contracts or agreements prescribing minimum or stipulated prices, for the resale of a commodity which bears, or the label or container of which bears, the trade-mark, brand, or name of the producer or distributor of such commodity and which is in free and open competition with commodities of the same general class produced or distributed by others, when contracts or agreements of that description are lawful as applied to intrastate transactions under any statute, law, or public policy now or hereafter in effect in any State, Territory, or the District of Columbia in which such resale is to be made, or to which the commodity is to be transported for such resale.

(3) Nothing contained in this Act or in any of the Antitrust Acts shall render unlawful the exercise or the enforcement of any right or right of action created by any statute, law, or public policy now or hereafter in effect in any State, Territory, or the District of Columbia, which in substance provides that willfully and knowingly advertising, offering for sale, or selling any commodity at less than the price or prices prescribed in such contracts or agreements whether the person so advertising, offering for sale, or selling is or is not a party to such a contract or agreement, is unfair competition and is actionable at the suit of any person damaged thereby.

(4) Neither the making of contracts or agreements as described in paragraph (2) of this subsection, nor the exercise or enforcement of any right or right of action as described in paragraph (3) of this subsection shall constitute an unlawful burden or restraint upon, or interference with, commerce.

(5) Nothing contained in paragraph (2) of this subsection shall make lawful contracts or agreements providing for the establishment or maintenance of minimum or stipulated resale prices on any commodity referred to in paragraph (2) of this subsection, between manufacturers, or between producers, or between wholesalers, or between brokers, or between factors, or between retailers, or between persons, firms, or corporations in competition with each other.

(6) The Commission is hereby empowered and directed to prevent persons, partnerships, or corporations, except banks, common carriers subject to the Acts to regulate commerce, air carriers and foreign air carriers subject to the Civil Aeronautics Act of 1938, and persons, partnerships, or corporations subject to the Packers and Stockyards Act, 1921, except as provided in section 406(b) of said Act, from using unfair methods of competition in commerce and unfair or deceptive acts or practices in commerce.[43]

(b) Whenever the Commission shall have reason to believe that any such person, partnership, or corporation has been or is using any unfair method of competition or unfair or deceptive act or practice in commerce, and if it shall appear to the Commission that a proceeding by it in respect thereof would be to the interest of the public, it shall issue and serve upon such person, partnership, or corporation a complaint stating its charges in that respect and containing a notice of a hearing upon a day and at a place therein fixed at least thirty days after the service of said complaint. The person, partnership, or corporation so complained of shall have the right to appear at the place and time so fixed and show cause why an order should not be entered by the Commission requiring such person, partnership, or corporation to cease and desist from the violation of the law so charged in said complaint. Any person, partnership, or corporation may make application, and upon good cause shown may be allowed by the Commission to intervene and appear in said proceeding by counsel or in person. The testimony in any

[42] 38 STAT. 719 (1914), as amended, 15 U.S.C. § 44 (1914).
[43] 38 STAT. 719 (1914), as amended by the McGuire Act, 66 STAT. 632, 15 U.S.C. § 45 (a). (1952).

such proceeding shall be reduced to writing and filed in the office of the Commission. If upon such hearing the Commission shall be of the opinion that the method of competition or the act or practice in question is prohibited by this Act, it shall make a report in writing in which it shall state its findings as to the facts and shall issue and cause to be served on such person, partnership, or corporation an order requiring such person, partnership, or corporation to cease and desist from using such method of competition or such act or practice. Until the expiration of the time allowed for filing a petition for review, if no such petition has been duly filed within such time, or, if a petition for review has been filed within such time then until the transcript of the record in the proceeding has been filed in a circuit court of appeals of the United States, as hereinafter provided, the Commission may at any time, upon such notice and in such manner as it shall deem proper, modify or set aside, in whole or in part, any report or any order made or issued by it under this section. After the expiration of the time allowed for filing a petition for review, if no such petition has been duly filed within such time, the Commission may at any time, after notice and opportunity for hearing, reopen and alter, modify, or set aside, in whole or in part, any report or order made or issued by it under this section, whenever in the opinion of the Commission conditions of fact or of law have so changed as to require such action or if the public interest shall so require: *Provided, however,* That the said person, partnership, or corporation may, within sixty days after service upon him or it of said report or order entered after such a reopening, obtain a review thereof in the appropriate circuit court of appeals of the United States, in the manner provided in subsection (c) of this section.

(c) Any person, partnership, or corporation required by an order of the Commission to cease and desist from using any method of competition or act or practice may obtain a review of such order in the circuit court of appeals of the United States, within any circuit where the method of competition or the act or practice in question was used or where such person, partnership, or corporation resides or carries on business, by filing in the court, within sixty days from the date of the service of such order, a written petition praying that the order of the Commission be set aside. A copy of such petition shall be forthwith served upon the Commission, and thereupon the Commission forthwith shall certify and file in the court a transcript of the entire record in the proceeding, including all the evidence taken and the report and order of the Commission. Upon such filing of the petition and transcript the court shall have jurisdiction of the proceeding and of the question determined therein, and shall have power to make and enter upon the pleadings, evidence, and proceedings set forth in such transcript a decree affirming, modifying, or setting aside the order of the Commission, and enforcing the same to the extent that such order is affirmed, and to issue such writs as are ancillary to its jurisdiction or are necessary in its judgment to prevent injury to the public or to competitors pendente lite. The findings of the Commission as to the facts, if supported by evidence, shall be conclusive. To the extent that the order of the Commission is affirmed, the court shall thereupon issue its own order commanding obedience to the terms of such order of the Commission. If either party shall apply to the court for leave to adduce additional evidence, and shall show to the satisfaction of the court that such additional evidence is material and that there were reasonable grounds for the failure to adduce such evidence in the proceeding before the Commission, the court may order such additional evidence to be taken before the Commission and to be adduced upon the hearing in such manner and upon such terms and conditions as to the court may seem proper. The Commission may modify its findings as to the facts, or make new findings, by reason of the additional evidence so taken, and it shall file such modified or new findings, which, if supported by evidence, shall be conclusive, and its recommendation, if any, for the modification or setting aside of its original order, with the return of such additional evidence. The judgment and decree of the court shall be final, except that the same shall be subject to review by the Supreme Court upon certiorari, as provided in section 347 of Title 28, U.S.C.

(d) The jurisdiction of the circuit court of appeals of the United States to affirm, enforce, modify, or set aside orders of the Commission shall be exclusive.

(e) Such proceedings in the circuit court of appeals shall be given precedence over other cases pending therein, and shall be in every way expedited. No order of the Commission or judgment of court to enforce the same shall in anywise relieve or absolve any person, partnership, or corporation from any liability under the Antitrust Acts.

(f) Complaints, orders, and other processes of the Commission under this section may be served by anyone duly authorized by the Commission, either (a) by delivering a copy thereof to the person to be served, or to a member of the partnership to be served, or the president, secretary, or other executive officer or a director of the corporation to be served; or (b) by leaving a copy thereof at the residence or the principal office or place of business of such person, partnership, or corporation; or (c) by registering and mailing a copy thereof addressed to such person, partnership, or corporation at his or its residence or principal office or place of business. The verified return by the person so serving said complaint, order, or other process setting forth the manner of said service shall be proof of the same, and the return post office receipt for said complaint, order, or other process registered and mailed as aforesaid shall be proof of the service of the same.

(g) An order of the Commission to cease and desist shall become final—

(1) Upon the expiration of the time allowed for filing a petition for review, if no such petition has been duly filed within such time; but the Commission may thereafter modify or set aside its order to the extent provided in the last sentence of subsection (b); or

(2) Upon the expiration of the time allowed for filing a petition for certiorari, if the order of the Commission has been affirmed, or the petition for review dismissed by the circuit court of appeals, and no petition for certiorari has been duly filed; or

(3) Upon the denial of a petition for certiorari, if the order of the Commission has been affirmed or the petition for review dismissed by the circuit court of appeals; or

(4) Upon the expiration of thirty days from the date of issuance of the mandate of the Supreme Court, if such Court directs that the order of the Commission be affirmed or the petition for review dismissed.

(h) If the Supreme Court directs that the order of the Commission be modified or set aside, the order of the Commission rendered in accordance with the mandate of the Supreme Court shall become final upon the expiration of thirty days from the time it was rendered, unless within such thirty days either party has instituted proceedings to have such order corrected to accord with the mandate, in which event the order of the Commission shall become final when so corrected.

(i) If the order of the Commission is modified or set aside by the circuit court of appeals, and if (1) the time allowed for filing a petition for certiorari has expired and no such petition has been duly filed, or (2) the petition for certiorari has been denied, or (3) the decision of the court has been affirmed by the Supreme Court, then the order of the Commission rendered in accordance with the mandate of the circuit court of appeals shall become final on the expiration of thirty days from the time such order of the Commission was rendered, unless within such thirty days either party has instituted proceedings to have such order corrected so that it will accord with the mandate, in which event the order of the Commission shall become final when so corrected.

(j) If the Supreme Court orders a rehearing; or if the case is remanded by the circuit court of appeals to the Commission for a rehearing, and if (1) the time allowed for filing a petition for certiorari has expired, and no such petition has been duly filed, or (2) the petition for certiorari has been denied, or (3) the decision of the court has been affirmed by the Supreme Court, then the order of the Commission rendered upon such rehearing shall become final in the same manner as though no prior order of the Commission had been rendered.

(k) As used in this section the term "mandate," in case a mandate has been recalled prior to the expiration of thirty days from the date of issuance thereof, means the final mandate. [44]

(l) Any person, partnership, or corporation who violates an order of the Commission to cease and desist after it has become final, and while such order is in effect, shall forfeit and pay to the United States a civil penalty of not more than $5,000 for each violation, which shall accrue to the United States and may be recovered in a civil action brought by the United States. Each separate violation of such an order shall be a separate offense, except that in the case of a violation through continuing failure or neglect to obey a final order of the Commission each day of continuance of such failure or neglect shall be deemed a separate offense. [45]

Sec. 6. The commission shall also have power—

(a) To gather and compile information concerning, and to investigate from time to time, the organization, business, conduct, practices, and management of any corporation engaged in commerce, excepting banks and common carriers subject to the Act to regulate commerce, and its relation to other corporations and to individuals, associations, and partnerships.

(b) To require, by general or special orders, corporations engaged in commerce, excepting banks and common carriers subject to the Act to regulate commerce, or any class of them, or any of them, respectively, to file with the commission in such form as the commission may prescribe annual or special, or both annual and special, reports or answers in writing to specific questions, furnishing to the commission such information as it may require as to the organization, business, conduct, practices, management, and relation to other corporations, partnerships, and individuals of the respective corporations filing such reports or answers in writing. Such reports and answers shall be made under oath, or otherwise, as the commission may prescribe, and shall be filed with the

---

[44] 38 STAT. 719 (1914), as amended, 15 U.S.C. § 45 (b)-(k) (1952).
[45] 38 STAT. 719 (1914), as amended, 15 U.S.C. § 45 (l) (Supp. IV, 1957).

commission within such reasonable period as the commission may prescribe, unless additional time be granted in any case by the commission.

(c) Whenever a final decree has been entered against any defendant corporation in any suit brought by the United States to prevent and restrain any violation of the antitrust Acts, to make investigation, upon its own initiative, of the manner in which the decree has been or is being carried out, and upon the application of the Attorney General it shall be its duty to make such investigation. It shall transmit to the Attorney General a report embodying its findings and recommendations as a result of any such investigation, and the report shall be made public in the discretion of the commission.

(d) Upon the direction of the President or either House of Congress to investigate and report the facts relating to any alleged violations of the antitrust Acts by any corporation.

(e) Upon the application of the Attorney General to investigate and make recommendations for the readjustment of the business of any corporation alleged to be violating the antitrust Acts in order that the corporation may thereafter maintain its organization, management, and conduct of business in accordance with law.

(f) To make public from time to time such portions of the information obtained by it hereunder, except trade secrets and names of customers, as it shall deem expedient in the public interest; and to make annual and special reports to the Congress and to submit therewith recommendations for additional legislation; and to provide for the publication of its reports and decisions in such form and manner as may be best adapted for public information and use.

(g) From time to time to classify corporations and to make rules and regulations for the purpose of carrying out the provisions of this Act.

(h) To investigate, from time to time, trade conditions in and with foreign countries where associations, combinations, or practices of manufactutrers, merchants, or traders, or other conditions, may affect the foreign trade of the United States, and to report to Congress thereon, with such recommendations as it deems advisable.[46]

Sec. 7. In any suit in equity brought by or under the direction of the Attorney General as provided in the antitrust Acts, the court may, upon the conclusion of the testimony therein, if it shall be then of opinion that the complainant is entitled to relief, refer said suit to the commission, as a master in chancery, to ascertain and report an appropriate form of decree therein. The commission shall proceed upon such notice to the parties and under such rules of procedure as the court may prescribe, and upon the coming in of such report such exceptions may be filed and such proceedings had in relation thereto as upon the report of a master in other equity causes, but the court may adopt or reject such report, in whole or in part, and enter such decee as the nature of the case may in its judgment require.[47]

Sec. 8. The several departments and bureaus of the Government when directed by the President shall furnish the commission, upon its request, all records, papers, and information in their possession relating to any corporation subject to any of the provisions of this Act, and shall detail from time to time such officials and employees to the commission as he may direct.[48]

Sec. 9. For the purposes of this Act the commission, or its duly authorized agent or agents, shall at all reasonable times have access to, for the purpose of examination, and the right to copy any documentary evidence of any corporation being investigated or proceeded against; and the commission shall have power to require by subpoena the attendance and testimony of witnesses and the production of all such documentary evidence relating to any matter under investigation. Any member of the commission may sign subpoenas, and members and examiners of the commission may administer oaths and affirmations, examine witnesses, and receive evidence.

Such attendance of witnesses, and the production of such documentary evidence, may be required from any place in the United States, at any designated place of hearing. And in case of disobedience to a subpoena the commission may invoke the aid of any court in the United States in requiring the attendance and testimony of witnesses and the production of documentary evidence.

Any of the district courts of the United States within the jurisdiction of which such inquiry is carried on may, in case of contumacy or refusal to obey a subpoena issued to any corporation or other person, issue an order requiring such corporation or other person to appear before the commission, or to produce documentary evidence if so ordered, or to give evidence touching the matter in question; and any failure to obey such order of the court may be punished by such court as a contempt thereof.

Upon the application of the Attorney General of the United States, at the request of the commission, the district courts of the United States shall have jurisdiction to

[46] 38 STAT. 721 (1914), 15 U.S.C. § 46 (1952). See also Executive Order No. 10544, 15 U.S.C. § 46 (Supp. IV, 1957).
[47] 38 STAT. 722 (1914), 15 U.S.C. § 47 (1952).
[48] 38 STAT. 722 (1914), 15 U.S.C. § 48 (1952).

issue writs of mandamus commanding any person or corporation to comply with the provisions of this Act or any order of the commission made in pursuance thereof.

The commission may order testimony to be taken by deposition in any proceeding or investigation pending under this Act at any stage of such proceeding or investigation. Such depositions may be taken before any person designated by the commission and having power to administer oaths. Such testimony shall be reduced to writing by the person taking the deposition, or under his direction, and shall then be subscribed by the deponent. Any person may be compelled to appear and depose and to produce documentary evidence in the same manner as witnesses may be compelled to appear and testify and produce documentary evidence before the commission as hereinbefore provided.

Witnesses summoned before the commission shall be paid the same fees and mileage that are paid witnesses in the courts of the United States, and witnesses whose depositions are taken and the persons taking the same shall severally be entitled to the same fees as are paid for like services in the courts of the United States.

No person shall be excused from attending and testifying or from producing documentary evidence before the commission or in obedience to the subpoena of the commission on the ground or for the reason that the testimony or evidence, documentary or otherwise, required of him may tend to criminate him or subject him to a penalty or forfeiture. But no natural person shall be prosecuted or subjected to any penalty or forfeiture for or on account of any transaction, matter, or thing concerning which he may testify, or produce evidence, documentary or otherwise, before the commission in obedience to a subpoena issued by it: *Provided,* That no natural person so testifying shall be exempt from prosecution and punishment for perjury committed in so testifying.[49]

Sec. 10. Any person who shall neglect or refuse to attend and testify, or to answer any lawful inquiry or to produce documentary evidence, if in his power to do so, in obedience to the subpoena or lawful requirement of the commission, shall be guilty of an offense and upon conviction thereof by a court of competent jurisdiction shall be punished by a fine of not less than $1,000 nor more than $5,000, or by imprisonment for not more than one year, or by both such fine and imprisonment.

Any person who shall willfully make, or cause to be made, any false entry or statement of fact in any report required to be made under this Act, or who shall willfully make, or cause to be made, any false entry in any account, record, or memorandum kept by any corporation subject to this Act, or who shall willfully neglect or fail to make, or cause to be made, full, true, and correct entries in such accounts, records, or memoranda of all facts and transactions appertaining to the business of such corporation, or who shall willfully remove out of the jurisdiction of the United States, or willfully mutilate, alter, or by any other means falsify any documentary evidence of such corporation, or who shall willfully refuse to submit to the commission or to any of its authorized agents, for the purpose of inspection and taking copies, any documentary evidence of such corporation in his possession or within his control, shall be deemed guilty of an offense against the United States, and shall be subject, upon conviction in any court of the United States of competent jurisdiction, to a fine of not less than $1,000 nor more than $5,000 or to imprisonment for a term of not more than three years, or to both such fine and imprisonment.

If any corporation required by this Act to file any annual or special report shall fail so to do within the time fixed by the commission for filing the same, and such failure shall continue for thirty days after notice of such default, the corporation shall forfeit to the United States the sum of $100 for each and every day of the continuance of such failure, which forfeiture shall be payable into the Treasury of the United States, and shall be recoverable in a civil suit in the name of the United States brought in the district where the corporation has its principal office or in any district in which it shall do business. It shall be the duty of the various district attorneys, under the direction of the Attorney General of the United States, to prosecute for the recovery of forfeitures. The costs and expenses of such prosecution shall be paid out of the appropriation for the expenses of the courts of the United States.

Any officer or employee of the commission who shall make public any information obtained by the commission without its authority, unless directed by a court, shall be deemed guilty of a misdemeanor, and, upon conviction thereof, shall be punished by a fine not exceeding $5,000, or by imprisonment not exceeding one year, or by fine and imprisonment, in the discretion of the court.[50]

Sec. 11. Nothing contained in this Act shall be construed to prevent or interfere with the enforcement of the provisions of the antitrust Acts or the Acts to regulate commerce, nor shall anything contained in the Act be construed to alter, modify, or repeal the said antitrust Acts or the Acts to regulate commerce or any part or parts thereof.[51]

---

[49] 38 STAT. 722 (1914), 15 U.S.C. § 49 (1952).
[50] 38 STAT. 723 (1914), 15 U.S.C. § 50 (1952).
[51] 38 STAT. 724 (1914), 15 U.S.C. § 51 (1952).

Sec. 12. (a) It shall be unlawful for any person, partnership, or corporation to disseminate, or cause to be disseminated, any false advertisement—

(1) By United States mails, or in commerce by any means, for the purpose of inducing, or which is likely to induce, directly or indirectly the purchase of food, drugs, devices, or cosmetics; or

(2) By any means, for the purpose of inducing, or which is likely to induce, directly or indirectly, the purchase in commerce of food, drugs, devices, or cosmetics.

(b) The dissemination or the causing to be disseminated of any false advertisement within the provisions of subsection (a) of this section shall be an unfair or deceptive act or practice in commerce within the meaning of section 5.[52]

Sec. 13. (a) Whenever the Commission has reason to believe—

(1) that any person, partnership, or corporation is engaged in, or is about to engage in, the dissemination or the causing of the dissemination of any advertisement in violation of section 12, and

(2) that the enjoining thereof pending the issuance of a complaint by the Commission under section 5, and until such complaint is dismissed by the Commission or set aside by the court on review, or the order of the Commission to cease and desist made thereon has become final within the meaning of section 5, would be to the interest of the public,

the Commission by any of its attorneys designated by it for such purpose may bring suit in a district court of the United States or in the United States court of any Territory, to enjoin the dissemination or the causing of the dissemination of such advertisement. Upon proper showing a temporary injunction or restraining order shall be granted without bond. Any such suit shall be brought in the district in which such person, partnership, or corporation resides or transacts business.

(b) Whenever it appears to the satisfaction of the court in the case of a newspaper, magazine, periodical, or other publication, published at regular intervals—

(1) that restraining the dissemination of a false advertisement in any particular issue of such publication would delay the delivery of such issue after the regular time therefor, and

(2) that such delay would be due to the method by which the manufacture and distribution of such publication is customarily conducted by the publisher in accordance with sound business practice, and not to any method or device adopted for the evasion of this section or to prevent or delay the issuance of an injunction or restraining order with respect to such false advertisement or any other advertisement,

the court shall exclude such issue from the operation of the restraining order or injunction.[53]

Sec. 14. (a) Any person, partnership, or corporation who violates any provision of section 12 (a) shall, if the use of the commodity advertised may be injurious to health because of results from such use under the conditions prescribed in the advertisement thereof, or under such conditions as are customary or usual, or if such violation is with intent to defraud or mislead, be guilty of a misdemeanor, and upon conviction shall be punished by a fine of not more than $5,000 or by imprisonment for not more than six months, or by both such fine or imprisonment; except that if the conviction is for a violation committed after a first conviction of such person, partnership, or corporation, for any violation of such section, punishment shall be by a fine of not more than $10,000 or by imprisonment for not more than one year, or by both such fine and imprisonment: *Provided,* That for the purposes of this section meats and meat food products duly inspected, marked, and labeled in accordance with rules and regulations issued under the Meat Inspection Act, approved March 4, 1907, as amended, shall be conclusively presumed not injurious to health at the time the same leave official "establishments."

(b) No publisher, radio-broadcast licensee, or agency or medium for the dissemination of advertising, except the manufacturer, packer, distributor, or seller of the commodity to which the false advertisement relates, shall be liable under this section by reason of the dissemination by him of any false advertisement, unless he has refused, on the request of the Commission, to furnish the Commission the name and post-office address of the manufacturer, packer, seller, distributor, or advertising agency, residing in the United States, who caused him to disseminate such advertisement. No advertising agency shall be liable under this section by reason of the causing by it of the dissemination of any false advertisement, unless it has refused, on the request of the Commission, to furnish the Commission the name and post-office address of the manufac-

---

[52] As added in 1938, 52 STAT. 114, 15 U.S.C. § 52 (1952).
[53] As added in 1938, 52 STAT. 114, 15 U.S.C. § 53 (1952).

turer, packer, distributor, or seller, residing in the United States, who caused it to cause the dissemination of such advertisement.[54]

Sec. 15. For the purposes of sections 12, 13 and 14—

(a) (1) The term "false advertisement" means an advertisement, other than labeling, which is misleading in a material respect; and in determining whether any advertisement is misleading, there shall be taken into account (among other things) not only representations made or suggested by statement, word, design, device, sound, or any combination thereof, but also the extent to which the advertisement fails to reveal facts material in the light of such representations or material with respect to consequences which may result from the use of the commodity to which the advertisement relates under the conditions prescribed in said advertisement, or under such conditions as are customary or usual. No advertisement of a drug shall be deemed to be false if it is disseminated only to members of the medical profession, contains no false representation of a material fact, and includes, or is accompanied in each instance by truthful disclosure of, the formula showing quantitatively each ingredient of such drug.

(2) In the case of oleomargarine or margarine an advertisement shall be deemed misleading in a material respect if in such advertisement representations are made or suggested by statement, word, device, grade designation, design, device, symbol, sound, or any combination thereof, that such oleomargarine or margarine is a dairy product, except that nothing contained herein shall prevent a truthful, accurate, and full statement in any such advertisement of all the ingredients contained in such oleomargarine or margarine.

(b) The term "food" means (1) articles used for food or drink for man or other animals, (2) chewing gum, and (3) articles used for components of any such article.

(c) The term "drug" means (1) articles recognized in the official United States Pharmacopoeia, official Homoeopathic Pharmacopoeia of the United States, or official National Formulary, or any supplement to any of them; and (2) articles intended for use in the diagnosis, cure, mitigation, treatment, or prevention of disease in man or other animals; and (3) articles (other than food) intended to affect the structure or any function of the body of man or other animals; and (4) articles intended for use as a component of any article specified in clause (1), (2), or (3); but does not include devices or their components, parts, or accessories.

(d) The term "device" (except when used in subsection (a) of this section) means instruments, apparatus, and contrivances, including their parts and accessories, intended (1) for use in the diagnosis, cure, mitigation, treatment, or prevention of disease in man or other animals; or (2) to affect the structure or any function of the body of man or other animals.

(e) The term "cosmetic" means (1) articles to be rubbed, poured, sprinkled, or sprayed on, introduced into, or otherwise applied to the human body or any part thereof intended for cleansing, beautifying, promoting attractiveness, or altering the appearance, and (2) articles intended for use as a component of any such article; except that such term shall not include soap.

(f) For the purposes of this section and section 407 of the Federal Food, Drug, and Cosmetic Act, as amended, the term "oleomargarine" or "margarine" includes—

(1) all substances, mixtures, and compounds known as oleomargarine or margarine;

(2) all substances, mixtures, and compounds which have a consistence similar to that of butter and which contain any edible oils or fats other than milk fat if made in imitation or semblance of butter.[55]

Sec. 16. Whenever the Federal Trade Commission has reason to believe that any person, partnership, or corporation is liable to a penalty under section 14 or under subsection (1) of section 5, it shall certify the facts to the Attorney General, whose duty it shall be to cause appropriate proceedings to be brought for the enforcement of the provisions of such section or subsection.[56]

Sec. 17. If any provision of this Act, or the application thereof to any person, partnership, corporation, or circumstance, is held invalid, the remainder of the Act and the application of such provision to any other person, partnership, corporation, or circumstance, shall not be affected thereby.[57]

Sec. 18. This Act may be cited as the "Federal Trade Commission Act."[58]

---

[54] As added in 1938, 52 STAT. 114, 15 U.S.C. § 54 (1952).
[55] As added in 1938, 52 STAT. 114, and as amended, 15 U.S.C. § 55 (1952).
[56] As added in 1938, 52 STAT. 114, 15 U.S.C. § 56 (1952).
[57] As added in 1938, 52 STAT. 114, 15 U.S.C. § 57 (1952).
[58] As added in 1938, 52 STAT. 114, 15 U.S.C. § 58 (1952).

TABLE OF CASES

Cases reprinted in full or in part are listed in *italics* with **bold-faced** page numbers, numbers of pages where they are only cited being in light face. Cases treated in the text or footnotes are listed in roman type.

A

B

C

J

K

L

M

N

O

P

T

U

V

W

INDEX

A

Acquisitions, *see* Mergers

Antitrust Division, *see* Department of Justice

Antitrust laws, federal:
  and international trade, 240-289
  and regulated industries, 203-239
  definition, 141-142
  purpose and underlying policy, 7, 8, 36, 83, 136-138, 140, 142-144, 147, 181, 240, 284-289
  text of, 290-306

Atomic energy industry, antitrust aspects, 229-239

Atomic Energy Commission, 230-239

Automobile dealer franchises, 98-101

B

Banking, commercial, antitrust aspects, 203-219

C

Cartel agreements, *see also* Restraints in international trade:
  allocating quotas, 261, 270, 271-272
  among foreign firms, 271-277
  and export associations, 261-262, 273
  and imports, 261, 266, 272
  dividing markets, 240-241, 249, 250-254, 256, 261, 265-266, 268, 270
  fixing prices, 249-251, 261-262, 270
  involving foreign Governments, 257-260, 272

involving patents, 254-257
  involving trademarks, 254-257
  legality of, 240-241, 247, 249-260, 261-262, 263-266, 268-272
  meaning of the term, 249
  oil cartel case, 220, 265-266
  typical example, 251-254

Cease and desist orders, *see* Enforcement

Civil suits, 179-194

Commerce:
  clause of the federal Constitution, 11
  foreign, restraints in, 260-267
  interstate, 11-27
  intrastate, 11-27
  meaning of, 11-22, 214

Competition:
  effective, 82
  in commercial banking, 203-205
  interindustry, 35
  oligopolistic, 44
  state of, in the U. S., 8
  substitute, 29-39, 72

Concentration, economic, 8, 47, 49

Conscious parallelism, 44

Consent decrees, 188-193, 225, 266

Conspiracy, 43, 44

Criminal suits:
  and civil suits, 195
  nolo contendere, 196-199
  penalties, 195-196
  procedures, 195
  statute of limitations, 199
  types of offenses prosecuted, 194

Cross-elasticity of demand, 29-39, 68

D

Damage suits, 199-202

Discrimination, *see* Price discrimination